A HISTORY OF SEA POWER

A HISTORY OF
SEA POWER

BY

WILLIAM OLIVER STEVENS
Formerly Professor in the United States Naval Academy

AND

ALLAN WESTCOTT
Senior Professor in the United States Naval Academy

WITH MAPS AND DIAGRAMS

DOUBLEDAY, DORAN & COMPANY, INC.

New York

MCMXLII

D
27
.S8
(2)

CONTENTS

CONTENTS

MAPS AND ILLUSTRATIONS

PAGE

MAPS AND ILLUSTRATIONS ix

CHAPTER I

EARLY MEDITERRANEAN SEA POWER

Introduction

THE term sea power, in its widest interpretation, must be taken to include not only the navies of nations but their total strength and interests on the sea—their extent of coast line, overseas bases and colonial possessions, merchant shipping and sea-borne trade. When the term is given this breadth of meaning, the history of sea power becomes not merely a record of naval warfare but an account of the rise and decline of the great maritime nations, and of their rivalry for sea trade and sea control. Among the western nations, this rivalry has always been a dominant motive, and naval history thus maintains an almost continuous relationship with the development of their commerce and the changes in their foreign policy.

This close contact with commercial and political history the present narrative has sought to keep constantly in mind, along with other guiding interests which belong more strictly to the naval field—such as progress in navigation, evolution of ships and weapons, changes in tactics and strategy, and qualities of leadership which have had a decisive influence in naval war. In the earlier periods especially, it has seemed best to illustrate these developments by somewhat detailed accounts of single typical campaigns, with only a more general indication of events in the long periods between. There is a resultant gain in simplicity of treatment, but with some loss in proportion and continuity, against which the reader is warned. The story naturally becomes fuller as it approaches our own time.

Though primarily historical, the treatment will inevitably illustrate certain fundamental principles of warfare, which for convenience of reference are here briefly stated at the outset.

As generally accepted, they include the principle of the *objective,* which calls for a sharply defined purpose and a testing of all measures by their contribution to this primary aim; *coördination,* which requires simplicity of plan and the understanding co-operation of all concerned; *surprise,* if possible; *security,* or guarding against surprise by one's opponents; the principle of the *offensive,* in so far as it may gain advantage in time and place of attack; *aggressiveness* in following up an advantage; *economy of forces; movement;* and the vital principle of *con-centration*—the last three of these being summed up in the homely phrase, "to get there first with the most men."

I. THE BEGINNINGS OF NAVIES

In all periods, since men first went down to the sea in ships, the waterways have served not only as frontiers and areas of conflict but also as avenues of intercourse between peoples and means for the spread of civilization. It is, for instance, the ocean routes, and not the impassable land barrier between them, which truly join the two American continents. So also in the Old World, the Mediterranean, though separating three continents, was the chief means for the contact and spread of the civilizations which grew up along its shores.

In the Mediterranean basin, at least for the western peoples, sea history properly begins. Its waters, broken by long peninsulas and islands, almost tideless, and with comparatively favorable weather conditions during a large part of the year, afforded easier and quicker communications than by land; and here trade, piracy, and organized sea warfare seem to have flourished from prehistoric times.

Homer pictures a period, perhaps twelve hundred years before Christ, when these conditions were already centuries old. It was the "greedy merchants" of Phœnicia who supplied the wardrobe of Priam's queen; and it is a plausible theory which makes the siege of Troy a trade war for control of the Euxine, and the tale of Ulysses' wanderings a poetical record of early Greek commercial adventures in strange seas.

Earlier than Homeric times, and in fact supplying the chief

source of its culture, there existed a remarkable civilization, based on sea power and centered in the island of Crete, which for a long period dominated the eastern Mediterranean. These early Ægean islanders were a white, non-Aryan race, akin perhaps to the modern Basques. In art and architecture, in costume, sanitation, sports, and even vices, they made astonishing advances, sometimes oddly suggestive of modern times. The old Greek legends of the Minotaur and of the Labyrinth

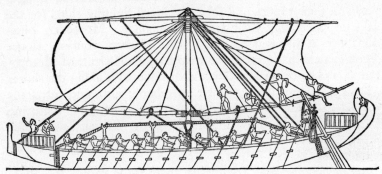

From Torr, *Ancient Ships.*

EGYPTIAN SHIP

bear witness to this period of Cretan dominance, when human tribute was levied on the peoples of the Ægean shores. The Cretan cities were open to the sea. For protection as well as for prosperity, they were dependent on their shipping; and though we know little of their history, their downfall, about 1400 B.C., appears to have been due to some great naval disaster which robbed them of sea control.

Their followers as sea traders were the Phœnicians, a Semitic people, thrust into a narrow strip of country between the mountains and seacoast along the eastern Mediterranean, and forced almost of necessity to find their living by the sea. To furnish wares for their trade, the Phœnicians attained high skill in the practical arts of weaving, dyeing, glassmaking, gem cutting, and working in wood and stone. Their famous "Tyrian dyes," obtained from two kinds of shellfish together with an alkali prepared from seaweed, were in demand throughout the known world, and, as we know from the Bible, many of the wonders of Solomon's temple were the work of these men of Sidon and Tyre. For timbers to be used in ship-building they could draw on the great forests of Lebanon; they learned something of ship construction from the Egyptians and Cretans, and something perhaps from the Assyrians of navigation by aid of the stars. Primarily a commercial people, they explored the Mediterranean and beyond for the sake of tapping new sources of wealth, they planted colonies for the sake of having trading posts on their routes, and they developed fighting ships for the sake of preserving their trade monopolies. Moreover, Phœnicia lay at the end of the Asiatic caravan routes. Hence Phœnician ships received the wealth of the Orient, of Mesopotamia, and of the Nile valley and distributed it along the shores of the Mediterranean. Their merchants also uncovered the wealth of Spain and the North African coast, and, venturing into the Atlantic, drew metals from the British Isles. For many centuries the Phœnicians were the chief traders of the western world.

In developing and organizing their trade routes the Phœnicians planted colonies on the islands of the Mediterranean—Malta, Sicily, Sardinia, and Corsica. They held both shores of the Straits of Gibraltar, and on the Atlantic coast of Spain established posts at Cadiz and Tarshish, the latter commonly supposed to have been situated just north of Cadiz at the mouth of the Guadalquivir River. Cadiz was their distributing point for the metals of northern Spain and the British Isles. Their most famous colony was Carthage, situated near the present city of Tunis. Carthage was founded in the 9th century before Christ, and on the decay of the parent state became in turn mistress of the western Mediterranean, holding sway until crushed by Rome in the Punic Wars.

Of the voyages and explorations of these most daring navigators of antiquity we should probably know more if it had not been their policy to keep their trade routes secret, but it is not difficult to believe the tale told by Herodotus, that in the 7th century B.C. they circumnavigated Africa, sailing first down the east coast and returning by Gibraltar after three years.

The story is made more credible by the comment of the ancient historian—"Others may believe, though I certainly do not, that in sailing around Africa they had the sun on their right hand."

Of the methods of the Phœnicians and their colonists in establishing trade with primitive peoples, Herodotus[1] also gives us an interesting picture, describing how the Carthaginians conducted business with barbarous tribes on the north coast of Africa: "When they (the Carthaginian traders) arrive, forthwith they unload their wares, and having disposed them in

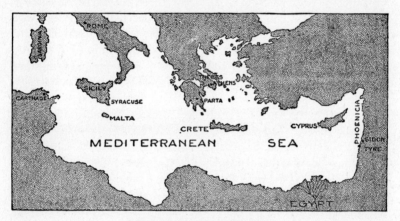

SCENE OF ANCIENT SEA POWER

orderly fashion on the beach, leave them, and returning aboard their ships, raise a great smoke. The natives, when they see the smoke, come down to the shore, and laying out to view so much gold as they think the wares to be worth, withdraw to a distance. The Carthaginians upon this come ashore and look. If they think the gold is enough they take it up and go their way; but if it does not seem sufficient they go aboard their ships once more and wait patiently. Then the others approach and add to the gold till the Carthaginians are satisfied. Neither party deals unfairly with the other . . ."

It is not easy to overstress the importance of these early mariners, such as the Cretans and Phœnicians, as builders of

[1]HISTORY, translated by Geo. Rawlinson, Vol. III, p. 144.

civilization. The venturesome explorer who brought his ship into some uncharted port not only opened up a new source of wealth but also established a reciprocal relation that quickened civilization at both ends of his route. The cargo ships that left the Nile delta distributed the arts of Egypt as well as its wheat, and the richest civilization of the ancient world, that of Greece, rose on foundation stones brought from Egypt, Assyria, and Phœnicia. It may be said of Phœnicia herself that she built up her advanced culture on ideas borrowed almost wholly from her customers. But control of the seas for trade involved control of the seas for war, and behind the merchantman stood the trireme. It is significant and appropriate that a Phœnician coin that has come down to us bears the relief of a ship of war.

In contrast with these early sea explorers and sea fighters stand the peoples of China and India. Having reached a high state of culture at an early period, they nevertheless sought no contact with the world outside and became stagnant for thousands of years. Indeed, among the Hindus the crossing of the sea was a crime to be expiated only by the most agonizing penance. Hence these peoples of Asia, the most numerous in the world, exercised no influence on the development of civilization compared with a mere handful of people in Crete or the island city of Tyre. And for the same reason China and India ceased to progress and became for centuries mere backwaters of history.

It is worth noting also that the Mediterranean, leading westwards from the early developed nations of Asia Minor and Egypt, opened a westward course to the advance of discovery and colonization, and this trend continued as the Pillars of Hercules led to the Atlantic and eventually to the new world. For every nation that bordered the Mediterranean illimitable highways opened out for expansion, provided it possessed the stamina and the skill to win them. And in those days they were practically the only highways; civilization followed the path of the sea. Even in these early beginnings it is easy to see that sea-borne commerce leads to the founding of colonies and the formation of an empire whose parts are linked together by trade routes, and finally, that the preservation of such an empire depends on the naval control of sea. This was as true of Crete and Phœnicia as it was later true of Venice, Holland, and England.

In the case of Phœnicia, a state with widespread colonies but little national solidarity or military strength, it was inevitable that the cities of the home land should come finally under the domination of the great empires that rose on their eastern border, first, in the 8th century, B.C., under the Assyrians, and later under the Babylonians and Persians. Their grip on their colonies was lost, and their commerce suffered some decline. But, with the Persians especially, their relation was not so much that of a conquered people as of voluntary naval allies. They aided the Persians in a campaign against Egypt in the late 6th century, and their navy was the chief instrument of Darius in subduing the revolt of his subject Greek cities in Asia Minor in 498 B.C., just before the great Graeco-Persian War.

2. THE CAMPAIGN OF SALAMIS

The campaign of Salamis, in this war, may well occupy our attention during the remainder of the chapter, both as an illustration of Greek naval developments and as one of the decisive campaigns of history. For it was the victory of Salamis—rather than the land battle of Marathon which preceded it, or of Platæa which followed it—that ended the real menace of Persia on European soil. Upon its issue depended the Greek civilization which reached its flower in the eighty years following, and which could hardly have come had Greece fallen under the demoralizing influence of eastern rule. The story of Salamis, as told by Herodotus who was a youth at the time and by the tragic poet Æschylus who fought in it, comes down to us in fairly authentic detail, and affords a clear picture of sea warfare in ancient times.

As for the causes of the war, there was the fact that Athens had aided her kindred cities across the Ægean in the revolt of a few years before. Both King Darius of Persia and his son Xerxes saw clearly, also, that without the defeat of the Greeks in Europe they could neither maintain a firm hold on their

Greek subjects in Asia Minor nor extend their rule beyond the Dardanelles.

The first Persian expedition against Greece, in 492, composed of a land force under Mardonius and a great fleet which followed the army along the northern coast of the Ægean, ended with the complete wreck of the navy in a storm off the dangerous promontory of Mt. Athos. The second, two years later, came by sea in 600 triremes, and was defeated by Miltiades at the bay of Marathon when the Persian army was only partly on shore. About 10,000 Greeks fought at Marathon, putting to rout a Persian force probably not more than twice as strong. The battle inflicted no very serious losses. Persia still controlled the sea, and ten years later, when conditions in the Asiatic empire became favorable, renewed the struggle on a grander scale.

Before taking up this final conflict, it is necessary to give some general account of the ancient fighting ships and their tactics. Very early in Mediterranean seafaring a differentiation had developed between the clumsy, broad-beamed, heavily timbered "round ship," or cargo vessel, dependent chiefly on sail propulsion, and the trim, narrow, sharp-lined "long ship," built for speed and war. The latter had a length as much as eight times her beam, and was propelled primarily by oars. Sails, rigged on one or two masts, were used in cruising or flight before the wind, but not in battle, so that to hoist sail became a Greek idiom for running away.

Coins and carvings show clearly that by the Phœnicians and almost certainly also by the Greeks the device was adopted of two banks of rowers, one above the other, thus doubling the motive power. The name *bireme,* supposedly, was applied to these craft with double banks of oars. At the time of Salamis the typical man-of-war was the so-called *trireme,* but whether the name refers to three superimposed banks of oars, or oars arranged in groups of three, or three men on each oar, remains a disputed question even to-day.[1]

---

[1] Cecil Torr, in ANCIENT SHIPS (1894), and many others follow the long-accepted theory of superimposed banks of oars; and a German writer, U. Tenne (KRIEGSCHIFFE ZU DEN ZEITEN DER ALTEN GREICHEN UND RÖMER), has worked out a plausible arrangement of at least three banks, one above another. More recent writers, notably H. W. Tarn in HELLENISTIC MILI-

The ordinary trireme was about 150 feet in length, 18 feet in beam, and from 4 to 6 feet in draught. The ship's company numbered about 200, of whom 170 were rowers. With its multitude of oarsmen a trireme could maintain a cruising speed of from 7 to 9 knots and increase it in emergencies to 12 or 15. Each night the craft was drawn ashore by the stern and the crew cooked and slept on land. Voyages skirted the coast,

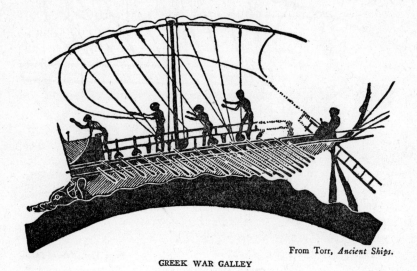

From Torr, *Ancient Ships.*

GREEK WAR GALLEY

and early history is replete with terrible disasters in which whole fleets of these frail vessels were wrecked by storms.

At the bow, under water, were one or more heavy, metal-shod, projecting timbers for ramming. This was the chief

TARY AND NAVAL DEVELOPMENTS (1930), argue ably in favor of an arrangement, known to have been used by the Venetians and called by them *a zenzile,* in which three rowers seated on a single bench pulled three oars of different lengths. This is clearly illustrated by the picture on p. 57. There is good evidence that the rectangular framework or outrigger shown in this illustration was used as early as Greek times. The alternative method of putting three or more men to a single oar was called *di scaloccio.* According to Tarn's theory, the quinquereme was a galley with five men to each oar, and in the larger types—16's, 20's, and even 40's—the two systems of grouped oars and of several men to an oar were combined. Usually the rowers were given some protection by bulwarks or shields.

mode of attack, though another was to dash close past the enemy's side, breaking oars and injuring rowers. The customary formation was in a long line abreast facing the enemy. Although at the time of Salamis the rowers were freemen, when vessels were boarded the fighting seems to have been left chiefly

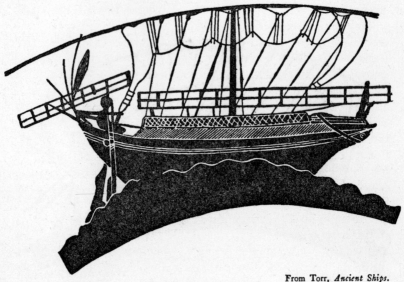

From Torr, *Ancient Ships.*

GREEK MERCHANT SHIP

to fourteen heavily armed hoplites and four bowmen stationed at bow and stern.

It is a mistake to suppose that the conflicts of these oar-driven vessels—from the trireme to the galley of the Middle Ages—were a crude business consisting simply of hand-to-hand combats as on land, after the vessels closed. True, they generally ended that way. But in Greek times the maneuvers of breaking the line (*diekplous*) and flanking (*periplous*) were common practice. Vast fleets of hundreds of units kept formation and executed maneuvers at signals from squadron commanders with a precision and speed not equaled till the days of steam. There was a so-called half-moon formation, and also a defensive formation in a circle with bows out, which the great Athenian admiral Phormio once broke up during the Peloponnesian War by rowing rapidly around it and suddenly concentrating on a weak point in the ring. To sum up the qualities of the ancient fighting ship, it had speed, maneuverability, and striking power, but lacked sea-keeping qualities and defensive strength.

To return to the story of Salamis, when King Xerxes gathered his forces in 480 B.C. for the final attack on the Greek city states he had 660 triremes and perhaps 100 smaller fighting craft, of which about 200 were Phœnician and the rest supplied by Egypt and the Greek subject cities of Asia Minor and adjacent islands.[1] These last seem to have fought loyally for the Persians, a fact less surprising when it is remembered that not all the western Greeks were united against the common foe.

An immense army, estimated by Herodotus at 1,700,000 effective infantry, but reduced by later students to 200,000 or 300,000, was to march by land. For its passage two bridges of boats were laid across the Hellespont. These were the work of Phœnician and Egyptian engineers; over them, as they swayed in the swift current, the troops of Asia marched for seven days and nights. The supply problem, which would seem almost insoluble to-day, was taken care of chiefly by a vast fleet of transports which followed the progress of the army along the shore.

In the face of this peril the salvation of the Greeks was centered in the great Athenian leader Themistocles. It was he who first saw clearly that the secret of victory over the Persian hordes lay in naval superiority which could cut their vital lines of communication by sea. It was he who persuaded his city to use the increased revenues from the silver mines of Attica to build a fleet of 200 triremes, which with the ships of other cities brought the total force available at Salamis to about 380. And though as a concession to the Peloponnesians the Spartan Eurybiades was given supreme command of this fleet, it was the brains and energy of Themistocles that really dominated the

[1] The larger estimates—from 1,000 to 1,200—given by Æschylus and Herodotus have been considerably lowered by modern students. Here and elsewhere in this chapter the figures in general follow the CAMBRIDGE ANCIENT HISTORY, Vol. IV.

campaign. His foresight, strategy, and quick judgment in emergencies give him a place with the great commanders of naval history.

As the Persians turned southward on the last stage of their long march from the Hellespont, the greater part of the Greek fleet was taken to the northern end of the island of Euboea, on the east coast of Greece, in order to protect the flank of the

ROUTE OF XERXES' FLEET TO BATTLE OF SALAMIS

small advance force under Leonidas which had been stationed to defend the pass of Thermopylæ. This, the only practicable gateway for the Persians into southern Greece, was a narrow road between mountains and shore, and here the whole land force of the Greeks might well have been concentrated. But Leonidas was ill supported by the military leaders of the Peloponnesus, who kept their main strength behind the four-mile line of fortifications at the Isthmus of Corinth, and seemed willing to leave Athens and all Greece north of the isthmus to their fate. The Peloponnesian troops under Leonidas appear to have been a sacrifice made to insure the good will of the Athenians and the help of their triremes. In any case, throughout the heroic struggle of Leonidas and his followers, the fleet in the waters outside kept his rear from being reached by sea.

Fearful as they were of the superior numbers of the approaching enemy fleet, and especially the traditional prowess of the Phœnicians in sea warfare, the Greek naval forces lying under the lee of Euboea were soon heartened by news of the loss of 200 Persian triremes, driven ashore along the rocky coast to northward in a severe northeast gale. During the next three days the two fleets were drawn up only a short distance apart in the waters north of the island. Each day there was sharp but indecisive fighting, and a large squadron of Persian vessels which had been sent to block the southern exit of the channel inside Euboea was swept to disaster in a second storm. As with the British in the later days of the Armada, it appeared as if the god of winds and waves were fighting on the side of Hellas.[1] But then came the news, swiftly conveyed to the fleet by a thirty-oared messenger boat, of the attack on Leonidas' rear by means of a mountain pathway, and the annihilation of his faithful band. Its first mission ended, the Greek fleet now retreated southward, taking its second stand at the strait within Salamis Island, just west of the port of Athens. The Persian fleet soon followed, keeping up with the advance on land, and assembled in the bay of Phalerum some eight miles east of Salamis.

On the approach of Xerxes' army, Athens was abandoned by the greater part of its citizens, and many of the refugees were taken to Salamis, where from the island heights they could still see the smoking citadel of their plundered city. They had accepted Themistocles' interpretation of the Delphic Oracle's prophecy that their safety lay in "wooden walls." For the redemption of their land, for their very lives, they must now trust the sharp-beaked fighting ships drawn up in the harbor below.

---

[1] "The gods so contriving that the Persian fleet might not greatly exceed the Greek, but be brought nearly to its level."—HERODOTUS, Vol. VIII, pp.12-13.

But at this critical moment the councils of the Greek sea leaders were torn with conflicting opinions as to what should be done.   Viewing with terror the pillage of Attica, the Peloponnesian contingent were overwhelmingly in favor of further retreat to the Isthmus of Corinth, where even if defeated they might join the defense on shore.   Against this course Themistocles spoke long and passionately.   It would mean the further advance of the Persian army, the complete abandonment of the

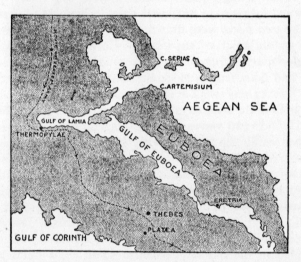

SCENE OF PRELIMINARY NAVAL OPERATIONS. CAMPAIGN OF SALAMIS

Athenian territory and the refugees at Salamis, the sacrifice also of their well-chosen defensive position in narrow waters where the enemy's superiority of numbers could not be brought to bear. It would very probably mean also the scattering of the fleet, each squadron sailing for the protection of its home harbor. To the taunt of a Corinthian that he no longer had a city to speak for, Themistocles replied that the 200 ships of Athens were his city, and that, if deserted by his allies, he would gather the Athenians and sail for new homes in Italy.   The last council, on the night before the battle, was ended by the news that a strong Egyptian force had been sent to block the western end of Salamis channel. To fight was now necessary, and to all it seemed best to fight with their face to the main foe.

At a meeting of the Persian leaders, presided over by Xerxes himself, the sentiment was almost unanimously in favor of an immediate attack. Only the sea queen Artemisia of Halicarnassus, who shares with Cleopatra the rare distinction of a woman in command of naval forces, advised the wiser policy of delay. The decision of the conference to engage at once was hastened by a last ruse of Themistocles, who saw only too clearly that a few days of inaction would be fatal to the Greek cause. One of his servants was sent to the Persian camp pretending desertion, with the plausible information that the Greeks were quarreling and about to disperse, and that by an immediate attack they could be destroyed at a blow.

The Persian fleet had been reduced by the disasters around Euboea to approximately 350 ships, or half its original strength, but the Greeks had also suffered losses and now numbered only about 300. The Persians had been occupied during the night watching the eastern exit, and at dawn both forces were forming their battle lines. On this September morning throngs of Greeks watched anxiously from the hills of the island; while on the opposite shore, surrounded by a bodyguard of troops, King Xerxes,

> ". . . sat on the rocky brow
> Which looks o'er sea-born Salamis,"

and viewed the channel filled with fighting ships of many races, drawn from every port of the eastern sea.

All the advantages of the defensive were with the Greeks, for they were fighting desperately for their homes and lives, in a steady formation awaiting attack, and in a narrow channel where the full strength of the enemy could not be used. Furthermore, a brisk morning wind from the west, which the Greeks had counted on, raised a choppy sea in the channel and hindered the enemy's approach. The Persian formation was also broken by a turn, and by the island of Psyttaleia, so that they poured into the straits in two confused streams. In his drama *The*

Persæ the first onset is thus described by the poet Æschylus who fought in the battle:

> "Ship on ship
> Dashed its bronze-pointed beak, and first a barque
> Of Hellas did the encounter fierce begin;
> And from Phœnician vessel crashes off
> Her carved prow.   And each against his neighbor
> Steers his own ship; and first the mighty flood
>   Of Persian host held out.   But when the ships
> Were crowded in the straits, nor could they give
>   Help to each other, they with mutual shocks,
>   With beaks of bronze, went crashing each the other,
> Shivering the rowers' benches.   And the ships
> Of Hellas, with maneuvering not unskillful
>   Charged circling round them."

Since the strait in its narrower parts was little over a mile wide, there could hardly have been a hundred ships in either front line.   As Æschylus says, the fighting was begun by the Athenians and Phœnicians who were on the southern or outer sides of their respective lines, while the Æginetans, placed next to the ships of Athens, soon fell on the Phœnician flank.   Somewhat later, Ionian Greeks from Ephesus, Miletus, Samos, Samothrace, and other cities under Persian rule met Greeks of the Peloponnesus at the northern end of the lines.   Advantage of position, rather than any marked superiority in seamanship or tactics, seems to have won the day, though in hand-to-hand fighting the heavier armor of the Greek hoplites was an important factor.   The Greeks backed water at first to draw the enemy into the strait, and then drove their rams again and again into the confused Persian line.   Amid wreckage and bodies of men swimming or drowning, the Persian ships fell backward, crashing into those astern.   Two of their number were driven ashore near King Xerxes, who in wrath ordered the beheading of their officers and crew.   On the island of Psyttaleia the Persian garrison was set upon by spearsmen under Aristides, the rival of Themistocles in Athens, and slain to the last man.

About half the Persian fleet was sunk in the battle, and an

indeterminate number captured. Their naval commander Aria-
bignes, brother of the king, was slain. The Greeks lost 40
ships, and as many more were disabled. Both fleets retired for
the night, the Greeks waiting for a renewal of the action on the
following day. But the decisive effect of Salamis was soon
evident. On the third day scouts reported that the Persian fleet
was in full retreat toward the Hellespont, and that, faced with

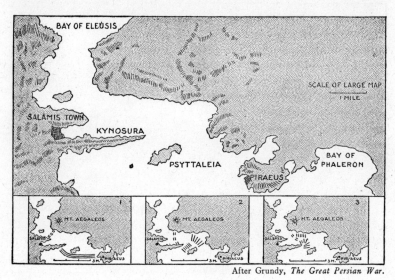

After Grundy, *The Great Persian War.*

THE BATTLE OF SALAMIS, 480 B. C.
1 The Original Position
2 The Advance
3 The Contact

starvation upon the rupture of their line of food supply from
Asia, Xerxes and the bulk of his army were retreating by land.
Under stress of famine, disease, and guerilla warfare, it was
only a broken and demoralized remnant of the great army that
reached the Hellespont. About 120,000 troops under Mardonius wintered in Thessaly, but were defeated in the next
summer at Platæa. The Greek fleet also cruised through the
Ægean during the next summer after Salamis, and at Mycale
on the Asia Minor coast destroyed the remainder of the Persian
fleet, which had been deserted by the Phœnicians and was drawn

up on the beach with a stockade built around it.   Here the last
of Xerxes' armada went up in flames.

Athens, the leading naval power among the Greeks who
fought at Salamis, was now supreme on the sea.   In the Delian
League formed a few years later, she assumed leadership over
the island cities of the Ægean and many communities on the

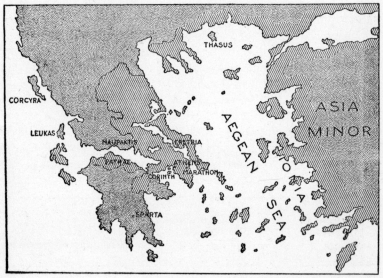

After Shepherd's *Historical Atlas.*

THE ATHENIAN EMPIRE AT ITS HEIGHT—ABOUT 450 B.C.

Asiatic shore, and soon made the confederacy merely an instrument for the extension of Athenian rule.   The Piræus was
fortified, the famous long walls were built to defend its connection with Athens, and it became a great naval base and center
of trade.   Hundreds of triremes were kept there, ready on short
notice to put to sea with highly trained crews.   Beset by her
land rival Sparta in the Peloponnesian Wars, Athens was long
able to hold her own by supremacy on the sea.   It was only
after the disastrous naval expedition to Sicily, 415–413 B.C.,
and the decisive naval defeat of Ægospotami in 405, cutting off
her trade and grain supply from the Black Sea, that Athenian

sea power fell into decay. Her trade was ultimately taken over by Rhodes and other island cities. Philip of Macedonia later conquered Athens and southern Greece by land. Alexander, in his Asiatic campaigns, though menaced somewhat by the superior sea forces under Persian control, was able, in 332 B.C., to strike effectively at the chief seat of Persian naval strength when the Phœnician cities of Byblius, Sidon, and Aradus surrendered and gave him the use of their ships in the famous siege and capture of Tyre.

The great period of Athenian maritime and commercial supremacy, as indicated in the preceding paragraph, came in the 5th century, between Salamis and the close of the Peloponnesian Wars, and in this period came also the culmination of Greek civilization in the Golden Age of Athens, with its inestimable achievements in philosophy, science, and the arts. Greeks of that age believed, as have historians of later times, that these achievements were assured to the world by the men who fought at Salamis; and if this is so, Salamis was truly a victory "not only for Greece but for mankind."

REFERENCES

(Note: The lists of books at the end of this and following chapters make no aim at completeness, but are intended merely to indicate some of the works of chief value in further study.)

CRETE, THE FORERUNNER OF GREECE, C. H. and H. B. Hawes, 1922.

THE SEA KINGS OF CRETE, J. Baikie, 1910.

THE ANCIENT HISTORY OF THE NEAR EAST, H. R. Hall, 1913.

HISTORY OF THE PERSIAN WARS, Herodotus, ed. and tr. by Geo. Rawlinson, 1862.

HISTORY OF THE PELOPONNESIAN WAR, Thucydides, ed. and tr. by Jowett.

THE GREAT PERSIAN WAR, G. B. Grundy, 1901.

THE MEDITERRANEAN IN THE ANCIENT WORLD, J. Holland Rose, 1933.

SEA POWER IN ANCIENT HISTORY, A. M. Shepard, 1924.

CAMBRIDGE ANCIENT HISTORY.

GEOGRAPHY OF THE MEDITERRANEAN REGION, E. C. Semple, 1931.

On ancient ships and methods of warfare see: ANCIENT SHIPS, C. TORR, 1894; DAS ANTIKE SEEWESEN, A. Köster, 1923; HELLENISTIC MILITARY AND NAVAL DEVELOPMENTS, W. W. Tarn, 1930; SHIPS AND WAYS OF OTHER DAYS, E. Keble Chatterton, 1913.

CHAPTER II

ROMAN SEA POWER

I. THE PUNIC WARS

Two centuries elapsed between the Greek victory over the Persians at Salamis and the Punic Wars, a second great struggle between alien races for Mediterranean control. Even before the Salamis campaign the commercial supremacy of the western Mediterranean, long held by the Phœnicians, had passed into the hands of Carthage, itself a Phœnician colony, admirably located for trade as an outlet to the rich grain region of northern Africa, and at the central narrows of the inland sea. Prior to the conflict with Rome, the Carthaginian commercial hegemony included the former Phœnician settlements westward along the African coast, the ports and mines of southern Spain, the islands of Malta, Sardinia, and Corsica, and the western portion of Sicily, where it met and clashed with the westward tide of Greek colonization.

Like the Phœnicians, the Carthaginians extended their trade to the bounds of the western world. Perhaps because of their secrecy regarding trade routes, we have few tales of their voyages, but through Greek sources has come the story of a certain Carthaginian named Hanno who pushed out past the Pillars of Hercules and down the African coast beyond Sierra Leone. Like the travel tales of the Middle Ages, his narrative is filled with the marvels and perils of these mysterious seas.

A treaty with Rome in 508 B.C., cited by the historian Polybius, shows Carthage's jealous guardianship of her trade monopoly. The Romans and their allies were not to sail "beyond the Fair Promontory [on the coast just west of Carthage] unless compelled by bad weather or an enemy," and later treaties shut them from the ports of Spain, Sardinia, and the African coast, limiting them to a direct trade with Carthage alone.

With the extension of Roman control over the Italian peninsula, completed in the 3rd century B.C., it was inevitable that these two nations should come into conflict. Sicily, midway between them and long a battleground of Greeks and Carthaginians, was the next step in Roman expansion. When in 264

SCENE OF THE PUNIC WARS

B.C. the Roman Senate decided to send an army into Sicily, at the appeal of a band of South Italian mercenaries established at Messina, it saw clearly that this meant trouble with Carthage; but it could hardly have foreseen the far-reaching consequences which within two centuries would make the voice of Rome dominant on every Mediterranean shore. The first great obstacle to the extension of Roman influence beyond the peninsula was Punic sea power, the overthrow of which was accomplished after three wars spread over more than a hundred years.

Each belligerent was strong in his special sphere. The Romans could count on the superior fighting quality of their legions, though Hannibal's extraordinary campaigns through the length and breadth of Italy in the second war demonstrated clearly enough that brilliant leadership could more than offset any inferiority in the rank and file.   On the other hand, Rome had little equipment, training, or natural bent for naval war, whereas her opponent had powerful military and commercial fleets and centuries of experience in seafaring and sea fighting. An even more vital contrast—and one that has an interest for nations to-day—lay in the character of the two peoples and their governments.   In Rome there was still a solidarity which could join senate and citizens in fortitude under adversity and in vigorous prosecution of national aims.   Carthage was a plutocracy, dependent on mercenaries for fighters, weakened by political factions, inclined to abandon leaders, waste opportunities, and upon any lightening of pressure let its armaments fall into decay.   This perhaps is what is meant by the statement of a British writer[1] that Rome had superior "fitness to win."   Both sides were prone to mistakes, sometimes due to political dictation in the choice and frequent changes of leaders, sometimes to the ignorance of the Roman commanders in sea warfare.   It was not mere chance that in the first war four great Roman fleets were lost in storms.

Of the three Punic Wars, naval interest centers almost wholly in the first, from 264 to 242 B.C.   Though defeated in Sicilian land fighting in the first stages of this conflict, and compelled to retire to their fortified bases in the west of the island, the Carthaginians used their naval forces to harry the enemy coast and paralyze its commerce.   The Romans were thus brought slowly to a realization that to win the war they must build a fleet and fight at sea.   But once realizing it, they moved with characteristic energy, taking a stranded enemy vessel, it is said, as a model for their new ships, recruiting crews from the maritime population of southern Italy, training them for rowing on huge platforms ashore, and launching 100 quinqueremes and 20 triremes in a few months' time.

The two fleets—about 100 on each side—met at Mylæ, on the north coast of Sicily, in 260 B.C.   Decisive in this engagement

[1] F. Jane, Heresies of Sea Power.

was the *corvus,* or "crow," a swinging gangway for boarding—
a novel device (though something similar had been used by
Alexander's ships at the siege of Tyre) which the Romans
adopted to counterbalance the enemy's superiority in ship handling and maneuvers. The corvus, as described by Polybius
(*General History,* Book I), was about 18 feet long and 4 feet
wide, guarded by rails, and swung by a topping lift from a short
mast which came up through a slot in the gangway about 6 feet
from its inner end. It was mounted in the bow and could be
dropped ahead or on either side. Beneath its outer end was a
sharp spike or beak—hence the name—to grapple and hold an
enemy vessel. Over the gangway soldiers protected by their
shields could throng aboard the enemy and convert the battle
into a combat as on land.[1]

Unaware of this new menace, and scornful of their awkward
opponents, the Carthaginians advanced rapidly into action without even stopping to range their craft in order. As they came
in contact, their leading ships were firmly grappled by the corvi,
and the first thirty were thus captured, in a mêlée on the decks
for which they could hardly have been well prepared. The remainder sheered off and attempted ramming tactics against the
Roman flanks and rear, but on finding they could not come to
close quarters without being grappled, they soon fled, "bewil-
dered," as Polybius says, "at the novelty of the occurrence, and
with the loss of 50 ships."

The victory was not decisive, but it gave the Romans a new
confidence in sea combat. Their commander, Duilius, was
accorded the first Roman naval "triumph," together with a
monument in the Forum modeled from the prows of captured
ships, and the privilege for life of returning from public ban-
quets preceded by a torchbearer and musicians. Their success
came as a result of their superiority in hand-to-hand fighting
and their ingenuity in bringing this advantage to bear, and it

[1]Some doubt has been expressed as to the use of this device, especially
by W. W. Tarn (HELLENISTIC MILITARY AND NAVAL DEVELOPMENTS) who
thinks the corvus would have been so bulky as to overset the light craft of
the time, and that Polybius was exercising his imagination in describing what
was merely some sort of grapnel. Polybius, however, is ordinarily trustworthy, and surely the corvus was not too heavy to operate on vessels
carrying from 300 to 500 men.

serves to illustrate what has often happened in naval history—
the defeat of a stronger and over-confident opponent by a novel
weapon or means of offense. Henceforth, just as Admiral
Jellicoe's tactics at Jutland were limited by the menace of torpedoes, the Carthaginian maneuvers were cramped through fear
of the corvi.

This was evident in the next important battle, the great naval

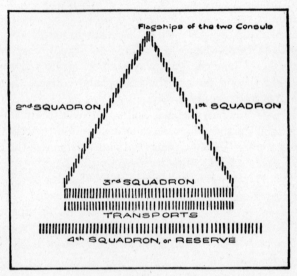

ROMAN FORMATION AT ECNOMUS

engagement of Ecnomus (256 B.C.). In the years between the
two battles, the Romans, though they had invaded Corsica and
Sardinia, had made little progress toward a decisive issue. Accordingly they now decided to carry the war into the Punic
homeland, and for this purpose equipped a fleet of 330 sail,
which, at the time it met the enemy, was manned by about
100,000 rowers and seamen and an advance force of 40,000
legionaries. The Carthaginian fleet of 350 quinqueremes carried at least an equal number, so that the total in the engagement
has been estimated at nearly 300,000 men. In recorded history,
no assembly of ships and men comparable in sheer numbers has
ever met at sea. The total of men in the British force at Tra-

falgar was a little over 10,000, and at Jutland less than 50,000.

From the heights of Mt. Ecnomus, or from the Roman army camp on the south coast of Sicily, the two vast fleets might have been seen advancing into battle, their thousands of oars in rhythmic stroke, their two formations stretched over miles of water. As shown in the diagram, the Carthaginians were in open order, the two wings somewhat ahead of the center. The two forward divisions of the Romans were in a slightly wedge-shaped formation, at the apex of which were the two heavier

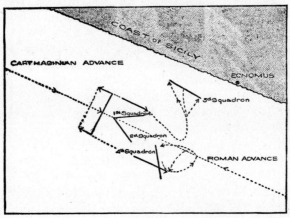

CARTHAGINIAN TACTICS AT THE BATTLE OF ECNOMUS, 256 B.C.

flagships of the consuls, Manlius and Regulus. Next came the third division, towing horse transports, and a fourth division guarded the rear.

As the two fleets closed, the Carthaginian center purposely fell back, drawing after it the two Roman forward divisions. Meantime the two Carthaginian wings swung rapidly around the enemy flanks, the left wing attacking the division hampered by the transports, while the right fell upon the Roman rear and drove it to seaward. The battle thus broke into three separate engagements, and if matters had developed as in certain combats of later times, notably in the great fleet actions of the Anglo-Dutch wars, each Roman division might have won or lost its own action without regard to mutual support.

Here, however, there was better cohesion. The commanders of the leading Roman divisions, having won their combat with the enemy center, turned back in time to aid the hard-pressed divisions left behind. The division with the transports had been driven toward shore in great disorder and some of its units had already been sunk. "Indeed," to quote Polybius, "they must all have long before been destroyed if the Carthaginians had not, through fear of the corvi, kept themselves at a distance, and declined a close engagement. But the consuls, now advancing together, surrounded the enemy and took fifty of their ships with all their crews. The rest, being fewer in number, steered close to the shore and saved themselves by flight."

The Carthaginian right division, threatened by a similar concentration, escaped to seaward. The Romans lost 24 ships, sunk; the Carthaginians, 94, of which over 60 were captured with their crews. No Roman vessel surrendered. Of special interest in the battle is the development shown in tactics, which here consisted of far more than the collision of two long lines. The Carthaginian plan was evidently to hold or "contain" the enemy center, while superior forces destroyed the transports and rear. Hannibal succeeded later with somewhat similar tactics in the great land battle of Cannæ (216 B.C.). At Ecnomus the Carthaginians were also on the verge of success when the two consuls, showing a spirit of teamwork which has always been associated with the Roman arms, returned to support the rear squadrons.

Though the victory opened the way for invasion of Africa, the subsequent land campaign there was badly managed. Time was wasted in pillage, part of the army was sent home too soon, and in the next year the Romans were defeated and compelled to evacuate Carthaginian territory. A fleet of 400 ships carried off the army, but on the southern coast of Sicily it was wrecked with a loss of 100,000 men, estimated at about 15 per cent of the total fighting strength of Rome. It was reported that the Roman leaders had disregarded the advice of their Greek pilots. This was but the first of a series of similar disasters. Two years later, in 253, a fleet of 150 ships was completely lost while attempting, again contrary to the advice

of experienced seamen, to steer directly from Panormus to
Ostia across the Tyrrhenean Sea. In 249 a force of 220 ships
was defeated by the Carthaginians at Drepanum, largely by
superior maneuvering, in their only major naval victory of the
war; and in the same year still another large Roman fleet was
driven ashore in a winter gale, and wrecked so completely that
scarcely a plank remained entire. Such fearful losses, though

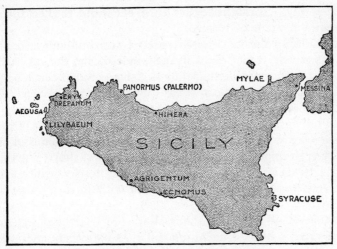

POINTS OF INTEREST IN THE FIRST PUNIC WAR

falling chiefly on the seafaring population, must have put Roman
wealth and man power to a severe strain; according to Mommsen (*History of Rome,* Vol. II, p. 52), in these five years, 252–
247, the roll of Roman citizens was reduced by one-sixth, or
40,000, without including the greater losses of non-citizens and
allies. Indeed for several years their operations were limited to
ineffective land attacks on the Punic sea fortresses of Drepanum
and Lilybæum.

At last, in 243, these indomitable Romans built another fleet
of 200 ships, constructed and equipped chiefly by private sub-
scription. With this they blockaded the enemy's Sicilian bases,
and in 241 at the Ægatian Islands, near Drepanum, defeated an
inferior force of enemy ships and transports in the last and

finally decisive battle of the war. "The Carthaginians at this time," according to Polybius, "were convinced that the Romans would never think of building up their navy again, and in their contemptuous feeling of security had greatly neglected their own." With his troops cut off from supplies and reduced to starvation, the Carthaginian general, Hamilcar, was now forced to sue for peace, the terms of which called for the evacuation of Sicily and the payment of 3,200 talents (over 3,000,000 dollars) as indemnity. As at the beginning, so at the end, the fleet turned the scales in favor of Rome.

Considering the vital importance of sea communications in this island war, it may seem strange, indeed, that the sea battles were not even more immediately decisive. But it must be remembered that in ancient times "command of the sea" was rarely achieved. Blockades, other than the actual occupation of an enemy harbor, were difficult to maintain. War craft were neither seaworthy nor "sea-keeping"; for food, drink, cooking, and even sleeping, they were dependent on the shore. Furthermore, defeats and disasters at sea were less decisive, since fleets and crews could apparently be replaced with an ease inconceivable to-day.

In the second and third Punic Wars (218–202 and 143–141 B.C.) there is little of naval interest. In both these later wars Roman sea power was clearly predominant, and though not very vigorously exercised, it restricted Carthaginian communications and forced the enemy to keep strong defensive garrisons both in Spain and in home territory. It was this sea control, apparently, which compelled Hannibal, early in the second war, to undertake the almost insuperable difficulties of the Alpine route from Spain into Italy, in surmounting which he lost half his army. And during his sixteen years of campaigning in Italy, it practically forbade his securing reënforcements and supplies from the mother country, though for this lack of support the indifference and weakness of his home government was probably as much to blame. It is important to note also that naval superiority enabled Rome to protect her own commerce and communications with Sicily and with the east, and finally to end both wars by carrying the campaign into Africa.

The second conflict ended with the defeat of Hannibal at Zama; the third ended with the razing of Carthage and the utter destruction of the Punic power, though the town itself rose again later to become third in population in the Roman Empire. Mistress of the western sea since the first war, and now enriched by great provinces in Sicily, Spain, and Africa, Rome could turn freely to the extension of her sway in the eastern Mediterranean.

2. WARFARE ON PIRACY

In the almost constant warfare that accompanied Rome's eastward expansion, already under way at the time of the second Punic War, sea communications were ever a vital factor, but were generally in the hands of the Roman forces, aided by their Rhodian and other maritime allies. Though the fleet was treated as a stepchild by Rome and often flagrantly neglected, as at the time of the Mithridatic Wars in the last century of the pre-Christian era, sufficient strength could be rallied in emergencies to clear the seas of enemy fleets, or at least cover the transport of the invincible legions to the area of warfare.

Even piracy, which since the decline of the earlier maritime states had long infested the Mediterranean and now preyed upon commerce at every strait and headland, felt at last the ordering influence of Roman primacy at sea. In 66 B.C. a campaign against the pirates was organized on a grand scale under Cneius Pompey, who was supplied with 500 ships and 125,000 men. (See Plutarch's *Life of Pompey*.) The Mediterranean was divided into thirteen districts with a squadron to each, while a *force d'élite* under Pompey's personal command ran down these sea brigands wherever they could be located. Within three months, we are told, 1,300 of their craft were captured, 10,000 corsairs were slain, and 20,000 surrendered.

The effect, however, was probably only transient. Twenty-five years later we find that Sextus Pompeius, a son of Pompey, had himself established a kind of semi-piratical empire, dominating Sicily and all the surrounding islands and threatening the food supply of Rome. At last, in 36 B.C., he was defeated by

Agrippa off Naulochus, Sicily, in a great sea battle rivaling in numbers the fleet actions of the first Punic War.

Piratical operations, whether of pursuit or escape, put a high premium on speed, and it is partly on account of this influence that, at Naulochus and thereafter, we find in fighting craft a trend toward lightness and rapidity of movement. Or perhaps it may be more truly said that the Mediterranean war vessels of the period showed a development along two divergent lines. The first was toward a low, light, relatively small craft, designed primarily for speed and quick maneuver; typical of these were the vessels built in the island of Rhodes, and also the so-called *liburni,* first used by a sea-roving tribe of that name on the east coast of the Adriatic. The second trend was toward greater strength and size, toward a type more heavily timbered and with higher freeboard, capable of carrying the tower-like structures, the catapults, ballistæ, grapnels, and other forms of ancient military machinery which were now coming into increased use in sea warfare.

3. THE CAMPAIGN OF ACTIUM

These new trends in types and weapons are all well illustrated in the battle of Actium, 31 B.C. From this famous battle something of the glory has been shorn away by modern research, so that it seems to represent in itself not so much a defeat as a débâcle, the last act of a tragedy. Yet it retains significance not only because of the historic and romantic interest of its chief figures but because it stands as a definite turning point in the evolution of Rome from a republic to an empire, and in the struggle between eastern and western influences for ascendancy in the Roman state.

From Plutarch, Shakespeare, and many other literary treatments, the main outlines of the story that ended at Actium are generally familiar—the assassination of Julius Cæsar in 44 B.C., the defeat of the conspirators in the ensuing civil war, the subsequent rivalry between Marc Antony and Cæsar's grand nephew Octavius, and the tragic downfall of Antony under the influence of the Greek princess who ruled in Egypt, Cleopatra. In glowing language Plutarch has pictured the first meeting, at Tarsus, Asia Minor, in 41 B.C., of the Egyptian queen, then in her twenty-ninth year, and the Roman triumvir, who was over forty; Cleopatra "sailing up the river Cydnus in a barge with gilded stern and outspread sails of purple, while oars of silver beat time to the music of flutes and pipes and lyres . . ."

Their liaison is usually portrayed as a passionate infatuation, at least on the part of Antony, in which principles and judgment were cast to the winds. Yet with both of them political motives were ever an important factor. Antony needed the wealth of Egypt for his eastern campaigns; Cleopatra desired Roman support to bolster her rule in Egypt. They were married by Egyptian rites in the year 36 at Antioch. Antony's subsequent open proclamation of the marriage, probably shortly before his divorce of Octavia, the sister of Octavius, in the year 32, marked his final decision that his quarrel with Octavius admitted no further compromise but must be settled in the field. The luxury of Egyptian life, the splendor of oriental royalty, and his devotion to the queen no doubt had a part in his decision. Very possibly, had he triumphed over Octavius, the seat of Roman rule might have been shifted to Alexandria. Certainly oriental influences, which were already strong in Rome, would have gained more permanent ascendancy, and the future of Rome and Europe would have been vastly changed. Such were the issues which at the time divided the Roman state into two great factions, and which reached a decision at Actium.

With Antony controlling the military resources of the Eastern provinces from the Euphrates to the Adriatic, and Octavius those of the west, the strength of the two contestants was perhaps equally matched, Antony's superiority in sheer numbers— he had about 500 ships and 30 legions, or 150,000 men—being counterbalanced by their weaker loyalty and inferior fighting quality. A glance at a map will show that the meeting place of their two spheres of influence, and hence the probable area of conflict, lay in the narrow waters between the heel of Italy and Greece. Here, when hostilities were opened in the autumn of the year 32, Antony and Cleopatra gathered their forces, making their headquarters at Patras on the Gulf of Corinth and their fleet base near the promontory of Actium, at the mouth of the Ambracian Gulf, or Gulf of Arta, further up the coast.

Thither also, early in the next spring, Octavius moved his fleet, establishing a fortified camp and naval anchorage just north of Actium.   At his first arrival he might easily have de-

SCENE OF BATTLE OF ACTIUM, 31 B.C.

stroyed the eastern fleet, which was far undermanned, but Antony, who had hastened northward, dressed his rowers as legionaries, stationed them on deck, and having propped the oars in position as if ready for an advance, led his cautious opponent to stand off.

Through the hot months of summer the two great armaments faced each other.   Antony, having concentrated his troops and moved them across to the north side of the strait, would at first willingly have trusted to his abler generalship in an engagement by land, could he have induced his wary foe to leave his defenses. But as time passed, Antony's prospects of victory grew more dubious, either by land or sea. Worse than the malaria and food shortage, which had depleted his crews and troops, was the internal dissension which split his camp—a long-standing, bitter strife between his Roman followers who favored a fight to the finish for supremacy in Rome, and the Egyptian faction led by Cleopatra, who now more than ever saw their interests best served by retreat to Egypt for a purely defensive campaign. Desertions multiplied, as it dawned on many Romans that they were fighting in an alien cause. By the close of the summer Antony's decision was made, or it would seem rather forced upon him—a naval battle, in which, however, the object was not victory but breaking through and escaping to Egypt.

Such was the policy behind Antony's movements when on the calm morning of September 2, under the eyes of the two armies on opposite sides of the strait, he drew up his fleet in battle lines at the mouth of the gulf. Owing to shortage of rowers, he had burned his poorer vessels and took into action only his best, probably less than 300 in number, though on this and other statistics of the battle the sources show a wide discrepancy. A rear squadron of 60 was under Cleopatra's personal command. Aboard his ships he placed 20,000 legionaries and 2,000 archers and slingers. Significant to the more suspicious was the fact that each vessel, instead of being fully cleared for action, was left with mast and sails; these, according to Antony, were for "pursuing the enemy," but all knew their more customary use was for running away.

Just as for months the two armies had lain inactive at Actium, so now the two fleets faced each other in almost motionless, compact battle lines, with the conventional three divisions, each awaiting the other's first move. The ships of Octavius were probably fewer in number—according to Plutarch, 250—and were certainly smaller in size. This latter contrast is, in fact, emphasized by all the ancient historians, Florus speaking of the ships of Antony's flotilla "with towers and high decks, that moved along like castles and cities." Plutarch also remarks upon "Antony's great octiremes and deciremes," whereas those of Octavius were "not pompous galleys, but light, swift, and perfectly manned." Many of these latter were liburni of the Adriatic, or pirate craft captured at Naulochus five years before. Their crews had been thoroughly drilled, and the western Romans possessed a tower of strength in the naval leader Agrippa, the victor at Naulochus, an experienced sea officer to whom Octavius turned over full command. It would appear that Agrippa, who had popularized the heavy ships by his success with them against the pirates, now chose the opposite type in dealing with a less skillful foe.

The inaction was broken about noon by a brisk breeze from the north. Either this or impatience set Antony's left flank into forward movement, and though Agrippa at first fell back to draw his enemy out of the narrows, the two fleets were soon engaged at all points. On neither side was there much use of ramming, for while Antony's craft were too slow and clumsy for the purpose, they were so well protected at the sides by heavy, iron-bolted timbers as to make such methods futile and even dangerous for the foe. Instead, as Plutarch describes it, the fighting resembled rather "the attack and defense of a walled town, for there were always three or four vessels of Caesar's about one of Antony's, pressing them with spears, javelins, poles, and several inventions of fire,[1] which they flung among them, Antony's men using catapults also, to pour down missiles from wooden towers."

Not the fighting, which at this point was indecisive, but rather a sudden movement of the Egyptian ships decided the fortunes of the day. Their purple sails set to the stiffening northern wind, these now streamed through the fighting lines and away toward the Peloponnesus. And in an act revealing the degeneration of those qualities that had won the devotion of his men in earlier times, Antony soon boarded a fast quinquereme and joined in the flight. Regardless or unaware of his defection, his heavy ships kept up the battle, and though worsted, most of them were able at nightfall to retire within the gulf. It was not until a week later that the remnant of the fleet and the

---

[1]Dio Cassius writes that "the assailants shot blazing missiles and with engines threw pots of flaming charcoal and pitch."

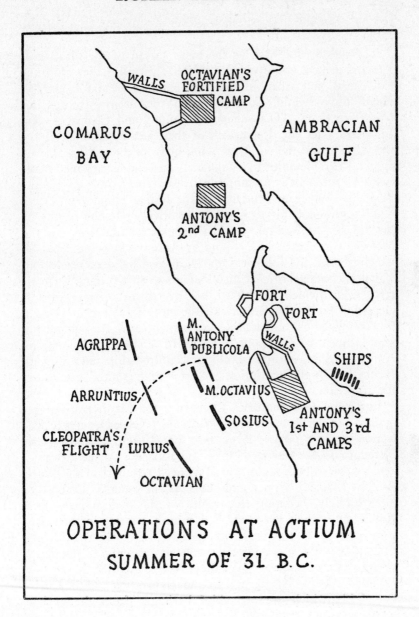

OPERATIONS AT ACTIUM
SUMMER OF 31 B.C.

troops, after the flight of their officers, went over in a body to Octavius.

Throughout the east, as the news spread of the disaster at Actium, princes and provinces shifted their allegiance from the lost cause, and when in the next summer Octavius invaded Egypt, the remaining ships and troops of Antony gave up after scarcely a blow. The suicide of Antony and Cleopatra soon followed, after the destruction of their last hopes. At Rome the victory, and the wealth flowing in from the subjugation of Egypt, lifted Octavius to a popularity and eminence which made easy his subsequent assumption of supreme power as Caesar Augustus, Imperator, the first of the Roman emperors.

To ascribe all this to naval superiority, or to the results of the fighting at Actium, would of course be fantastic, for the outcome was shaped beforehand by Antony's two-faced policy, which divided his followers and weakened his own resolution. Yet it is characteristic of men's minds to fasten upon the concrete event which signalized his overthrow. And since it pleased Octavius also to cultivate the idea of a triumph in arms, he recognized the momentous consequences of Actium by the establishment of Nicopolis, the City of Victory, on the site of Antony's camp, with the beaks of captured ships adorning its forum, and by the institution of "the Actian games," celebrated for 200 years.

For some four centuries thereafter, the Mediterranean remained for the Romans *Mare Nostrum* (our sea). As a protection against piracy, large fleet bases were established at Misenum on the Bay of Naples and Ravenna on the Adriatic, and smaller squadrons operated as need required in the Black Sea, the British Channel, and other distant waters. Commerce moved freely, bringing the wealth of the eastern peoples to Rome and with it their arts and culture, whence in turn they were carried to the barbarian peoples of northern Europe. Control over the seas and waterways was essential to the maintenance of the empire. Over these routes, guarded by the *Pax Romana,* spread Hellenic and Roman civilization and the Christian faith, which are our chief heritages from the ancient world.

Naval control naturally declined with the slow crumbling of the empire. Against the Teutonic invasions of Britain and Gaul beginning in the 5th century, little defense was offered. The Vandals, crossing at Gibraltar and settling in the old Carthaginian domain, sent out piratical fleets which swept the Mediterranean, and under their leader Gaiseric anchored in 445 A.D. in the Tiber and pillaged Rome for fourteen days. Though the Vandal state was destroyed a century later by a fleet and army of the Eastern Roman Empire, the shift of the capital to Constantinople meant a general weakening of Roman influence in the western Mediterranean, which became a haunt of piracy and a battleground of Christian and Moslem down, one might almost say, to our own times.

REFERENCES

HISTORY OF ROME, Theodor Mommsen, tr. by W. P. Dickson, 1867.

GENERAL HISTORY, Polybius, tr. by Hampton, 1823.

THE GREATNESS AND DECLINE OF ROME, G. Ferrero, tr. by A. E. Zemmern, 1909.

CHARACTERS AND EVENTS OF ROMAN HISTORY, G. Ferrero, 1909.

THE ARCHITECT OF THE ROMAN EMPIRE, T. R. Holmes, 1928.

CAMBRIDGE ANCIENT HISTORY, especially Vols. VII, VIII.

SEA POWER IN ANCIENT HISTORY, A. M. Shepard, 1924.

PIRACY IN THE ANCIENT WORLD, H. A. Ormund, 1924.

FLEETS OF THE FIRST PUNIC WAR, W. W. Tarn, in *Journal of Hellenistic Studies*, 1907.

INFLUENCE OF SEA POWER ON THE ROMAN REPUBLIC (Harvard Doctoral Dissertation), F. W. Clark, 1915.

CHAPTER III

THE EASTERN ROMAN EMPIRE

In 328 A.D. the Emperor Constantine the Great, first of the Roman rulers to adopt the Christian faith, shifted his capital from Rome to Byzantium, or Constantinople, to give it the name by which it has since commonly been known. The change was the outcome of a general gravitation of imperial interests to the eastward, and brought the emperor's seat of government closer to his campaigns on the weak Danube and Asiatic frontiers. In contrast to Rome, moreover, the location of Constantinople combined strategic and commercial advantages of the highest order, in ancient as in modern times—at the meeting place of Europe and Asia, on the narrow waters joining the Black Sea and the Mediterranean, and in a position to command the chief trade routes from the Orient to the western world.

Situated on a point of land between the Sea of Marmora and a narrow inlet from the Bosphorus known as the Golden Horn, the city was defended on its land side by massive fortifications, stretching four miles from the Marble Tower on the Propontis or Sea of Marmora to the Xylo Porta on the Horn, and consisting of a 60-foot moat and three great walls, the innermost of which averaged 50 feet in height and 15 feet in thickness, with 97 projecting bastions or towers. These defenses were practically impregnable to the siege methods of earlier days. The shore line also was protected by a single wall and some 300 towers. It is important to note, however, that for defense of outlying possessions and communications, and especially for assurance of its food supply, the city was primarily dependent on command of the sea.

After the separation of the Eastern and Western Roman Empires at the close of the 4th century, and the breakup of the western portion into smaller independent kingdoms, the Eastern or Byzantine Empire remained for many centuries the strongest state in Christendom, a preserver of the cultural inheritance from Greece and Rome, a civilizing influence among the Slavic peoples to the northward, and the great bulwark of Europe against the assaults of Moslem power.   In this latter struggle, its navy, as will be seen, played an important and even decisive rôle.

In its earlier warfare with the Persians, and also with the

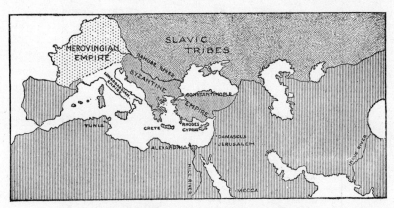

THE SARACEN EMPIRE AT ITS HEIGHT, ABOUT 715 A.D.

Slavs and Bulgars on the west, Constantinople had stood safe behind its fleet and its great walls.   Not until the tremendous assaults of Islam in the late 7th and early 8th centuries were the city and the empire seriously threatened by both land and sea.

The rapid rise and spread of the Arabic Moslem peoples in this period is a phenomenon which, though it had parallels in the earlier and contemporary migrations of the more northern races, seems scarcely explicable to-day.   Religious fanaticism combined with the poverty of their homeland to send these peoples, hitherto scattered and insignificant, on an irresistible surge of expansion, eastward to India and westward along the south shore of the Mediterranean to Gibraltar, where it crossed and extended through Spain to the Pyrenees, like a great scimitar threatening the whole Christian world.   The prophet

Mohammed's brief ascendancy at Mecca had covered less than a decade before his death in 632; his successors carved out this vast empire within the next hundred years.   Persia was conquered, and the provinces of Syria and Egypt were torn from the Eastern Roman Empire before 650.   The conquest of these latter provinces gave to Islam a means for the development of sea power, which was accomplished, as Rome had accomplished

EUROPE'S EASTERN FRONTIER

it in an earlier day, by drawing upon the ships and seafaring populations of the subject lands.   With forces thus created, a Christian fleet sent to reconquer Egypt was defeated in 652 at the mouth of the Nile.   Cyprus was put under tribute; the islands of Rhodes and Cos were plundered; and in a naval battle in 655 off Phaselis, on the southern coast of Asia Minor, an Eastern Roman fleet of 400 ships suffered defeat in a hard-fought battle in which the Christian Emperor himself, Constantine IV, escaped capture only by a wild leap from his ship after it had been boarded by the enemy.   As has already been said, the Eastern Empire was now threatened by a power that was formidable on both land and sea.

Before taking up the two great Saracen assaults on Constantinople, in 673–677 and 717–718, we may here pause briefly to consider the ships and weapons of the time. There is every evidence that the so-called *dromon* (fast sailer), and the smaller types of various nomenclature also employed in this period, were direct descendants of the Roman ships that fought at Actium. Like the ancient vessels, they were long and narrow, equipped with rams, and provided with two masts and lateen sails, though they were dependent for propulsion primarily on the oar. They had crews of about 300, of whom 230 were rowers. The later craft were probably of stronger build and somewhat higher freeboard, and they carried tower-like timber structures amidships and forward, which were armed with ancient types of artillery and means of projecting Greek fire. This last was their most distinctive and effective weapon. The secret of its composition is said to have been brought to Constantinople by a Syrian Christian named Callinicus during the first siege in 673, and it was thereafter jealously guarded for centuries. According to the best accounts of modern investigators, the substance was a semi-fluid mixture of sulphur, pitch, niter, petroleum, and other more obscure elements which was ejected, possibly by gunpowder, through tubes or "siphons", and also thrown in more primitive fashion by means of earthen pots, hand grenades, and arrows wrapped with flaming tow. This "fire resembling the lightning from heaven" burned even on water, and could be fought only by means of vinegar, wine, or sand. The Venetians in later times are reported to have protected the sides of their galleys by hides soaked in vinegar.

As for the Saracen ships, they came from former Roman provinces and were similar in general type, though probably smaller and without the weapon of Greek fire.

Of the first great thrust against Constantinople, planned though not actually led by the Caliph Muaviah, we have from contemporary chroniclers only the barest records. In March, 673, a strong Saracen fleet entered the Dardanelles, apparently unopposed, and established a base at Cyzicus on the Sea of

Marmora.   An army was landed on the European shores and a kind of intermittent siege of Constantinople was established which continued for five years.   Each summer there were fighting outside the walls, and successful raids on the Saracen navy

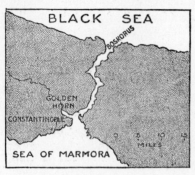

CONSTANTINOPLE AND VICINITY

by the Christian ships sallying out unexpectedly from their shelter in the Golden Horn. Each winter the Arab fleet and army retired to Cyzicus, while down the Bosphorus the city replenished its grain and general food supply for the ordeal of the next year.   Not until the summer of 677 was the Christian fleet ready to strike a decisive blow against the besiegers.   Now, equipped with the new and terrible weapon of Greek fire—and also, we must suppose, with some means of projecting it so that it would not be as dangerous to themselves as the enemy—they directed an attack in full strength against the fleet below the city.   The result, as one might expect from a well-equipped fleet taking the offensive in home waters, with a novel weapon, and with longer experience in sea warfare, was a signal victory.

The remnants of the Arab flotilla escaped through the Dardanelles, but after suffering from a storm on the Lycian coast, were again set upon by Christian forces and almost completely destroyed; while the army, retreating through Asia Minor, was attacked and defeated with a loss of 30,000.   The caliph now agreed to a truce which continued for fifteen years, and also to annual tribute of 3000 pounds of gold, 50 Arab horses, and 50 slaves.

Had the Eastern Empire at this time taken full advantage of its superiority in weapons and other facilities to build up a strong permanent navy, it might apparently have held indefinitely not only the Dardanelles but its Asia Minor coast line and the Ægean shores and islands.   Despite the well-known limitations of early sea power, it might even have prevented the expansion of the Saracens into Carthage, Sicily, and the West, since this expansion was dependent largely on sea communications. But the empire was in these years plunged in a period of bloody dynastic turmoil, such as too frequently occurred throughout its history. Moreover, in neglecting to maintain an adequate naval force, the empire fell into a mistake by no means confined to ancient times.

In the last quarter of the 7th century the westward expansion just mentioned continued rapidly. Carthage was permanently taken over in 698, and Spain was occupied in 711–12. But at the Pyrenees the energies behind this far-flung western movement seem to have been in large part expended, and the famous victory over the Saracens won by Charles Martel between Tours and Poictiers in 732 is now regarded by historians as having ended a raid rather than a serious threat against northern Europe.

In the east, however, the situation was indeed critical at the time of the second great Moslem onslaught on Constantinople in 717–18, when for two years the attacks were continued on a grand scale. It was fortunate that on the very eve of these invasions the Byzantine throne was taken over by an able emperor, Leo III, called "the Isaurian" from his native province, who in character and achievements is truly comparable to Martel and Charlemagne among the great leaders of his century.

After two years of preparation, a vast fleet of 1800 vessels, of which at least 400 were fighting craft, sailed from Syria for the Hellespont in the spring of 717, while an army of 80,000 pierced the Taurus Mountains and advanced on Constantinople by land. By mid-August these forces had invested the city by land and sea. Two weeks later a portion of the Saracen naval armada advanced up the Bosphorus to block the northern approaches to the city. This was the long-awaited moment for the first Byzantine offensive. Their forces up to this time had remained within the shelter of the Golden Horn, protected by a boom of logs and chains. The boom was now swung open and the Christian fleet poured out, ramming, boarding, and utilizing to the utmost its terrifying Greek fire. Before the main body of the Arabs could work up against the current to the rescue, the Christians had destroyed 20 enemy ships and taken a number of prizes back into the Horn. Elated with his success, Leo now ordered the boom opened wide, and, lying in battle order at the mouth of the Horn, he challenged the enemy to attack. But the latter, despite their great superiority in numbers, declined to close. Instead they withdrew from the Bosphorus and thereafter followed the less risky policy of blockade. This initial success of the Christians had the important effect of keeping open the water route to the Black Sea, by means of which supplies could still reach the beleaguered city.

After a lull in operations during the winter, an Egyptian fleet of 400 vessels and a squadron from Carthage and the west numbering 360 brought the blockaders what must have seemed an overwhelming reënforcement, and moored in the Bosphorus in an immense, confused mass of ships on the Asiatic shore. The situation for the defenders was indeed desperate, for the presence of these new arrivals in the upper straits threatened to close the last inlet to the city. Here, however, a new element entered. Many of the crews of the newcomers, as presumably of the whole Arab fleet, were either still Christians or else recent and dubious converts to Islam. There were frequent desertions, and important information was conveyed to the emperor regarding the disposition of the Arab ships. Acting on this knowledge, Leo again took his ships from the shelter of the boom and attacked the Egyptian and African squadrons across the strait. What followed was a massacre rather than a battle. The Christian members of the crews deserted wholesale and turned upon their Moslem officers. Ship after ship was rammed by the Christian dromons or set on fire by the terrible substance which every Arab regarded with superstitious dread. Some were driven ashore, others captured, and many more were sunk or burned to the water's edge. Of a total of nearly 800 vessels practically nothing was left.

Leo followed up this spectacular naval victory by transporting troops to the Asiatic shore, attacking the army encamped there, and driving it in rout. In response to the emperor's appeal a Bulgarian force also came to his aid at this time by attacking another portion of the Saracen army engaged in besieging Adrianople, and beat them back with great slaughter. The fugitives served to throw into a panic the troops encamped round the walls of Constantinople, already demoralized by disease, the death of their leaders, and the annihilation of the African and Egyptian fleets.

The great retreat began. After taking the remains of the army to the eastern side of the strait, the Saracen fleet cleared the Dardanelles, but paralleling the fate of the retreating forces in 677, it suffered from a storm in the Ægean and was almost completely wiped out in a subsequent battle. Christian ships picked off many of the survivors, and the islands destroyed others that sought shelter in any port. It is said that out of the original armada of 1800 vessels only five returned to Syria! And of the army which had numbered 180,000 only a sixth part survived the retreat through Asia Minor. Thus this supreme effort of the Saracens ended in one of the great military disasters of history.

Throughout the campaign the Christian fleet was the decisive factor. To quote a historian of the Eastern Empire:

"The fleet won most of the credit for the fine defense; it invariably fought with admirable readiness and discipline, and was handled in the most masterful manner. It checked the establishment of a naval blockade at the very outset, and broke it when it was temporarily formed in 718; it enabled the army to operate at will on either shore of the Bosphorus, and it followed up the retreating Saracens and completed the ruin of the great armament . . . Leo had won the greatest success in Roman history."[1]

It was a victory of inestimable value to Europe. Had Constantinople been conquered, the way would have been open for a westward movement which the weak European states of that epoch could scarcely have repelled. Certainly all eastern Europe to the Danube and Carpathians would have been subjected to Islam—a subjection which was thus postponed for 700 years, or longer than from 1453 to our own time.

Whether or not from the blow suffered at Constantinople,

[1]Edward Foord, THE BYZANTINE EMPIRE, p. 170.

and the defeat inflicted fourteen years later by Charles Martel in southern France, a decline of the Saracen power set in during the eighth century, and Constantinople was not again seriously threatened until the rise of the Ottoman Turk. On the other hand, the Persian Gulf and the Indian Ocean, which fell into the hands of the Arabs as soon as they took to the water, remained in their hands down to the times of the Portuguese. In those waters, because they were cut off from the Mediterranean, the Saracen had no competitor. As early as the eighth century Ceylon was an Arab trading base, and when the Portuguese explorers arrived at the end of the fifteenth century they found the Arabs still dominating the water routes of India and Asia, holding as they had held for seven centuries a monopoly of the commerce of the east.

Of the Mediterranean during the struggle between Christian and Saracen a recent English writer makes the following suggestive comment:

"The function of the Mediterranean has thus undergone a change. In early times it had been a barrier; later, under the Phœnicians, it became a highway, and to the Greeks a defense. We find that the Romans made it a basis for sea power and subdued all the lands on its margin. With the weakening of Rome came a weakening of sea power. The Barbary states and Spain became Saracen only because the naval power of the eastern empire was not strong enough to hold the whole sea, but neither was the Saracen able to gain supreme control. Thus the conditions were the same as in the earlier days of the conflict between Rome and Carthage: the Mediterranean became a moat separating the rivals, though first one and then the other had somewhat more control. The islands became alternately Saracen and Christian. Crete and Sicily were held for centuries before they were regained by a Christian power."[1]

In the centuries of intermittent frontier and sea warfare that followed between the Saracen sieges of Constantinople and the final downfall of the Eastern Empire, its fleets rendered frequent though less outstanding service. As an instance may be

[1]Fairgrieve, GEOGRAPHY AND WORLD POWER, p. 125.

cited the prominent part taken by the navy in a great expedition sent out in 959 for the reconquest of the island of Crete, which had been seized by corsairs from Egypt 150 years before and had thereafter remained a stronghold of piracy.

A second episode, especially illustrating the effectiveness of Greek fire, was the naval victory in 941 over the Varangians, or Vikings, a branch of these Scandinavian rovers who had advanced along the Russian rivers and established a strong state centering about Novgorod and Kiev. With an immense number of their swift open boats, estimated at no fewer than 1,500, an army of the Varangians entered the Bosphorus and, finding the Roman forces occupied in distant regions, proceeded upon a wild campaign of plunder around the outskirts of Constantinople. In this emergency the military governor, Theophanes the Patrician, armed a few antiquated dromons—not more than fifteen altogether—on both bow and broadsides with Greek-fire tubes and advanced up the Bosphorus to attack the swarm of pirate craft. A strange battle ensued, like those of later times in which single English or Dutch ships beat off whole squadrons of Mediterranean galleys. In this case, the Greek fire did its work, even against these Norse barbarians who must have been hardier fighters than the Arabs, for they fled in confusion up the strait after the loss of a large part of their flotilla, while their detachments on shore were hunted down and put to the sword.

This exploit of Theophanes may serve incidentally to refute the libel of the historian Gibbon and other writers that the Byzantines were inherently a nation of cowards. And it may serve also to draw attention to the many contacts, friendly as well as hostile, which the Byzantine Empire had with the peoples to the northward, and to the part it played in the religious and cultural development of eastern Europe.

The decline of the empire was largely a matter of internal decay. The loss of its eastern Mediterranean provinces to the Moslems cut deeply into its trade and revenues, as well as into its resources of men and materials for maintaining a strong navy, while such wealth as remained, instead of being used for adequate defense measures, was squandered by a corrupt court and ruling class.   More and more Constantinople became dependent on the Italian maritime cities, especially Venice and Genoa, for the transport of its trade and even for its sea protection.   Needless to say, such trust was sadly misplaced.   The Italian cities bullied and fought with the empire for trading privileges, and also, like dogs over a stolen bone, they fought over these privileges among themselves.

The death blow of the empire came in the year 1204, when the Fourth Crusade was diverted into an attack on the Christian city of Constantinople.   Two years earlier a great company of French, Flemish, and Italian barons and their retainers had gathered at Venice for an expedition to the Holy Land, having struck a bargain with the aged Doge Dandolo for transport thither upon payment of 85,000 marks (about $850,000) and a promise of a half share in all conquests.   From the first, however, among both Venetians and crusaders, mercenary motives mingled with religious zeal.   Venice, for her part, could see no advantage in disrupting her friendly trade relations with the Saracens by an invasion of Palestine, and, at the same time, was bitterly hostile toward the empire because of recent warfare and loss of trading concessions.   Delays had meantime eaten into the crusaders' funds.   In these circumstances the wily Dandolo easily persuaded them to pay their passage by the siege and plunder of the city of Zara on the Adriatic; and, when this was accomplished, he persuaded them with equal ease to an attack on Constantinople.   The affair was to be a mere episode in their eastward progress and was made doubly attractive by the offer of an exiled Byzantine prince, Alexius, to pay them 200,000 marks for assisting him to take over the imperial throne.

Against the 100 Venetian galleys and the force of about 40,000 Venetians and crusaders, Constantinople at this time could offer little defense save her massive walls.   Having reached the city and landed the army, the galleys broke through the boom to gain the Golden Horn, and from this point the attackers were able to get possession of a portion of the sea wall and burn the northern quarter of the city.   A truce, marked by a series of governmental upsets and constant quarrels between the citizens and their unwelcome guests, was followed by a renewal of hostilities in the next spring. With their long experience in this type of amphibian warfare, the Venetians, on April 12, 1204, again led an assault on the city, attacking its sea face outside the Horn, and flinging ladders and flying bridges from scaffolds on their galleys lashed in pairs. By these and other means they finally captured four towers and poured into the city.

In this fashion fewer than 40,000 men made themselves masters of a metropolis of a million people, with its immense accumulated wealth, literature, and art, which was subjected to massacre and plunder on an unparalleled scale. Four-fifths of the city was burned; three-fourths of the population fled or perished; the actual wealth seized by the invaders and not destroyed was estimated at 900,000 marks, or fourteen times as much as the annual government revenues of England in that day. A so-called "Latin Empire" was set up under Count Baldwin of Flanders, which lasted for sixty years. As part of her spoils, which she held long afterward, Venice took Crete, and many fine ports and islands of the Ægean. Though the empire was later reëstablished under Byzantine rulers it retained but a shadow of its former extent and power. In her short-sighted greed, Venice had helped to destroy a bulwark that might otherwise possibly have stayed the progress of the second westward sweep of Mohammedanism under the Ottoman Turks.[1]

Of the final capture of Constantinople by the Turkish ruler Mohammed II in 1453 little need be told, since it belongs only indirectly to sea history. Zealous converts to Islam, like the Seljuk Turks who had preceded them into southwestern Asia, the Ottoman Turks had already pushed across into Europe and established a capital at Adrianople, so populating the surrounding country that by 1400 there were more Turks west than there were east of the Dardanelles. Constantinople was an island in

---

[1]"If the Eastern Empire had not been mortally wounded and reduced to the ranks of a petty state by the greed and brutality of the western brigands who called themselves crusaders, it is probable that the Turks might never have gained a footing in Europe."—J. B. Bury, CAMBRIDGE MEDIEVAL HISTORY, Vol. IV (Introduction).

a sea of Islam.   In the final siege of the city the tiny defending force of about 8000 led by the last Emperor Constantine held out for seven weeks, until at last the fortifications on the land side were broken down by the Turkish siege artillery of 200 cannon, the largest of which was an immense mortar of 46-inch bore throwing a stone ball of 1200 pounds.   Thereafter the city became the capital and center of Moslem rule.   Though their advance into Europe was finally halted at the gates of Vienna, the Turks held the whole Balkan peninsula down to the 19th century, and Thrace and the straits to our own time.

Through many dark centuries of invasion from northward and eastward, and chaos in Europe, the Eastern Empire had cherished its heritage of ancient Greek and Roman civilization and added a rich art and architecture of its own.   Even in its ruin it sent its fugitives westward with the manuscripts of a language and literature then little known, the Greek, and thereby added greatly to the growing impetus of the Renaissance.   It is significant also that during its thousand years of life, so long as it kept its hold on the sea it stood firm.   When it yielded that, its empire dwindled to a mere city fortress whose doom was assured long before it fell.

REFERENCES

CAMBRIDGE MEDIEVAL HISTORY, Vol. II, 1913.

HISTORY OF THE DECLINE AND FALL OF THE ROMAN EMPIRE, Edward Gibbon, ed. by J. B. Bury.

HISTORY OF THE EASTERN ROMAN EMPIRE, J. B. Bury, 1912.

THE BYZANTINE EMPIRE, E. A. Foord, 1911.

HISTORY OF EUROPE, 476–918 (Periods of European History Series), Chas. Oman, 1895.

THE SEA POWER OF NEW ROME, A. M. Shepard (used in manuscript through the kindness of the author).

CHAPTER IV

VENICE AND THE TURK

THE early history of Venice has been touched upon in the preceding chapter, for the sea trade of the Italian city-states was closely related with the Eastern Empire, and grew as that of the empire declined. Beginning amid the islets and lagoons of the Adriatic as a city of refugees from the barbarian invasions of Italy, Venice early capitalized the advantages of her location between East and West. She developed her salt works and fisheries, established trading stations and political overlordship along the Dalmatian coast, and soon sent out her trading galleys to Sicily and the Levant.

Like Phœnicia, Carthage, and Athens, Venice was a "natural sea power", whose interests were centered in maritime commerce, and whose naval strength was developed as a vital necessity for the protection and extension of her trade. In earlier and later times her mercantile interests dominated her foreign policy. From Charlemagne in the early 9th century she obtained advantageous trading concessions which opened the markets of his vast domains in Italy and beyond the Alps. Naval assistance which she extended to the Eastern Empire secured for her a practical independence politically and a highly favored position in the Constantinople trade; while with the Saracens, and later with the Crusaders established in the Levant, she combined force and policy to promote her commerce and gain access to their ports which were the termini of caravan routes from the East. In Constantinople at the close of the 12th century there were 18,000 resident Venetian traders, and in all the important Levantine cities there was a Venetian quarter.

For thus guiding her foreign policy to promote the wealth and prosperity of her citizens Venice has suffered severe criti-

cism.   Yet it is a policy which has been consistently followed
by later mercantile nations.   And it is indeed open to censure
only when it sacrifices permanent for immediate interests, as
instanced by Venice in her guilty part in the downfall of the
Eastern Empire, and also in her long warfare with Genoa,
which weakened the resistance of both against the advance of
the Turks.

We have already noted that, as a part of her booty after the

THEATER OF OPERATIONS, VENICE AND THE TURK

pillage of Constantinople in 1204, Venice took Crete, which remained hers for nearly 400 years.   Cyprus was seized in 1479,
and her political control was also extended to Treviso, Padua,
Verona, and other cities of northern Italy.   After 1350 both
her trading and her war galleys were owned by the state, and
with them she commanded the carrying trade of the Mediterranean.   Great fleets under naval escort set forth each year, two
going to Alexandria, and others to Syria, Constantinople, and
the Barbary states, while one or more large merchant galleys
voyaged each summer to the Biscay coast, England, and Antwerp, laden with spices, silks, drugs, cloths, and other wares of

the Orient for the peoples of northern Europe. To quote the
lines of Byron in *Childe Harold,*

> ". . . Her daughters had their dowers
> From spoils of nations, and the exhaustless East
> Poured in her lap all gems in sparkling showers."

By 1400 Venice was at the height of her prosperity. In the
city's population of 200,000 there were 38,000 seamen. There
were over 3,000 Venetian ships. In the Great Arsenal of
Venice, three miles in circumference, with 6,000 workmen, and
with building and storage facilities comparable to a modern
navy yard, were constructed and outfitted the galleys which represented her maritime power.

Wealth and luxury, if one may venture to generalize from
history, carry in themselves the germs of decay. But the decline of Venice, which had already begun in the 15th century,
was a slow process with many contributing factors,—most conspicuous among which was the rise of Turkish power on land
and sea. These virile people, of Mongolian stock from the
steppes of central Asia, had, as we have seen, taken over and
extended the old Saracen Empire, and carried their domain
across the straits into Europe. Like the Saracens, they were no
seafarers, but used the Egyptian, Syrian, and other subject
peoples to build and man their fleets. After 1411 the Venetians
paid them regular tribute for trade protection, and between the
Turkish capture of Negropont (Euboea) in 1470 and the battle
of Lepanto a hundred years later the Turkish sea power sustained no decisive defeat. This was the period of their great
corsair leaders Keyr-ed-din or Barbarossa, Dragut, and Uluch
Ali. The advance of the Turks on land was halted finally at
the Danube. On the sea the decisive engagement was the
famous battle of Lepanto in 1571.

The Campaign of Prevesa

Preliminary to Lepanto, however, the campaign of Prevesa,
thirty-three years earlier, has a special interest as the beginning
of combined Christian resistance to the Turks on the sea, a re-

sistance headed in this instance by the great Emperor Charles V of Spain, who had long suffered from the depredations of the Barbary corsairs and now saw the need of striking directly at the central Turkish power. The campaign is significant also in that it illustrates a new type of fighting craft, and brings into opposition the two most celebrated naval leaders of the age. The Turkish forces at Prevesa in 1538 were headed by Barbarossa (Red Beard), the son, reputedly, of Christian parents on the island of Lesbos, who had risen in piratical warfare to become king of Algiers and since 1534 had held supreme command in the fleet of the Turkish sultan, Soliman "the Magnificent." At his first meeting with the sultan he had uttered a saying that might stand as a text for all the writings of Mahan: "Sire, he who is master of the sea will very shortly become master on the land." Against him was pitted Andrea Doria, scion of a distinguished line of Genoese sea leaders, who had long held high command in the fleets of Spain. It may help to explain the rather puzzling tactics of the Prevesa encounter that both these leaders were old men, Doria over seventy and Barbarossa eighty-two.

Doria commanded a fleet of 166 galleys and 64 *nefs* or sailing ships, of which the Venetians had provided 80 galleys and a squadron of *nefs* led by the great *Galleon of Venice,* a sailing vessel of a new type in Mediterranean warfare, high-sided, 16 feet in draught, and armed at all points with 128 "mouths of fire," or cannon. Though slow in assembling, the allied Christian forces were at last gathered at Corfu in September, and proceeded to blockade the smaller force of 122 Turkish galleys lying under the guns of Prevesa, a Turkish base just inside the Gulf of Arta, near the scene of the battle of Actium almost 1600 years before.

In view of the lateness of the season and their exposed position outside the gulf, the Christian fleet might soon have been forced to withdraw. Their problem was simplified, however, by Barbarossa, who was regarded as something of an interloper by his Turkish subordinates, and who, upon their insinuations of cowardice, was goaded into taking the offensive. Accordingly, on the morning of September 27, when the Christian fleet had moved some twenty miles to the southward, he left the harbor with his entire force. At this time the slow-moving *Galleon of Venice* lay becalmed, about midway between the two fleets.

Seizing upon this obvious chance for concentration, Barbarossa closed in on her, while Doria, disregarding her danger, went through curious parade movements with the rest of the fleet some ten miles away. Doria's aim, as he explained afterward, was to induce the enemy to close with him in such a manner that he might use the heavy guns of his nefs to break up their initial attack—an interesting development in tactics employed successfully with galleasses, later at Lepanto. But in this instance it was absurd to expect an inferior opponent to be drawn into battle on such unfavorable terms. Overcaution, probably combined with an intense Genoese dislike of the Venetians, marked Doria's conduct throughout this strange engagement, in which all the glory went to the *Galleon of Venice* and her gallant commander, Condulmiero.

Amid a beating of tambours and a din of war cries, a division of Turkish galleys bore down on the *Galleon,* whose crew were ordered to lie flat upon her decks protected by her high sides and bulwarks. Not until the Turks were at point-blank range were they assailed by a terrific fire of arquebus and artillery, which literally mowed down the exposed rowers and fighters of the Turkish craft. One galley was sunk by a single shot through the bow. The division drew off as fast as it had come, and subsequent attacks were made more cautiously, the galleys advancing in "waves" of 20 to deliver their artillery fire and then withdraw. In this way the battle continued from about 1 P.M. till near nightfall. With 13 killed and 40 wounded, and their deck strewn with wreckage, the Venetians now prepared for a final desperate defense against boarders; but this last attack Barbarossa failed to push home, content instead to capture a number of isolated smaller craft, and with the intention, no doubt, of renewing the battle next day.

During the night, however, Doria, taking advantage of a fair wind, picked up the battered *Galleon* and made off with all his forces toward Corfu. Next morning his fleet was nowhere to be seen, and Barbarossa, with shouts of laughter, declared that Doria had put out the poop lanterns of his flagship to conceal his flight. Thus ingloriously for the Christians ended the Prevesa campaign.

In view of the clearly demonstrated superiority of the heavily armed sailing ship in the Prevesa fighting—scarcely credible unless one compares it with the later similar feats of single

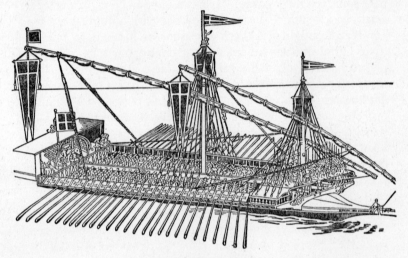

16TH CENTURY GALLEY

Dutch and English ships against galleys—one may well wonder that the galley should have continued long afterward as the chief fighting type in the Mediterranean. In explanation, it may be pointed out that the strength of the galleon or sailing ship was in those days primarily defensive. It lacked speed and maneuverability, and was useless for commerce defense against corsairs, a primary requirement for the inland sea. Don Juan, at Lepanto, thanked God that the few nefs of his fleet had fallen behind and were not with him in the battle, for he feared they would impede his attack. It is perhaps something approaching a principle of warfare that "like fights like." It is a curious fact, moreover, that Venice in the 17th century had to send to England for her first "ship of the line."

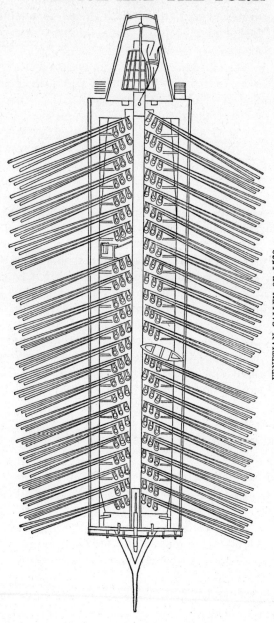

VENETIAN GALLEY OF 1539

A reconstruction by Fincati, which shows the arrangement of oars in groups of three called a *zenzili*.

Of the characteristics of the galley as the typical fighting craft of this period little need be added to what has already been said of the triremes and the dromons of earlier days. Though they varied in size, the typical galley was from 120 to 130 feet over all, with a beam of 16 to 20 feet, and with about 200 rowers arranged in a single bank with three or more men to an oar. This last was the usual scheme, though the *zenzile* arrangement (see p. 8 and the illustration on p. 57) provided smaller oars in groups of three, each pulled by one rower.

At Lepanto, in addition to the 200 rowers, each Christian galley had 100 soldiers and as many as 60 officers and other men with special duties. The fighters had their station in the bow, and sometimes also amidships, the benches there being removed during battle. Among the officers, quartered at the stern, were included the commander, pilot, and slave master. The latter, with one or two subordinates, took station, lash in hand, along a narrow midship gangway which led from stem to stern. The strokes of the oars were kept in time by the music of drum, timbrils, and trumpet. Ordinarily, the rowers were war captives or felons; and the life of the galley slaves, chained to their benches, has become proverbial for its hardships. One account of their sea diet gives a daily ration of 30 ounces of biscuit and water, with soup every other day, and meat and wine four times a year. Sickness was generally fatal, but for this and other reasons an effort was made to maintain decent food and living conditions in the better-ordered fleets.

For offensive armament the galley still depended on a metal beak projecting from the bow. After the advent of gunpowder, cannon were mounted in the bow and stern, for fore and aft fire, and could be discharged as many as three times while the opposing forces were coming into action, each, as usual, in line abreast. Though the coördinated movement of galleys was highly perfected, so that they could advance, back water, maintain a line, and turn with the precision of modern destroyers, the battle after the first collision usually developed into a close mêlée, in which the issue was decided with arquebus, bow, lance, and cutlass.

The Campaign of Lepanto

After Prevesa, the Venetians made a peace with the Turks, with a renewal of 236,000 ducats in annual tribute for trade security, which lasted precariously for the next 30 years. It was broken finally when Sultan Selim "the Drunkard", who had succeeded Soliman in 1566, demanded the surrender of Cyprus, the last possession of Venice in the eastern sea and a highly valuable base for her trade. In the ensuing struggle for the island, the capital city, Nicosia, surrendered to the Turk in 1570, and Famagusta, the chief seaport, was captured in August of the next year, after a heroic defense of 55 days. Enraged by the loss of 50,000 men in the siege, the Turks violated the terms of capitulation and massacred the captive officers and men. News of this, and of the torture and flaying alive of the commander, Bragadino, reached the Christian fleet in the midst of the Lepanto campaign.

To the urgent appeals for assistance which had been sent by Venice to all the states of Christendom at the outbreak of the war, the responses were at first disappointing. France was troubled with civil strife, and moreover had cultivated friendly relations with the sultan in her rivalry with Spain. Other powers felt that Venice deserved her fate, for she had stood neutral during the terrible Turkish siege of Malta in 1565, which had failed after four months only through the indomitable defense of the Knights of St. John.

Pope Pius V, however, had set his heart on joint action against the Turks as the scourges of the whole Christian world, and it was chiefly through his energetic and able efforts that a "Holy League" was finally organized and a naval force of Spanish, Papal, and Venetian galleys was gathered at Crete in the late summer of 1570. Unfortunately this force had no unified command. Though it moved on to the Asia Minor coast, it accomplished nothing. All matters were decided, or rather left undecided, by futile councils of war, which revealed chiefly the reluctance of Spain to risk ships or men in a Venetian cause.

The next year the league remedied this defect by the selection of a single supreme commander, and fixed its choice happily on Don Juan of Austria, illegitimate son of Charles V, a handsome and high-spirited young nobleman, twenty-four years of age, who despite his youth had commanded the Spanish army in suppressing a revolt of the Moors and had also had some naval experience as captain general of the Spanish fleet. Though Don Juan profited by the guidance of older and more experienced subordinates, it was his will to fight and will to win, combined with tact and good judgment in handling the discordant elements of which his fleet was composed, that contributed most toward the success of the ensuing campaign.

The rendezvous was Messina in Sicily, and here the allied forces slowly gathered. First to arrive were the 12 galleys of the Pope. Then came the 105 galleys and 6 galleasses furnished by the Venetians. Owing to the situation in the East, they had been in two divisions, one at Crete and one at Corfu; and the latter division had with difficulty slipped past a superior Turkish force operating under Uluch Ali at the mouth of the Adriatic. Last to arrive, in detachments of varying size, were the 80 or more galleys from the Spanish and western Italian maritime cities, most of which flew the flag of King Philip of Spain. Over the exact numbers of so large a force there must inevitably be some discrepancy. For the ships that actually took part in the battle the figures generally given are 203 Christian galleys and 6 galleasses, manned by 13,000 seamen, 43,000 rowers, and about 29,000 soldiers, most of whom were Spanish and Italian, or troops from central Europe in Spanish pay. In a juvenile poem on the battle by James VI of Scotland (later James I of England) the assembly of fighting men and ships is thus picturesquely described:

> "There came eight thousand Spaniards brave,
> From hotte and barren Spaine,
> Good order keepers, cold in fight,
> With proud disdainfull braine.
> From pleasant fertill Italie
> There came twelve thousand als,
> With subtill sprites bent to revenge

By craftie meanes and false . . .
 From divers parts did also come
Three thousand venturers brave,
 All volunteers of conscience moved,
And would no wages have.
 Arm'd galleys twice a hundr' and eight,
Six ships all wondrous great,
 And five and twentie loadened ships
With baggage and with meate.
 With forty other little barks
And pretty galeots small,
 Of these aforesaide was compound
The Christian Navie all."

The "wondrous great" ships were of course the Venetian galleasses, each with 180 cannon and 500 arquebusiers. They were a hybrid type, more strongly built and loftier than the galleys and dependent largely on sails, but with long sweeps for use in calm or in narrow waters. At Lepanto they were towed into action.

Don Juan's arrival at Messina had been delayed until August 24 by the fêtes and ceremonials held in his honor on the journey thither; and after his coming there was still a question whether, at this late date, the fleet should set out. The feelings of the Spanish monarch were well known. He had joined the league at the Pope's call, but preferred to save his galleys for use against the Moors of the Barbary coast, rather than risk them in what was chiefly a Venetian cause. Undoubtedly Doria and the other Spanish officers were fully informed of their royal master's desires in this expedition as in the one of the year before. They were to avoid battle if they could. Opposed to this sentiment was Don Juan's spirit of sincere religious zeal and youthful desire for aggressive action, mingled also with a not unworthy ambition for the personal fame which a victory would ensure in every Christian land. In this spirit he was seconded by thousands of young nobles and soldiers of fortune from Spain and Italy, who had flocked to his standard like the knights errant of the age of chivalry, burning to distinguish themselves against the infidel. Among these, stationed in one of the Venetian galleys, was a young Spaniard, Miguel de Cervantes, who, though he lost his left hand in the battle, wrote with the other an immortal romance ridiculing the fantastic tales of chivalry, but filled with devotion to knightly courage and Christian faith.

When the great armada finally sailed from Messina in mid-September, each ship had been assigned its exact place in the fighting line, and the fleet itself had been divided into squadrons—right, left, center or "main battle," and a reserve of 30 galleys—each squadron with its distinctive colors, green, blue, orange, and white. In cruising, an advance guard moved 20 miles ahead, closing at night to 8 miles, and a rear guard was placed 1 mile astern. In battle the 6 galleasses were to take station at intervals considerably in advance of the battle line, acting as floating fortresses to break up the enemy's formation. The fighting line itself was given cohesion by the fact that the main or center division was not only considerably larger than the others but was strengthened at its mid point by the great *Reale,* or "galley royal", of the commander in chief, with the flagship of the Papal commander, Colonna, on its right, and that of Veniero, the Venetian leader, on the left. Most writers have also commended Don Juan's plan of scattering the ships of the different nations among all four divisions in order to prevent the jealousy, rivalry, and possible treachery that might result if the ships of each nationality operated as distinct groups.

Even so, during the slow ten-day cruise eastward from Messina to Corfu, these dangers became manifest, for in quelling a wild fray between Spanish soldiers and Venetian sailors that broke out on Veniero's flagship, the aged Venetian admiral, who was a notorious martinet, executed summary justice by hanging three Spaniards at the masthead. Don Juan, angry at what appeared a usurpation of authority, refused to receive the Venetian at his subsequent councils aboard the *Reale*— a prohibition which Veniero declared he was only too glad to observe.

In the meantime, while these slow Christian preparations and movements had been going on, the Turkish fleet after the fall of Cyprus had advanced westward into the Adriatic, partly to protect their Greek possessions, partly to fall upon the Venetians in detail as they moved to the Messina rendezvous. Failing in this by a narrow margin, they had plundered the Adriatic coast, almost to the lagoons of Venice itself, and had finally returned to their base in the Gulf of Corinth, or Lepanto.[1]

With a force of 208 galleys and some 60 galliots and other smaller types, the Turks were about equal in number of fighting vessels, but decidedly inferior in the strength of troops aboard, which came to about 25,000, and also in the number and size of artillery. On the other hand, they had the advantages of greater national unity, of self-confidence born of their recent victories in Cyprus, and of at least equal skill and experience at sea, for it must be remembered that their crews were for the most part not Turks by race but Moors, Greeks, Syrians, Egyptians, and other seafaring peoples of the Mediterranean. The commander in chief was Ali Pasha, like Don Juan a youthful officer elevated to his position only the year before. Like Don Juan also, he had his station in the center of the Turkish line. Uluch Ali, the celebrated Barbary corsair, led the left wing, and Scirocco, the viceroy of Egypt, commanded the right.

Early in October the Christian fleet moved slowly down the Dalmatian coast. Scouting forces at this time and later operated on both sides with great daring; a Turkish corsair named Kara Khodja, painting his 22-oared galliot black, actually rowed on a dark night into the very midst of the Christian fleet. Owing to temporary detachments, however, he considerably underestimated its strength. Partly perhaps on this account, partly through an over-confidence created by Prevesa and the naval operations of the year before, the Turkish council of war, though divided in opinion, decided to leave the shelter of their base and meet the enemy in the open sea.

On the morning of October 7 the two fleets came in sight of each other at the mouth of the Gulf of Lepanto near Cape Schropha, afterward named in Turkish "the Cape of Blood." As the Christian forces rounded the cape to form their battle

[1] Lepanto is the modern name of the ancient Naupaktis, a town on the northern side of the gulf, and is also used as a name for the gulf.

line, Don Juan hoisted at the stern of his flagship the great
white banner of the Holy League, with the figure of Christ on
the cross, while from the Turkish flagship rose another white
standard emblazoned in gold with texts from the Koran. Religious faith rather than patriotism stirred the hearts of the
fighters of that day; and Don Juan's words, "There is no Para-

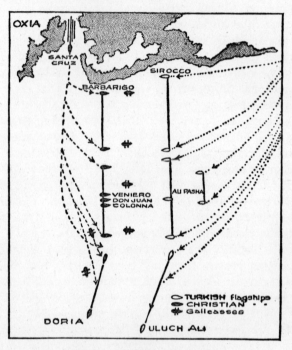

BATTLE OF LEPANTO, OCT. 7, 1571
Formation of the two fleets just before contact, about 11 a. m.

dise for poltroons," no doubt had many echoes in both the
fighting lines. As the fleets drew closer, the wind, which had
been against the Christians, fell calm. Don Juan, crucifix in
hand, passed in a light *fregatta* or rowing boat along the left
and center giving last words of encouragement, and greeting
even Veniero with a friendly salute.

Owing to the turn already mentioned, the Christian right
wing and rear were delayed in reaching their station, and it was

the left and center that bore the brunt of the first attack, their four galleasses standing like piers of a bridge to break the current of the enemy's advance. In trying to avoid them, the Turks fell into some confusion, and suffered from an effective close-range fire as they swept past. This was an important service of the galleasses, but as they were too unwieldy for close maneuvering, we hear no more of them in the day's action.

Once past this barrier, the Turkish right came into close contact amid a tumult of shouting and furious plying of oars. With a better knowledge of the water, Scirocco threatened to outflank Barbarigo, the Venetian commander of the Christian left wing, by thrusting a stream of galleys between him and the shore. The Venetian, however, swung his line toward them, and after an hour or more of fierce fighting, in which both division commanders were killed and the Turkish flagship was stormed and captured, the Turkish ships were either put to flight or driven ashore. The greater part of the fighting and the losses at Lepanto came on this side of the two lines.

In the center, the flagships of the two chief commanders steered straight toward each other. There was time for but three discharges of cannon as the opponents closed. The Turkish flagship, somewhat higher than the *Reale,* drove her ram into the latter as far as the fourth rowers' bench, then wrenched away and came alongside. Attack and counter attack between Spanish infantry and Turkish Janissaries now swayed back and forth from one galley to another amid a terrific uproar. Once the *Reale* was nearly taken, but Colonna jammed the bows of his galley alongside and saved the situation by a counter attack. On the other side of the flagship Veniero was also at one time in grave peril but was saved by the timely assistance of his comrades. Though wounded in the leg, this veteran of seventy fought throughout the action as stoutly as the youngest soldier.

The prompt action of Colonna turned the tide in the center, for after clearing the Turks from the deck of the *Reale,* the Christians, now reënforced, made a supreme effort that swept the length of Ali Pasha's galley and left the Turkish commander in chief among the slain. In fighting of this character no quarter was given; of the 400 men on the Turkish flagship not one was spared.   Don Juan immediately hoisted the banner of the league to the masthead of the captured ship.   This sign of victory broke the spirit of the Turks and nerved the Christians to redoubled efforts.   As on the left wing so in the center the offensive now passed to the allies.   Thus after two hours' fighting the Turks were already beaten on left and center, though fighting still went on hotly in tangled and scattered groups of ships.

Meanwhile, in the outboard or seaward divisions of the two fleets, there was more complicated maneuvering on the part of the two veteran commanders, Gian Andrea Doria, a great nephew of the Doria who fought at Prevesa, and Uluch Ali. Doria, with a somewhat smaller force than Ali's (about 50 to 65), was slower in coming into position, and as he did so he thought he detected an intention on the part of his opponent either to outflank him or escape altogether.   He therefore followed Ali's movements, swinging far out and leaving a broad gap between his own force and the Christian right center. Seizing the opportunity offered, Ali at this moment dashed suddenly at the ships of the Knights of Malta and the 10 Venetian galleys in this part of the main body.   One after another these were taken by superior forces, until it looked as if the Turks might "roll up" the entire flank.   The flagship of Malta was attacked by seven of the enemy and all but three on board were killed.   But by this time Santa Cruz with the rear division was coming into action, and relief was available also from Doria and Don Juan.   Signaling retreat, Ali was able to draw off toward the gulf with some 35 galleys, bearing with him the captured flag of the Knights of Malta, which he could later lay at the feet of the sultan as some consolation for the terrible defeat inflicted on the Moslem arms.

The fighting did not end till evening.   By that time the Christians could report 117 galleys and 20 galliots captured, and about 50 ships of various sorts either sunk or burned.   Since little quarter was given on either side, one may possibly accept the seemingly incredible report of 30,000 Turks killed, wounded, or captured on this fatal day.   The Christian loss was placed at 7,500 men.

Among the factors accounting for the victory were the greater number of soldiers on the Christian ships, their better equipment, especially in the way of body armor, and probably also the better fighting quality of the Spanish infantry. The galleasses counted for something, and also the fact that the bows and sterns of the Christian vessels were covered so as to form a protection, while those of the Turks were completely exposed. In the preparation for and the planning of the battle, much credit must go to the energetic leadership of Don Juan. In the outcome there was small honor for Gian Andrea Doria, as there had been little for the elder Doria at Prevesa. Whatever the purpose or skill of his maneuvering, it had left an opening so serious as almost to threaten the success of the Christian arms.

The material results of Lepanto may have seemed somewhat disappointing. Fighting flotillas and man power were in those days more easily replaced, and Uluch Ali was at sea with another fleet of 250 galleys in the next spring. Twice, however, he refused a challenge to battle with the forces of the league. Late in 1572 Venice, whose trade was suffering, negotiated a separate peace with the Turks which lasted till 1635, and in which she renewed her tribute for commercial privileges and confirmed the surrender of Cyprus. The moral effect of the victory, on the other hand, was more decisive and lasting. Not again did the Turks seriously threaten the domination of the Mediterranean, though the Barbary corsairs preyed upon commerce down to the close of the Napoleonic Wars. It was at Lepanto, to quote Cervantes, that "the world and all the nations were disabused of the error that the Turks were invincible at sea."

The decline of Venice as a sea power had, as already stated, begun a hundred years before. The hostility of the Turks had increased the obstacles to her trade in the Levant; but far more serious in its effect upon her commerce was the opening of the ocean route to the East, by which the heavier wares of the West could be carried directly to the Orient and a reciprocal trade established free from Turkish interference and the heavier costs of partial transport by land. This diverted trade from the Mediterranean until the construction of a canal at Suez. The Venetian Republic fell gradually back into the ranks of petty states, until its existence was finally ended in the French Revolutionary War.

REFERENCES

LA GUERRE DE CHYPRE ET LA BATAILLE DE LÉPANTE, J. P. Jurien de la Gravière, 1888.

By the same author, DORIA ET BARBEROUSSE, 1886.

HISTORY OF THE REIGN OF PHILIP THE SECOND, Vol. III, W. H. Prescott, 1858.

SEA WOLVES OF THE MEDITERRANEAN, E. Hamilton Currey. This contains a full bibliography.

THE NAVY OF VENICE, Alethea Wiel, 1910.

THE EASTERN QUESTION, Chap. V, J. A. R. Marriott, 1917.

BARBARY CORSAIRS, Story of the Nations Series, Lane-Poole, 1890.

DRAKE AND THE TUDOR NAVY (Introduction), J. S. Corbett, 1898.

GEOGRAPHY AND WORLD POWER, James Fairgrieve, 1917.

CHAPTER V

OPENING THE OCEAN ROUTES

I. PORTUGAL AND THE NEW ROUTE TO INDIA

FROM the days of the Phœnicians to the close of the 15th century, all trade between Europe and Asia crossed the land barrier east of the Mediterranean. Delivered by Mohammedan vessels at the head of the Persian Gulf or the ports of the Red Sea, merchandise followed thence the caravan routes across Arabia or Egypt to the Mediterranean, quadrupling in value in the transit. Intercourse between East and West, active under the Romans, was again stimulated by the crusades and by Venetian traders, until in the 14th and the 15th centuries the dyes, spices, perfumes, cottons, muslins, silks, and jewels of the Orient were in demand throughout the western world. This assurance of a ready market and large profits, combined with the capture of Constantinople by the Turks (1453), their piratical attacks in the Mediterranean which continued unchecked until Lepanto, and their final barring of all trade routes through the Levant, revived among nations of western Europe the old legends of all-water routes to Asia, either around Africa or directly westward across the unknown sea.

With the opening of ocean routes and the discovery of America, a rivalry in world trade and colonial expansion set in which has continued increasingly down to the present time, forming a dominant element in the foreign policies of maritime nations and a primary motive for the possession and use of navies. The development of overseas trade, involving the factors of merchant shipping, navies, and control of the seas, is thus an integral part of the history of sea power. The great voyages of discovery are also not to be disregarded, supplying as they did the basis for colonial claims, and illustrating at the same time the progress of nautical science and geographical knowledge.

The art of navigation, though still crude, had by the 15th century so advanced that the sailor was no longer compelled to skirt the shore, with only rare ventures across open stretches of sea. The use of the compass, originating in China, had

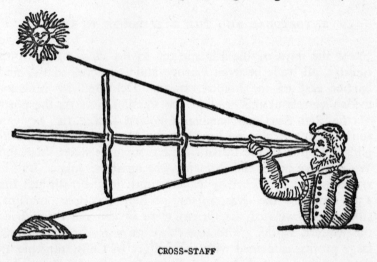

CROSS-STAFF

been learned from the Arabs by the crusaders, and is first mentioned in Europe towards the close of the 12th century. An Italian in England, describing a visit to the philosopher Roger Bacon in 1258, writes as follows: "Among other things he showed me an ugly black stone called a magnet . . . upon which, if a needle be rubbed and afterward fastened to a straw so that it shall float upon the water, the needle will instantly turn toward the pole-star; though the night be never so dark, yet shall the mariner be able by the help of this needle to steer his course aright. But no master-mariner," he adds, "dares to use it lest he should fall under the imputation of being a magician." [1]   By the end of the 13th century

[1] Dante's tutor Brunetto Latini, quoted in THE DISCOVERY OF AMERICA, Fiske, Vol. I. p. 314.

the compass was coming into general use; and when Columbus sailed he had an instrument divided as in later times into 360 degrees and 32 points, as well as a quadrant, sea-astrolabe, and other nautical devices. The astrolabe, an instrument for determining latitude by measuring the altitude of the sun or other heavenly body, was suspended from the finger by a ring and held upright at noon till the shadow of the sun passed the sights. The cross-staff, more frequently used for the same purpose by sailors of the time, was a simpler affair less affected by the ship's roll; it was held with the lower end of the cross-piece level with the horizon and the upper adjusted to a point on a line between the eye of the observer and the sun at the zenith. By these various means the sailor could steer a fixed course and determine latitude. He had, however, as yet no trustworthy means of reckoning longitude and no accurate gauge of distance traveled. The log-line was not invented until the 17th century, and accurate chronometers for determining longitude did not come into use until still later. A common practice of navigators, adopted by Columbus, was to steer first north or south along the coast and then due west on the parallel thought to lead to the destination sought.

With the revival of classical learning in the Renaissance, geographical theories also became less wildly imaginative than in the medieval period, the charts of which, though beautifully colored and highly decorated with fauna and flora, show no such accurate knowledge even of the old world as do those of the great geographer Ptolemy, who lived a thousand years before. Ptolemy (200 A.D.), in company with the majority of learned men since Aristotle, had declared the earth to be round and had even estimated its circumference with substantial accuracy, though he had misled later students by picturing the Indian Ocean as completely surrounded by Africa, which he conceived to extend indefinitely southward and join Asia on the southeast, leaving no sea-route open from the Atlantic. There was another body of opinion of long standing, however, which outlined Africa much as it actually is. Friar Roger Bacon, whose interest in the compass has already been mentioned, collected statements of class-

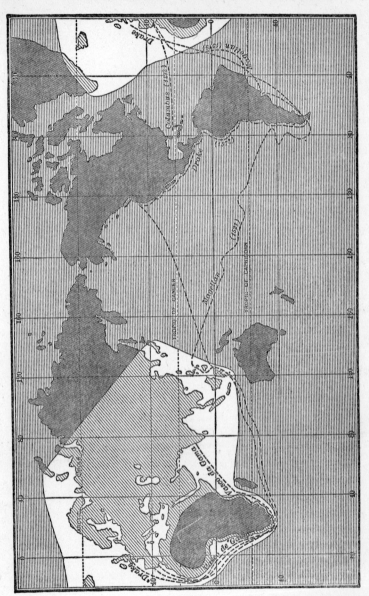

THE KNOWN AND UNKNOWN WORLD IN 1450, SHOWING THE VOYAGES OF COLUMBUS, VASCO DA GAMA, MAGELLAN, AND DRAKE

ical authorities and other evidence to show that Asia could be reached by sailing directly westward, and that the distance was not great; and this material was published in Paris in a popular *Imago Mundi* of 1410 In general, the best geographical knowledge of the period, though it underestimated the distance from Europe westward to Asia and was completely ignorant of the vast continents lying between, gave support to the theories which the voyages of Diaz, Vasco da Gama, and Columbus magnificently proved true.

When the best sailors of the time were Italians, and when astronomical and other scientific knowledge of use in navigation was largely monopolized by Arabs and Jews, it seems strange that the isolated and hitherto insignificant country of Portugal should have taken, and for a century or more maintained primacy in the great epoch of geographical discovery. The fact is explained, not so much by her proximity to the African coast and the outlying islands in the Atlantic, as by the energetic and well-directed patronage which Prince Henry the Navigator (1394-1460) extended to voyages of exploration and to the development of every branch of nautical art. The third son of John the Great of Portugal, and a nephew on his mother's side of Henry IV of England, the prince in 1415 led an armada to the capture of Ceuta from the Moors, and thereafter, as governor of the conquered territory and of the southern province of Portugal, settled at Saigres near Cape St. Vincent. On this promontory, almost at the western verge of the known world, Henry founded a city, Villa do Iffante, erected an observatory on the cliff, and gathered round him the best sailors, geographers and astronomers of his age.

Under this intelligent stimulus, Portuguese navigators within a century rounded the Cape of Good Hope, opened the sea route to the Indies, discovered Brazil, circumnavigated the globe, and made Portugal the richest nation in Europe, with a great colonial empire and claims to dominion over half the seas of the world. Portuguese ships carried her flag from Labrador (which reveals its discoverers in its name) and Nova Zembla to the Malay Archipelago and Japan.

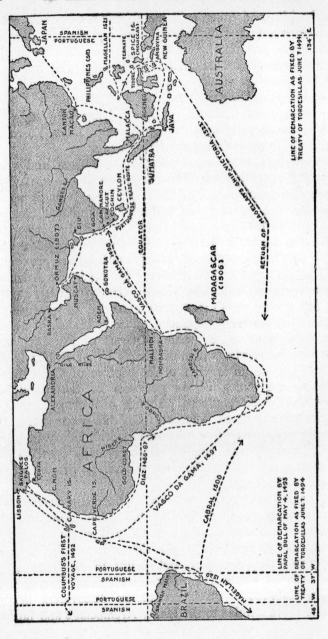

PORTUGUESE VOYAGES AND POSSESSIONS

It is characteristic of the crusading spirit of the age that Prince Henry's first ventures down the African coast were in pursuance of a vague plan to ascend one of the African rivers and unite with the legendary Christian monarch Prester John (Presbyter or Bishop John, whose realm was then supposed to be located in Abyssinia) in a campaign against the Turk. But crusading zeal changed to dreams of wealth when his ships returned from the Senegal coast between 1440 and 1445 with elephants' tusks, gold, and negro slaves. The Gold Coast was already reached; the fabled dangers of equatorial waters—serpent rocks, whirlpools, liquid sun's rays and boil-ing rivers—were soon proved unreal; and before 1480 the coast well beyond the Congo was known.

The continental limits of Africa to southward, long clearly surmised, were verified by the voyage of Bartolomeo Diaz, in 1487. Diaz rounded the cape, sailed northward some 200 miles, and then, troubled by food shortage and heavy weather, turned backward. But he had blazed the trail. The cape he called *Tormentoso* (tempestuous) was re-named by his sovereign, João II, Cape *Bon Esperanto*—the Cape of Good Hope. The Florentine professor Politian wrote to congratulate the king upon opening to Christianity "new lands, new seas, new worlds, dragged from secular dark-ness into the light of day."

It was not until ten years later that Vasco da Gama set out to complete the work of Diaz and establish contact be-tween east and west. The contour of the African coast was now so well understood and the art of navigation so advanced that Vasco could steer a direct course across the open sea from the Cape Verde Islands to the southern extremity of Africa, a distance of 3770 miles (more than a thousand miles greater than that of Columbus' voyage from the Canaries to the Bahamas), which he covered in one hundred days. After touching at Mozambique, he caught the steady monsoon winds for Calicut, on the western coast of the peninsula of India, then a great *entrepôt* where Mohammedan and Chinese fleets met each year to exchange wares. Thwarted here by the in-trigues of Mohammedan traders, who were quick to realize the danger threatening their commercial monopoly, he moved on to Cannanore, a port further north along the coast, took cargo, and set sail for home, reaching the Azores in August of 1499, with 55 of his original complement of 148 men. They came back, in the picturesque words of the Admiral, "With the pumps in their hands and the Virgin Mary in their mouths," completing a total voyage of 13,000 miles. The profits are said to have been sixty-fold.

The ease with which in the next two decades Portugal extended and consolidated her conquest of eastern trade is readily accounted for. She was dependent indeed solely upon sea communications, over a distance so great as to make the task seem almost impossible. But the craft of the east were frail in construction and built for commerce rather than for warfare. The Chinese junks that came to India are described as immense in size, with large cabins for the officers and their families, vegetable gardens growing on board, and crews of as many as a thousand men; but they had sails of matted reed that could not be lowered, and their timbers were loosely fastened together with pegs and withes. The Arab ships, according to Marco Polo, were also built without the use of nails. Like the Portuguese themselves, the Arab or Mohammedan merchants belonged to a race of alien invaders, little liked by the native princes who retained petty sovereignties along the coast. But the real secret of Portuguese success lay in the fact that their rivals were traders rather than fighters, who had enjoyed a peaceful monopoly for centuries, and who could expect little aid from their own countries harassed by the Turk. The Portuguese on the other hand inherited the traditions of Mediterranean seamanship and warfare, and, above all, were engaged in a great national enterprise, led by the best men in the land, with enthusiastic government support.

After Vasco's return, fleets were sent out each year, to open the Indian ports by either force or diplomacy, destroy Moslem merchant vessels, and establish factories and garrisons. In 1505 Francisco de Almeida set sail with the largest fleet as yet fitted out (sixteen ships and sixteen caravels), an appointment as Viceroy of Cochin, Cannanore, and Quilon, and supreme authority from the Cape to the Malay Peninsula. Almeida in the next four years defeated the Mohammedan traders, who with the aid of Egypt had by this time organized to protect themselves, in a series of naval engagements, culminating on February 3, 1509, in the decisive battle of Diu.

Mir Hussain, Admiral of the Gran Soldan of Egypt and commander in chief of the Mohammedan fleet in this battle, anchored his main force of more than a hundred ships in the mouth of the channel between the island of Diu and the mainland, designing to fall back before the Portuguese attack towards the island, where he could secure the aid of shore batteries and a swarm of 300 or more foists and other small craft in the harbor. Almeida had only 19 ships and 1300 men, but against his vigorous attack the flimsy vessels of the east were of little value. The battle was fought at close quarters in the old Mediterranean style, with saber, cutlass, and culverin; ramming, grappling, and boarding. Before nightfall Almeida had won. This victory ensured Portugal's commercial control in the eastern seas.

Alfonso d'Albuquerque, greatest of the Portuguese conquistadores, succeeded Almeida in 1509. Establishing headquarters in a central position at Goa, he sent a fleet eastward to Malacca, where he set up a fort and factory, and later fitted out expeditions against Ormuz and Aden, the two strongholds protecting respectively the entrances to the Persian Gulf and the Red Sea. The attack on Aden failed, but Ormuz fell in 1515. Albuquerque died in the same year and was buried in his capital at Goa. His successor opened trade and founded factories in Ceylon. In 1526 a trading post was established at Hugli, near the mouth of the Ganges. Ormuz became a center for the Persian trade, Malacca for trade with Java, Sumatra, and the Spice Islands. A Portuguese envoy, Fernam de Andrada, reached Canton in 1517—in the first European ship to enter Chinese waters—and Pekin three years later. Another adventurer named Mendez Pinto spent years in China and in 1548 established a factory near Yokohama, Japan. Brazil, where a squadron under Cabral had touched as early as 1502, was by 1550 a prosperous colony, and in later centuries a chief source of wealth. Mozambique, Mombassa, and Malindi, on the southeastern coast of Africa, were taken and fortified as intermediate bases to protect the route to Asia. The muslins of Bengal, the calicoes of Calicut, the spices from the islands, the pepper of Malabar, the teas and silks of China and Japan, now found their way by direct ocean passage to the Lisbon quays.

A few strips along the African coast, tenuously held by sufferance of the great powers, and bits of territory at Goa, Daman, and Diu in India, are the twentieth century remnants of Portugal's colonial empire. The greater part of it fell away between 1580 and 1640, when Portugal was under Spanish rule. But her own system of colonial administration, or rather exploitation, was if possible worse than Spain's. Her scanty resources of man power were exhausted in colonial warfare. The expulsion of Protestants and Jews deprived her of elements in her population that might have known how to utilize wealth from the colonies to build up home trade and industries. Her situation was too distant from the European markets; and the raw materials landed at Lisbon were transshipped in Dutch bottoms for Amsterdam and Antwerp, which became the true centers of manufacturing and exchange. Cervantes, in 1607, could still speak of Lisbon as the greatest city in Europe,[1] but her greatness was already decaying; and her fate was sealed when Philip of Spain closed her ports to Dutch shipping, and Dutch ships themselves set sail for the east.

But the period of Portugal's maritime ascendancy cannot be left without recording, even if in barest outline, the circumnavigation of the globe by Fernão da Magalhães, or Magellan, who, though he made this last voyage of his under the Spanish flag, was Portuguese by birth and had proved his courage and iron resolution under Almeida and Albuquerque in Portugal's eastern campaigns. Seeking a westward passage to the Spice Islands, the five vessels of 75 to 100 tons composing his squadron cleared the mouth of the Guadalquivir

[1] PERSILES AND SIGISMUDA, III, i.

on September 20, 1519. They established winter quarters in the last of March at Port St. Julian on the coast of Patagonia. Here, on Easter Sunday, three of his Spanish captains mutinied. Magellan promptly threw a boat's crew armed with cutlasses aboard one of the mutinous ships, killed the leader, and overcame the unruly element in the crew. The two other ships he forced to surrender within 24 hours. One of the guilty captains was beheaded and the other marooned on the coast when the expedition left in September. Five weeks were now spent in the labyrinths of the strait which has since borne the leader's name. "When the capltayne Magalianes," so runs the contemporary English translation of the story of the voyage, "was past the strayght and sawe the way open to the other mayne sea, he was so gladde thereof that for joy the teares fell from his eyes."

He had sworn he would go on if he had to eat the leather from the ships' yards. With three vessels—one had been shipwrecked in the preceding winter and the other deserted in the straits—they set out across the vast unknown expanse of the Pacific. "In three monethes and xx dayes they sailed foure thousande leagues in one goulfe by the sayde sea called Pacificum. . . . And havying in this tyme consumed all their bysket and other vyttayles, they fell into such necessitie that they were inforced to eate the pouder that remayned thereof being now full of woormes. . . . Theyre freshe water was also putryfyed and become yellow. They dyd eate skynnes and pieces of lether which were foulded about certeyne great ropes of the shyps." On March 6, 1521, they reached the Ladrones, and ten days later, the Philippines, even these islands having never before been visited by Europeans. Here the leader was killed in a conflict with the natives. One ship was now abandoned, and another was later captured by the Portuguese. Of the five ships that had left Spain with 280 men, a single vessel, "with tackle worn and weather-beaten yards," and 18 gaunt survivors reached home. "It has not," writes the historian John Fiske of this voyage, "the unique historic position of the first voyage of Columbus, which brought together two streams of human life that had been disjoined since the glacial period. But as an achievement in ocean navigation that voyage of Columbus sinks into insignificance beside it. . . . When we consider the frailness of the ships, the immeasurable extent of the unknown, the mutinies that were prevented or quelled, and the hardships that were endured, we can have no hesitation in speaking of Magellan as the prince of navigators." [1]

2. SPAIN AND THE NEW WORLD

It is generally taken for granted that the great movement of the Renaissance, which spread through western Europe in the 15th and the 16th centuries, quickening men's interest in the world about them rather than the world to come, and inspiring them with an eagerness and a confident belief in their own power to explore its hidden secrets, was among the forces which brought about the great geographical discoveries of the period. Its influence in this direction is evident enough in England and elsewhere later on; but, judging by the difficulties of Columbus in securing support, it was not in his time potent with those in control of government policy and government funds. The Italian navigator John Cabot and his son Sebastian made their voyages from England in 1498 and 1500 with very feeble support from Henry VII, though it was upon their discoveries that England later based her American claims. Even in Spain there seems to have been little eagerness to emulate the methods by which her neighbor Portugal had so rapidly risen to wealth and power.

But the influence of revived classical information on geographical matters was keenly felt; and the idea of a direct westerly passage to India was suggested, not only by Portugal's monopoly of the Cape route, but by classical authority, generally accepted by the best geographers of the time. The *Imago Mundi* of 1410, already mentioned, embodying Roger Bacon's arguments that the Atlantic washed the shores of Asia and that the voyage thither was not long, was a book

[1] THE DISCOVERY OF AMERICA, Vol. II, p. 210.

carefully studied by Columbus. Paul Toscanelli, a Florentine physicist and astronomer, adopting and developing this theory, sent in 1474 to Alfonso V of Portugal a map of the world in which he demonstrated the possibilities of the western route. The distance round the earth at the equator he estimated almost exactly to be 24,780 statute miles, and in the latitude of Lisbon 19,500 miles; but he so exaggerated the extent of Europe and Asia as to reduce the distance between them by an Atlantic voyage to about 6500 miles, putting the east coast of China in about the longitude of Oregon. This distance he still further shortened by locating Cipango (Japan) far to the eastward of Asia, in about the latitude of the Canary Islands and distant from them only 3250 miles.

With all these opinions Columbus was familiar, for the list of his library and the annotations still preserved in his own handwriting, show that he was not an ignorant sailor, nor yet a wild visionary, but prepared by closest study for the task to which he gave his later years. His earlier career, on the other hand, had supplied him with abundant practical knowledge. Born in Genoa, a mother city of great seamen, probably in the year 1436, he had received a fair education in Latin, geography, astronomy, drafting, and other subjects useful to the master-mariner of those days. He had sailed the Mediterranean, and prior to his great adventure, had been as far north as Iceland, and on many voyages down the African coast. Following his brother Bartholomew, who was a mapmaker in the Portuguese service, he came about 1470 to Lisbon, even then a center of geographical knowledge and maritime activity. Probably as early as this time the idea of a western voyage was in his mind.

Skepticism may account for Portugal's failure to listen to his proposals; and her interest was already centered in the route around Africa under her exclusive control. The tale of his years of search for assistance is well known. Indeed, while the fame of Columbus rests rightly enough upon his discovery of a new world, of whose existence he had never dreamed and which he never admitted in his lifetime, his greatness is best shown by his faith in his vision, and the steadfast energy and fortitude with which he pushed towards its practical accomplishment, during years of vain supplication, and amid the trials of the voyage itself. He had actually left Granada, when Isabella of Spain at last agreed to support his venture. In the contract later drawn up he drove a good bargain, contingent always upon success; he was to be admiral and viceroy of islands and continents discovered and their surrounding waters, with control of trading privileges and a tenth part of the wealth of all kinds derived.

With the explorations of Columbus on his first and his three later voyages (in 1496, 1498, and 1502) we are less concerned than with the first voyage itself as an illustration of the problems and dangers faced by the navigator of the time, and with the effect of the discovery of the new world upon Spain's rise as a sea power. The three caravels in which he sailed were typical craft of the period. The *Santa Maria,* the largest, was like the other two, a single-decked, lateen-rigged, three-masted vessel, with a length of about 90 feet, beam of about 20 feet, and a maximum speed of perhaps 6½ knots. She was of 100 tons burden and carried 52 men. The *Pinta* was somewhat smaller. The *Niña* (Baby) was a tiny, half-decked vessel of 40 tons. Heavily timbered and seaworthy enough, the three caravels were short provisioned and manned in part from the rakings of the Palos jail.

Leaving Palos August 3, 1492, Columbus went first to the Canaries, and thence turned his prow directly westward, believing that he was on the parallel that touched the northern end of Japan. By a reckoning even more optimistic than Toscanelli's, he estimated the distance thither to be only 2500 miles. Thence he would sail to Quinsay (Hang Chow), the ancient capital of China, and deliver the letter he carried to the Khan of Cathay. The northeast trade winds bore them steadily westward, raising in the minds of the already fear-stricken sailors the certainty that against these head winds they could never beat back. At last they entered the vast expanse of the Sargasso Sea, six times as large as France, where they lay for a week almost becalmed, amid tangled masses of floating seaweeds. To add to their perplexities, they had passed the line of no variation, and the needle now swung to the left of the pole-star instead of the right.   On the last day of the outward voyage they were 2300 miles to the westward according to the information Columbus shared with his officers and men; according to his secret log they were 2700 miles from the Canaries, and well beyond the point where he had expected to strike the islands of the Asiatic coast.   The mutinous and

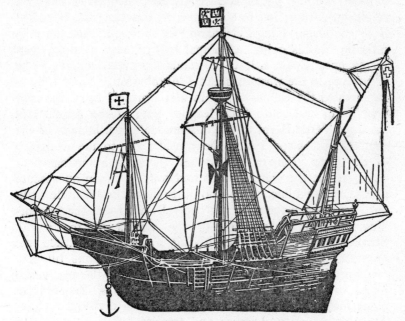

FLAGSHIP OF COLUMBUS

panic-stricken spirit of his subordinates, the uncertainty of Columbus himself, turned to rejoicing when at 2:00 A.M. of Friday, October 12, a sailor on the *Pinta* sighted the little island of the Bahamas, which, since the time of the Vikings, was the first land sighted by white men in the new world.

The three vessels cruised southward, in the belief, expressed by the name Indian which they gave the natives, that they were in the archipelago east of Asia.   Skirting the northern coast of Cuba and Hayti, they sought for traces of gold, and information as to the way to the mainland. The *Santa Maria* was wrecked on Christmas Day; the *Pinta* became separated; Columbus returned in the little *Niña,* putting in first at the Tagus, and reaching Palos on March 15, 1493.

Though his voyage gave no immediate prospect of immense profits, yet it was the general belief that he had reached Asia, and by a route three times as short as that by the Cape of Good Hope. The Spanish court celebrated his return with rejoicing. Appealing to the Pope, at this time the Spaniard Rodrigo Borgia, King Ferdinand lost no time in securing holy sanction for his gains. A Papal bull of May 3, 1493, conferred upon Spain title to all lands discovered or yet to be discovered in the western ocean. Another on the day following divided the claims of Spain and Portugal by a line running north and south "100 leagues west of the Azores and the Cape Verde Islands" (an obscure statement in view of the fact that the Cape Verdes lie considerably to the westward of the other group), and granted to Spain a monopoly of commerce in the waters "west and south" (again an obscure phrase) of this line, so that no other nation could trade without license from the power in control. This was the extraordinary Papal decree dividing the waters of the world. Small wonder that the French king, Francis I, remarked that he refused to recognize the title of the claimants till they could produce the will of Father Adam, making them universal heirs; or that Elizabeth, when a century later England became interested in world trade, disputed a division contrary not only to common sense and treaties but to "the law of nations." The Papal decree, intended merely to settle the differences of the two Catholic states, gave rise to endless disputes and preposterous claims.

The treaty of Tordesillas (1494) between Spain and Portugal fixed the line of demarcation more definitely, 370 miles west of the Cape Verde Islands, giving Portugal the Brazilian coast, and by an additional clause it made illegitimate trade a crime punishable by death. Another agreement in 1529 extended the line around to the Eastern Hemisphere, 17 degrees east of the Moluccas, which, if Spain had abided by it, would have excluded her from the Philippines. After Portugal fell under Spanish rule in 1580, Spain could claim dominion over all the southern seas.

The enthusiasm and confident expectation with which Spain set out to exploit the discoveries of Columbus's first voyage changed to disappointment when subsequent explorations revealed lands of continental dimensions to be sure, but populated by ignorant savages, with no thoroughfare to the ancient

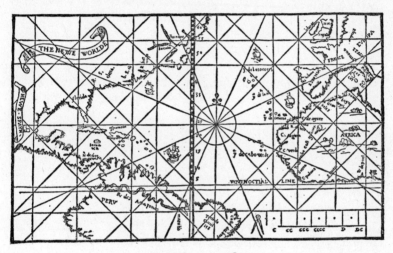

CHART OF A.D. 1589
Showing Papal line of Demarcation

civilization and wealth of the East, and no promise of a solid, lucrative commerce such as Portugal had gained. Mines were opened in the West Indies, but it was not until the conquest of Mexico by Cortez (1519-1521) laid open the accumulated wealth of seven centuries that Spain had definite assurance of the treasure which was to pour out of America in a steadily increasing stream. The first two vessels laden with Mexican treasure returned in 1523. Ten years later the exploration and conquest of Peru by Pizarro trebled the influx of silver and gold. The silver mines of Europe were abandoned. The Emperor Charles, as Francis I said, could fight his European campaigns on the wealth of the Indies alone.

But between Spain and her "sinews of war" lay 3000 miles of ocean. To hold the colonies themselves, to guard the plate fleets against French, Dutch, and English raiders, to protect her own coastline and maintain communications with her possessions in Italy and the Low Countries, to wage war against the Turk in the Mediterranean, Spain felt the need of a navy. Indeed, in view of these varied motives for maritime strength, it is surprising that Spain depended so largely on impressed merchant vessels, and had made only the beginnings of a royal navy at the time of the Grand Armada.[1] Not primarily a nation of traders or sailors, she had, by grudging assistance to the greatest of sea explorers, fallen into a rich colonial empire, to secure and make the most of which called for sea power.

It is possible, however, to lay undue stress on the factor just mentioned in accounting for both the rise and the decay of Spain. Her ascendancy in Europe in the 16th century was due chiefly to the immense territories united with her under Charles the Fifth (1500-1558), who inherited Spain, Burgundy, and the Low Countries, and added Austria with her German and Italian provinces by his accession to the imperial throne. Under Charles's powerful leadership Spain became the greatest nation in Europe; but at the same time her resources in men and wealth were exhausted in the almost constant warfare of his long reign. The treasures of America flowed through the land like water, in the expressive figure of a German historian, "not fertilizing it but laying it waste, and leaving sharper dearth behind."[2] The revenues of the plate fleet were pledged to German or Genoese bankers even before they reached the country, and were expended in the purchase of foreign luxuries or in waging imperial wars,

---

[1] "For the kings of England have for many years been at the charge to build and furnish a navy of powerful ships for their own defense, and for the wars only; whereas the French, the Spaniards, the Portugals, and the Hollanders (till of late) have had no proper fleet belonging to their princes or state." Sir Walter Raleigh, A DISCOURSE OF THE INVENTION OF SHIPS.

[2] DAS ZEITALTER DER FUGGER, Vol. II, p. 150.

rather than in the encouragement of home agriculture, trade, and industry. While the vast possessions of church and nobility escaped taxation, the people were burdened with levies on the movement and sale of commodities and on the common necessities of life. Prohibition of imports to keep gold in the country was ineffectual, for without the supplies brought in by Dutch merchantmen Spain would have starved, and Philip II often had to connive in violations of his own restrictions. Prohibition of exports to keep prices down was an equally Quixotic measure, the chief effect of which was to kill trade. Spain could not supply the needs of her own colonies, and in fact illustrates the truth that a nation cannot, in the end, profit greatly by colonies unless it develops industries to utilize their raw materials and supply their demands.

For some time before the Armada Spain was on the downward path, as a result of the conditions mentioned. On the other hand, while the Armada relieved England of a terrible danger and dashed Spain's hope of domination in the north, it was not of itself a fatal blow. The war still continued, with other Spanish expeditions organized on a grand scale, and ended in 1604, so far as England was concerned, with that country's renunciation of trade to the Indies and aid to the Dutch.

But even if Spain's rise and decline were not primarily a result of sea power, still, taking the term to include the extension of shipping and maritime trade as well as the employment of naval forces in strictly military operations, there are lessons to be drawn from the use or neglect of sea power by both sides in Spain's long drawn-out struggle with Holland and England.

REFERENCES

General

THE EXPANSION OF EUROPE, a History of the Foundations of the Modern World, by Prof. W. C. Abbot, 1918.
THE STORY OF GEOGRAPHICAL DISCOVERY, J. Jacobs, 1913.
SHIPS AND THEIR WAYS OF OTHER DAYS, E. Keble Chatterton, 1906.

The Dawn of Navigation, Thomas G. Ford, U. S. Naval Institute Proceedings, Vol. XXXIII., 1-3.
The Dawn of Modern Geography, 2 vols., C. Raymond Beazley, 1904.

Portugal

Prince Henry the Navigator, C. Raymond Beazley, 1895.
Vasco da Gama and His Successors, 1460-1580, K. G. Jayne, 1910.
Rise of Portuguese Power in India, R. S. Whiteway, 1910.
Cambridge Modern History, Vol. I., Ch. I.
History of the Indian Navy, Lieut. C. R. Low, 1877.

Spain

The Discovery of America, John Fiske, 1893.
Spain in America, E. G. Bourne, American Nation Series, 1909.
Spain, Martin Hume, Cam. Modern Hist. Series, 1898.

CHAPTER VI

SEA POWER IN THE NORTH: HOLLAND'S STRUGGLE FOR INDEPENDENCE

THE first sea-farers in the storm-swept waters of the north, at least in historic times, were the Teutonic tribes along the North Sea and the Baltic. On land the Teutons held the Rhine and the Danube against the legions of Rome, spread later southward and westward, and founded modern European states out of the wreckage of the Roman Empire. On the sea, Angles, Saxons, and Jutes in the 5th century began plundering the coasts of what is now England, and, after driving the Celts into mountain fastnesses, established themselves in permanent control.

The Vikings

These Teutonic voyagers were followed toward the close of the 8th century by their Scandinavian kindred to the northward, the Vikings—superb fighting men and daring sea-rovers who harried the coasts of western Europe for the next 200 years. There were no navies to stop them. "These sea dragons," exclaimed Charlemagne, "will tear my kingdom asunder!" In England no king before Alfred had a navy; and Alfred was compelled to organize a strong sea force to bring the invaders to terms.

Elsewhere the Vikings met little opposition. Wherever they found lands that attracted them, they conquered and settled down. Thus Normandy came into being. They swept up the rivers, burning and looting where they pleased, from the Elbe to the Rhone. They carried their raids as far south as Sicily and the Mediterranean coast of Africa, and as far north and west as Iceland, Greenland, and the American continent. In the east, by establishing a Viking colony at Nishni Novgorod, they laid the foundations of the Russian empire, and their leader, Rus, gave it his name. Following river courses, others penetrated inland as far as Constantinople, where, being bought off by the emperor, they took service as imperial guards.

Their extraordinary voyages were made in boats that resemble so closely Greek and Roman models—even Phœnician, for that matter—as to suggest that the Vikings learned their ship-building from Mediterranean traders who forced their way into the Baltic in very early times. For example, the Viking method of making a rib in three parts is identical with the method of the Greeks and Romans. The chief points of difference are that Viking ships were sharp at both ends—like a canoe, were round-bottomed instead of flat, and had one steering oar instead of two. The typical Viking ship was only about 75 feet in length; but a royal vessel—the *Dragon* of the chief—sometimes attained a length of 300 feet, with sixty pairs of oars.

If the Vikings had had national organization under one head, they might well have laid the rest of Europe under tribute. In the 11th century, Cnut, a descendant of the Vikings, ruled in person over England, Denmark, and Norway. But their ocean folk-wanderings seem to have ended as suddenly as they began, and the effects were social rather than political. Where they settled, they brought a strain of the hardiest racial stock in Europe to blend with that of the conquered peoples.

The Hanseatic League

During the Middle Ages, peaceful trading gradually gained the upper hand over piracy and conquest. From the Italian cities the wares of the south and the Orient came over the passes of the Alps and down the German rivers, where trading cities grew up to act as carriers of merchandise and civilization among the nations of the north. The merchant guilds of these cities, banded together in the Hanseatic League, for at least three centuries dominated the northern seas.

Perhaps the most extensive commercial combination ever formed for the control of sea trade, the Hanseatic League began with a treaty between Lübeck and Hamburg in 1174, and at the height of its power in the 14th and 15th centuries it included from 60 to 80 cities, of which Lübeck, Cologne, Brunswick, and Danzig were among the chief. The league cleared northern waters of pirates, and used embargo and naval power to subdue rivals and promote trade. It established factories or trading stations from Nishni Novgorod to Bergen, London, and Bruges. From Russia it took cargoes of fats, tallows, wax, and wares brought into Russian markets from the east; from Scandinavia, iron and copper; from England, hides and wool; from Germany, fish, grain, beer, and manufactured goods of all kinds. The British pound sterling (Österling) and pound avoirdupois, in fact the whole British system of weights and coinage, are legacies from the German merchants who once had their headquarters in the Steelyard, London.

In the early 15th century the league attempted to shut Dutch ships from the Baltic trade by restricting their cargoes to wares produced in their own country, and by coercing Denmark into granting the league special privileges on the route through the Sound. This policy, culminating in the destruction of the Dutch grain fleet in 1437, led to a naval struggle which extended over four years and ended in a truce by which the Dutch secured the freedom of the Baltic. It was a typical naval war for sea control and commercial advantage, in which the Dutch as a rule seem to have got the better, and in which the legend first made its appearance of a Dutch admiral sweeping the seas with a broom nailed to his mast.

From this time the power of the Hansa declined. This was partly because the free cities came more and more under the rule of German princes with no interest in, or knowledge of, commerce; partly because of rivalry arising from the union of the Scandinavian states (1397) and the growth of

England, France, and the Low Countries to national strength and commercial independence; and partly also because of the decline of German fisheries when the herring suddenly shifted from the Baltic to the North Sea. Underlying these varied causes, however, and significant of the far-reaching effect of changing trade-routes upon the progress and prosperity of nations, was the fact that, when the Mediterranean trade route was closed by the Turks, and also the route through Russia by Ivan III, the German cities were side-tracked. Antwerp and Amsterdam were not only more centrally located for the distribution of trade, but also much nearer for Atlantic traffic—an advantage which Germany has ever since keenly envied.

Long before the rise of the Low Countries as a maritime power, Ghent and Bruges had enjoyed an early preëminence owing to their development of cloth manufacture, and the latter city as a terminus for the galleys of Venice and Genoa. After the silting up of the port of Bruges (1432), Antwerp grew in importance, and in the 16th century became the chief market and money center of Europe. Its inhabitants numbered about 100,000, with a floating population of upwards of 50,000 more. It contained the counting-houses of the great bankers of Europe—the Fuggers of Germany, the Pazzi of Florence, the Dorias of Genoa. Five thousand merchants were registered on the Bourse, as many as 500 ships often left the city in a single day, and two or three thousand more might be seen anchored in the Scheldt or lying along the quays.[1] Amsterdam by 1560 was second to Antwerp with a population of 40,000, and forged ahead after the sack of Antwerp by Spanish soldiers in 1576 and the Dutch blockade of the Scheldt during the struggle with Spain.

This early prosperity of the Netherland cities may be attributed less to aggressive maritime activity than to their flourishing industries, their natural advantages as trading centers at the mouths of the Rhine, Scheldt, and Meuse, and the privileges of self-government enjoyed by the middle classes under the House of Burgundy and even under Charles the

[1] Blok, HISTORY OF THE PEOPLE OF THE NETHERLANDS, Part II, Ch. XII.

Fifth. Charles taxed them heavily—his revenues from the Low Countries in reality far exceeded the treasure he drew from America; but he was a Fleming born, spoke their language, and accorded them a large measure of political and religious freedom. The grievances which after his death led to the Dutch War of Independence, are almost personified in the son who succeeded him in 1555—Philip II, a Spaniard born and bred, who spoke no Flemish and left Brussels for the last time in 1573, dour, treacherous, distrustful, fanatical in religion; a tragic character, who, no doubt with great injustice to the Spanish, has somehow come to represent the character of Spain in his time.

The Dutch Struggle for Freedom

The causes of the long war in the Netherlands, which began in 1566 and ended with their independence 43 years later, is best explained in terms of general principles rather than specific grievances. "A conflict in which the principle of Catholicism with unlimited royal autocracy as Spain recognized it, was opposed to toleration in the realm of religion, with a national government according to ancient principles and based on ancient privileges,"—so the Dutch historian Blok sums up the issues at stake. The Prince of Orange, just before he was cut down by an assassin, asserted in his famous *Defense* three fundamental principles: freedom to worship God; withdrawal of foreigners; and restoration of the charters, privileges, and liberties of the land. The Dutch fought for political, religious, and also for economic independence. England gave aid, not so much for religious motives as because she saw that her political safety and commercial prosperity hinged on the weakening of Spain.

Resembling our American Revolution in the character of the struggle as well as the issues at stake—though it was far more bloody and desperate—the Dutch War of Independence was fought mainly within the country itself, with the population divided, and the Spanish depending on land forces to maintain their rule; but, as in the American war, control of the sea was a vital factor. For munitions, supplies, gold, for the transport of the troops themselves, Spain had to depend primarily on the sea. It is true one could continue on Spanish territory from Genoa, which was Spain's watergate into Italy, across the Mont Cenis Pass, and through Savoy, Burgundy, Lorraine, and Luxembourg to Brussels, and it was by this route that Parma's splendid army of 10,000 "Blackbeards" came in 1577. But this was an arduous three months' march for troops and still more difficult for supplies. To cross France was as a rule impossible; when Don Juan of Austria went to Flanders for the brief period of leadership ended by his death of camp fever in 1578, he passed through French territory disguised as a Moorish slave. By the sea route, upon which Spain was after all largely dependent, and the complete control of which would have made her task infinitely easier, she was constantly exposed to Huguenot, Dutch, and English privateers. These gentry cared little whether or not their country was actually at war with Spain, but took their letters of marque, if they carried them, from any prince or ruler who would serve their turn.

With this opportunity to strike at Spanish communications, it will appear strange that the Dutch should not have immediately seized their advantage and made it decisive. One curious difficulty lay in the fact that throughout the war Dutch shipping actually carried the bulk of Spanish trade and drew from it immense profits. Even at the close of the century, while the war was still continuing, nine-tenths of Spain's foreign trade and five-sixths of her home trade was in foreign—and most of it in Dutch—hands. Hence any form of sea warfare was sure to injure Dutch trade. The Revolution, moreover, began slowly and feebly, with no well-thought-out plan of campaign, and could not at once fit out fully organized forces to cope with those of Spain. The Dutch early took to commerce warfare, but it was at first semi-piratical, and involved the destruction of ships of their own countrymen.

The Sea Beggars—*Zee Geuzen* or *Gueux der Mer*—made their appearance shortly after the outbreak of rebellion.

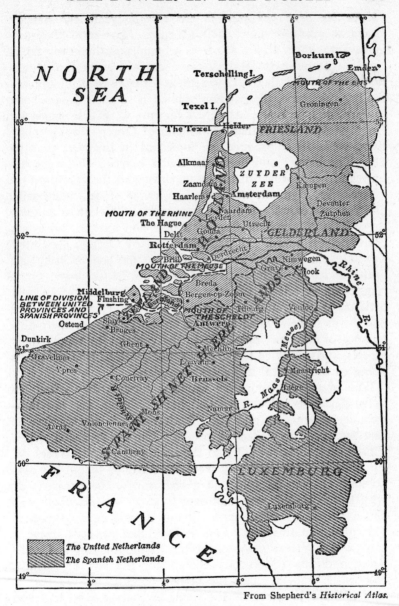

NORTH
SEA

N O R T H
S E A

Borkum I.

Terschelling I.

Emden

MOUTH OF THE EMS

Texel I.

Groningen

The Texel   Helder

FRIESLAND

Alkmaar

ZUYDER
ZEE

Kampen

Zaandam

Deventer

Haarlem   Amsterdam

Zutphen

Naarden

MOUTH OF THE RHINE   Leyden

The Hague   Gouda   Utrecht

Delft   GELDERLAND

Rotterdam

Nimwegen

Brill   Dordrecht

MOUTH OF THE MEUSE   Grave   Mook   Rhine

Middelburg   Breda

LINE OF DIVISION   Flushing   Bergen-op-Zoom

BETWEEN UNITED   MOUTH OF   Tilburg   Venloo

PROVINCES AND   Sluys   THE SCHELDT

SPANISH PROVINCES   Antwerp

Ostend   Mechlin   Maas (Meuse)

Dunkirk   Louvain   Maastricht

Gravelines   Ghent   Liege

Ypres   Brussels

Courtray   Namur R. Maas

Arras   Mons

Valenciennes   Namur

Cambray   LUXEMBURG

FRANCE   Luxemburg

The United Netherlands
The Spanish Netherlands

From Shepherd's *Historical Atlas.*

THE NETHERLANDS IN THE 16TH CENTURY

"Vyve les geus par mer et par terre," wrote the patriot Count van Brederode as early as 1566. The term "beggar" is said to have arisen from a contemptuous remark by a Spanish courtier to Margaret of Parma, when the Dutch nobles presented their grievances in Brussels. Willingly accepting the name, the patriots applied it to their forces both by land and by sea. Letters of marque were first issued by Louis of Nassau, brother of William of Orange, and in 1569 there were 18 ships engaged, increased in the next year to 84. The bloody and licentious De la Marck, who wore his hair and beard unshorn till he had avenged the execution of his relative, Egmont, was a typical leader of still more wild and reckless crews. It was no uncommon practice to go over the rail of a merchant ship with pike and ax and kill every Spaniard on board. In 1569 William of Orange appointed the Seigneur de Lumbres as admiral of the beggar fleet, and issued strict instructions to him to secure better order, avoid attacks on vessels of friendly and neutral states, enforce the articles of war, and carry a preacher on each ship. The booty was to be divided one-third to the Prince for the maintenance of the war, one-third to the captains to supply their vessels, and one-third to the crews, one-tenth of this last share going to the admiral in general command.

The events of commerce warfare, though they often involve desperate adventures and hard fighting, are not individually impressive, and the effectiveness of this warfare is best measured by collective results. On one occasion, when a fleet of transports fell into the hands of patriot forces off Flushing in 1572, not only were 1000 troops taken, but also 500,000 crowns of gold and a rich cargo, the proceeds of which, it is stated, were sufficient to carry on the whole war for a period of two years. Again it was fear of pirates (Huguenot in this case) that in December of 1568 drove a squadron of Spanish transports into Plymouth, England, with 450,000 ducats ($960,000) aboard for the pay of Spanish troops. Elizabeth seized the money (on the ground that it was still the property of the Genoese bankers who had lent it and that she might as well borrow it as Philip), and minted

it into English coin at a profit of £3000. But Alva at Antwerp, with no money at all, was forced to the obnoxious
"Hundreds" tax—requiring a payment of one per cent on all
possessions, five per cent on all real estate transfers, and 10
per cent every time a piece of merchandise was sold—a
typical tax after the Spanish recipe, which, though not finally
enforced to its full extent, aroused every Netherlander as a
fatal blow at national prosperity. To return to the general
effect of commerce destruction, it is estimated that Spain thus
lost annually 3,000,000 ducats ($6,400,000), a sum which
of course meant vastly more then than now. When the Duke
of Alva retired from command in 1578, the pay of Spanish
troops was 6,500,000 ducats in arrears.

Among the exploits of organized naval forces, the earliest
was the capture of Brill, by which, according to Motley, "the
foundations of the Dutch republic were laid." Driven out
of England by Elizabeth, who upon the representations of
the Spanish ambassador ordered her subjects not to supply
the Beggars with "meat, bread or beer," a fleet of 25 vessels
and 300 or 400 men left Dover towards the end of March,
1572, with the project of seizing a base on their own coast.
On the afternoon of April 1, they appeared off the town of
Brill, located on an island at the mouth of the Meuse. The
magistrates and most of the inhabitants fled; and the Beggars battered down the gates, occupied the town, and put to
death 13 monks and priests. When Spanish forces attempted
to recapture the city, the defenders opened sluice gates to
cut off the northern approach, and at the same time set fire
to the boats which had carried the Spanish to the island. The
Spanish, terrorized by both fire and water, waded through
mud and slime to the northern shore. During the same week
Flushing was taken, and before the end of June the Dutch
were masters of nearly the entire Zealand coast.

In the north the Spanish at first found an able naval leader in
Admiral Bossu, himself a Hollander, who for a time kept the
coast clear of Beggars. In October, 1573, however, 30 of
his ships were beaten in the Zuyder Zee by 25 under Dirkzoon,
who captured five of the Spanish vessels and scattered the rest

with the exception of the flagship. The latter, a 32-gun ship terrifyingly named the *Inquisition* and much stronger than any of the others on either side, held out from three o'clock in the afternoon until the next morning. Three patriot vessels closed in on her, attacking with the vicious weapons of the period—pitch, boiling oil, and molten lead. By morning the four combatants had drifted ashore in a tangled mass. When Bossu at last surrendered, 300 men, out of 382 in his ship's complement, were dead or disabled.

Though not yet able to stand up against Spanish infantry, the Dutch in naval battles were usually successful. In the Scheldt, January 29, 1574, 75 Spanish vessels were attacked by 64 Dutch under Admiral Boisot. After a single broadside, the two fleets grappled, and in a two-hour fight at close quarters eight of the Spanish ships were captured, seven destroyed, and 1200 Spaniards killed. The Spanish commander, Julian Romero, who escaped through a port-hole, is said to have remarked afterwards, "I told you I was a land fighter and no sailor; give me a hundred fleets and I would fare no better."

In September following, Admiral Boisot brought some of his victorious ships and sailors to the relief of Leyden, whose inhabitants and garrison had been reduced by siege to the very last extremities. The campaign that followed was typical of this amphibious war. Boisot's force, with those already on the scene, numbered about 2500, equipped with some 200 shallow-draft boats and row-barges mounting an average of ten guns each. Among them was the curious *Ark of Delft,* with shot-proof bulwarks and paddle-wheels turned by a crank. As a result of ruthless flooding of the country, ten of the fifteen miles between Leyden and the outer dyke were easily passed; but five miles from the city ran the Landscheidung or inner dyke, which was above water, and beyond this an intricate system of canals and flooded polders, with forts and villages held by a Spanish force four times as strong. The most savage fighting on decks, dykes, and bridges marked every step forward; the Dutch in their native element attacking with cutlass, boathook and harpoon, while the superior military discipline of the Spanish could not

come in play.   But at least 20 inches of water were necessary
to float the Dutch vessels, and it was not until October 3 that
a spring tide and a heavy northwest gale made it possible to
reach the city walls.   In storm and darkness, terrified by the
rising waters, the Spanish fled.   The relief of the city marked
a turning-point in the history of the revolt.

During the six terrible years of Alva's rule in the Netherlands (1567-1573) the Dutch sea forces contributed heavily
toward the maintenance of the war, assured control of the
Holland and Zealand coasts, and more than once, as at Brill
and Leyden, proved the salvation of the patriot cause.   Holland and Zealand, the storm-centers of rebellion, were not
again so devastated, though the war dragged on for many
years, maintained by the indomitable spirit of William of
Orange until his assassination in 1584, and afterward by the
military skill of Maurice of Nassau and the aid of foreign
powers.   The seven provinces north of the Scheldt, separating from the Catholic states of the south, prospered in trade
and industry as they shook themselves free from the stifling
rule of Spain.   By a twelve-year truce, finally ratified in 1609,
they became "free states over which Spain makes no pretensions," though their independence was not fully recognized
until the Peace of Westphalia in 1648.   The war, while it
ruined Antwerp, increased the prosperity of Holland and
Zealand, which for at least twenty years before the truce were
busily extending their trade to every part of the world.

Growth of Dutch Commerce

The story of this expansion of commerce is a striking record.   The grain and timber of the Baltic, the wines of France
and Spain, the salt of the Cape Verde Islands, the costly
wares of the east, came to the ports of the Meuse and Zuyder
Zee.   In 1590 the first Dutch traders entered the Mediterranean, securing, eight years later, the permission of the Sultan to engage in Constantinople trade.   In 1594 their ships
reached the Gold Coast, and a year later four vessels visited
Madagascar, Goa, Java, and the Moluccas or Spice Islands.

A rich Zealand merchant had a factory at Archangel and a regular trade into the White Sea. Seeking a reward of 25,000 florins offered by the States for the discovery of a northeast passage, Jacob van Heimskirck sailed into the Arctic and wintered in Nova Zembla; Henry Hudson, in quest of a route northwestward, explored the river and the bay that bear his name and died in the Polar Seas.

Statistics, while not very trustworthy and not enlightening unless compared with those for other nations, may give some idea of the preponderance of Dutch shipping. At the time of the truce she is said to have had 16,300 ships, about 10,000 of which were small vessels in the coasting trade. Of the larger, 3000 were in the Baltic trade, 2000 in the Spanish, 600 sailed to Italy, and the remainder to the Mediterranean, South America, the Far East, and Archangel. The significance of these figures may be made clearer by citing Colbert's estimate that at a later period (1664) there were 20,000 ships in general European carrying trade, 16,000 of which were Dutch. Throughout the 17th century Dutch commerce continued to prosper, and did not reach its zenith until early in the century following.

In the closing years of the 16th century several private companies were founded in Amsterdam, Rotterdam and Zealand to engage in eastern trade. These were combined in 1602 into the United East Indies Company, which sent large fleets to the Orient each year, easily ousted the Portuguese from their bases on the coast and islands, and soon established almost a monopoly, leaving to England only a small share of trade with Persia and northwest India. The relative resources invested by English and Dutch in Eastern ventures is suggested by the fact that the British East Indies Company founded in 1600 had a capital of £80,000, while the Dutch Company had £316,000. By 1620 the shares of the Dutch company had increased to three times their original value, and they paid average dividends of 18 per cent for the next 200 years.

In this Dutch conquest of eastern trade, like that of the Portuguese a century earlier, we have an illustration of what

has since been a guiding principle in the history of sea power
—a national policy of commercial expansion sturdily backed
by foreign policy and whenever necessary by naval force.
The element of national policy is evident in the fact that
Holland—and England until the accession of James I in
1603—preferred war rather than acceptance of Spanish pretensions to exclusive rights in the southern seas. The Dutch,
like the Portuguese, saw clearly the need of political control.
They made strongholds of their trading bases, and gave their
companies power to oust competitors by force. As a concession to Spanish pride, the commerce clause in the Truce
of 1609 was made intentionally unintelligible—but the Dutch
interpreted it to suit themselves. As for the element of force,
every squadron that sailed to the east was a semi-military
expedition. The Dutch seaman was sailor, fighter, and trader
combined. The merchant was truly, in the phrase of the age,
a "merchant adventurer," lucky indeed and enriched if, after
facing the perils of navigation in strange waters, the possible
hostility of native rulers, and the still greater danger from
European rivals, half his ships returned. The last statement
is no hyperbole; of 9 ships sent to the East from Amsterdam
in 1598, four came back, and just half of the 22 sent out
from the entire Netherlands.

From time to time, either to maintain the blockade of the
Scheldt and assist in operations on the Flanders coast, or to
protect their trade and strike a direct blow at Spain, the
Dutch fitted out purely naval expeditions. One of the most
effective, from the standpoint of actual fighting, was that
led by van Heimskirck, already famous for Arctic exploration and exploits in the Far East. In 1607 he took 21 converted merchantmen and 4 transports to the Spanish coast to
protect Dutch vessels from the east and the Mediterranean.
Encountering off Gibraltar an enemy force of 11 large galleons and as many galleys under Alvarez d'Avila, a veteran
of Lepanto, he destroyed half the Spanish force and drove
the rest into port, killing about 2000 Spanish and coming out
of the fight with the loss of only 100 men. Heimskirck
concentrated upon the galleons and came to close action after

the fashion which seems to have been characteristic of the Dutch in naval engagements throughout the war. "Hold your fire till you hear the crash," he cried, as he drove his prow into the enemy flagship; and the battle was won after a struggle yard-arm to yard-arm. Both admirals were killed.

Portugal, broken by the Spanish yoke, could offer little resistance in the Far East. In 1606 a Dutch fleet of 12 ships under Matelieff de Jonge laid siege to Malacca, and gave up the attempt only after destroying 10 galleons sent to relieve the town. Matelieff then sailed to the neighboring islands, and established the authority of the company at Bantam, Amboyna, Ternate, and other centers of trade.

Other fleets earlier and later promoted the interests of the company by the same means. English traders, with scanty government encouragement from the Stuart kings, were not as yet dangerous rivals. A conflict occurred with them in 1611 off Surat; and at Amboyna in 1623 the Dutch seized the English Company's men, tortured ten of them, and broke up the English base. For more than a century Holland remained supreme in the east; she has retained her colonial empire down to the 20th century; and she did not surrender her commercial primacy until exhausted by the combined attacks of England and France. Less successful than England in the development of colonies, she has stood out as the greatest of trading nations.

REFERENCES

The Vikings

THE VIKING AGE, H. F. Du Chaillu, 1889.

The Hansa

THE HANSA TOWNS, H. Zimmerman, 1889.
HISTORY OF COMMERCE, Clive Day, 1913 (bibliography).
CIVILIZATION DURING THE MIDDLE AGES, George Burton Adams, 1918.
CAMBRIDGE MODERN HISTORY, Vols. I and II.

Dutch Sea Power

MOTLEY'S RISE OF THE DUTCH REPUBLIC (still the best source in English for political and naval history of the period).

HISTORY OF THE PEOPLE OF THE NETHERLANDS, P. J. Blok, trans. Ruth Putnam, 1898-1912.

HISTORY OF COMMERCE IN EUROPE, W. H. Gibbins, 1917.

THE SEA BEGGARS, Dingman Versteg, 1901.

SOME EXPLOITS OF THE OLD DUTCH NAVY, Lieut. H. H. Frost, U. S. Naval Institute Proceedings, January, 1919.

CHAPTER VII

ENGLAND AND THE ARMADA

By reason of England's insularity, it is an easy matter to find instances from even her early history of the salutary or fatal influence of sea power. Romans, Saxons, Danes swept down upon England from the sea. By building a fleet, King Alfred, said to have been the true father of the British navy, kept back the Danes. It was the dispersion of the English fleet by reason of the lateness of the season that enabled William the Conqueror, in the small open vessels interestingly pictured in the Bayeux tapestry, to win a footing on the English shore.

But during the next three centuries, with little shipping and little trade save that carried on by the Hansa, with no enemy that dangerously threatened her by sea, England had neither the motives nor the national strength and unity to develop naval power. She claimed, it is true, dominion over the narrow waters between her and her possessions in France, and also over the "four seas" surrounding her; and as early as 1201 an ordinance was passed requiring vessels in these waters to lower sails ("vail the bonnet") and also to "lie by the lee" when so ordered by King's ships. But though these claims were revived in the 17th century against the Dutch, and though the requirement that foreign vessels strike their topsails to the British flag remained in the Admiralty Instructions until after Trafalgar, they were at this time enforced chiefly to rid the seas of pirates—the common enemies of nations. During this period there were a few "king's ships," the sovereign's personal property, forming a nucleus around which a naval force of fishing and merchant vessels could be assembled in time of war. The Cinque Ports, originally Dover, Sandwich, Hastings, Romney and Hythe, long enjoyed certain trading privileges in return 'for the agreement that when the king passed overseas they would "rigge up fiftie and seven ships" (according to a charter of Edward I) with 20 armed soldiers each, and maintain them for 15 days.

An attack in 1217 by such a fleet, under the Governor of Dover Castle, affords perhaps the earliest instance of maneuvering for the weather-gage. The English came down from the windward and, as they scrambled aboard the enemy, threw quicklime into the Frenchmen's eyes. At Sluis, in 1340, to take another instance of early English naval warfare, Edward III defeated a large French fleet and a number of hired Genoese galleys lashed side by side in the little river Eede in Flanders. Edward came in with a fair wind and tide and fell upon the enemy as they lay aground at the stern and unmanageable. This victory gave control of the Channel for the transport of troops in the following campaign. But like most early naval combats, it was practically a land battle over decks, and, although sanguinary enough, it is from a naval standpoint interesting chiefly for such novelties as a scouting force of knights on horseback along the shore.

The beginnings of a permanent and strong naval establishment, as distinct from merchant vessels owned by the king or in his service, must be dated, however, from the Tudors and the period of national rehabilitation following the Hundred Years' War (1337-1453) and the War of the Roses (1455-1485). One reason for this was that the employment of artillery on shipboard and the introduction of port-holes made it increasingly difficult to convert merchant craft into dependable men-of-war. Henry VIII took a keen interest in his navy, devoted the revenues of forfeited church property to its expansion, established the first Navy Board (1546), and is even credited with the adoption of sailing vessels as the major units of his fleet.

From Oar to Sail

The use of heavy ordnance, already mentioned, as well as the increasing size and efficiency of sail-craft that came with

the spread of ocean commerce and navigation, naturally
pointed the way to this transition in warfare from oar to sail.
The galley was at best a frail affair, cumbered with oars,
benches and rowers, unable to carry heavy guns or withstand
their fire. Once sailing vessels had attained reasonable maneuvering qualities, their superior strength and size, reduced number of non-combatant personnel, and increased seaworthiness

GALLEON

and cruising radius gave them a tremendous superiority. That
the change should have begun in the north rather than in the
Mediterranean, where naval and military science had reached
its highest development, must be attributed not only to the
rougher weather conditions of the northern seas, and the difficulty of obtaining slaves as rowers, but also to the fact that
the southern nations were more completely shackled by the
traditions of galley warfare.

Yet for the new type it was the splendid trading vessels of
Venice that supplied the design. For the Antwerp and Lon-

don trade, and in protection against the increasing danger from pirates, the Venetians had developed a compromise between the war-galley and the round-ship of commerce, a type with three masts and propelled at least primarily by sails, with a length about three times its beam and thus shorter and more seaworthy than the galley, but longer, lower and swifter than the clumsy round-ship. To this new type the names *galleass* and *galleon* were both given, but in English and later usage *galleass* came to be applied to war vessels combining oar and sail, and *galleon* to either war or trading vessels of medium size and length and propelled by sail alone.

The Spanish found the galleon useful in the Atlantic carrying trade, but, as shown at Lepanto, they retained the galley in warfare; whereas Henry VIII of England was probably the first definitely to favor sail for his men-of-war. An English navy list of 1545 shows four clumsy old-fashioned "greatships" of upwards of 1000 tons, but second to these a dozen newer vessels of distinctly galleon lines, lower than the greatships, flush-decked, and sail-driven. Though in engagements with French galleys during the campaign of 1545 these were handicapped by calm weather, they seem to have held their own both in battle and in naval opinion. Of the royal ships at the opening of Elizabeth's reign (1558), there were 11 large sailing vessels of 200 tons and upwards, and 10 smaller ones, but only two galleys, and these "of no continuance and not worth repair." [1] In comment on these figures, it should be added that there were half a hundred large ships available from the merchant service, and also that pinnaces and other small craft still combined oar and sail.

In England the superiority of sail propulsion was soon definitely recognized, and discussion later centered on the relative merits of the medium-sized galleon and the big "great-ship." The characteristics of each are well set forth in a contemporary naval treatise by Sir William Monson: the former with "flush deck fore and aft, sunk and low in the water; the other lofty and high-charged, with a half-deck, forecastle, and copper-idge-heads [athwartship bulkheads where light guns were

[1] DRAKE AND THE TUDOR NAVY, Corbett, Vol. I, p. 133.

mounted to command the space between decks]." The advantages of the first were that she was speedy and "a fast ship by the wind" so as to avoid boarding by the enemy, and could run in close and fire effective broadsides between wind and water without being touched; whereas the big ship was more terrifying, more commodious, stronger, and could carry more and heavier guns.   Monson, like many a later expert, suspended judgment regarding the two types; but Sir Walter Raleigh came out strongly for the smaller design.   "The greatest ships," he writes, "are the least serviceable. . . ., less nimble, less maniable; 'Grande navi grande fatiga,' saith the Spaniard.   A ship of 600 tons will carry as good ordnance as a ship of 1200 tons; and though the greater have double her number, the lesser will turn her broadsides twice before the greater can wind once."   And elsewhere: "The high charging of ships makes them extreme leeward, makes them sink deep in the water, makes them labor, and makes them overset. Men may not expect the ease of many cabins and safety at once in sea-service." [1]

These statements were made after the Armada; but the trend of English naval construction away from unwieldy ships such as used by the Spanish in the Armada, is clearly seen in vessels dating from 1570-1580—the *Foresight, Bull,* and *Tiger* (rebuilt from galleasses), the *Swiftsure, Dreadnought, Revenge,* and others of names renowned in naval annals. These were all of about the dimensions of the *Revenge,* which was of 440 tons, 92 feet over all, 32 feet beam, and 15 feet from deck to keel.   That is to say, their length was not more than three times their beam, and their beam was about twice their depth in the hold—the characteristic proportions of the galleon type.

The progressiveness of English ship construction is highly significant, for to it may be attributed in large measure the Armada victory.   Spain had made no such advances; in fact, until the decade of the Armada, she hardly had such a thing as a royal navy.   The superiority of the English ships was generally recognized.   An English naval writer in 1570 de-

[1] WORKS, Oxford ed. 1829, Vol. VIII, p. 338.

clared the ships of his nation so fine "none of any other region may seem comparable to them"; and a Spaniard some years later testified that his people regarded "one English ship worth four of theirs."

Though not larger than frigates of Nelson's time, these ships were crowded with an even heavier armament, comprising guns of all sizes and of picturesque but bewildering nomenclature. According to Corbett,[1] the ordnance may be divided into four main classes based on caliber, the first two of the "long gun" and the other two of the carronade or mortar type.

I. Cannon proper, from 16 to 28 caliber, of 8.5-inch bore and 12 feet in length, firing 65-pound shot. The demi-cannon, which was the largest gun carried on ships of the time, was 6.5 inches by 9 feet and fired 30-pound shot.

II. Culverins, 28 to 34 caliber long guns, 5 inches by 12 feet, firing 17-pound shot. Demi-culverins were 9-pounders. Slings, bases, sakers, port-pieces, and fowlers belonged to this class.

III. Perriers, from 6 to 8 caliber, firing stone-balls, shells, fire-balls, etc.

IV. Mortars, of 1.5 caliber, including petards and murderers.

The "great ordnance," or cannon, were muzzle-loading. The secondary armament, mounted in tops, cageworks, bulkheads, etc., were breech-loading; but these smaller pieces fell out of favor as time went on owing to reliance on long-range fire and rareness of boarding actions. Down to the middle of the 19th century there was no great improvement in ordnance, save in the way of better powder and boring. Even in Elizabeth's day the heaviest cannon had a range of three miles.

These advances in ship design and armament were accompanied by some changes in naval administration. In 1546 the Navy Board was created, which continued to handle matters of what may be termed civil administration until its functions were taken over by the Board of Admiralty in the reorganization of 1832. The chief members of the Navy Board, the

[1] DRAKE AND THE TUDOR NAVY, Vol. I, p. 384.

Treasurer, Comptroller, Surveyor of Ships, Surveyor of Ordnance, and Clerk of Ships, were in Elizabethan times usually experienced in sea affairs. To John Hawkins, Treasurer from 1578 to 1595, belongs chief credit for the excellent condition of ships in his day. The Lord High Admiral, a member of the nobility, exercised at least nominal command of the fleet in peace and war. For vice admiral under him a man of practical experience was ordinarily chosen. On shipboard, the only "gentleman" officers were the captains; the rest—masters, master's mates, pilots, carpenters, boatswains, coxswains, and gunners—were, to quote a contemporary description, "mechanick men that had been bred up from swabbers." But owing to the small proportion of soldiers on board, the English ships were not like those of Spain, which were organized like a camp, with the soldier element supreme and the sailors "slaves to the rest."

The Political Situation

The steps taken to build up the navy in the decade or more preceding the Armada were well justified by the political and religious strife in western Europe and the dangers which on all sides threatened the English realm. France, the Netherlands, and Scotland were torn by religious warfare. In England the party with open or secret Catholic sympathies was large, amounting to perhaps half the population, the strength of whose loyalty to Elizabeth it was difficult to gage. Since 1568 Elizabeth had held captive Mary Queen of Scots, driven out of her own country by the Presbyterian hierarchy, and a Catholic with hereditary claims to the English throne. Before her death, Philip of Spain had conspired with her to assassinate the heretic Elizabeth; after Mary's execution in 1587 he became heir to her claims and entered the more willingly upon the task of conquering England and restoring it to the faith. For years, in fact, there had been a state of undeclared hostility between England and Spain, and acts which, with sovereigns less cautious and astute than both Elizabeth and Philip, would have meant war. In 1585 Elizabeth formed an alliance with the Netherlands, and sent her favorite, Leicester, there as governor-general, and Sir Philip Sidney as Governor of Flushing, which with two other "cautionary towns" she took as pledges of Dutch loyalty. The motives for this action are well stated in a paper drawn up by the English Privy Council in 1584, presenting a situation interesting in its analogy to that which faced the United States when it entered the World War:

"The conclusion of the whole was this: Although her Majesty should thereby enter into the war presently, yet were she better to do it now, while she may make the same out of her realm, having the help of the people of Holland, and before the King of Spain shall have consummated his conquest of those countries, whereby he shall be so provoked by pride, solicited by the Pope, and tempted by the Queen's own subjects, and shall be so strong by sea; and so free from all other actions and quarrels—yea, shall be so formidable to all the rest of Christendom, as that her Majesty shall no wise be able, with her own power, nor with the aid of any other, neither by land nor sea, to withstand his attempts, but shall be forced to give place to his insatiable malice, which is most terrible to be thought of, but miserable to suffer."

These were the compelling reasons for England's entry into the war. The aid to Holland and the execution of Mary, on the other hand, were sufficient to explain Philip's attempted invasion. The grievance of Spain owing to the incursions of Hawkins and Drake into her American possessions, and England's desire to break Spain's commercial monopoly, were at the time relatively subordinate, though from a naval standpoint the voyages are interesting in themselves and important in the history of sea control and sea trade.

Hawkins and Drake

John Hawkins was a well-to-do ship-owner of Plymouth, and as already stated, Treasurer of the Royal Navy, with a contract for the upkeep of ships. His first venture to the Spanish Main was in 1562, when he kidnapped 300 negroes on

the Portuguese coast of Africa and exchanged them at His-
panola (Haiti), for West Indian products, chartering two additional vessels to take his cargo home. Though he might have
been put to death if caught by either Portugal or Spain, his
profits were so handsome by the double exchange that he tried
it again in 1565, this time taking his "choice negroes at £160
each" to Terra Firme, or the Spanish Main, including the
coasts of Venezuela, Colombia, and the Isthmus. When the
Spanish authorities, warned by their home government, made
some show of resistance, Hawkins threatened bombardment,
landed his men, and did business by force, the inhabitants con-
niving in a contraband trade very profitable to them.

On his third voyage he had six vessels, two of which, the
Jesus of Lubeck and the *Minion,* were Queen's ships hired
out for the voyage. The skipper of one of the smaller vessels, the *Judith,* was Francis Drake, a relative and protégé of
the Hawkins family, and then a youth of twenty-two. On
September 16, 1567, after a series of encounters stormier
than ever in the Spanish settlements, the squadron homeward
bound was driven by bad weather into the port of Mexico City
in San Juan de Ulua Bay. Here, having a decided superiority
over the vessels in the harbor, Hawkins secured the privilege
of mooring and refitting his ships inside the island that formed
a natural breakwater, and mounted guns on the island itself.
To his surprise next morning, he beheld in the offing 13 ships
of Spain led by an armed galleon and having on board the
newly appointed Mexican viceroy. Hawkins, though his guns
commanded the entrance, took hostages and made some sort
of agreement by which the Spanish ships were allowed to
come in and moor alongside. But the situation was too tense
to carry off without an explosion. Three days later the English were suddenly attacked on sea and shore. They at once
leaped into their ships and cut their cables, but though they
hammered the Spanish severely in the fight that followed, only
two English vessels, the *Minion* and the *Judith,* escaped, the
Minion so overcrowded that Hawkins had to drop 100 of his
crew on the Mexican coast. Drake made straight for Plymouth, nursing a bitter grievance at the alleged breach of

faith, and vowing vengeance on the whole Spanish race. "The case," as Drake's biographer, Thomas Fuller, says, "was clear in sea-divinity, and few are such infidels as not to believe doctrines which make for their own profit." [1]

In the next three years, following the example of many a French Huguenot privateersman before him, and forsaking trade for semi-private reprisal (in that epoch a few degrees short of piracy), he made three voyages to the Spanish Indies. On the third, in 1572, he raided Nombre de Dios with fire and sword. Then, leaguing himself with the mixed-breed natives or cameroons, he waylaid a guarded mule-train bearing treasure across the Isthmus, securing 15 tons of silver which he buried, and as much gold as his men could stagger away under. It was on this foray that he first saw the Pacific from a height of the Cordilleras, and resolved to steer an English squadron into this hitherto unmolested Spanish sea.

The tale of Drake's voyage into the Pacific and circumnavigation of the globe is a piratical epic, the episodes of which, however, find some justification in the state of virtual though undeclared hostilities between England and Spain, in the Queen's secret sanction, and in Spain's own policy of ruthless spoliation in America. Starting at the close of 1577 with five small vessels, the squadron was reduced by shipwreck and desertion until only the flagship remained when Drake at last, on September 6 of the next year, achieved his midwinter passage of the Straits of Magellan and bore down, "like a visitation of God" as a Spaniard said, upon the weakly defended ports of the west coast. After ballasting his ship with silver from the rich Potosi mines, and rifling even the churches, he hastened onward in pursuit of a richly laden galleon nicknamed *Cacafuego*—a name discreetly translated *Spitfire,* but which, to repeat a joke that greatly amused Drake's men at the time, it was proposed to change to *Spitsilver,* for when overtaken and captured the vessel yielded 26 tons of silver, 13 chests of pieces of eight, and gold and jewels sufficient to swell the booty to half a million pounds sterling.

For 20 years the voyage across the northern Pacific had been

[1] THE HOLY STATE, Bk. II, Ch. XXII.

familiar to the Spanish, who had studied winds and currents, laid down routes, and made regular crossings. Having picked up charts and China pilots, and left the whole coast in panic fear, Drake sailed far to the northward, overhauled his ship in a bay above San Francisco, then struck across the Pacific, and at last rounded Good Hope and put into Plymouth in September of the third year. It suited Elizabeth's policy to countenance the voyage. She put the major part of the treasure into the Tower, took some trinkets herself, knighted Drake aboard the *Golden Hind,* and when the Spanish ambassador talked war she told him, in a quiet tone of voice, that she would throw him into a dungeon.

This red-bearded, short and thickset Devon skipper, bold of speech as of action, was now the most renowned sailor of England, with a name that inspired terror on every coast of Spain. It was inevitable, therefore, that when Elizabeth resolved upon open reprisals in 1585, Drake should be chosen to lead another, and this time fully authorized, raid on the Spanish Indies. Here he sacked the cities of San Domingo and Carthagena, and, though he narrowly missed the plate fleet, brought home sufficient spoils for the individuals who backed the venture. In the year 1587 with 23 ships and orders permitting him to operate freely on Spain's home coasts, he first boldly entered Cadiz, in almost complete disregard of the puny galleys guarding the harbor, and destroyed some 37 vessels and their cargoes. Despite the horrified protests of his Vice Admiral Borough (an officer "of the old school" to be found in every epoch) at these violations of traditional methods, he then took up a position off Saigres where he could harry coastwise commerce, picked up the East Indiaman *San Felipe* with a cargo worth a million pounds in modern money, and even appeared off Lisbon to defy the Spanish Admiral Santa Cruz. Thus he "singed the King of Spain's beard," and set, in the words of a recent biographer, "what to this day may serve as the finest example of how a small, well-handled fleet, acting on a nicely timed offensive, may paralyze the mobilization of an overwhelming force." [1]

---

[1] DRAKE AND THE TUDOR NAVY, Corbett, Vol. II, p. 108.

The Grand Armada

At the time of this Cadiz expedition Spanish preparations for the invasion of England were already well under way, Philip being now convinced that by a blow at England all his aims might be secured—the subjugation of the Netherlands, the safety of Spanish America, the overthrow of Protestantism, possibly even his accession to the English throne. As the secret instructions to Medina Sidonia more modestly stated, it was at least believed that by a vigorous offensive and occupation of English territory England could be forced to cease her opposition to Spain. For this purpose every province of the empire was pressed for funds. Pope Sixtus VI contributed a million gold crowns, which he shrewdly made payable only when troops actually landed on English soil. Church and nobility were squeezed as never before. The Cortes on the eve of the voyage voted 8,000,000 ducats, secured by a tax on wine, meat, and oil, the common necessities of life, which was not lifted for more than two hundred years.

To gain control of the Channel long enough to throw 40,000 troops ashore at Margate, and thereafter to meet and conquer the army of defense—such was the highly difficult objective, to assure the success of which Philip had been led to hope for a wholesale defection of English Catholics to the Spanish cause. Twenty thousand troops were to sail with the Armada; Alexander Farnese, Duke of Parma, was to add 17,000 veterans from Flanders and assume supreme command. With the Spanish infantry once landed, under the best general in Europe, it was not beyond reason that England might become a province of Spain.

What Philip did not see clearly, what indeed could scarcely be foreseen from past experience, was that no movement of troops should be undertaken without first definitely accounting for the enemy fleet. The Spanish had not even an open base to sail to. With English vessels thronging the northern ports of the Channel, with 90 Dutch ships blockading the Scheldt and the shallows of the Flanders coast, it would be necessary to clear the Channel by a naval victory, and maintain control until it was assured by victory on land. The leader first selected, Santa Cruz—a veteran of Lepanto—at least put naval considerations uppermost and laid plans on a grand scale, calling for 150 major ships and 100,000 men, 30,000 of them sailors. But with his death in 1587 the campaign was again thought of primarily from the army standpoint. The ships were conceived as so many transports, whose duty at most was to hold the English fleet at bay. Parma was to be supreme. To succeed Santa Cruz as naval leader, and in order, it is said, that the gray-haired autocrat Philip might still control from his cell in the Escorial, the Duke of Medina Sidonia was chosen—an amiable gentleman of high rank, but consciously ignorant of naval warfare, uncertain of purpose, and despondent almost from the start. Medina had an experienced Vice Admiral in Diego Flores de Valdes, whose professional advice he usually followed, and he had able squadron commanders in Recalde, Pedro de Valdes, Oquendo, and others; but such a commander-in-chief, unless a very genius in self-effacement, was enough to ruin a far more auspicious campaign.

Delayed by the uncertain political situation in France, even more than by Drake's exploits off Cadiz, the Armada was at last, in May of 1588, ready to depart. The success of the Catholic party under the leadership of the Duke of Guise gave assurance of support rather than hostility on the French flank. There were altogether some 130 ships, the best of which were 10 war galleons of Portugal and 10 of the "Indian Guard" of Spain. These were supported by the Biscayan, Andalusian, Guipuscoan, and Levantine squadrons of about 10 armed merchantmen each, four splendid Neapolitan galleasses that gave a good account of themselves in action, and four galleys that were driven upon the French coast by storms and took no part in the battle—making a total (without the galleys) of about 64 fighting ships. Then there were 35 or more pinnaces and small craft, and 23 *urcas* or storeships of little or no fighting value. The backbone of the force was the 60 galleons, large, top-lofty vessels, all but 20 of them from the merchant service, with towering poops and forecastles that made them terrible to look upon but hard to handle. On board were 8,000 sailors and 19,000 troops.

Dispersed by a storm on their departure from Lisbon, the fleet again assembled at Corunna, their victuals already rotten, and their water foul and short. Medina Sidonia even now counseled abandonment; but religious faith, the fatalistic pride of Spain, and Philip's dogged fixity of purpose drove them on. Putting out of Corunna on July 22, and again buffeted by Biscay gales, they were sighted off the Lizard at daybreak of July 30, and a pinnace scudded into Plymouth with the alarm.

For England the moment of supreme crisis had come. Elizabeth's policy of paying for nothing that she might expect her subjects to contribute had left the royal navy short of what the situation called for, and the government seems also, even throughout the campaign, to have tied the admirals to the coast and kept them from distant adventures by limited supplies of munitions and food. But in the imminent danger, the nobility, both Catholic and Protestant, and every coastwise city, responded to the call for ships and men. Their loyalty was fatal to Philip's plan. The royal fleet of 25 ships and a dozen pinnaces was reënforced until the total craft of all descriptions numbered 197, not more than 140 of which, however, may be said to have had a real share in the campaign. For a month or more a hundred sail had been mobilized at Plymouth, of which 69 were greatships and galleons. These were smaller in average tonnage than the Spanish ships, but more heavily armed, and manned by 10,000 capable seamen. Lord Henry Seymour, with Palmer and Sir William Winter under him, watched Parma at the Strait of Dover, with 20 ships and an equal number of galleys, barks and pinnaces. The Lord High Admiral, Thomas Howard of Effingham, a nobleman of 50 with some naval experience and of a family that had long held the office, commanded the western squadron, with Drake as Vice Admiral and John Hawkins as Rear Admiral. The *Ark* (800 tons), *Revenge* (500), and *Victory* (800) were their respective flagships. Martin Frobisher in the big 1100-ton *Triumph,* Lord Sheffield in the *White Bear* (1000), and Thomas Fenner in the *Nonpareil* (500) were included with the Admi-

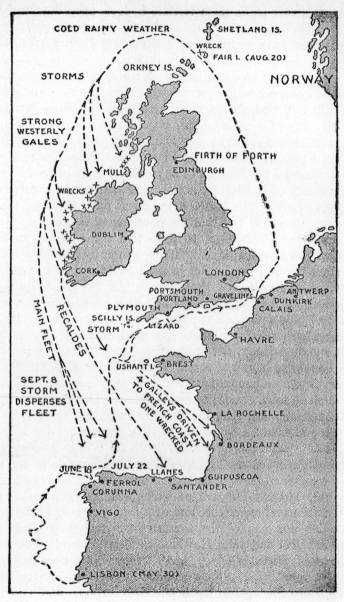

CRUISE OF THE SPANISH ARMADA

rals in Howard's inner council of war. "Howard," says Thomas Fuller, "was no deep-seaman, but he had skill enough to know those who had more skill than himself and to follow their instructions." As far as was possible for a commoner, Drake exercised command.

On the morning of the 31st the Armada swept slowly past Plymouth in what has been described as a broad crescent, but which, from a contemporary Italian description, seems to have

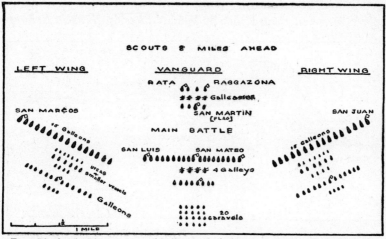

From Pigafetta's *Discorso sopro l'Ordinanza dell' Armata Catholico* (Corbett's *Drake,* Vol. II, p. 213),

ORIGINAL "EAGLE" FORMATION OF THE ARMADA, PROBABLY ADOPTED WITH SOME MODIFICATIONS AND SHOWING THE INFLUENCE OF GALLEY WAR-FARE

been the "eagle" formation familiar to galley warfare, in line abreast with wide extended wings bent slightly forward, the main strength in center and guards in van and rear. Howard was just completing the arduous task of warping his ships out of the harbor. Had Medina attacked at once, as some of his subordinates advised, he might have compelled Howard to close action and won by superior numbers. But his orders suggested the advisability of avoiding battle till he had joined with Parma; and for the Duke this was enough. As the Armada continued its course, Howard fell in astern and to windward, inflicting serious injuries to two ships of the enemy rear.

A week of desultory running battle ensued as the fleets moved slowly through the Channel; the English fighting "loose and large," and seeking to pick off stragglers, still fearful of a general action, but taking advantage of Channel flaws to close with the enemy and sheer as swiftly away; the Spanish on the defensive but able to avoid disaster by better concerted action and fleet control. Only two Spanish ships were actually lost, one of them Pedro de Valdes' flagship *Neustra Señora*

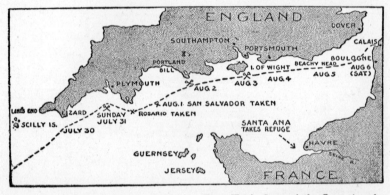

From Hale's *Story of the Great Armada.*

THE COURSE OF THE ARMADA UP THE CHANNEL

del Rosario, which had been injured in collision and surrendered to Drake without a struggle on the night of August 1, the other the big *San Salvador* of the Guipuscoan squadron, the whole after part of which had been torn up by an explosion after the fighting on the first day. But the Spanish inferiority had been clearly demonstrated and they had suffered far more in morale than in material injuries when on Sunday, August 7, they dropped anchor in Calais roads. The English, on their part, though flushed with confidence, had seen their weakness in organized tactics, and now divided their fleet into four squadrons, with the flag officers and Frobisher in command.

It betrays the fatuity of the Spanish leader, if not of the whole plan of campaign, that when thus practically driven to refuge in a neutral port, Medina Sidonia thought his share of the task accomplished, and wrote urgent appeals to Parma to join or send aid, though the great general had not enough flat-boats and barges to float his army had he been so foolhardy as to embark, or the Dutch so benevolent as to let him go. But the English, now reënforced by Seymour's squadron, gave the Duke little time to ponder his next move. At midnight eight fire hulks, "spurting flames and their ordnance explod-ing," were borne by wind and tide full upon the crowded Spanish fleet. Fearful of *maquinas de minas* such as had wrought destruction a year before at the siege of Antwerp, the Spanish made no effort to grapple the peril but slipped or cut cables and in complete confusion beat off shore.

At dawn the Spanish galleons, attempting with a veering wind from the southward and westward to form in order off Gravelines, were set upon in the closest approach to a general engagement that occurred in the campaign. While Howard and several of his ships were busy effecting the capture of a beached galleass, Drake led the attack in the *Revenge,* seeking to force the enemy to leeward and throw the whole body upon the shallows of the Flanders coast. With splendid discipline, the Spanish weather ships, the flagship *San Martin* among them, fought valiantly to cover the retreat. But it was an unequal struggle, the heavier and more rapid fire of the Eng-lish doing fearful execution on decks crowded with men-at-arms. Such artillery combat was hitherto unheard of. Though warned of the new northern methods, the Spanish were ob-sessed by tradition; they were prepared for grappling and boarding, and could they have closed, their numbers and disci-pline would have told. Both sides suffered from short ammu-nition; but the Armada, with no fresh supplies, was undoubt-edly in the worse case. "They fighting with their great ord-nance," writes Medina Sidonia, "and we with harquebus fire and musketry, the distance being very small." Six-inch guns against bows and muskets tells the tale.

A slackening of the English pursuit at nightfall after eight hours' fighting, and an off-shore slant of wind at daybreak, prevented complete disaster. One large galleon sank and two more stranded and were captured by the Dutch. These losses were not indeed fatal, but the remaining ships staggering away to leeward were little more than blood-drenched wrecks. Fifteen hundred had been killed and wounded in the day's action, and eleven ships and some eight thousand men sacrificed thus far in the campaign. The English, on the other hand, had suffered no serious ship injuries and the loss of not above 100 men. In the council held next day beyond the Straits of Dover, only a few of the Spanish leaders had stomach for further fighting; the rest preferred to brave the perils of a return around the Orkneys rather than face again these defenders of the narrow seas. Beforr a fair wind they stood northward, Drake still at their heels, chough by reason of short supplies he left them at the Firth of Forth.

In October, fifty ships, with 10,000 starved and fever-stricken men, trailed into the Biscay ports of Spain. Torn by September gales, the rest of the Armada had been sunk or stranded on the rough coasts of Scotland and Ireland. "The wreckers of the Orkneys and the Faroes, the clansmen of the Scottish isles, the kernes of Donegal and Galway, all had their part in the work of murder and robbery. Eight thousand Spaniards perished between the Giant's Causeway and the Blaskets. On a strand near Sligo an English captain numbered eleven hundred corpses which had been cast up by the sea." [1]

"Flavit Deus, et dissipati sunt"—"The Lord sent His wind, and scattered them." So ran the motto on the English medal of victory. But storms completed the destruction of a fleet already thoroughly defeated. Religious faith, courage, and discipline had availed little against superior ships, weapons, leadership, and nautical skill. "Till the King of Spain had war with us," an Englishman remarked, "he never knew what war by sea meant." [2] It might be said more accurately that the battle gave a new meaning to war by sea.

From the standpoint of naval progress, the campaign demonstrated definitely the ascendancy of sail and artillery. For the old galley tactics a new system now had to be developed. Since

---

[1] HISTORY OF THE ENGLISH PEOPLE, Green, Vol. II, p. 448.
[2] Sir Wm. Monson, NAVAL TRACTS, Purchas, Vol. III, p. 121.

between sailing vessels head-on conflict was practically eliminated, and since guns mounted to fire ahead and astern were of little value save in flight or pursuit, the arrangement of guns in broadside soon became universal, and fleets fought in column, or "line ahead," usually close-hauled on the same or opposite tacks.   While these were lessons for the next generation, there is more permanent value in the truth, again illustrated, that fortune favors the belligerent quicker to forsake outworn methods and to develop skill in the use of new weapons.   The Spanish defeat illustrates also the necessity of expert planning and guidance of a naval campaign, with naval counsels and requirements duly regarded; and the fatal effect of failure to concentrate attention on the enemy fleet.   It is doubtful, however, whether it would have been better, as Drake urged, and as was actually attempted in the month before the Armada's arrival, if the English had shifted the war to the coast of Spain.   The objections arise chiefly from the difficulties, in that age, of maintaining a large naval force far from its base, all of which the Spanish encountered in their northward cruise.   It is noteworthy that, even after the brief Channel operations, an epidemic caused heavy mortality in the English fleet.   Finally, the Armada is a classic example of the value of naval defense to an insular nation.   In the often quoted words of Raleigh, "To entertain the enemy with their own beef in their bellies, before they eat of our Kentish capons, I take it to be the wisest way, to do which his Majesty after God will employ his good ships at sea."

Upon Spain, already tottering from inherent weakness, the Armada defeat had the effect of casting down her pride and confidence as leader of the Catholic world.   Though it was not until three centuries later that she lost her last colonies, her hold on her vast empire was at once shaken by this blow at her sea control.   While she maintained large fleets until after the Napoleonic Wars, she was never again truly formidable as a naval power. But the victory lifted England more than it crushed Spain, inspiring an intenser patriotism, an eagerness for colonial and commercial adventure, an exaltation of spirit

manifested in the men of genius who crowned the Elizabethan
age.

The Last Years of the War

The war was not ended; and though Philip was restrained
by the rise of Protestant power in France under Henry of
Navarre, he was still able to gather his sea forces on almost
as grand a scale. In the latter stages of the war the naval
expeditions on both sides were either, like the Armada, for the
purpose of landing armies on foreign soil, or raids on enemy
ports, colonies and commerce. Thus Drake in 1589 set out
with a force of 18,000 men, which attacked Corunna, moved
thence upon Lisbon, and lost a third or more of its number in
a fruitless campaign on land. Both Drake and the aged
Hawkins, now his vice admiral, died in the winter of 1595-96
during a last and this time ineffective foray upon the Spanish
Main. Drake was buried off Puerto Bello, where legend has
it his spirit still awaits England's call—

"Take my drum to England, hang et by the shore,
Strike et when your powder's running low.
  If the Dons sight Devon, I'll leave the port of Heaven,
An' drum them up the Channel as we drummed them long
      ago."[1]

We are still far from the period when sea control was
thought of as important in itself, apart from land operations,
or when fleets were kept in permanent readiness to take
the sea. It is owing to this latter fact that we hear of large
flotillas dispatched by each side even in the same year, yet not
meeting in naval action. Thus in June of 1596 the Essex expedition, with 17 English and 18 Dutch men-of-war and numerous auxiliaries, seized Cadiz and burned shipping to the value
of 11,000,000 ducats. There was no naval opposition, though
Philip in October of the same year had ready a hundred ships
and 16,000 men, which were dispersed with the loss of a
quarter of their strength in a gale off Finisterre. Storms also

[1] DRAKE'S DRUM, Sir Henry Newbolt.

scattered Philip's fleet in the next year; in 1598, Spanish transports landed 5,000 men at Calais; and England's fears were renewed in the year after that by news of over 100 vessels fitting out for the Channel, which, however, merely protected the plate fleet by a cruise to the Azores. As late as 1601, Spain landed 3500 troops in Ireland.

But if these major operations seem to have missed contact, there were many lively actions on a minor scale, the well-armed trading vessels of the north easily beating off the galley squadrons guarding Gibraltar and the routes past Spain. Among these lesser encounters, the famous "Last Fight of the Revenge," which occurred during operations of a small English squadron off the Azores in 1591, well illustrates the fighting spirit of the Elizabethan Englishman and the ineptitude which since the Armada seems to have marked the Spaniard at sea. In Drake's old flagship, attacked by 15 ships and surrounded by a Spanish fleet of 50 sail, a bellicose old sea-warrior named Sir Richard Grenville held out from nightfall until eleven the next day, and surrendered only after he had sunk three of the enemy, when his powder was gone, half his crew dead, the rest disabled, and his ship a sinking wreck. "Here die I, Richard Grenville," so we are given his last words, "with a joyful and a quiet mind, for that I have ended my life as a good soldier ought to do, who has fought for his country and his queen, his honor and his religion."

The naval activities mentioned in the immediately preceding paragraphs had no decisive effect upon the war, which ended, for England at least, with the death of Elizabeth in 1603 and the accession of James Stuart of Scotland to the English throne. James at once adopted a policy of *rapprochement* with Spain, which while it guaranteed peace during the 22 years of his reign, was by its renunciation of trade with the Indies, aid to the Dutch, and leadership of Protestant Europe, a sorry sequel to the victory of fifteen years before.

The Armada nevertheless marks the decadence of Spanish sea power. With the next century begins a new epoch in naval warfare, an age of sail and artillery, in which Dutch,

English, and later French fleets contested for the sea mastery deemed essential to colonial empire and commercial prosperity.

REFERENCES

DRAKE AND THE TUDOR NAVY, Sir Julian Corbett, 2 vols., 1898.
THE SUCCESSORS OF DRAKE, Sir Julian Corbett, 1900.
THE STORY OF THE GREAT ARMADA, J. R. Hale, no date.
ARMADA PAPERS, Sir John Knox Laughton, 2 vols., Navy Records Society, 1894.
LA ARMADA INVENCIBLE, Captain Fernandez Duro, 1884.
A HISTORY OF THE ADMINISTRATION OF THE ROYAL NAVY, 1509-1660, by M. Oppenheim, 1896.
A HISTORY OF THE ROYAL NAVY, William Laird Clowes, Vol. I., 1897.
THE GROWTH OF ENGLISH COMMERCE AND INDUSTRY, W. Cunningham, 1907.
THE DEVELOPMENT OF TACTICS IN THE TUDOR NAVY, Capt. G. Goldingham, United Service Magazine, June, 1918.

CHAPTER VIII

RISE OF ENGLISH SEA POWER: WARS WITH THE DUTCH.

In the Dutch Wars of the 17th century the British navy may be said to have caught its stride in the march that made Britannia the unrivaled mistress of the seas. The defeat of the Armada was caused by other things besides the skill of the English, and the steady decline of Spain from that point was not due to that battle or to any energetic naval campaign undertaken by the English thereafter. In fact, save for the Cadiz expedition of 1596, in which the Dutch coöperated, England had a rather barren record after the Armada campaign down to the middle of the 17th century. During that period the Dutch seized the control of the seas for trade and war. They appropriated what was left of the Levantine trade in the Mediterranean, and contested the Portuguese monopoly in the East Indies and the Spanish in the West. Indeed the Dutch were at this time freely acknowledged to be the greatest sea-faring people of Europe.[1]

When the Commonwealth came into power in England the new government turned its attention to the navy, which had languished under the Stuarts. A great reform was accomplished in the bettering of the living conditions for the seamen. Their pay was increased, their share of prize money enlarged, and their food improved. At the same time, during the years 1648-51, the number of ships of the fleet was practically doubled, and the new vessels were the product of the

---

[1] "Dutch exports reached a figure in the 17th century, which was not attained by the English until 1740. Even the Dutch fisheries, which employed over 2000 boats, were said to be more valuable than the manufactures of France and England combined." A HISTORY OF COMMERCE, Clive Day, p. 194.

highest skill in design and honest work in construction. The turmoil between Roundhead and Royalist had naturally disorganized the officer personnel of the fleet. Prince Rupert, nephew of Charles I, had taken a squadron of seven Royalist ships to sea, hoping to organize, at the Scilly Islands or at Kinsdale in Ireland, bases for piratical raids on the commerce of England, and it was necessary to bring him up short. Moreover, Ireland was still rebellious, Barbados, the only British possession in the West Indies, was held for the King, and Virginia also was Royalist. To establish the rule of the Commonwealth Cromwell needed an efficient fleet and an energetic admiral.

For the latter he turned to a man who had won a military reputation in the Civil War second only to that of the great Oliver himself, Robert Blake, colonel of militia. Blake was chosen as one of three "generals at sea" in 1649. As far as is known he had never before set foot on a man of war; he was a scholarly man, who had spent ten years at Oxford, where he had cherished the ambition of becoming a professor of Greek. At the time of his appointment he was fifty years old, and his entire naval career was comprised in the seven or eight remaining years of his life, and yet he so bore himself in those years as to win a reputation that stands second only to that of Nelson among the sea-fighters of the English race.

Blake made short work of Rupert's cruising and destroyed the Royalist pretensions to Jersey and the Scillies. One of his' rewards for the excellent service rendered was a position in the Council of State, in which capacity he did much toward the bettering of the condition of the sailors, which was one of the striking reforms of the Commonwealth. His test, however, came in the first Dutch War, in which he was pitted against Martin Tromp, then the leading naval figure of Europe.

In the wars with Spain, English and Dutch had been allies, but the shift of circumstances brought the two Protestant nations into a series of fierce conflicts lasting throughout the latter half of the 17th century. The outcome of these was that England won the scepter of the sea which she has ever since held. The main cause of the war was the rivalry of the two nations on the sea. There were various other specific reasons for bad feeling on both sides, as for instance a massacre by the Dutch of English traders at Amboyna in the East Indies, during the reign of James I, which still rankled because it had never been avenged. The English on their side insisted on a salute to their men of war from every ship that passed through the Channel, and claimed the rights to a tribute of all herrings taken within 30 miles off the English coast.

Cromwell formulated the English demands in the Navigation Act of 1651. The chief of these required that none but English ships should bring cargoes to England, save vessels of the country whence the cargoes came. This was frankly a direct blow at the Dutch carrying trade, one to which the Dutch could not yield without a struggle.

For this struggle the Netherlanders were ill prepared. The Dutch Republic was a federation of seven sovereign states, lacking a strong executive and torn by rival factions. Moreover, her geographical position was most vulnerable. Pressed by enemies on her land frontiers, she was compelled to maintain an army of 57,000 men in addition to her navy. As the resources of the country were wholly inadequate to support the population, her very life depended on the sea. For the Holland of the 17th century, as for the England of the 20th, the fleets of merchantmen were the life blood of the nation. Unfortunately for the Dutch, this life blood had to course either through the Channel or else round the north of Scotland. Either way was open to attacks by the British, who held the interior position. Further, the shallows of the coasts and bays made necessary a flat bottomed ship of war, lighter built than the English and less weatherly in deep water.

In contrast the British had a unity of government under the iron hand of Cromwell, they had the enormous advantage of position, they were self-sustaining, and their ships were larger, stouter and better in every respect than those of their enemies. Hence, although the Dutch entered the conflict with the naval prestige on their side, it is clear that the odds were decidedly against them.

The First Dutch War

The fighting did not wait for a declaration of war. Blake
met Tromp, who was convoying a fleet of merchantmen, off
Dover on May 19, 1652. On coming up with him Blake fired
guns demanding the required salute. Tromp replied with a

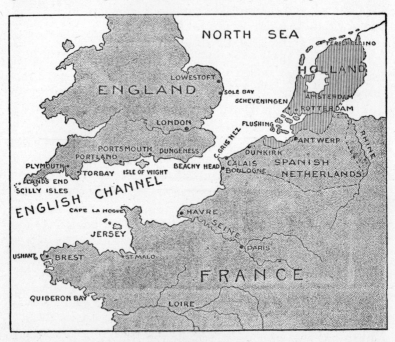

SCENE OF THE PRINCIPAL NAVAL ACTIONS OF THE 17TH CENTURY BETWEEN
ENGLAND AND HOLLAND AND ENGLAND AND FRANCE

broadside. Blake attacked with his flagship, well ahead of his
own line, and fought for five hours with Tromp's flagship and
several others. The English were outnumbered about three
to one, and Blake might have been annihilated had not the
English admiral, Bourne, brought his squadron out from
Dover at the sound of the firing and fallen upon Tromp's
flank. As the Dutch Admiral's main business was to get his
convoy home, he fell back slowly toward the coast of France,

both sides maintaining a cannonade until they lost each other in the darkness. Apparently there was little attempt at formation after the first onset; it was close quarters fighting, and only the wild gunnery of the day saved both fleets from enormous losses. As it was, Blake's flagship was very severely hammered.

Following this action, Tromp reappeared with 100 ships, but failed to keep Blake from attacking and ruining the Dutch herring fisheries for that year. This mistake temporarily cost Tromp his command. He was superseded by DeWith, an able man and brave, but no match for Blake. On September 28, 1652, Blake met him off the "Kentish Knock" shoal at the mouth of the Thames. In order to keep the weather gage, which would enable him to attack at close quarters, Blake took the risk of grounding on the shoal. His own ship and a few others did ground for a time, but they served as a guide to the rest. In the ensuing action Blake succeeded in putting the Dutch between two fires and inflicting a severe defeat. Only darkness saved the Dutch from utter destruction.

The effect of this victory was to give the English Council of State a false impression of security. In vain Blake urged the upkeep of the fleet. Two months later, November 30, 1652, Tromp, now restored to command, suddenly appeared in the Channel with 80 ships and a convoy behind him. Blake had only 45 and these only partly manned, but he was no man to refuse a challenge and boldly sailed out to meet him. It is said that during the desperate struggle—the "battle of Dungeness"—Blake's flagship, supported by two others, fought for some time with twenty of the Dutch. As Blake had the weather gage and retained it, he was able to draw off finally and save his fleet from destruction. All the ships were badly knocked about and two fell into the hands of the enemy. Blake came back so depressed by his defeat that he offered to resign his command, but the Council of State would not hear of such a thing, handsomely admitted their responsibility for the weakness of the fleet, and set at work to refit. Meanwhile for the next three months the Channel was in Tromp's hands.

This is the period when the legend describes him as hoisting a broom to his masthead.

By the middle of February the English had reorganized their fleet and Blake took the sea with another famous Roundhead soldier, Monk, as one of his divisional commanders. At this time Tromp lay off Land's End waiting for the Dutch merchant fleet which he expected to convoy to Holland. On the 18th the two forces sighted each other about 15 miles off Portland. Then followed the "Three Days' Battle," or the battle of Portland, one of the most stubbornly contested fights in the war and its turning point.

In order to be sure to catch Tromp, Blake had extended his force of 70 or 80 ships in a cross Channel position. Under cover of a fog Tromp suddenly appeared and caught the English fleet divided. Less than half were collected under the immediate command of Blake, only about ten were in the actual vicinity of his flagship, and the rest were to eastward, especially Monk's division which he had carelessly permitted to drift to leeward four or five miles. As the wind was from the west and very light, Monk's position made it impossible for him to support his chief for some time. Tromp saw his opportunity to concentrate on the part of the English fleet nearest him, the handful of ships with Blake. The latter had the choice of either bearing up to make a junction with Monk and the others before accepting battle or of grappling with Tromp at once, trusting to his admirals to arrive in time to win a victory. It was characteristic of Blake that he chose the bolder course.

The fighting began early in the afternoon and was close and furious from the outset. Again Blake's ship was compelled to engage several Dutch, including Tromp's flagship. De Ruyter, the brilliant lieutenant of Tromp, attempted to cut Blake off from his supports on the north, and Evertsen steered between Blake and Penn's squadron on the south. (See diagram 1.) Blake's dozen ships might well have been surrounded and taken if his admirals had not known their business. Penn tacked right through Evertsen's squadron to come to the side of Blake, and Lawson foiled de Ruyter by bearing away till he

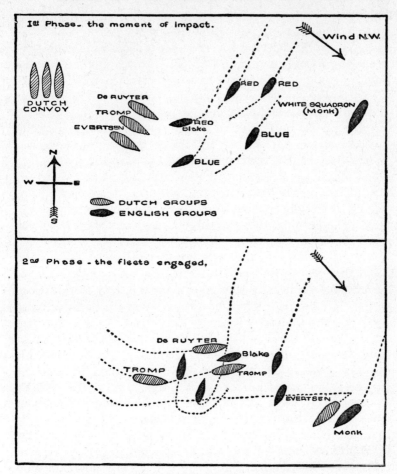

Based on diagram of Mahan's in Clowes, *The Royal Navy,* Vol. II, p. 180-1.

THE BATTLE OF PORTLAND, FEB. 18, 1653

had enough southing to tack in the wake of Penn and fall upon Tromp's rear (diagram 2). Evertsen then attempted to get between Monk and the rest of the fleet and two hours after the fight in the center began Monk also was engaged. When the lee vessels of the "red" or center squadron came on the scene about four o'clock, they threatened to weather the

Dutch and put them between two fires. To avoid this and to protect his convoy, Tromp tacked his whole fleet together—an exceedingly difficult maneuver under the circumstances—and drew off to windward. Darkness stopped the fighting for that day. All night the two fleets sailed eastward watching each other's lights, and hastily patching up damages.

Morning discovered them off the Isle of Wight, with the English on the north side of the Channel. As Tromp's chief business was to save his convoy and as the English force was now united, he took a defensive position. He formed his own ships in a long crescent, with the outward curve toward his enemy, and in the lee of this line he placed his convoy. The wind was so light that the English were unable to attack until late. The fighting, though energetic, had not proved decisive when darkness fell.

The following day, the 20th, brought a fresh wind that enabled the English to overhaul the Dutch, who could not move faster than the heavily laden merchantmen, and force a close action. Blake tried to cut off Tromp from the north so as to block his road home. Vice Admiral Penn, leading the van, broke through the Dutch battle line and fell upon the convoy, but Blake was unable to reach far enough to head off his adversary before he rounded Cape Gris Nez under cover of darkness and found anchorage in Calais roads. That night, favored by the tide and thick weather, Tromp succeeded in carrying off the greater part of his convoy unobserved. Nevertheless he had left in Blake's hand some fifty merchantmen and a number of men of war variously estimated from five to eighteen. At the same time the English had suffered heavily in men and ships. On Blake's flagship alone it is said that 100 men had been killed and Blake and his second in command, Deane, were both wounded, the former seriously.

The result of this three days' action was to encourage the English to press the war with energy and take the offensive to the enemy's own coast. English crews had shown that they could fight with a spirit fully equal to that of the Dutch, and English ships and weight of broadside, as de Ruyter frankly declared to his government, were decidedly superior. The fact that the shallow waters of the Dutch coast made necessary a lighter draft man of war than that of the English proved a serious handicap to the Dutch in all their conflicts with the British.   Both fleets were so badly shot up by this prolonged battle that there was a lull in operations until May.

In that month Tromp suddenly arrived off Dover and bombarded the defenses.   The English quickly took the sea to hunt him down.   As Blake was still incapacitated by his wound, the command was given to Monk.   The latter, with a fleet of over a hundred ships, brought Tromp to action on June 2 (1653) in what is known as the "Battle of the Gabbard" after a shoal near the mouth of the Thames, where the action began.   Tromp was this time not burdened with a convoy but his fleet was smaller in numbers than Monk's and, as he well knew, inferior in other elements of force.   Accordingly, he adopted defensive tactics of a sort that was copied afterwards by the French as a fixed policy.   He accepted battle to leeward, drawing off in a slanting line from his enemy with the idea of catching the English van as it advanced to the attack unsupported by the rest of the fleet, and crippling it so severely that the attack would not be pressed. As it turned out, a shift of the wind gave him the chance to fall heavily upon the English van, but a second shift gave back the weather gage to the English and the two fleets became fiercely engaged at close quarters.   Blake, hearing the guns, left his sick bed and with his own available force of 18 ships sailed out to join battle.   The sight of this fresh squadron flying Blake's flag, turned the fortune of battle decisively.   The Dutch escaped destruction only by finding safety in the shallows of the Flemish coast, where the English ships could not follow.

After this defeat the Dutch were almost at the end of their resources and sued for peace, but Cromwell's ruthless demands amounted to a practical loss of independence, which even a bankrupt nation could not accept.   Accordingly, every nerve was strained to build a fleet that might yet beat the English. The latter, for their part, were equally determined not to lose the fruits of their hard won victories.   Since Blake's active share in the battle of the Gabbard aggravated his wound so severely that he was carried ashore more nearly dead than alive, Monk retained actual command.

Monk attempted to maintain a close blockade of the Dutch coast and to prevent a junction between Tromp's main fleet at Flushing and a force of thirty ships at Amsterdam. In this, however, he was outgeneraled by Tromp, who succeeded in taking the sea with the greatest of all Dutch fleets, 120 men of war. The English and the Dutch speedily clashed in the last, and perhaps the most furiously contested, battle of the war, the "Battle of Scheveningen." The action began at six in the morning of July 30, 1653. Tromp had the weather gage, but Monk, instead of awaiting his onslaught, tacked towards him and actually cut through the Dutch line. Tromp countered by tacking also, in order to keep his windward position, and this maneuver was repeated three times by Tromp and Monk, and the two great fleets sailed in great zigzag courses down the Dutch coast a distance of forty miles, with bitter fighting going on at close range between the two lines. Early in the action the renowned Tromp was killed, but his flag was kept flying and there was no flinching on the part of his admirals. About one o'clock a shift of the wind gave the weather gage to the English. Some of the Dutch captains then showed the white feather and tried to escape. This compelled the retirement of DeWith, who had succeeded to the command, and who, as he retreated, fired on his own fugitives as well as on the English. As usual in those battles with the Dutch, the English had been forced to pay a high price for their victory. Their fleet was so shattered that they were obliged to lift the blockade and return home to refit. But for the Dutch it was the last effort. Again they sued for peace. Cromwell drove a hard bargain; he insisted on every claim England had ever made against the Netherlands before the war, but on this occasion he agreed to leave Holland her independence.

Thus in less than two years the First Dutch War came to an end. In the words of Mr. Hannay,[1] the English historian,

[1] A SHORT HISTORY OF THE ROYAL NAVY, Vol. I, p. 217.

its "importance as an epoch in the history of the English Navy can hardly be exaggerated. Though short, for it lasted barely twenty-two months, it was singularly fierce and full of battles. Yet its interest is not derived mainly from the mere amount of fighting but from the character of it. This was the first of our naval wars conducted by steady, continuous, coherent campaigns. Hitherto our operations on the sea had been of the nature of adventures by single ships and small squadrons, with here and there a great expedition sent out to capture some particular port or island."

As to the intensity of the fighting, it is worth noting that in this short period six great battles took place between fleets numbering as a rule from 70 to 120 ships on a side. By comparison it may be remarked that at Trafalgar the total British force numbered 27 ships of the line and the Allies, 33. Nor were the men of war of Blake and Tromp the small types of an earlier day. In 1652 the ship of the line had become the unit of the fleet as truly as it was in 1805. It is true that Blake's ships were not the equal of Nelson's huge "first rates," because the "two-decker" was then the most powerful type. The first three-decker in the English navy was launched in the year of Blake's death, 1657. The fact remains, however, that these fleet actions of the Dutch Wars took place on a scale unmatched by any of the far better known engagements of the 18th or early 19th century.

A curious naval weapon survived from the day when Howard drove Medina Sidonia from Calais roads, the fireship, or "brander." This was used by both English and Dutch. Its usefulness, of course, was confined to the side that held the windward position, and even an opponent to leeward could usually, if he kept his head, send out boats to grapple and tow the brander out of harm's way. In the battle of Scheveningen, however, Dutch fireships cost the English two fine ships, together with a Dutch prize, and very nearly destroyed the old flagship of Blake, the *Triumph*. She was saved only by the extraordinary exertions of her captain, who received mortal injury from the flames he fought so courageously.

This First Dutch War is interesting in what it reveals of the advance in tactics. Tromp well deserves his title as the "Father of Naval Tactics," and he undoubtedly taught Blake and Monk a good deal by the rough schooling of battle, but they proved apt pupils. From even the brief summary of these great battles just given, it is evident that Dutch and English did not fight each other in helter skelter fashion. In fact, there is revealed a great advance in coördination over the work of the English in the campaign of the Armada. These fleets worked as units. This does not mean that they were not divided into squadrons. A force of 100 ships of the line required division and subdivision, and considerable freedom of movement was left to division and squadron commanders under the general direction of the commander in chief, but they were all working consciously together. Just as at Trafalgar Nelson formed his fleet in two lines (originally planned as three) and allowed his second in command a free hand in carrying out the task assigned him, so Tromp and Blake operated their fleets in squadrons—Tromp usually had five—and expected of their subordinates responsibility and initiative. All this is in striking contrast with the practice that paralyzed tactics in the latter 17th and 18th centuries, which sacrificed everything to a rigid line of battle in column ahead, and required every movement to emanate from the commander in chief.

Although details about the great battles of the First Dutch War are scanty, there is enough recorded to show that both sides used the line ahead as the normal battle line. It is equally clear, however, that they repeatedly broke through each other's lines and aimed at concentration, or destroying in detail. These two related principles, which had to be rediscovered toward the end of the 18th century, were practiced by Tromp, de Ruyter, and Blake. Their work has not the advantage of being as near our day as the easy, one-sided victories over the demoralized French navy in the Revolutionary and Napoleonic era, but the day may come when the British will regard the age of Blake as the naval epoch of which they have the most reason to be proud. Then England met the greatest seamen of the day led by one of the greatest admirals of history and won a bitterly fought contest by virtue of better ships and the spirit of Cromwell's "Ironsides."

Porto Farina and Santa Cruz

Nor did the age of Blake end with the First Dutch War. As soon as the admiral was able to go aboard ship, Cromwell sent him with a squadron into the Mediterranean to enforce respect for the Commonwealth from the Italian governments and the Barbary states. He conducted his mission with eminent success. Although the Barbary pirates did not course the sea in great fleets as in the palmy days of Barbarossa, they were still a source of peril to Christian traders. Blake was received civilly by the Dey of Algiers but negotiations did not result satisfactorily. At Tunis he was openly flouted. The Pasha drew up his nine cruisers inside Porto Farina and defied the English admiral to do his worst. Blake left for a few days to gain the effect of surprise and replenish provisions. On April 4, 1655, he suddenly reappeared and stood in to the attack.

The harbor of Porto Farina was regarded as impregnable. The entrance was narrow and the shores lined with castles and batteries. As Blake foresaw, the wind that took him in would roll the battle smoke upon the enemy. In a short time he had silenced the fire of the forts and then sent boarding parties against the Tunisian ships, which were speedily taken and burnt. Then he took his squadron out again, having destroyed the entire Tunisian navy, shattered the forts, and suffered only a trifling loss. This exploit resounded throughout the Mediterranean. Algiers was quick to follow Tunis in yielding to Blake's demands. It is characteristic of this officer that he should have made the attack on Tunis entirely without orders from Cromwell, and it is equally characteristic of the latter that he was heartily pleased with the initiative of his admiral in carrying out the spirit rather than the letter of his instructions.

Meanwhile Cromwell had been wavering between a war

against France or Spain. The need of a capture of money perhaps influenced him to turn against Spain, for this country still drew from her western colonies a tribute of gold and silver, which naturally would fall a prey to the power that controlled the sea. One month after Blake's exploit at Tunis, another English naval expedition set out to the West Indies to take Santo Domingo. Although Jamaica was seized and thereafter became an English possession, the expedition as a whole was a disgraceful failure, and the leaders, Penn and Venables, were promptly clapped by Cromwell into the Tower on their return. This stroke against Spain amounted to a declaration of war, and on Blake's return to England he was ordered to blockade Cadiz. One detachment of the plate fleet fell into the hands of his blockading ships and the silver ingots were dispatched to London. Blake continued his blockade in an open roadstead for six months, through autumn and winter, an unheard of thing in those days and exceedingly difficult. Blake was himself ill, his ships were not the copper-bottomed ones of a hundred years later, and there was not, as in later days, an English base at Gibraltar. But he never relaxed his vigilance.

In April (1657) he learned that another large plate fleet had arrived at Santa Cruz, Teneriffe. Immediately he sailed thither to take or destroy it. If Porto Farina had been regarded as safe from naval attack, Santa Cruz was far more so. A deep harbor, with a narrow, funnel entrance, and backed by mountains, it is liable to dead calms or squally bursts of wind from the land. In addition to its natural defenses it was heavily fortified. Blake, however, reckoned on coming in with a flowing tide and a sea breeze that, as at Porto Farina, would blow his smoke upon the defenses. He rightly guessed that if he sailed close enough under the castles at the harbor entrance their guns could not be sufficiently depressed to hit his ships, and as he saw the galleons and their escorts lined up along the shore he perceived also that they were masking the fire of their own shore batteries. For the most difficult part of his undertaking, the exit from the harbor, he trusted to the ebbing tide with the chance of a shift in the wind in his favor.

Early on the morning of April 20th (1657) he sailed in. As he had judged, the fire of the forts did little damage. By eight o'clock the English ships were all at their appointed stations and fighting. During the entire day Blake continued his work of destruction till it was complete, and at dusk drifted out on the ebb. Some writers mention a favoring land breeze that helped to extricate the English, but according to Blake's own words, "the wind blew right into the bay." In spite of this head wind the ships that were crippled were warped or towed out and not one was lost. The English suffered in the entire action only 50 killed and 120 wounded, and repairs were so easily made that Blake returned to his blockading station at once.

This was the greatest of Blake's feats as it also was his last. All who heard of it—friend or enemy—pronounced it as without parallel in the history of ships. A few months later Blake was given leave to return home. He had long been a sick man, but his name alone was worth a fleet and Cromwell had not been able to spare him. As it happened, he did not live long enough to see England again. Cromwell, who knew the worth of his faithful admiral, gave him a funeral of royal dignity and interment in Westminster Abbey.

Blake never showed, perhaps, great strategic insight— Tromp and de Ruyter were his superiors there, as was also Nelson—but he, more than any other, won for England her mastery of the sea, and no other can boast his record of great victories. These he won partly by skill and forethought but chiefly by intrepidity. We can do no better than leave his fame in the words of the Royalist historian, Clarendon—a political enemy—who says: "He quickly made himself signal there (on the sea) and was the first man who declined the old track . . . and disproved those rules that had long been in practice, to keep his ships and men out of danger, which had been held in former times a point of great ability and circumspection, as if the principal requisite in the captain of a ship had been to come home safe again. He was the first man who brought ships to contemn castles on shore, which had been thought ever very formidable. . . . He was the first that infused that proportion of courage into the seamen by making them see what mighty things they could do if they were resolved, and taught them to fight in fire as well as on water. And though he hath been very well imitated and followed, he was the first that drew the copy of naval courage and bold resolute achievement."

The chaos that followed the death of the Protector resulted in Monk's bringing over the exiled Stuart king—Charles II. Thereafter Round Head and Royalist served together in the British navy. An important effect of the Restoration was organization of a means of training the future officers of the fleet. The Navy as a profession may be said to date from this time, in contrast with the practice of using merchant skippers and army officers, which had prevailed to so great a degree hitherto. Under the new system "young gentlemen" were sent to sea as "King's Letter Boys"—midshipmen—to learn the ways of the navy and to grow up in it as a preparation for command. This was an excellent reform but it resulted in making the navy the property of a social class from that day to this, and it made promotion, for a century and more, largely subject to family influence.

Another effect of the Restoration was to break down the fighting efficiency of the fleet as it had been in the days of Blake. The veterans of the First Dutch War fought with their old time courage and discipline, but the newer elements did not show the same devotion and initiative. The effect on the material was still worse, for the fleet became a prey to the cynical dishonesty that Charles II inspired in every department of his government.

The Second Dutch War

Five years after Charles II became king, England was involved in another war with the Netherlands. There was still bad feeling between the two peoples, and trading companies in the far east or west kept up a guerilla warfare which flooded both governments with complaints. The chief cause seems to have been the desire of the English Guinea Company to get rid of their Dutch competitors who persistently undersold them in the slave markets of the West Indies. Before there was any declaration of war an English squadron was sent out to attack the Dutch company's settlement on the West African coast. After this it crossed the Atlantic and took New Amsterdam, which thereafter became New York. The Dutch retaliated by sending out one of their squadrons to retake their African post and threaten the Atlantic colonies. In March, 1665, war was declared.

In this conflict the relative strengths of the two navies were about the same as in the previous war. The Dutch had made improvements in their ships, but they still suffered from the lack of unity in organization and spirit. The first engagement was the battle of Lowestoft, on June 3, 1665. The English fleet was under the personal command of the Duke of York, later James II; the Dutch were led by de Ruyter. The two forces numbered from 80 to 100 ships each, and strung out as they were, must have extended over nearly ten miles of sea. The Duke of York formed his fleet in the pattern that he set by his own "Fighting Instructions," which governed the tactics of all navies thereafter for a hundred years, namely, the entire force drawn up in single line. This line bore down abreast toward the enemy until it reached gunshot, then swung into line ahead and sailed on a course parallel to that of the enemy. De Ruyter arranged his fleet accordingly, and the two long lines passed each other on opposite tacks three times, cannonading furiously at close range. This meant that the force was distributed evenly along the enemy's line and as against an evenly matched force these tactics could result, as a rule, only in mere inconclusive artillery duels which each side would claim as victories. In the battle of Lowestoft, however, several of the captains in the Dutch center flinched at the third passing and bore up to leeward, leaving a wide gap in de Ruyter's line. The English broke through at this point and hammered the weakened Dutch line in the center with a superior force. This was the decisive point in the battle and de Ruyter was forced to retreat. The Dutch would have suffered even greater loss than they did had it not been for the masterly fashion in which Cornelius Tromp—son of the famous Martin Tromp—covered the retreat.

The defeat of the Dutch was due to the bad conduct of the captains in the center, four of whom were shot by order of de Ruyter and others dismissed from the service. It is interesting to note that while the first half of the battle was fought on the formal lines that were soon to be the cast iron rule of conduct for the British navy, and led to nothing conclusive; the second half was characterized by the breaking of the enemy's line, in the older style of Blake, and led to a pronounced victory.

At this time Louis XIV had pledged himself to give aid to the Netherlands in case of attack by a third Power. But when the Dutch and his own ministers called on him to make good his promise he offered more promises and no fulfillment. The rumor of an approaching French squadron, which was to make junction with de Ruyter, who had now been placed in command of the Dutch fleet, caused the English government to make the grave mistake of detaching Prince Rupert with 20 ships to look for the mythical French force. This division left Monk, who was again in command of the fleet, with only 57 ships. Hearing that de Ruyter was anchored on the Flanders coast, Monk went out to find him. De Ruyter left his anchorage to meet the English, and on June 1, 1666, the two forces met in mid-Channel, between Dunkirk and the Downs. As the Dutch force heavily outnumbered him—nearly two to one—Monk might have been expected to avoid fighting, but he acted in the spirit of Blake. Having the windward position he decided that he could strike the advanced division under Tromp and maul it severely before the rest of the Dutch could succor it. Accordingly he boldly headed for the enemy's van. When Monk attacked he had only about 35 ships in hand, for the rest were straggling behind too far to help. Thus began the famous "Four Days' Battle," characterized by Mahan as "the most remarkable, in some of its aspects that has ever been fought upon the ocean." [1]

The fighting was close and furious and in its unparalleled duration numbers were bound to tell. On the third day Monk retreated to the Thames, but on being joined by Rupert's squadron immediately sallied forth to do battle again. On this day, June 4, the Dutch succeeded in cutting through his formation and putting him between two fires. Indeed Monk escaped destruction only by breaking through his ring of enemies and finding refuge in the Thames. The Dutch had won a great victory, for the English had lost some twenty ships and 5000 in killed and wounded. But Monk was right in feeling a sense of pride in the fight that he had made against great odds. The losses that he had inflicted were out of all proportion to the relative strength of the two forces. Unfortunately the new spirit that was coming into the navy of the Restoration was evidenced by the fact that a number of English captains, finding the action too hot for them, deserted their commander in chief. On the Dutch side de Ruyter's handling of his fleet was complicated by the conduct of Cornelius Tromp. This officer believed that he, not de Ruyter, should have been made commander of the Dutch fleet and in this action as in the next, acted with no regard for his chief's orders.

As a consequence of the Four Days' Battle, Dutchmen again controlled the Channel and closed the mouth of the Thames to trade. The English strained every nerve to create a fleet that should put an end to this humiliating and disastrous situation. The preparations were carried out with such speed that on July 22 (1666), Monk and Rupert anchored off the end of the Gunfleet shoal with a fleet of about 80 ships of the line and frigates. On the 25th the English sighted de Ruyter, with a fleet slightly larger in numbers, in the broad part of the Thames estuary. Monk, forming his fleet in the long line ahead, sailed to the attack. The action that followed is called the "Battle of St. James's Day" or the "Gunfleet."

Whether or not Monk was influenced by his princely col-

[1] THE INFLUENCE OF SEA POWER UPON HISTORY, p. 125.

league it is impossible to say, but the tactics of this engagement do not suggest the Monk of earlier battles. He followed the "Fighting Instructions" and in spite of them won a victory, but it might have been far more decisive. The English bore down in line abreast, then formed line ahead on reaching gunshot, the van, center, and rear, engaging respectively the Dutch van, center, and rear. In these line ahead attacks the

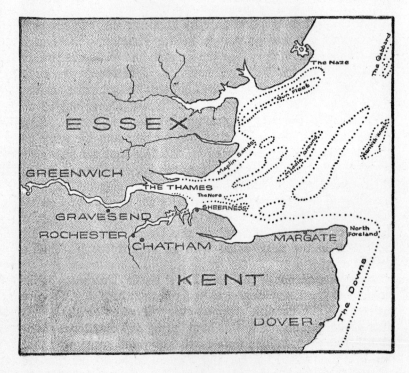

THE THAMES ESTUARY

rear usually straggled. Tromp, commanding the Dutch rear, saw his chance to attack Smith, commanding the English rear, before his squadron was in proper formation. Smith retreated, and Tromp, eager to win a victory all by himself, abandoned the rest of the Dutch fleet and pursued Smith. Thus the action broke into two widely separated parts. The

English van and center succeeded in forcing the corresponding Dutch divisions to retreat, and if Monk had turned to the help of Smith he might have taken or destroyed all of the 39 ships in Tromp's division. Instead, he and Rupert went careering on in pursuit of the enemy directly ahead of them. Eventually de Ruyter's ships found refuge in shallow water and then Monk turned to catch Tromp. But the latter proved too clever for his adversaries and slipped between them to an anchorage alongside of de Ruyter.

Although the victory was not nearly so decisive as it should have been with the opportunity offered, nevertheless it served the need of the hour. De Ruyter was no longer able to blockade the Thames and the Straits of Dover. And Monk, following up his success, carried the war to the enemy's coast, where he burned a merchant fleet of 160 vessels in the roadstead of the island of Terschelling, and destroyed one of the towns. Early in 1666 active operations on both sides dwindled down, and Charles, anxious to use naval appropriations for other purposes, allowed the fleet to fall into a condition of unreadiness for service. One of the least scandals in this corrupt age was the unwillingness or inability of the officials to pay the seamen their wages. In consequence large numbers of English prisoners in Holland actually preferred taking service in the Dutch navy rather than accepting exchange, on the ground that the Dutch government paid its men while their own did not.

Early in June, 1667, de Ruyter took advantage of the condition of the English fleet by inflicting perhaps the greatest humiliation on England that she had ever suffered. Entering the Thames unopposed, he was prevented from attacking London only by unfavorable wind and tide. He then turned his attention to the dockyards of Chatham and burnt or captured seven great ships of the line, besides numerous smaller craft, carried off the naval stores at Sheerness, and then for the next six weeks kept a blockade on the Thames and the eastern and southern coasts of England. This mortifying situation continued until the signing of the "Peace of Breda" concluded the war.

The Third Dutch War

Less than five years later Charles again made war on the Netherlands. For this there was not the shadow of excuse, but Louis XIV saw fit to attack the Dutch, and Charles was ever his willing vassal. The English began hostilities without any declaration of war by a piratical attack on a Dutch convoy.

At this juncture Holland was reduced to the last extremity. Attacked on her land frontiers by France, then the dominating military power, and on her sea frontiers by England, the strongest naval power, she seemed to have small chance to survive. But her people responded with a heroism worthy of her splendid history. They opened their dykes to check the armies of invasion and strained every nerve to equip a fleet large enough to cope with the combined navies of France and England. In this Third Dutch War four great naval battles were fought: that of Solebay, May 28, 1672, the two engagements off Schooneveldt, May 28 and June 4, 1673, and that of the Texel, August 11, 1673.

In all of these the honors go to the Dutch and their great admiral, de Ruyter. Since these actions did not restore the Netherlands to their old-time position or check the ascendancy of England, they need not be discussed individually here. The outstanding feature of the whole story is the surpassing skill and courage of de Ruyter in the face of overwhelming odds. In this war he showed the full stature of his genius as never before, and won his title as the greatest seaman of the 17th century. After his death one must wait till the day of Suffren and Nelson to find men worthy to rank with him.

In this campaign de Ruyter showed his powers not only as a tactician but as a strategist. In the words of Mahan, the Dutch "made a strategic use of their dangerous coast and shoals, upon which were based their sea operations. To this they were forced by the desperate odds under which they were fighting; but they did not use their shoals as a mere shelter,—

the warfare they waged was the defensive-offensive. When the wind was fair for the allies to attack, de Ruyter kept under cover of his islands, or at least on ground where the enemy dared not follow; but when the wind served so that he might attack in his own way he turned and fell upon them." [1] That is, instead of accepting the tame rôle of a "fleet in being" and hiding in a safe harbor, de Ruyter took and held the sea, always on the aggressive, always alert to catch his enemy in a position of divided forces or exposed flank and strike hard. His master, Martin Tromp, is regarded as the father of the line ahead formation for battle, but he undoubtedly taught de Ruyter its limitations as well as its advantages, and there is no trace of the stupid formalism of the Duke of York's regulations in de Ruyter's brilliant work.

At this time he had no worthy opponent. As Monk was dead, the Duke of York had again assumed active command with Rupert as his lieutenant. Although the Duke was honestly devoted to the navy he was dull-witted, and in spite of the advantage of numbers and the dogged courage of officers and men which so often in English history has made up for stupid leadership, he was wholly unable to cope with de Ruyter's genius. As for the French navy, their ships were superb, the best in Europe, but their officers had no experience and apparently small desire for close fighting. At all events, despite the odds against him, de Ruyter defeated the allies in all four battles, prevented their landing an army of invasion, and broke up their attempt to blockade the coast.

The war was unpopular in England and as it met with ill success it became more so. After the battle of the Texel, in 1673, active operations died down to practically nothing, and at the beginning of the year England made peace. By this time Holland had managed to find other allies on the Continent—Spain and certain German states—and while she had to continue her struggle against Louis XIV by land she was relieved of the menace of her great enemy on the sea. Fifteen years later, by a curious freak of history, a Dutch

---

[1] INFLUENCE OF SEA POWER UPON HISTORY, p. 144.

prince became King William III of England, and the two old enemies became united in alliance. But the Netherlands had exhausted themselves by their protracted struggle. They had saved their independence, but after the close of the 17th century they ceased to be a world power of any consequence.

The persistent enmity of the French king for the Dutch gained nothing for France but everything for England. Unwittingly he poured out his resources in money and men to the end that England should become the great colonial and maritime rival of France. As a part of her spoils England had gained New York and New Jersey, thus linking her northern and southern American colonies, and she had taken St. Helena as a base for her East Indies merchantmen. She had tightened her hold in India, and by repeatedly chastising the Barbary pirates had won immunity for her traders in the Mediterranean. At the beginning of the Second Dutch War Monk had said with brutal frankness, "What matters this or that reason? What we want is more of the trade which the Dutch have." This, the richest prize of all, fell from the hands of the Dutch into those of the English. During the long drawn war which went on after the English peace of 1674, while Holland with her allies fought against Louis XIV, the great bulk of the Dutch carrying trade passed from the Dutch to the English flag. The close of the 17th century, therefore, found England fairly started on her career as an ocean empire, united by sea power. Her navy, despite the vices it had caught from the Stuart régime, had become firmly established as a permanent institution with a definite organization. By this time every party recognized its essential importance to England's future.

Nevertheless, whatever satisfaction may be felt by men of English speech in this rapid growth of England's power and prestige as a result of the three wars with the Dutch, one cannot avoid the other side of the picture. A people small in numbers but great in energy and genius was hounded to the point of extinction by the greed of its powerful neighbors.

Peace-loving, asking merely to be let alone, the only crime of the Dutch was to excite the envy of the English and the French.

REFERENCES

See page 244.

CHAPTER IX

RISE OF ENGLISH SEA POWER [*Continued*]. WARS WITH FRANCE TO THE FRENCH REVOLUTION

THE effect of the expulsion of James II from the throne of England coupled with the accession of the Dutch prince, William of Orange, was to make England change sides and take the leadership in the coalition opposed to Louis XIV. From this time on, for over 125 years, England was involved in a series of wars with France. They began with the threat of Louis to dominate Europe and ended with the similar threat on the part of Napoleon. In all this conflict the sea power of England was a factor of paramount importance. Even when the fighting was continental rather than naval, the ability of Great Britain to cut France off from her overseas possessions resulted in the transfer of enormous tracts of territory to the British Empire. During the 18th century, the territorial extent of the Empire grew by leaps and bounds, with the single important loss of the American colonies. And even this brought no positive advantage to France for it did not weaken her adversary's grip on the sea.

The War of the League of Augsburg

The accession of William III was the signal for England's entry into the war of the League of Augsburg (1688-1697) against France, and the effort of the French king to put James II back again upon the English throne. By this time the French navy had been so greatly strengthened that at the outset it outnumbered the combined fleets of the English and the Dutch. It boasted the only notable admiral of this period,

Tourville, but it missed every opportunity to do something decisive. It failed to keep William from landing in England with an army; it failed also to keep the English from landing and supplying an army in Ireland, where they raised the siege of Londonderry and won the decisive victory of the Boyne. On the other hand the British navy was handled with equal irresolution and blindness in strategy. It accomplished what it did in keeping communications open with Ireland through

THREE-DECKED SHIP OF THE LINE, 18TH CENTURY

the mistakes of the French, and its leaders seemed to be equally unaware of the importance of winning definitely the control of the sea.

If the naval strategy on both sides was feeble the tactics were equally so. The contrast between the fighting of Blake, Monk, Tromp and de Ruyter and that of the admirals of this period is striking. For example, on May 1, 1689, the English admiral Herbert and the French admiral Châteaurenault fought an indecisive action in Bantry Bay, Ireland. After considerable powder had been shot away without the loss of a ship on either side, the French went back to protect their transports in the bay; Herbert also withdrew, and was made Earl of Torrington for his "victory." This same officer commanding a Dutch and English fleet encountered the French under Tourville off Beachy Head on the south coast of England (July 10, 1690). It is true that Tourville's force was stronger, but Torrington acted with no enterprise and was thoroughly beaten. At the same time the French admiral showed lack of push in following up his victory, which might have been crushing. By this time the line ahead order of fighting had become a fetich on both sides. The most noted naval battle of this war is that of La Hogue (May 29, 1692), which has been celebrated as a great British victory. In this action an allied fleet of 99 were opposed to a French fleet of 44 under Tourville. Tourville offered battle under such odds only because he had imperative orders from his king to fight the enemy. During the action the French did not lose a single ship, but in the four days' retreat the vessels became separated in trying to find shelter and fifteen were destroyed or taken. This was a severe blow to the the French navy but by no means decisive. The subsequent inactivity of the fleet was due to the demands of the war on land.

As the war became more and more a continental affair, Louis was compelled to utilize all his resources for his military campaigns. For this reason the splendid fleet with which he had begun the war gradually disappeared from the sea. Some of these men of war were lent to great privateersmen like Jean Bart and Du Guay Trouin, who took out powerful squadrons of from five to ten ships of the line, strong enough to overcome the naval escorts of a British convoy, and ravaged English commerce. In this matter of protecting shipping the naval strategy was as vacillating and blind as in everything else. Nevertheless no mere commerce destroying will serve to win the control of the sea, and despite the losses in trade and the low ebb to which English naval efficiency had sunk, the British flag still dominated the ocean routes while the greater part of the French fleet rotted in port.

In this war of the League of Augsburg, Louis XIV was fighting practically all Europe, and the strain was too great for a nation already weakened by a long series of wars. By the terms of peace which he found himself obliged to accept, he lost nearly everything that he had gained by conquest during his long reign.

Wars of the Spanish and the Austrian Succession

After a brief interval of peace war blazed out again over the question whether a French Bourbon should be king of Spain,—the War of the Spanish Succession, 1702-1713. England's aim in this war was to acquire some of the Spanish colonies in America and to prevent any loss of trading privileges hitherto enjoyed by the English and the Dutch. But as it turned out nothing of importance was accomplished in the western hemisphere except by the terms of peace. The French and Spanish attempted no major operations by sea. But the English navy captured Minorca, with its important harbor of Port Mahon, and Rooke, with more initiative than he had ever shown before in his career, took Gibraltar (August 4, 1704). These two prizes made Great Britain for the first time a Mediterranean power, and the fact that she held the gateway to the inland sea was of great importance in subsequent naval history.

In addition to these captures the terms of peace (the Treaty of Utrecht) yielded to England from the French Newfoundland, the Hudson Bay territory, and Nova Scotia. All that the French had left on the eastern coast of Canada was Cape Breton Island, with Louisburg, which was the key to the St. Lawrence. As for commercial privileges, England had gained from the Portuguese, who had been allies in the war, a practical monopoly of their carrying trade; and from France she had taken the entire monopoly of the slave trade to the Spanish American colonies which had been formerly granted by Spain to France. Holland got nothing out of the war as affecting her interests at sea,—not even a trading post. Her alliance with Great Britain had become as some one has called it, that of "the giant and the dwarf." At the conclusion of the War of the Spanish Succession, to quote the words of Mahan, "England was *the* sea power; there was no second."

In this war as in the preceding, French privateersmen made great inroads on British commerce, and some of these privateering operations were conducted on a grand scale. For example, Du Guay Trouin took a squadron of six ships of the line and two frigates, together with 2000 troops, across the Atlantic and attacked Rio Janeiro. He had little difficulty in forcing its submission and extorting a ransom of $400,000. The activities of the privateers led to a clause in the treaty of peace requiring the French to destroy the fortifications of the port of Dunkirk, which was notorious as the nest of these corsairs.

The War of the Austrian Succession, 1740-1748, was another of the dynastic quarrels of this age, with France and Spain arrayed against England. It has no naval interest for our purposes here. The peace of 1748, however, leaving things exactly as they were when the war began, settled none of the existing grudge between Great Britain and France. Eight years later, hostilities began again in the Seven Years' War, 1756-1763, in which Great Britain entered on the side of Prussia against a great coalition of Continental powers headed by France.

The Seven Years' War

The naval interest of this war is centered in the year 1759, when France, having lost Louisburg on account of England's control of the sea, decided to concentrate naval and military forces on an invasion of England. Before the plans for this projected thrust were completed, Quebec also had fallen to the British. The attempted invasion of 1759 is not so well known as that of Napoleon in 1805, but it furnished the pattern that Napoleon copied and had a better chance of success than his. In brief, a small squadron under the famous privateer Thurot was to threaten the Scotch and Irish coasts, acting as a diversion to draw off the British fleet. Meanwhile the squadron at Toulon was to dodge the British off that port, pass the Straits and join Conflans, who had the main French fleet at Brest. The united forces were then to cover the crossing of the troops in transports and flatboats to the English coast.

This plan was smashed by Admiral Hawke in one of the most daring feats in British naval annals. Thurot got away but did not divert any of the main force guarding the Channel. The Toulon fleet also eluded the English for a time but went to pieces outside the Straits largely on account of mismanagement on the part of its commander. The remnants were either captured or driven to shelter in neutral ports by the English squadron under Boscawen. On November 9, a heavy gale and the necessities of the fleet compelled Hawke to lift his blockade of Brest and take shelter in Torbay, after leaving four frigates to watch the port. On the 14th, Conflans, discovering that his enemy was gone, came out, with the absurd idea of covering the transportation of the French army before Hawke should appear again. That very day Hawke returned to renew the blockade, and learning that Conflans had been seen heading southeast, decided rightly that the French admiral was bound for Quiberon Bay to make an easy capture of a small British squadron there under Duff before beginning the transportation of the invading army.

For five days pursuer and pursued drifted in calms. On the 19th a stiff westerly gale enabled Hawke to overtake Conflans, who was obliged to shorten sail for fear of arriving at his destination in the darkness. The morning of the 20th found the fleets in sight of each other but scattered. All the forenoon the rival admirals made efforts to gather their units for battle. A frigate leading the British pursuit fired signal guns to warn Duff of the enemy's presence, and the latter, cutting his cables, was barely able to get out in time to escape the French fleet and join Hawke. Conflans then decided that the English were too strong for him, and abandoning his idea of offering battle, signaled a general retreat and led the way into Quiberon Bay.

Hawke instantly ordered pursuit. The importance of this signal can be realized only by taking into account the tremendous gale blowing and the exceedingly dangerous character of the approach to Quiberon Bay, lined as it was with sunken rocks.   Hawke had little knowledge of the channels but he reasoned that where a French ship could go an English one could follow, and the perils of the entry could not outweigh in his mind the importance of crushing the navy of France then and there.   The small British superiority of numbers which Conflans feared was greatly aggravated by the conditions of his flight.   The slower ships in his rear were crushed by the British in superior force and the English coming alongside the French on their lee side were able to use their heaviest batteries while the French, heeled over by the gale, had to keep their lowest tier of ports closed for fear of being sunk.   One of their ships tried the experiment of opening this broadside and promptly foundered.

Darkness fell on a scene of wild confusion.   Two of the British vessels were lost on a reef, but daylight revealed the fact that the French had scattered in all directions.   Only five of their ships had been destroyed and one taken, but the organization and the morale were completely shattered.   The idea of invasion thus came to a sudden end in Quiberon Bay. The daring and initiative of Hawke in defying weather and rocks in his pursuit of Conflans is the admirable and significant fact of this story, for the actual fighting amounted to little.   It is the sort of thing that marked the spirit of the Dutch Wars and of Blake at Santa Cruz, and is strikingly different from the tame and stupid work of other admirals, English or French, in his own day.

The Seven Years' War ended in terms of the deepest humiliation for France—a "Carthaginian peace."   She was compelled to renounce to England all of Canada with the islands of the St. Lawrence, the Ohio valley and the entire area east of the Mississippi except New Orleans.   Spain, which had entered the war on the side of France in 1761, gave up Florida in exchange for Havana, captured by the English, and in the West Indies several of the Lesser Antilles came under the British flag.   It is hardly necessary to point out that the loss of these overseas possessions on such a tremendous scale was

due to the ability of the British navy to cut the communications between them and the mother country.

Naval administration in England at this time was corrupt,
and the admirals, with the notable exception of Hawke, were
lacking in enterprise; they were still slaves to the "Fighting
Instructions." But in all these respects the French were far
worse, and the British government never lost sight of the
immense importance of sea power. Its strategy was sound.

The War of American Independence

The peace of 1763 was so humiliating that every patriotic
Frenchman longed for the opportunity of revenge. This offered itself in the revolt of the American colonies against
the North Ministry in 1775. From the outset French neutrality as regards the American rebels was most benevolent;
nothing could be more pleasing to France than to see her
old enemy involved in difficulties with the richest and most
populous of her colonies. For the first two or three years
France gave aid surreptitiously, but after the capture of Bur-
goyne in 1777, she decided to enter the war openly and draw
in allies as well. She succeeded in enlisting Spain in 1779
and Holland the year following. The entrance of the latter
was of small military value, perhaps, but at all events France
so manipulated the rebellion in the colonies as to bring on
another great European war. In this conflict for the first
time she had no enemies to fight on the Continent; hence she
was free to throw her full force upon the sea, attacking British possessions in every quarter of the world. The War of
the American Revolution became therefore a maritime war,
the first since the conflicts with the Dutch in the 17th century.

While Paul Jones was in Paris waiting for his promised
command, he forwarded to the Minister of Marine a plan
for a rapid descent in force on the American coast. If his
plan had been followed and properly executed the war might
have been ended in America at one blow. But this project
died in the procrastination and red tape of the Ministry of
Marine, and a subsequent proposal for an attack on Liverpool

dwindled into the mere commerce-destroying cruise which is memorable only for Jones's unparalleled fight with the *Serapis*. Eventually the navy of France was thrown into the balance to offset that of Great Britain, and it is largely to this fact that the United States owes its independence; men and munitions came freely from overseas and on one momentous occasion, the Battle of the Virginia Capes, the French navy performed its part decisively in action. But on a score of other occasions it failed pitiably on account of the lack of a comprehensive strategic plan and the want of energy and experience on the part of the commanding officers.

It is true that the French navy had made progress since the Seven Years' War. In 1778, it possessed 80 good line of battle ships. To this force, a year later, Spain was able to contribute nearly sixty. But England began the war with 150. Thus even if the French and Spanish personnel had been as well trained and as energetic as the British they would have had a superior force to contend with, particularly as the allied fleet was divided between the ports of Spain and France, and under dual command. But in efficiency the French and Spanish navies were vastly inferior to the British. Spanish efficiency may be dismissed at the outset as worthless. For the French officer the chief requisite was nobility of birth. The aristocracy of England furnished the officers for its service also, but in the French navy, considerations of social grade outweighed those of naval rank, a condition that never obtained in the British. In consequence, discipline—the principle of subordination animated by the spirit of team work—was conspicuously wanting in the French fleets. Individual captains were more concerned about their own prerogatives than about the success of the whole. This condition is illustrated by the conduct of the captains under Suffren in the Bay of Bengal, where the genius of the commander was always frustrated by the wilfulness of his subordinates. Finally in the matter of tactics the French were brought up on a fatally wrong theory, that of acting on the defensive, of avoiding decisive action, of saving a fleet rather than risking it for the sake of victory. Hence, though they were skilled in maneuvering, and ahead of the British in signaling, though their ships were as fine as any in the world, this fatal error of principle prevented their taking advantage of great opportunities and sent them to certain defeat in the end.

Thus it is clear that the sea power of France and Spain was not formidable if the English had taken the proper course of strategy. This should have been to bottle up French and Spanish fleets in their own ports from Brest to Cadiz. Such a policy would have left enough ships to attend to the necessities of the army in America and the pursuit of French and American privateers, and accomplished the primary duty of preventing the arrival of French squadrons and French troops on the scene of war. Here the British government made its fatal mistake. Instead of concentrating on the coast of France and Spain, it tried to defend every outlying post where the flag might be threatened. Thus the superior English fleet was scattered all over the world, from Calcutta to Jamaica, while the French fleets came and went at will, sending troops and supplies to America and challenging the British control of the sea. Had the French navy been more efficient and energetic in its leadership France might have made her ancient enemy pay far more dearly for her strategic blunder. As it was, England lost her colonies in America.

Instead of the swift stroke on the American coast which Paul Jones had contemplated, a French fleet under d'Estaing arrived in the Delaware about five months after France had entered the war and after inexcusable delays on the way. In spite of the loss of precious time he had an opportunity to beat an inferior force under Howe at New York and seize that important British base, but his characteristic timidity kept him from doing anything there. From the American coast he went to the West Indies, where he bungled every opportunity of doing his duty. He allowed St. Lucia to fall into British hands and failed to capture Grenada. Turning north again, he made a futile attempt to retake Savannah, which had fallen to the English. Then at the end of 1779, at about the darkest hour of the American cause, he returned to France, leaving the colonists in the lurch. D'Estaing was by training an infantry officer, and his appointment to such an important naval command is eloquent of the effect of court influence in demoralizing the navy. "S'il avait été aussi marin que brave," was the generous remark of Suffren on this man. It is true that on shore, where he was at home, d'Estaing was personally fearless, but as commander of a fleet, where he was conscious of inexperience, he showed timidity that should have brought him to court martial.

In March, 1780, the French fleet in the West Indies was put under the command of de Guichen, a far abler man than d'Estaing, but similarly indoctrinated with the policy of staying on the defensive. His rival on the station was Rodney, a British officer of the old school, weakened by years and illness, but destined to make a name for himself by his great victory two years later. In many respects Rodney was a conservative, and in respect to an appetite for prize money he belonged to the 16th century, but his example went a long way to cure the British navy of the paralysis of the Fighting Instructions and bring back the close, decisive fighting methods of Blake and de Ruyter.

In this same year in which Rodney took command of the West Indies station, a Scotch gentleman named Clerk published a pamphlet on naval tactics which attracted much attention. It is a striking commentary on the lack of interest in the theory of the profession that no British naval officer had ever written on the subject. This civilian, who had no military training or experience, worked out an analysis of the Fighting Instructions and came to the conclusion that the whole conception of naval tactics therein contained was wrong, that decisive actions could be fought only by concentrating superior forces on inferior. One can imagine the derision heaped on the landlubber who presumed to teach admirals their business, but there was no dodging the force of his point. Of course the mathematical precision of his paper victories depended on the enemy's being passive while the attack was carried out, but fundamentally he was right. The history of the past hundred years showed the futility of an unbroken line ahead, with van, center, and rear attempting to engage the corresponding divisions of the enemy. Decisive victories could be won only by close, concentrated fighting. It may be true, as the British naval officers asserted, that they were not influenced by Clerk's ideas, but the year in which his book appeared marks the beginning of the practice of his theory in naval warfare.

At the time of the American Revolution the West Indies represented a debatable ground where British interests clashed with those of her enemies, France, Spain, and Holland. It was very rich in trade importance; in fact, about one fourth of all British commerce was concerned with the Caribbean. Moreover, it contained the rival bases for operations on the American coast. Hence it became the chief theater of naval activity. Rodney's business was to make the area definitely British in control, to protect British possessions and trade and to capture as much as possible of enemy possessions and trade. On arriving at his station in the spring of 1780, he sought de Guichen. The latter had shown small enterprise, having missed one opportunity to capture British transports and another to prevent the junction of Rodney's fleet with that of Parker who was awaiting him. Even when the junction was effected, the British total amounted to only 20 ships of the line to de Guichen's 22, and the French admiral might still have offered battle. Instead he followed the French strategy of his day, by lying at anchor at Fort Royal, Martinique, waiting for the British to sail away and give him an opportunity to capture an island without having to fight for it.

Rodney promptly sought him out and set a watch of frigates off the port. When de Guichen came out on April 15 (1780) to attend to the convoying of troops, Rodney was immediately in pursuit, and on the 17th the two fleets were in contact. Early that morning the British admiral signaled his plan "to attack the enemy's rear," because de Guichen's ships were strung out in extended order with a wide gap between rear and center. De Guichen, seeing his danger, wore together and closed the gap. This done, he again turned northward and the two fleets sailed on parallel courses but out of gunshot.

THE WEST INDIES

About eleven o'clock, some four hours after his first signal, Rodney again signaled his intention to engage the enemy, and shortly before twelve he sent up the order, "for every ship to bear down and steer for her opposite in the enemy's line, agreeable to the 21st article of the Additional Fighting Instructions." Rodney had intended to concentrate his ships against their *actual* opposites at the time,—the rear of the French line, which was still considerably drawn out; but the captain of the leading ship interpreted the order to mean the *numerical* opposites in the enemy's line, after the style of fighting provided for by the Instructions from time immemorial. Rodney's first signal informing the fleet that he intended to attack the enemy's rear meant nothing to his captain at this time. Accordingly he sailed away to engage the first ship in the French van, followed by the vessels immediately astern of him, and thus wrecked the plan of his commander in chief.

Nothing could illustrate better the hold of the traditional style of fighting on the minds of naval officers than this blunder, though it is only fair to add that there was some excuse in the ambiguity of the order. Rodney was infuriated and expressed himself with corresponding bitterness. He always regarded this battle as the one on which his fame should rest because of what it might have been if his subordinates had given him proper support. The interesting point lies in the fact that he designed to throw his whole force on an inferior part of the enemy's force—the principle of concentration. In a later and much more famous battle, as we shall see, Rodney departed still further from the traditional tactics by "breaking the line," his own as well as that of the French, and won a great victory.

Meanwhile there occurred another operation not so creditable. Rodney had spent a large part of his life dodging creditors, and it was due to the generous loan of a French gentleman in Paris that he did not drag out the years of this war in the Bastille for debt. When Holland entered the war he saw an opportunity to make a fortune by seizing the island of St. Eustatius, which had been the chief depot in the West

Indies for smuggling contraband into America. To this purpose he subordinated every other consideration. The island was an easy prize, but the quarrels and lawsuits over the distribution of the booty broke him down and sent him back to England at just the time when he was most needed in American waters, leaving Hood in acting command.

In March, 1781, de Grasse sailed from Brest with a fleet of 26 ships of the line and a large convoy. Five of his battleships were detached for service in the East, under Suffren, of whom we shall hear more later. The rest proceeded to the Caribbean. On arriving at Martinique de Grasse had an excellent opportunity to beat Hood, who had an inferior force; but like his predecessors, d'Estaing and de Guichen, he was content to follow a defensive policy, excusing himself on the ground of not exposing his convoy. While at Cape Haitien he received messages from Rochambeau and Washington urging his coöperation with the campaign in America. To his credit be it said that on this occasion he acted promptly and skillfully, and the results were of great moment.

At this time the British had subdued Georgia and South Carolina, and Cornwallis was attempting to carry the conquest through North Carolina. In order to keep in touch with his source of supplies the sea, however, he was compelled to fall back to Wilmington. From there, under orders from General Clinton, he marched north to Yorktown, Virginia, where he was joined by a small force of infantry. Washington and Rochambeau had agreed on the necessity of getting the coöperation of the West Indies fleet in an offensive directed either at Clinton in New York or at Cornwallis at Yorktown. Rochambeau preferred the latter alternative, because it involved fewer difficulties, and the message to de Grasse was accompanied by a private memorandum from him to the effect that he preferred the Chesapeake as the scene of operations. Accordingly de Grasse sent the messenger frigate back with word of his intention to go to Chesapeake Bay. He then made skillful arrangements for the transport of all available troops, and set sail with every ship he could muster, steering by the less frequented Old Bahama Channel in order to screen his movement.

On August 30 (1781) de Grasse anchored in Lynnhaven Bay, just inside the Chesapeake Capes, with 28 ships of the line. The two British guard frigates were found stupidly at anchor inside the bay; one was taken and the other chased up the York river. De Grasse then landed the troops he had

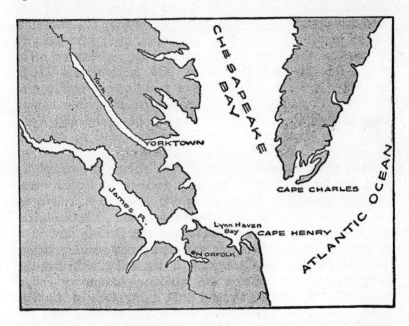

SCENE OF THE YORKTOWN CAMPAIGN

brought with him, and these made a welcome reënforcement to Lafayette, who was then opposing Cornwallis. At the same time Washington was marching south to join Lafayette, and word had been sent to the commander of a small French squadron at Newport to make junction with de Grasse, bringing the siege artillery necessary to the operations before Yorktown. Thus the available forces were converging on Cornwallis in superior strength, and his only route for supplies and reënforcements lay by sea. All depended on whether the British could succeed in forcing the entrance to Chesapeake Bay.

Hood, with 14 ships of the line, had followed on the trail of de Grasse, and as it happened looked into Chesapeake Bay just three days before the French admiral arrived. Finding no sign of the French, Hood sailed on to New York and joined Admiral Graves, who being senior, took command of the combined squadrons. As it was an open secret at that time that the allied operations would be directed at Cornwallis, Graves immediately sailed for the Capes, hoping on the way to intercept the Newport squadron which was known to be bound for the same destination. On reaching the Capes, September 5, he found de Grasse guarding the entrance to the bay with 24 ships of the line, the remaining four having been detailed to block the mouths of the James and York rivers. To oppose this force Graves had only 19 ships of the line, but he did not hesitate to offer battle.

In de Grasse's mind there were two things to accomplish: first, to hold the bay, and secondly, to keep the British occupied far enough at sea to allow the Newport squadron to slip in. Of course he could have made sure of both objects and a great deal more by defeating the British fleet in a decisive action, but that was not the French naval doctrine. The entrance to the Chesapeake is ten miles wide but the main channel lies between the southern promontory and a shoal called the Middle Ground three miles north of it. The British stood for the channel during the morning and the French, taking advantage of the ebbing tide at noon, cleared the bay, forming line of battle as they went. As they had to make several tacks to clear Cape Henry, the ships issued in straggling order, offering an opportunity for attack which Graves did not appreciate. Instead he went about, heading east on a course parallel to that of de Grasse, and holding the windward position. When the two lines were nearly opposite each other the British admiral wore down to attack.

Graves's method followed the orthodox tradition exactly, and with the unvarying result. As the attacking fleet bore down in line ahead at an angle, the van of course came into action first, unsupported for some time by the rest. As the signal for close action was repeated, this angle was made sharper, and in attempting to close up the line several ships got bunched in such a way as to mask their fire. Meanwhile the rear, the seven ships under Hood, still trailing along in line ahead, never got into the action at all. Graves had signaled for "close action," but Hood chose to believe that the

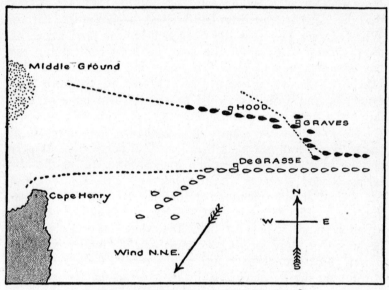

BATTLE OF THE VIRGINIA CAPES, SEPT. 5, 1781

(After diagram in Mahan's *Major Operations in the War of American Independence*, p. 180.)

order for line ahead still held until the signal was repeated, whereupon he bore down. As the French turned away at the same time, to keep their distance, Hood contributed nothing to the fighting of the day. At sunset the battle ended. The British had lost 90 killed and 246 wounded; the French, a total of 200. Several of the British ships were badly damaged, one of which was in a sinking condition and had to be burned. The two fleets continued on an easterly course about three miles apart, and for five days more the two maneuvered without fighting. Graves was too much injured by the first day's encounter to attack again and de Grasse was content to let him alone. Graves still had an opportunity to cut back and enter the bay, taking a position from which it would have been hard to dislodge him and effecting the main object of the expedition by holding the mouth of the Chesapeake. But this apparently did not occur to him. De Grasse, who had imperiled Washington's campaign by cruising so far from the entrance, finally returned on the 11th, and found that the Newport squadron had arrived safely the day before. When Graves saw that the French fleet was now increased to 36 line-of-battle ships, he gave up hope of winning the bay and returned to New York, leaving Cornwallis to his fate. A little over a month later, October 19, the latter surrendered, and with his sword passed the last hope of subduing the American revolution.

This battle of the Capes, or Lynnhaven, has never until recent times been given its true historical perspective, largely because in itself it was a rather tame affair. But as the historian Reich [1] observes, "battles, like men, are important not for their dramatic splendor but for their efficiency and consequences. . . . The battle off Cape Henry had ultimate effects infinitely more important than Waterloo." Certainly there never was a more striking example of the "influence of sea power" on a campaign. Just at the crisis of the American Revolution the French navy, by denying to the British their communications by sea, struck the decisive blow of the war. This was the French *revanche* for the humiliation of 1763.

The British failure in this action was due to a dull commander in chief carrying out a blundering attack based on the Fighting Instructions. Blame must fall also on his second in command, Hood, who, though a brilliant officer, certainly failed to support his chief properly when there was an obvious thing to do. Perhaps if the personal relations between the two had been more cordial Hood would have taken the initiative. But in those days the initiative of a subordinate was not encouraged, and Hood chose to stand on his dignity.

Although the war was practically settled by the fall of

[1] FOUNDATIONS OF MODERN EUROPE, p. 24.

Yorktown, it required another year or so to die out. In this final year a famous naval battle was fought which went far toward establishing British predominance in the West Indies, and which revealed something radically different in naval tactics from the practice of the time.

In the spring of 1782, Rodney was back in command of the West Indian station, succeeding Hood, who continued to serve as commander of a division. The British base was Gros Islet Bay in Santa Lucia. De Grasse was at Fort Royal, Martinique, waiting to transport troops to Santo Domingo, where other troops and ships were collected. There, joining with a force of Spaniards from Cuba, he was to conduct a campaign against Jamaica. It was Rodney's business to break up this plan. During a period of preparation on both sides, reënforcements joined the rival fleets, that of the British amounting to enough to give Rodney a marked superiority in numbers. Moreover his ships were heavier, as he had five 3-deckers to the French one, and about 200 more guns. The superiority of speed, as well, lay with Rodney because more of his ships had copper sheathing. A still further advantage lay in the fact that he was not burdened with the problem of protecting convoys and transports as was de Grasse. Thus, in the event of conflict, the advantages lay heavily with the British.

On the morning of April 8, the English sentry frigate off Fort Royal noted that the French were coming out, and hastened with the news to Rodney at Santa Lucia. The latter put to sea at once. He judged rightly that de Grasse would steer for Santo Domingo, in order to get rid of his transports at their destination as soon as possible, and on the morning of the 9th he sighted the French off the west coast of the island of Dominica. On the approach of the English fleet, de Grasse signaled his transports to run to the northwest, while he took his fleet on a course for the channel between the islands of Dominica and Guadeloupe. As the British would be sure to pursue the fleet, this move would enable the convoy to escape.

The channel toward which de Grasse turned his fleet is

known as the Saints' Passage from a little group of islands, "les isles des Saintes," lying to the north of it. In the course of the pursuit, Hood, with the British van division of nine ships, had got ahead of the rest and offered a tempting opening for attack in superior force. If de Grasse had grasped his opportunity he might have inflicted a crushing blow on Rodney and upset the balance of superiority. But the lack of aggressiveness in the French doctrine was again fatal to French success. De Grasse merely sent his second in command to conduct a skirmish at long range—and thus threw his chance away.

The light winds and baffling calms kept both fleets idle for a day. On the 11th de Grasse tried to work his fleet through the channel on short tacks. Just as he had almost accomplished his purpose he discovered several of his vessels still so far to westward as to be in danger of capture. In order to rescue these he gave up the fruits of laborious beating against the head wind and returned. The following morning, April 12 (1782), discovered the two fleets to the west of the strait and so near that the French could no longer evade battle. The French came down on the port tack and the British stood toward them, with their admiral's signal flying to "engage to leeward." When the two lines converged to close range, the leading British ship shifted her course slightly so as to run parallel with that of the French, and the two fleets sailed past each other firing broadsides. So far the battle had followed traditional line-ahead pattern.

Just as the leading ship of the British came abreast of the rearmost of the French, the wind suddenly veered to the southward, checking the speed of the French ships and swinging their bows over toward the English line. At best a line of battle in the sailing ship days was an uneven straggling formation, and the effect of this flaw of wind, dead ahead, was to break up the French line into irregular groups separated by wide gaps. One of these opened up ahead as Rodney's flagship, the *Formidable,* forged past the French line. His fleet captain, Douglas, saw the opportunity and pleaded with Rodney to cut through the gap. "No," he replied, "I will not break my line." Douglas insisted. A moment later, as the *Formidable* came abreast of the opening, the opportunity proved too tempting and Rodney gave his consent. His battle signal, "engage the enemy to leeward," was still flying, but the *Formidable* luffed up and swung

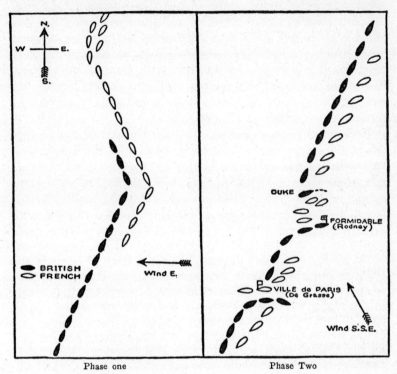

Phase one   Phase Two

BATTLE OF THE SAINTS' PASSAGE, APRIL 12, 1782

After diagram in Mahan's *Influence of Sea Power Upon History*, p. 486.

through the French line followed by five others. The ship immediately ahead of the *Formidable* also cut through a gap, and the sixth astern of the flagship went through as well, followed by the entire British rear. As each vessel pierced the broken line she delivered a terrible fire with both broadsides at close range.

The result of this maneuver was that the British fleet found

itself to windward of the French in three groups, while the
French ships were scattered to leeward and trying to escape
before the wind, leaving three dismasted hulks between the
lines.   An isolated group of six ships in the center, including
de Grasse's *Ville de Paris,* offered a target for attack, but the
wind was light and Rodney indolent in pursuit.   Of these,
one small vessel was overhauled and the French flagship was
taken after a heroic defense, that lasted until sunset, against
overwhelming odds.   De Grasse's efforts to reform his fleet
after his line was broken had met with failure, for the van
fled to the southwest and the rear to the northwest, apparently
making little effort to succor their commander in chief or
retrieve the fortunes of the day.

Rodney received a peerage for this day's work but he certainly did not make the most of his victory.   Apparently content with the five prizes he had taken, together with the person of de Grasse, he allowed the bulk of the French fleet to
escape when he had it in his power to capture practically all.
On this point his subordinate, Hood, expressed himself with
great emphasis:

"Why he (Rodney) should bring the fleet to because the
Ville de Paris was taken, I cannot reconcile. He did not pursue under easy sail, so as never to have lost sight of the enemy,
in the night, which would clearly and most undoubtedly have
enabled him to have taken almost every ship the next day. . . .
Had I had the honor of commanding his Majesty's noble fleet
on the 12th, I may, without much imputation of vanity, say
the flag of England should now have graced the sterns of *upwards* of twenty sail of the enemy's ships of the line." [1]

Sir Charles Douglas, who had been responsible for Rodney's breaking the line, warmly agreed with Hood's opinion
on this point.   Nevertheless, although the victory was not
half of what it might have been in younger hands, it proved
decisive enough to shatter the naval organization of the
French in the West Indies.   It stopped the projected cam-

---

[1] Quoted by Mahan, THE ROYAL NAVY (Clowes), Vol. III, p. 535.

paign against Jamaica and served to write better terms for England in the peace treaty of January 20, 1783.

Tactically this battle has become famous for the maneuver of "breaking the line," contrary to the express stipulations of the Fighting Instructions. Certainly the move was not premeditated. Rodney may well be said to have been pushed into making it, and two of his captains made the same move on their own initiative. Indeed it is quite likely that, after the event, too much has been made of this as a piece of deliberate tactics, for the sudden shift of wind had paid off the bows of the French ships so that they were probably heading athwart the course of the British line, and the British move was obviously the only thing to do. But the lesson of the battle was clear,—the decisive effect of close fighting and concentrated fire. In the words of Hannay, "It marked the beginning of that fierce and headlong yet well calculated style of sea fighting which led to Trafalgar and made England undisputed mistress of the sea." [1] It marked, therefore, the end of the Fighting Instructions, which had deadened the spirit as well as the tactics of the British navy for over a hundred years.

The tactical value of "breaking the line" is well summarized by Mahan in the following passage:

"The effect of breaking an enemy's line, or order-of-battle, depends upon several conditions. The essential idea is to divide the opposing force by penetrating through an interval found, or made, in it, and then to concentrate upon that one of the fractions which can be least easily helped by the other. In a column of ships this will usually be the rear. The compactness of the order attacked, the number of the ships cut off, the length of time during which they can be isolated and outnumbered, will all affect the results. A very great factor in the issue will be the moral effect, the confusion introduced into a line thus broken. Ships coming up toward the break are stopped, the rear doubles up, while the ships ahead continue their course. Such a moment is critical, and calls for instant action; but the men are rare who in an unforeseen

[1] Rodney (ENGLISH MEN OF ACTION SERIES), p. 213.

emergency can see, and at once take the right course, especially if, being subordinates, they incur responsibility. In such a scene of confusion the English, without presumption, hoped to profit by their better seamanship; for it is not only 'courage and devotion,' but skill, which then tells. All these effects of 'breaking the line' received illustration in Rodney's great battle in 1782."[1]

Before we leave the War of American Independence mention should be made of Commodore Suffren who, as we have seen, left de Grasse with five ships of the line to conduct a campaign in the Indian Ocean in the spring of 1781. His purpose was to shake the British hold on India, which had been fastened by the genius of Clive in the Seven Years' War. But the task given to Suffren was exceedingly difficult. His squadron was inadequate—for instance, he had only two frigates for scout and messenger duty—and he had no port that he could use as a base in Indian waters. To conduct any campaign at all he was compelled to live off his enemy and capture a base. These were risky prospects for naval operations several thousand miles from home, and for the faintest hope of success required an energy and initiative which had never before appeared in a French naval commander. In addition to these handicaps of circumstance Suffren soon discovered that he had to deal with incorrigible slackness and insubordination in his captains.

In spite of everything, however, Suffren achieved an amazing degree of success. He succeeded in living off the prizes taken from the British, and he took from them the port of Trincomalee for a base. He fought five battles off the coast of India against the British Vice Admiral Hughes, in only one of which was the latter the assailant, and in all of which Suffren bore off the honors. He was constantly hampered, however, by the inefficiency and insubordination of his captains. On four or five occasions, including an engagement at the Cape Verde Islands on his way to India, it was only this misconduct that saved the British from the crushing attack that

[1] THE INFLUENCE OF SEA POWER UPON HISTORY, pp. 380-381.

Suffren had planned. Unfortunately for him his victories were barren of result, for the terms of peace gave nothing in India to the French which they had not possessed before. As Trincomalee had belonged to the Dutch before the British captured it, this port was turned back to Holland.

Nevertheless Suffren deserves to be remembered both for what he actually accomplished under grave difficulties and what he might have done had he been served by loyal and efficient subordinates. Among all the commanders of this war he stands preëminent for naval genius, and this eminence is all the more extraordinary when one realizes that his resourcefulness, tenacity, aggressiveness, his contempt of the formal, parade tactics of his day, were notoriously absent in the rest of the French service. Such was the admiration felt for him by his adversaries that after the end of the war, when the French squadron arrived at Cape Town on its way home and found the British squadron anchored there, all the British officers, from Hughes down, went aboard the French flagship to tender their homage.[1]

Although the War of American Independence was unsuccessfully fought by Great Britain and she was compelled to recognize the independence of her rebellious colonies, she lost comparatively little else by the terms of peace. As we have seen, her hold in India was unchanged. The stubborn defense of Gibraltar throughout the war, aided by occasional timely relief by a British fleet, saved that stronghold for the English flag. To Spain England was forced to surrender Florida and Minorca. France got back all the West Indian islands she had lost, with the exception of Tobago, but gained nothing besides. The war therefore did not restore to France her colonial empire of former days or make any change in the relative overseas strength of the two nations. Despite the

---

[1] "If ever a man lived who justified Napoleon's maxim that war is an affair not of men but of a man, it was he. It was by his personal merit that his squadron came to the very verge of winning a triumphant success. That he failed was due to the fact that the French Navy . . . was honeycombed by the intellectual and moral vices which were bringing France to the great Revolution—corruption, self-seeking, acrid class insolence, and skinless, morbid vanity."—THE ROYAL NAVY, David Hannay, II, 287.

blunders of the war no rival sea power challenged that of Great Britain at the conclusion of peace.

Meanwhile, just before the war and during its early years, an English naval officer was laying the foundation for an enormous expansion of the British empire in the east. This was James Cook, a man who owed his commission in the navy and his subsequent fame to nothing in family or political influence, but to sheer genius. Of humble birth, he passed from the merchant service into the navy and rose by his extraordinary abilities to the rank of master. Later he was commissioned lieutenant and finally attained the rank of post captain.[1] Such rank was hardly adequate recognition of his great powers, but it was unusually high for a man who was not born a "gentleman."

At the end of the Seven Years' War he distinguished himself, by his work in surveying and sounding on the coasts of Labrador and Newfoundland, as a man of science. In consequence, he was detailed to undertake expeditions for observing the transit of Venus and for discovering the southern continent which was supposed to exist in the neighborhood of the Antarctic circle. In the course of this work Cook practically established the geography of the southern half of the globe as we know it to-day. And by his skill and study of the subject he conquered the great enemy of exploring expeditions, scurvy. Thirty years before, another British naval officer, Anson, had taken a squadron into the Pacific and lost about three-fourths of his men from this disease. When the war of the American Revolution broke out, Cook was abroad on one of his expeditions, but the French and American governments issued orders to their captains not to molest him on account of his great service to the cause of scientific knowledge. Unfortunately he was killed by savages at the Sandwich Islands in 1779.

The bearing of his work on the British empire lies chiefly in his careful survey of the east coast of Australia, which he laid claim to in the name of King George, and the circumnavi-

---

[1] Full captain's rank, held only by a captain in command of a vessel of at least 20 guns.

gation of New Zealand, which later gave title to the British claim on those islands. Thus, while the American colonies in the west were winning their independence, another territory in the east, far more extensive, was being brought under British sway, destined in another century to become important dominions of the empire. The Dutch had a claim of priority in discovery through the early voyages of Tasman, but they attempted no colonization and Dutch sea power was too weak to make good a technical claim in the face of England's navy.

Finally, when the results of a century of wars between France and England are summarized, we find that France had lost all her great domain in America except a few small islands in the West Indies and near Newfoundland. In brief, it is due to British control of the sea during the 18th century that practically all of the continent north of the Rio Grande is English in speech, laws, and tradition.

This control of the sea exercised by England was not the gift of fortune. It was a prize gained, in the main, by wise policy in peace and hard fighting in war. France had the opportunity to wrest from England the control of the sea as England had won it from Holland, for France at the close of the 17th century dominated Europe. In population and in wealth she was superior to her rival. But the arrogance of her king kept her embroiled in futile wars on the Continent, with little energy left for the major issue, the conquest of the sea. Finally, when the war of American Independence left her a free hand to concentrate on her navy as against that of England, France lost through the fatal weakness of policy which corrupted all her officers with the single brilliant exception of Suffren. The French naval officer avoided battle on principle, and when he could not avoid it he accepted the defensive. To the credit of the English officer be it said that, as a rule, he sought the enemy and took the aggressive; he had the "fighting spirit." This difference between French and British commanders had as much to do with the ultimate triumph of England on the sea as anything else. It retrieved many a blunder in strategy and tactics by sheer hard hitting.

The history of the French navy points a moral applicable

to any service and any time. When a navy encourages the idea that ships must not be risked, that a decisive battle must be avoided because of what might happen in case of defeat, it is headed for the same fate that overwhelmed the French.

REFERENCES

INFLUENCE OF SEA POWER UPON HISTORY, A. T. Mahan, 1890.
A SHORT HISTORY OF THE ROYAL NAVY, David Hannay, 1909.
THE ROYAL NAVY (vols. II, III), W. L. Clowes et al., 1903.
ADMIRAL BLAKE, English Men of Action Series, David Hannay, 1909.
RODNEY, English Men of Action Series, David Hannay, 1891.
MONK, English Men of Action Series, Julian Corbett, 1907.
ENGLAND IN THE SEVEN YEARS' WAR, J. S. Corbett, 1907.
THE GRAVES PAPERS, F. E. Chadwick, 1916.
STUDIES IN NAVAL HISTORY, BIOGRAPHIES, J. K. Laughton, 1887.
FROM HOWARD TO NELSON, ed. by J. K. Laughton, 1899.
MAJOR OPERATIONS IN THE WAR OF AMERICAN INDEPENDENCE, A. T Mahan, 1913.
SEA KINGS OF BRITAIN, Geoffrey Callender, 1915.

CHAPTER X

THE NAPOLEONIC WARS: THE FIRST OF JUNE AND CAMPERDOWN

TEN years after the War of American Independence, British sea power was drawn into a more prolonged and desperate conflict with France. This time it was with a France whose navy, demoralized by revolution, was less able to dispute sea control, but whose armies, organized into an aggressive, empire-building force by the genius of Napoleon, threatened to dominate Europe, shaking the old monarchies with dangerous radical doctrines, and bringing all Continental nations into the conflict either as enemies or as allies. The dismissal of the French envoy from England immediately after the execution of Louis XVI (Jan. 21, 1793) led the French Republic a week later to a declaration of war, which continued with but a single intermission—from October, 1801, to May, 1803—through the next 22 years.

The magnitude of events on land in this period, during which French armies fought a hundred bloody campaigns, overthrew kingdoms, and remade the map of Europe, obscures the importance of the warfare on the sea. Yet it was Great Britain by virtue of her navy and insular position that remained Napoleon's least vulnerable and most obstinate opponent, forcing him to ever renewed and exhausting campaigns, reviving continental opposition, and supporting it with subsidies made possible by control of sea trade. In Napoleon's own words the effect of this pressure is well summarized: "To live without ships, without trade, without colonies, is to live as no Frenchman can consent to do." The Egyptian campaign, conceived as a thrust at British sources of wealth in the East, and defeated at the Nile; the organization of the northern neutrals against England, overthrown at Copenhagen; the direct invasion of the British Isles, repeatedly planned and thwarted at St. Vincent, Camperdown, and Trafalgar; the final and most nearly successful effort to ruin England by closing her continental markets and thus, in Napoleon's phrase, "defeating the sea by the land"—these were the successive measures by which he sought to shake the grip of sea power.

The following narrative of these events is in three divisions: the first dealing with the earlier engagements of the First of June and Camperdown, fought by squadrons based on home ports; the second with the war in the Mediterranean and the rise of Nelson as seen in the campaigns of St. Vincent, the Nile, and Copenhagen; the third with the Trafalgar campaign and the commercial struggle to which the naval side of the war was later confined. The career of Nelson is given an emphasis justified by his primacy among naval leaders and the value of his example for later times.

The effect of land events in obscuring the naval side of the war, already mentioned, is explained not merely by their magnitude, but by the fact that, though Great Britain was more than once brought to the verge of ruin, this was a consequence not of the enemy's power on the sea, but of his victories on land. Furthermore, the slow process which ended in the downfall of Napoleon and the reduction of France to her old frontiers was accomplished, not so conspicuously by the economic pressure of sea power, as by the efforts of armies on battlefields from Russia to Spain. On the sea British supremacy was more firmly established, and the capacities of France and her allies were far less, than in preceding conflicts of the century.

The French Navy Demoralized

The explanation of this weakness of the French navy involves an interesting but somewhat perplexing study of the influences which make for naval growth or decay. That its ineffectiveness was due largely to an inferior national instinct or genius for sea warfare, as compared with England, is discredited by the fact that the disparity was less obvious in previous wars; for, as Lord Clowes has insisted, England won no decisive naval victory against superior forces from the second Dutch War to the time of Nelson. The familiar theory that democracy ruined the French navy will be accepted nowadays only with some qualifications, especially when it is remembered that French troops equally affected by the downfall of caste rule were steadily defeating the armies of monarchical powers. It is true, however, that navies, as compared with armies, are more complicated and more easily disorganized machines, and that it would have taxed even Napoleonic genius to reorganize the French navy after the neglect, mutiny, and wholesale sweeping out of trained personnel to which it was subjected in the first furies of revolution. Whatever the merits of the officers of the old régime, selected as they were wholly from the aristocracy and dominated by the defensive policy of the French service, three-fourths of them were driven out by 1791, and replaced by officers from the merchant service, from subordinate ratings, and from the crews. Suspicion of aristocracy was accompanied in the navy by a more fatal suspicion of skill. In January, 1794, the regiments of marine infantry and artillery, as well as the corps of seamen-gunners, were abolished on the ground that no body of men should have "the exclusive privilege of fighting the enemy at sea," and their places were filled by battalions of the national guard. Figures show that as a result, French gunnery was far less efficient than in the preceding war.

The strong forces that restored discipline in the army had more difficulty in reaching the navy; and Napoleon's gift for discovering ability and lifting it to command was marked by its absence in his choice of leaders for the fleets. Usually he fell back on pessimistic veterans of the old régime like Brueys, Missiessy, and Villeneuve. An exception, Allemand, showed by his cruise out of Rochefort in 1805 what youth, energy, and daring could accomplish even with inferior means. Considering the importance of leadership as a factor in success, we may well believe that, had a French Nelson, or even a Suffren, been discovered in this epoch, history would tell a different tale. If further reasons for the decadence of the navy are needed, they may be found in the extreme difficulty of securing naval stores and timber from the Baltic, and in the fact that, though France had nearly three times the population of the British Isles, her wealth, man-power, and genius were absorbed in the war on land.

Aside from repulsion at the violence of the French revolution and fear of its contagion, England had a concrete motive for war in the French occupation of the Austrian Netherlands and the Scheldt, the possession of which by an ambitious maritime nation England has always regarded as a menace to her safety and commercial prosperity. "This government," declared the British Ministry in December, 1792, "will never view with indifference that France shall make herself, directly or indirectly, sovereign of the Low Countries or general arbitress of the rights and liberties of Europe."

In prosecuting the war, Great Britain fought chiefly with her main weapon, the navy, leaving the land war to her allies. A contemporary critic remarked that she "worked with her navy and played with her army"; though the latter did useful service in colonial conquests and in Egypt, the two expeditionary forces to the Low Countries in 1793 and 1799 were ill-managed and ineffective. The tasks of the fleet were to guard the British Isles from raids and invasion, to protect British commerce in all parts of the world, and, on the offensive, to seize enemy colonies, cut off enemy trade, and coöperate in the Mediterranean with allied armies. To accomplish these aims, which called for a wide dispersion of forces, the British naval superiority over France was barely adequate. According to the contemporary naval historian James, the strength of the two fleets at the outbreak of war was as follows:

	Ships of the line	Guns	Aggregate broadsides
British	115	8,718	88,957
French	76	6,002	73,057

Of her main fighting units, the ships-of-the-line, England could put into commission about 85, which as soon as possible were distributed in three main spheres of operation: in the Mediterranean and its western approaches, from 20 to 25; in the West Indies, from 10 to 12; in home waters, from the North Sea to Cape Finisterre, from 20 to 25, with a reserve of some 25 more in the home bases on the Channel. Though this distribution was naturally altered from time to time to meet changes in the situation, it gives at least an idea of the general disposition of the British forces throughout the war. France, with no suitable bases in the Channel, divided her fleet between the two main arsenals at Brest and Toulon, with minor squadrons at Rochefort and, during the Spanish alliance, in the ports of Spain.

Distant Operations

In the West Indies and other distant waters, France could offer but little effective resistance, and operations there may hence be dismissed briefly, but with emphasis on the benefit which naval control conferred upon British trade, the main guaranty of England's financial stability and power to keep up the war. Fully one-fifth of this trade was with the West Indies. Consequently, both to swell the volume of British commerce and protect it from privateering, the seizure of the French West Indian colonies—"filching the sugar islands," as Sheridan called it—was a very justifiable war measure, in spite of the scattering of forces involved. Hayti was lost to France as a result of the negro uprising under Toussaint l'Ouverture. Practically all the French Antilles changed hands twice in 1794, the failure of the British to hold them arising from a combination of yellow fever, inadequate forces of occupation, and lax blockade methods on the French coast, which permitted heavy reënforcements to leave France. General Abercromby, with 17,000 men, finally took all but Guadaloupe in the next year. As Holland, Spain, and other nations came under French control, England seized their colonies likewise—the Dutch settlements at the Cape of Good Hope and Ceylon in 1795; the Moluccas and other Dutch islands in the East Indies in 1796; Trinidad (Spanish) in 1797; Curaçao (Dutch) in 1800; and the Swedish and Danish West Indies in 1801. By the Treaty of Amiens in 1802 all these except Trinidad and Ceylon were given back, and had to be retaken in the later period of the war, Guadaloupe remaining a privateers' nest until its final capture in 1810. Though French trade was ruined, it was impossible to stamp out privateering, which grew with the growth of British commerce which it preyed upon, and the extent of which is indicated by the estimate that in 1807 there were from 200 to 300 privateers on the coasts of Cuba and Hayti alone. As for the captured islands, Great Britain in 1815 retained only Malta, Heligoland, and the Ionian Islands in European waters; Cape Colony, Mauritius, and Ceylon on the route to the East; and in the Caribbean, Demerara on the coast, Santa Lucia, Trinidad, and Tobago—some of them of little intrinsic value, but all useful outposts for an empire of the seas.

In the Channel and Bay of Biscay, the first year of war passed quietly. Lord Howe, commanding the British Channel fleet, had behind him a long, fine record as a disciplinarian and tactician; he had fought with Hawke at Quiberon Bay, protected New York and Rhode Island against d'Estaing in 1778, and later thrown relief into Gibraltar in the face of superior force. Now 68 years of age, he inclined to cautious, old-school methods, such as indeed marked activities on both land and sea at this time, before Napoleon had injected a new desperateness into war. Both before and after the "Glorious First of June" the watch on the French coast was merely nominal; small detachments were kept off Brest, but the main fleet rested in Portsmouth throughout the winter and took only occasional cruises during the remainder of the year.

The Battle of the First of June

Though there had been no real blockade, the interruption of her commerce, the closure of her land frontiers, and the bad harvest of 1793, combined to bring France in the spring following to the verge of famine, and forced her to risk her fleet in an effort to import supplies from overseas. On April 11 an immense flotilla of 120 grain vessels sailed from the Chesapeake under the escort of two ships-of-the-line, which were to be strengthened by the entire Brest fleet at a rendezvous 300 miles west of Belleisle. Foodstuffs having already been declared subject to seizure by both belligerents, Howe was out on May 2 to intercept the convoy. A big British merchant fleet also put to sea with him, to protect which he had to detach 8 of his 34 ships, but with orders to 6 of these that they should rejoin his force on the 20th off Ushant. Looking into Brest on the 19th, Howe found the French battle fleet already at sea. Not waiting for the detachment, and thus losing its help in the battle that was to follow, he at once turned westward and began sweeping with his entire fleet the waters in which the convoy was expected to appear.

The French with 26 ships-of-the-line—and thus precisely equal to Howe in numbers—had left Brest two days before. The crews were largely landsmen; of the flag officers and captains, not one had been above the grade of lieutenant three years before, and nine of them had been merchant skippers with no naval experience whatever. On board were two delegates of the National Convention, whose double duties seem to have been to watch the officers and help them command. To take the place of experience there was revolutionary fervor, evidenced in the change of ship-names to such resounding appellations as *La Montagne, Patriote, Vengeur du Peuple, Tyrannicide,* and *Revolutionnaire.* There was also more confidence than was ever felt again by French sailors during the war. "Intentionally disregarding subtle evolutions," said the delegate Jean Bon Saint Andrée, "perhaps our sailors will think it more appropriate and effective to resort to the boarding tactics in which the French were always victorious, and thus astonish the world by new prodigies of valor." "If they had added to their courage a little training," said the same commissioner after the battle, "the day might have been ours."

The commander in chief, Villaret de Joyeuse, who had won his lieutenancy and the esteem of Suffren in the American war, was no such scorner of wary tactics. Thus when the two fleets, more by accident than calculation on either side, came in contact on the morning of May 28, 1794, about 400 miles west of Ushant, it would have been quite possible for him to have closed with the British, who were 10 miles to leeward in a fresh southerly wind. But his orders were not to fight unless it were essential to protect the convoy, and since this was thought to be close at hand, he first drew away to the eastward, with the British in pursuit.

The chase continued during the remainder of this day and the day following, with partial engagements and complicated maneuvering, the net result of which was that in the end Howe, in spite of the superior sailing qualities of the French ships, had kept in touch with them, driven his own vessels through their line to a windward position, and forced the withdrawal of four units, with the loss of but one of his own. Two days of thick weather followed, during which both fleets stood to the northwest in the same relative positions, the French, very fortunately indeed, securing a reënforcement of four fresh ships from detachments earlier at sea.

Now 26 French to 25 British, the two fleets on the morning of the final engagement were moving to westward on the still southerly wind, in two long, roughly parallel lines. Confident of the individual superiority of his ships, the British admiral had no wish for further maneuvering, in which his own captains had shown themselves none too reliable and the enemy commander not unskilled. Possibly also he feared the confusion of a complicated plan, for it was notorious (as may be verified by looking over his correspondence) that Howe had the greatest difficulty in making himself intelligible with tongue or pen. His orders were therefore to bear up together toward the enemy and attack ship to ship, without effort at concentration, and with but one noteworthy departure from the time-honored tactics in which he had been schooled. This was that the battle should be close and decisive. The instructions were that each ship should if possible break through the line astern of her chosen opponent, raking the ships on each side as she went through, and continue the action to leeward, in position to cut off retreat. "I don't want the ships to be bilge to bilge," said Howe to the officers of his flagship, the *Queen Charlotte,* "but if you can lock the yardarms, so much the better; the battle will be the quicker decided." The approach was leisurely, nearly in line abreast, on a course slightly diagonal to that of the enemy. At 10 A. M. the *Queen Charlotte,* in the center of the British line, shoved past just under the stern of Villaret's flagship, the *Montagne,* raking her with a terrible broadside which is said to have struck down 300 of her men. As was likely to result from the plan of attack, the ships in the van of the attacking force were more closely and promptly engaged than those of the rear; only six ships actually broke through, but there was hot fighting all along the line.

Famous among the struggles in the mêlée was the epic three-hour combat of the *Brunswick,* next astern of Howe, and the *Vengeur,* both 74's. With the British vessel's anchors hooked in her opponent's port forechannels, the two drifted away to leeward, the *Brunswick* by virtue of flexible rammers alone able to use her lower deck guns, which were given alternately extreme elevation and depression and sent shot tearing through the *Vengeur's* deck and hull; whereas the *Vengeur,* with a superior fire of carronades and musketry, swept the enemy's upper deck. When the antagonists wrenched apart, the *Brunswick* had lost 158 of her complement of 600 men. The *Vengeur* was slowly sinking and went down at 6 P. M., with a loss of 250 killed and wounded and 100 more drowned. "As we drew away," wrote a survivor, "we heard some of our comrades still offering prayers for the welfare of their country; the last cries of these unfortunates were, 'Vive la République!' They died uttering them."

Out of the confusion, an hour after the battle had begun, Villaret was able to form a column of 16 ships to leeward, and though ten of his vessels lay helpless between the lines, three drifted or were towed down to him and escaped. Howe has been sharply criticized for letting these cripples get away; but the battered condition of his fleet and his own complete physical exhaustion led him to rest content with six prizes aside from the sunken *Vengeur.* The criticism has also been made that he should have further exerted himself to secure a junction with the detachment on convoy duty, which on May 19 was returning and not far away. If he had at that time held his 32 ships between Brest and Rochefort, with scouts well distributed to westward, he would have been much more certain to intercept both Villaret's fleet and the convoy, which would have approached in company, and both of which, with the British searching in a body at sea, stood a good chance of

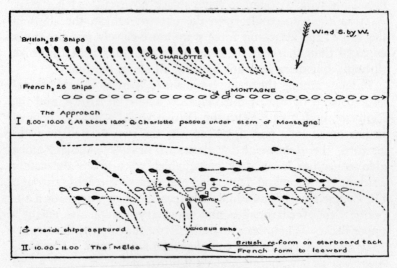

BATTLE OF THE FIRST OF JUNE, 1794

(Based on diagram in Mahan's *Influence of Sea Power upon the French Revolution,* Vol. I, p. 136.)

escape. Howe's hope, no doubt, was to meet the convoy unguarded. The latter, protected by fog, actually crossed on May 30 the waters fought over on the 29th, and twelve days later safely reached the French coast. Robespierre had told Villaret that if the convoy were captured he should answer for it with his life. Hence the French admiral declared years later that the loss of his battleships troubled him relatively little. "While Howe amused himself refitting them, I saved the convoy, and I saved my head."

Though the escape of the convoy enabled the French to

boast a "strategic victory," the First of June in reality established British prestige and proved a crushing blow to French morale. A British defeat, on the other hand, might have brought serious consequences, for within a year's time the Allied armies, including the British under the Duke of York, were driven out of Holland, the Batavian Republic was established in league with France (February, 1795), and both Spain and Prussia backed out of the war. Austria remained England's only active ally.

During the remainder of 1794 and the year following only minor or indecisive encounters occurred in the northern theater of war, lack of funds and naval supplies hampering the recovery of the French fleet from the injuries inflicted by Howe. Ill health forcing the latter's retirement from sea duty, he was succeeded in the Channel by Lord Bridport, who continued his predecessor's easy-going methods until the advent of Jervis in 1798, instituted a more rigorous régime. It was not yet recognized that the wear and tear on ships and crews during sea duty was less serious than the injurious effect of long stays in port upon sea spirit and morale.

French Projects of Invasion

With their fleets passive, the French resorted vigorously to commerce warfare, and at the same time kept England constantly perturbed by rumors, grandiose plans, and actual undertakings of invasion. That these earlier efforts failed was due as much to ill luck and bad management as to the work of Bridport's fleet. Intended, moreover, primarily as diversions to keep England occupied at home and sicken her of the war, they did not altogether fail of their aim. Some of these projects verged on the ludicrous, as that of corraling a band of the criminals and royalist outlaws that infested France and dropping them on the English coast for a wild campaign of murder and pillage. Fifteen hundred of these *Chouans* were actually landed at Fishguard in February of 1798, but promptly surrendered, and France had to give good English prisoners in

exchange for them on the threat that they would be turned
loose again on French soil.

Much more serious was General Hoche's expedition to Ireland of the winter before. Though Hoche wished to use for
the purpose the army of over 100,000 with which he had subdued revolt in the Vendée, the Government was willing to venture a force of only 15,000, which set sail from Brest, December 15, 1796, in 17 ships-of-the-line, together with a large
number of smaller war-vessels and transports. Heavy weather
and bad leadership, helped along by British frigates with false
signals, scattered the fleet on the first night out. It never
again got together; and though a squadron with 6,000 soldiers
on board was actually for a week or more in the destination,
Bantry Bay, not a man was landed, and by the middle of January nearly all of the flotilla was back in France. The British
squadron under Colport, which had been on the French coast
at the time of the departure, had in the meanwhile been obliged
to make port for supplies. Bridport with the main fleet left
Portsmouth, 250 miles from the scene of operations, four days
after news of the French departure. During the whole affair
neither he nor Colport took a single prize.

Even so small a force coöperating with rebellion in Ireland
might have proved a serious annoyance, though not a grave
danger. Invasion on a grand scale, which Napoleon's victorious campaign in Italy and the peace with Austria (preliminaries at Loeben, April, 1797) now made possible, was
effectually forestalled by two decisive victories at sea. Bonaparte, who was to lead the invasion, did not minimize its difficulties. "To make a descent upon England without being master of the sea," he wrote at this time, "is the boldest and most
difficult operation ever attempted." Yet the flotilla of small
craft necessary was collected, army forces were designated, and
in February of 1798 Bonaparte was at Dunkirk. All this
served no doubt to screen the Egyptian preparations, which
amid profound secrecy were already under way. The Egyptian campaign was an indirect blow at England; but the direct
blow would certainly have been struck had not the naval engagements of Cape St. Vincent (February, 1797) and Cam-

perdown (October, 1797) settled the question of mastery of the sea by removing the naval support of Spain and Holland on the right and left wings.

The Battle of Camperdown

Admiral Duncan's victory of Camperdown, here taken first as part of the events in northern waters, is noteworthy in that it was achieved not only against ever-dangerous opponents, but with a squadron which during the preceding May and June had been in the very midst of the most serious mutiny in the history of the British navy. In Bridport's fleet at Portsmouth this was not so much a mutiny as a well organized strike, the sailors it is true taking full control of the ships, and forcing the Admiralty and Parliament to grant their well justified demands for better treatment and better pay. Possibly a secret sympathy with their grievances explains the apparent helplessness of the officers. The men on their part went about the business quietly, and even rated some of their former officers as midshipmen, in special token of esteem. At the Nore, however, and in Duncan's squadron at Yarmouth, the mutiny was marked by bloodshed and taint of disloyalty, little surprising in view of the disaffected Irish, ex-criminals, impressed merchant sailors, and other unruly elements in the crews. In the end 18 men were put to death and many others sentenced.

Duncan faced the trouble with the courage but not the mingling of fair treatment and sharp justice which marked its suppression by that great master of discipline, Jervis, in the fleet off Spain. On his own ship and another, Duncan drew up the loyal marines under arms, spoke to the sailors, and won their allegiance, picking one troublesome spirit up bodily and shaking him over the side. But the rest of the squadron suddenly sailed off two days later to join the mutineers at the Nore, where all the ships were then in the hands of the crews. With his two faithful ships, Duncan made for the Texel, swearing that if the Dutch came out he would go down with colors flying. Fortunately he was rejoined before that event by the rest of his squadron, the mutinous ships having been either retaken by the officers or voluntarily surrendered by the men.

The whole affair, among the ships in Thames mouth, was over in a month's time, from mid-May to mid-June, so quickly that the enemy had little chance to seize the advantage. The Dutch, driven willy-nilly into alliance with France and not too eager to embark upon desperate adventures in the new cause, were nevertheless not restrained from action by any kind feel-

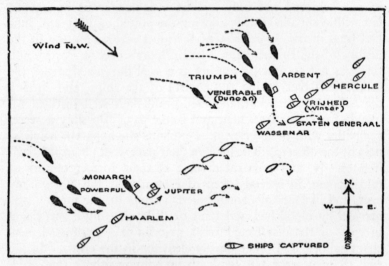

BATTLE OF CAMPERDOWN, OCTOBER II, 1797, ABOUT 12:30 P.M.
British, 16 of the line; Dutch, 15 of the line.

ing for England, who had seized their ships and colonies and ruined their trade. When at last, during a brief withdrawal of Duncan, their fleet under Admiral de Winter attempted a cruise, it was in a run-down condition. Aside from small units, it consisted of 15 ships (4 of 74 guns, 5 of 68, 2 of 64, and 4 under 60), against Duncan's stronger force of 16 (7 of 74, 7 of 64 and 2 of 50). The Dutch ships were flat-bottomed and light-draft for navigation in their shallow coastal waters, and generally inferior to British vessels of similar rating, even though the latter were left-overs from the Channel Fleet.

On the morning of the Battle of Camperdown, October 11,

1797, the Dutch were streaming along their coast on a northwest wind bent on return into the Texel. Pressing forward in pursuit, Duncan when in striking distance determined to prevent the enemy's escape into shallow water by breaking through their line and attacking to leeward. The signal to this effect, however, was soon changed to "Close action," and only the two leading ships eventually broke through. The two British divisions—for they were still in cruising formation and strung out by the pursuit—came down before the wind. Onslow, the second in command, in the *Monarch*, struck the line first at 12:30 and engaged the Dutch *Jupiter*, fourth from the rear. Eighteen minutes later Duncan in the *Venerable* closed similarly to leeward of the *Staten Generaal*, and afterward the *Vrijheid*, in the Dutch van.

The two leaders were soon supported—though there was straggling on both sides; and the battle that ensued was the bloodiest and fiercest of this period of the war. The British lost 825 out of a total of 8221 officers and men,[1] more than half the loss occurring in the first four ships in action. The British ships were also severely injured by the gruelling broadsides during the onset, but finally took 11 prizes, all of them injured beyond repair. Though less carefully thought out and executed, the plan of the attack closely resembles that of Nelson at Trafalgar. The head-on approach seems not to have involved fatal risks against even such redoubtable opponents as the Dutch, and it insured decisive results.

Duncan's otherwise undistinguished career, and the somewhat unstudied methods of his one victory, may explain why he has not attained the fame which the energy displayed and results achieved would seem to deserve. "He was a valiant officer," writes his contemporary Jervis, "little versed in subtleties of tactics, by which he would have been quickly confused. When he saw the enemy, he ran down upon them, without thinking of a fixed order of battle. To conquer, he counted

---

[1] As compared with this loss of 10%, the casualties in Nelson's three chief battles were as follows: Nile, 896 out of 7401, or 12.1%; Copenhagen, 941 out of 6892, or 13.75%; Trafalgar, 1690 out of 17,256, or 9.73%.

on the bold example he gave his captains, and the event completely justified his hopes."

Whatever its tactical merits, the battle had the important strategic effect of putting the Dutch out of the war. The remnants of their fleet were destroyed in harbor during an otherwise profitless expedition into Holland led by the Duke of York in 1799. By this time, when naval requirements and expanding trade had exhausted England's supply of seamen, and forced her to relax her navigation laws, it is estimated that no less than 20,000 Dutch sailors had left their own idle ships and were serving on British traders and men-of-war.[1]

[1]For references, see end of Chapter XII, page 244.

CHAPTER XI

THE NAPOLEONIC WARS [*Continued*] : THE RISE OF NELSON

In the Mediterranean, where the protection of commerce, the fate of Italy and all southern Europe, and the exposed interests of France gave abundant motives for the presence of a British fleet, the course of naval events may be sufficiently indicated by following the work of Nelson, who came thither in 1793 in command of the *Agamemnon* (64) and remained until the withdrawal of the fleet at the close of 1796. Already marked within the service, in the words of his senior, Hood, as "an officer to be consulted on questions relative to naval tactics," Nelson was no doubt also marked as possessed of an uncomfortable activity and independence of mind. Singled out nevertheless for responsible detached service, he took a prominent part in the occupation of Corsica, where at the siege of Calvi he lost the sight of his right eye, and later commanded a small squadron supporting the left flank of the Austrian army on the Riviera.

In these latter operations, during 1795 and 1796, Nelson felt that much more might have been done. The Corniche coast route into Italy, the only one at first open to the French, was exposed at many points to fire from ships at sea, and much of the French army supplies as well as their heavy artillery had to be transported in boats along the coast. "The British fleet could have prevented the invasion of Italy," wrote Nelson five years later, "if our friend Hotham [who had succeeded Hood as commander in chief in the Mediterranean] had kept his fleet on that coast." [1] Hotham felt, perhaps rightly, that the necessity of watching the French ships at Toulon made this impos-

[1] DISPATCHES, June 6, 1800.

sible. But had the Toulon fleet been destroyed or effectually crippled at either of the two opportunities which offered in 1795, no such need would have existed; the British fleet would have dominated the Mediterranean, and exercised a controlling influence on the wavering sympathies of the Italian states and Spain. At the first of these opportunities, on the 13th and 14th of March, Hotham said they had done well enough in capturing two French ships-of-the-line. "Now," remarked Nelson, whose aggressive pursuit had led to the capture, "had we taken 10 sail and allowed the 11th to escape, when it had been possible to have got at her, I should not have called it well done." And again of the second encounter: "To say how much we wanted Lord Hood on the 13th of July, is to say, 'Will you have all the French fleet, or no action?'" History, and especially naval history, is full of might-have-beens. Aggressive action establishing naval predominance might have prevented Napoleon's brilliant invasion and conquest of Italy; Spain would then have steered clear of the French alliance; and the Egyptian campaign would have been impossible.

The succession of Sir John Jervis to the Mediterranean command in November, 1795, instituted at once a new order of things, in which inspiring leadership, strict discipline, and closest attention to the health of crews, up-keep of vessels, and every detail of ship and fleet organization soon brought the naval forces under him to what has been judged the highest efficiency attained by any fleet during the war. Jervis had able subordinates—Nelson, Collingwood and Troubridge, to carry the list no further; but he may claim a kind of paternal share in molding the military character of these men.

Between Jervis and Nelson in particular there existed ever the warmest mutual confidence and admiration. Yet the contrast between them well illustrates the difference between all-round professional and administrative ability, possessed in high degree by the older leader, and supreme fighting genius, which, in spite of mental and moral qualities far inferior, has rightly won Nelson a more lasting fame. As a member of parliament before the war, as First Lord of the Admiralty from 1801 to 1803, and indeed in his sea commands, Jervis displayed a breadth of judgment, a knowledge of the world, a mastery of details of administration, to which Nelson could not pretend. In the organization of the Toulon and the Brest blockades, and in the suppression of mutiny in 1797, Jervis better than Nelson illustrates conventional ideals of military discipline. When appointed to the Channel command in 1799 he at once adopted the system of keeping the bulk of the fleet constantly on the enemy coast "well within Ushant with an easterly wind." Captains were to be on deck when ships came about at whatever hour. In port there were no night boats and no night leave for officers. To one officer who ventured a protest Jervis wrote that he "ought not to delay one day his intention to retire." "May the discipline of the Mediterranean never be introduced in the Channel," was a toast on Jervis's appointment to the latter squadron. "May his next glass of wine choke the wretch," was the wish of an indignant officer's wife. Jervis may have been a martinet, but it was he, more than any other officer, who instilled into the British navy the spirit of war.

In the Mediterranean, however, he arrived too late. There, as in the Atlantic, the French Directory after the experiments of 1794 and 1795 had now abandoned the idea of risking their battleships; and while these still served effectively in port as a fleet in being, their crews were turned to commerce warfare or transport flotilla work for the army. Bonaparte's ragged heroes were driving the Austrians out of Italy. Sardinia made peace in May of 1796. Spain closed an offensive and defensive alliance with the French Republic in August, putting a fleet of 50 of the line (at least on paper) on Jervis's communications and making further tenure of the Mediterranean a dangerous business. By October, 26 Spanish ships had joined the 12 French then at Toulon. Even so, Jervis with his force of 22 might have hazarded action, if his subordinate Mann, with a detached squadron of 7 of these, had not fled to England. Assigning to Nelson the task of evacuating Corsica and later Elba, Jervis now took station outside the straits, where on February 13, 1797, Nelson rejoined his chief, whose strength still consisted of 15 of the line.

The Battle of Cape St. Vincent

The Spanish fleet, now 27, was at this time returning to Cadiz, as a first step toward a grand naval concentration in the north. A stiff Levanter having thrown the Spanish far beyond their destination, they were returning eastward when on February 14, 1797, the two fleets came in contact within sight of Cape St. Vincent. In view of the existing political situation, and the known inefficiency of the Spanish in sea fighting, Jervis decided to attack. "A victory," he is said to have remarked, "is very essential to England at this hour."

As a fresh westerly wind blew away the morning fog, the Spanish were fully revealed to southward, running before the wind, badly scattered, with 7 ships far in advance and thus to leeward of the rest. After some preliminary pursuit, the British formed in a single column (Troubridge in the *Culloden* first, the flagship *Victory* seventh, and Nelson in the *Captain* third from the rear), and took a southerly course which would carry them between the two enemy groups. As soon as they found themselves thus separated, the Spanish weather division hauled their wind, opened fire, and ran to northward along the weather side of the British line; while the lee division at first also turned northward and made some effort to unite with the rest of their company by breaking through the enemy formation, but were thrown back by a heavy broadside from the *Victory*. Having accomplished his first purpose, Jervis had already, at about noon, hoisted the signal to "tack in succession," which meant that each ship should continue her course to the point where the *Culloden* came about and then follow her in pursuit of the enemy weather division. This critical and much discussed maneuver appears entirely justified. The British by tacking in succession kept their column still between the parts of the enemy, its rear covering the enemy lee division, and the whole formation still in perfect order and control, as it would not have been had the ships tacked simultaneously. Again, if the attack had been made on the small group to leeward, the Spanish weather division could easily have run

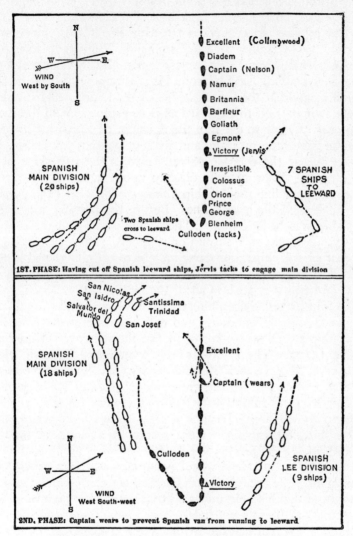

BATTLE OF CAPE ST. VINCENT, FEBRUARY 14, 1797

BRITISH: 15 ships, 1232 guns. SPANISH: 27 ships, 2286 guns.

down into the action and thus brought their full strength to bear.

But against an enemy so superior in numbers more was needed to keep the situation in hand. Shortly before one o'clock, when several British vessels had already filled away on the new course, Nelson from his position well back in the column saw that the leading ships of the main enemy division were swinging off to eastward as if to escape around the British rear. Eager to get into the fighting, of which his present course gave little promise, and without waiting for orders, he wore out of the column, passed between the two ships next astern, and threw himself directly upon the three big three-deckers, including the flagship *Santisima Trindad* (130 guns), which headed the enemy line. Before the fighting was over, his ship was badly battered, "her foretopmast and wheel shot away, and not a sail, shroud or rope left"; [1] but the *Culloden* and other van ships soon came up, and also Collingwood in the *Excellent* from the rear, after orders from Jervis for which Nelson had not waited. Out of the mêlée the British emerged with four prizes, Nelson himself having boarded the *San Nicolas* (80), cleared her decks, and with reënforcements from his own ship passed across her to receive the surrender of the *San Josef* (112). The swords of the vanquished Spanish, Nelson says, "I gave to William Fearney, one of my bargemen, who placed them with the greatest *sangfroid* under his arm."

For Nelson's initiative (which is the word for such actions when they end well) Jervis had only the warmest praise, and when his fleet captain, Calder, ventured a comment on the breach of orders, Jervis gave the tart answer, "Ay, and if ever you offend in the same way I promise you a forgiveness beforehand." Jervis was made Earl St. Vincent, and Nelson, who never hid his light under a bushel, shared at least in popular acclaim. It was not indeed a sweeping victory, and there is little doubt that had the British admiral so chosen, he might have done much more. But enough had been accomplished to discourage Spanish naval activities in the French cause for a long time to come. They were hopelessly outclassed; but in

[1] Nelson's DISPATCHES, Vol. II, p. 345.

their favor it should be borne in mind that their ships were miserably manned, the crews consisting of ignorant peasants of whom it is reported that they said prayers before going aloft, and with whom their best admiral, Mazzaredo, had refused to sail. Moreover, they were fighting half-heartedly, lacking the inspiration of a great national cause, without which victories are rarely won.

The defeat of the Spanish, as Jervis had foreseen, was timely. Mantua had just capitulated; British efforts to secure an honorable peace had failed; consols were at 51, and specie payments stopped by the Bank of England; Austria was on the verge of separate negotiations, the preliminaries of which were signed at Loeben on April 18; France, in the words of Bonaparte, could now "turn all her forces against England and oblige her to a prompt peace." [1] The news of St. Vincent was thus a ray of light on a very dark horizon. Its strategic value, along with the Battle of Camperdown, has already been made clear.

The British fleet, after refitting at Lisbon, took up a blockade of the Spanish at Cadiz which continued through the next two years. Discontent and mutiny, which threatened with each fresh ship from home, was guarded against by strict discipline, careful attention to health and diet, and by minor enterprises which served as diversions, such as the bombardment of Cadiz and the unsuccessful attack on Santa Cruz in the Canary Islands, July 24-25, 1797, in which Nelson lost his right arm.

The Battle of the Nile

Nelson's return to the Cadiz blockade in May, 1798, after months of suffering in England, was coincident with the gathering of a fresh storm cloud in the Mediterranean, though the direction in which it threatened was still completely concealed. While Sicily, Greece, Portugal and even Ireland were mentioned by the British Admiralty as possible French objectives, Egypt was apparently not thought of. Yet its strategic position between three continents remained as important as

[1] CORRESPONDENCE, III, 346.

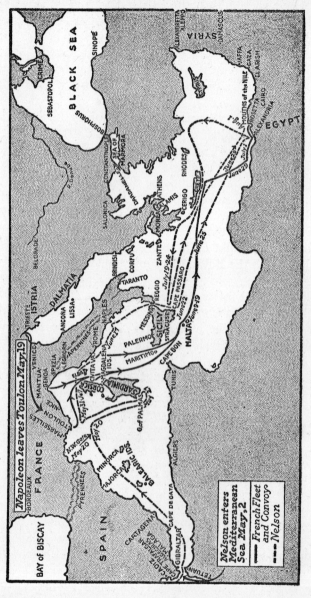

THE NILE CAMPAIGN, MAY-AUGUST. 1798

in centuries past, controlling the trade of the Levant and threatening India by land or sea. "The time is not far distant," Bonaparte had already written, "when we shall feel that truly to destroy England we must take possession of Egypt." In point of fact the strength of England rested not merely on the wealth of the Indies, but on her merchant fleets, naval control, home products and manufactures, in short her whole industrial and commercial development, too strong to be struck down by a blow in this remote field. Still, if the continued absence of a British fleet from the Mediterranean could be counted on, the Egyptian campaign was the most effective move against her that offered at the time. It was well that the British Admiralty rose to the danger. Jervis, though he pointed out the risks involved, was directed to send Nelson with an advance squadron of 3 ships, later strengthened to 14, to watch the concentration of land and naval forces at Toulon. "The appearance of a British fleet in the Mediterranean," wrote the First Lord, Spencer, in urging the move, "is a condition on which the fate of Europe may be stated to depend."

Before a strong northwest wind the French armada on May 19 left Toulon—13 of the line, 13 smaller vessels, and a fleet of transports which when joined by contingents from Genoa, Corsica, and Civita Vecchia brought the total to 400 sail, crowded with over 30,000 troops. Of the fighting fleet there is the usual tale of ships carelessly fitted out, one-third short-handed, and supplied with but two months' food—a tale which simply points the truth that the winning of naval campaigns begins months or years before.

The gale from which the French found shelter under Sardinia and Corsica fell later with full force on Nelson to the westward of the islands. His flagship the *Vanguard* lost her foremast and remaining topmasts, while at the same time his four frigates, so essential in the search that followed, were scattered and failed to rejoin. Having by extraordinary exertions refitted in Sardinia in the short space of four days, he was soon again off Toulon, but did not learn of the enemy's departure until May 31, and even then he got no clue as to where they had gone.   Here he was joined on June 7 by the promised reënforcements, bringing his squadron to 13 74's and the *Leander* of 50 guns.

The ensuing search continued for two months, until August 1, the date of the Battle of the Nile.   During this period, Nelson appears to best advantage; in the words of David Hannay, he was an "embodied flame of resolution, with none of the vulgar bluster that was to appear later."

Moving slowly southward, the French flotilla had spent ten days in the occupation of Malta—the surrender of which was chiefly due to French influence among the Knights of St. John who held the island—and departed on June 19 for their destination, following a circuitous route along the south side of Crete and thence to the African coast 70 miles west of Alexandria.

Learning off Cape Passaro on the 22d of the enemy's departure from Malta, Nelson made direct for Alexandria under fair wind and press of sail.   He reached the port two days ahead of Bonaparte, and finding it empty, at once set out to retrace his course, his impetuous energy betraying him into what was undoubtedly a hasty move.   The two fleets had been but 60 miles apart on the night of the 25th.   Had they met, though Bonaparte had done his utmost by organization and drill to prepare for such an emergency, a French disaster would have been almost inevitable, and Napoleon, in the amusingly partisan words of Nelson's biographer Southey, "would have escaped those later crimes that have incarnadined his soul."   Nelson had planned in case of such an encounter to detach three of his ships to attack the transports.

The trying month that now intervened, spent by the British fleet in a vain search along the northern coast of the Mediterranean, a brief stop at Syracuse for water and supplies, and return, was not wholly wasted, for during this time the commander in chief was in frequent consultation with his captains, securing their hearty support, and familiarizing them with his plans for action in whatever circumstances a meeting might occur.   An interesting reference to this practice of Nelson's appears in a later characterization of him written by the

French Admiral Décres to Napoleon. "His boastfulness," so the comment runs, "is only equalled by his ineptitude, but he has the saving quality of making no pretense to any other virtues than boldness and good nature, so that he is accessible to the counsels of those under him." As to who dominated these conferences and who profited by them we may form our own opinion. It was by such means that Nelson fostered a spirit of full coöperation and mutual confidence between himself and his subordinates which justified his affectionate phrase, "a band of brothers."

The result was seen at the Nile. If rapid action lost the chance of battle a month before, it did much to insure victory when the opportunity came, and it was made possible by each captain's full grasp of what was to be done. "Time is everything," to quote a familiar phrase of Nelson; "five minutes may spell the difference between victory and defeat." It was two in the afternoon when the British, after looking into Alexandria, first sighted the French fleet at anchor in Aboukir Bay, and it was just sundown when the leading ship *Goliath* rounded the *Guerrier's* bows. The battle was fought in darkness. In the face of a fleet protected by shoals and shore batteries, with no trustworthy charts or pilots, with ships still widely separated by their varying speeds, a less thoroughly drilled force under a less ardent leader would have felt the necessity of delaying action until the following day. Nelson never hesitated. His ships went into action in the order in which they reached the scene.

The almost decisive advantage thus gained is evident from the confusion which then reigned in Aboukir Bay. In spite of the repeated letters from Bonaparte urging him to secure his fleet in Alexandria harbor, in spite of repeated soundings which showed this course possible, the French Admiral Brueys with a kind of despondent inertia still lay in this exposed anchorage at the Rosetta mouth of the Nile. Mortars and cannon had been mounted on Aboukir point, but it was known that their range did not cover the head of the French line. The frigates and scout vessels that might have given more timely warning were at anchor in the bay. Numerous water

parties were on shore and with them the ships' boats needed
to stretch cables from one vessel to another and rig gear
for winding ships, as had been vaguely planned. At a hurried council it was proposed to put to sea, but this was given
up for the sufficient reason that there was no time. The French
were cleared for action only on the out-board side. Their
admiral was chiefly fearful of attack in the rear, a fear reasonable enough if his ships had been sailing before the wind
at sea; but at anchor, with the Aboukir batteries ineffective
and the wind blowing directly down the line, attack upon the

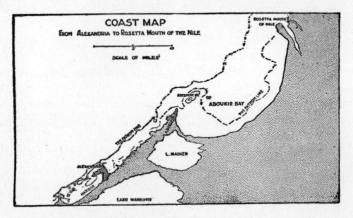

van would be far more dangerous, since support could less
easily be brought up from the rear.

It was on the head of the line that the attack came. Nelson
had given the one signal that "his intention was to attack
the van and center as they lay at anchor, according to the
plan before developed." This plan called for doubling, two
ships to the enemy's one. With a fair wind from the north-
northwest Captain Foley in the *Goliath* at 6 p. m. reached the
Guerrier, the headmost of the thirteen ships in the enemy line.
Either by instant initiative, or more likely in accordance with
previous plans in view of such an opportunity, he took his ship
inside the line, his anchor dragging slightly so as to bring
him up on the quarter of the second enemy vessel, the *Conquérant.* The *Zealous,* following closely, anchored on the

bows of the *Guerrier;* the *Orion* engaged inside the fifth ship; the *Theseus* inside the third; and the *Audacious,* passing between the first two of the enemy, brought up on the *Conquérant's* bow. With these five engaged inside, Nelson in the *Vanguard* and the two ships following him engaged respectively outside the third, fourth and fifth of the enemy. Thus the concentration on the van was eight to five.

About a half hour later the *Bellerophon* and the *Majestic* attacked respectively the big flagship *Orient* (110) in the center and the *Tonnant* (80) next astern, and against these superior antagonists suffered severely, losing in killed and wounded 390 men divided about equally between them, which was nearly half the total loss of 896 and greater than the total at Cape St. Vincent. Both later drifted almost helpless down the line. The *Culloden* under Troubridge, a favorite of both Jervis and Nelson, had unfortunately grounded and stuck fast on Aboukir shoal; but the *Swiftsure* and the *Alexander* came up two hours after the battle had begun as a support to the ships in the centre, the *Swiftsure* engaging the *Orient,* and the *Alexander* the *Franklin* next ahead, while the smaller *Leander* skillfully chose a position where she could rake the two. By this time all five of the French van had surrendered; the *Orient* was in flames and blew up about 10 o'clock with the loss of all but 70 men. Admiral Brueys, thrice wounded, died before the explosion. Of the four ships in the rear, only two, the *Guillaume Tell* under Admiral Villeneuve and the *Généreux,* were able to cut their cables next morning and get away. Nelson asserted that, had he not been incapacitated by a severe scalp wound in the action, even these would not have escaped. Of the rest, two were burned and nine captured. Among important naval victories, aside from such one-sided slaughters as those of our own Spanish war, it remains the most overwhelming in history.

The effect was immediate throughout Europe, attesting clearly the contemporary importance attached to sea control. "It was this battle," writes Admiral de la Gravière, "which for two years delivered over the Mediterranean to the British and called thither the squadrons of Russia, which shut up our

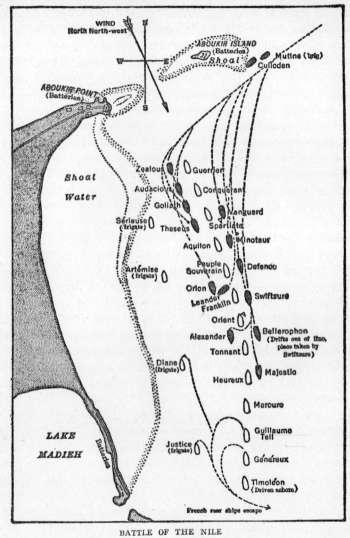

BATTLE OF THE NILE

● ▬ BRITISH   ◯ FRENCH

army in the midst of a hostile people and led the Porte to declare against us, which put India beyond our reach and thrust France to the brink of ruin, for it rekindled the hardly extinct war with Austria and brought Suvaroff and the Austro-Russians to our very frontiers." [1]

The whole campaign affords an instance of an overseas expedition daringly undertaken in the face of a hostile fleet (though it should be remembered that the British were not in the Mediterranean when it was planned), reaching its destination by extraordinary good luck, and its possibilities then completely negatived by the reëstablishment of enemy naval control. The efforts of the French army to extricate itself northward through Palestine were later thwarted partly by the squadron under Commodore Sidney Smith, which captured the siege guns sent to Acre by sea and aided the Turks in the defense of the fortress. In October of 1799 Bonaparte escaped to France in a frigate. French fleets afterwards made various futile efforts to succor the forces left in Egypt, which finally surrendered to an army under Abercromby, just too late to strengthen the British in the peace negotiations of October, 1801.

Nelson's subsequent activities in command of naval forces in Italian waters need not detain us. Physically and nervously weakened from the effects of his wound and arduous campaign, he fell under the influence of Lady Hamilton and the wretched court of Naples, lent naval assistance to schemes of doubtful advantage to his country, and in June of 1800 incurred the displeasure of the Admiralty by direct disobedience of orders to send support to Minorca. He returned to England at the close of 1800 with the glory of his victory somewhat tarnished, and with blemishes on his private character which unfortunately, as will be seen, affected also his professional reputation.

The Copenhagen Campaign

Under the rapid scene-shifting of Napoleon, the political stage had by this time undergone another complete change from

[1] GUERRES MARITIMES, II, 129.

that which followed the battle of the Nile. Partly at least as a consequence of that battle, the so-called Second Coalition had been formed by Great Britain, Russia, and Austria, the armies of the two latter powers, as already stated, carrying the war again to the French frontiers. It required only the presence of Bonaparte, in supreme control after the *coup d'état* of the Eighteenth *Brumaire* (9 Nov., 1799), to turn the tide, rehabilitate the internal administration of France, and by the victories of Marengo in June and Hohenlinden in December of 1800 to force Austria once more to a separate peace. Paul I of Russia had already fallen out with his allies and withdrawn his armies and his great general, Suvaroff, a year before. Now, taken with a romantic admiration for Napoleon, and angry when the British, after retaking Malta, refused to turn it over to him as Grand Master of the Knights of St. John, he was easily manipulated by Napoleon into active support of the latter's next move against England.

This was the Armed Neutrality of 1800, the object of which, from the French standpoint, was to close to England the markets of the North, and combine against her the naval forces of the Baltic. Under French and Russian pressure, and in spite of the fact that all these northern nations stood to suffer in one way or another from rupture of trade relations with England, the coalition was accomplished in December, 1800; Russia, Prussia, Sweden, and Denmark pledging themselves to resist infringements of neutral rights, whether by extension of contraband lists, seizure of enemy goods under neutral flag, search of vessels guaranteed innocent by their naval escort, or by other methods familiar then as in later times. These were measures which England, aiming both to ruin the trade of France and to cut off her naval supplies, felt bound to insist upon as the belligerent privileges of sea power.

To overcome this new danger called for a mixture of force and diplomacy, which England supplied by sending to Denmark an envoy with a 48-hour ultimatum, and along with him 20 ships-of-the-line, which according to Nelson were "the best negotiators in Europe." The commander in chief of this squadron was Sir Hyde Parker, a hesitant and mediocre leader who could be trusted to do nothing (if that were necessary), and Nelson was made second in command. Influence, seniority, a clean record, and what-not, often lead to such choices, bad enough at any time but indefensible in time of war. Fortunately for England, when the reply of the Danish court showed that force was required, the two admirals virtually changed places with less friction than might have been expected, and Nelson "lifted and carried on his shoulders the dead weight of his superior," [1] throughout the ensuing campaign.

When the envoy on March 23 returned to the fleet, then anchored in the Cattegat, he brought an alarming tale of Danish preparations, and an air of gloom pervaded the flagship when Nelson came aboard for a council of war. Copenhagen, it will be recalled, is situated on the eastern coast of Zealand, on the waterway called the Sound leading southward from the Cattegat to the Baltic. Directly in front of the city, a long shoal named the Middle Ground separates the Sound into two navigable channels, the one nearer Copenhagen known as the King's Deep (*Kongedyb*). The defenses of the Danish capital, so the envoy reported, were planned against attack from the northward. At this end of the line the formidable Trekroner Battery (68 guns), together with two ships-of-the-line and some smaller vessels, defended the narrow entrance to the harbor; while protecting the city to the southward, along the flats at the edge of the King's Deep, was drawn up an array of about 37 craft ranging from ships-of-the-line to mere scows, mounting a total of 628 guns, and supported at some distance by batteries on land. Filled with patriotic ardor, half the male population of the city had volunteered to support the forces manning these batteries afloat and ashore.

Nelson's plan for meeting these obstacles, as well as his view of the whole situation, as presented at the council, was embodied in a memorandum dated the following day, which well illustrates his grasp of a general strategic problem. The

[1] Mahan, INFLUENCE OF SEA POWER UPON FRENCH REVOLUTION AND EMPIRE, II, 52.

Government's instructions, as well as Parker's preference, were apparently to wait in the Cattegat until the combined enemy forces should choose to come out and fight. Instead, the second in command advocated immediate action. "Not a moment," he wrote, "should be lost in attacking the enemy; they will every day and hour be stronger." The best course, in his opinion, would be to take the whole fleet at once into the Baltic against Russia, as a "home stroke," which if successful would bring down the coalition like a house of cards. If the Danes must first be dealt with, he proposed, instead of a direct attack, which would be "taking the bull by the horns," an attack from the rear. In order to do so, the fleet could get beyond the city either by passing through the Great Belt south of Zealand, or directly through the Sound. Another resultant advantage, in case the five Swedish sail of the line or the 14 Russian ships at Revel should take the offensive, would be that of central position, between the enemy divisions.

"Supposing us through the Belt," the letter concludes, "with the wind northwesterly, would it not be possible to either go with the fleet or detach ten Ships of three and two decks, with one Bomb and two Fireships, to Revel, to destroy the Russian squadron at that place? I do not see the great risk of such a detachment, and with the remainder to attempt the business at Copenhagen. The measure may be thought bold, but I am of the opinion that the boldest measures are the safest; and our Country demands a most vigorous assertion of her force, directed with judgment."

Here was a striking plan of aggressive warfare, aimed at the heart of the coalition. The proposal to leave part of the fleet at Copenhagen was indeed a dangerous compromise, involving divided forces and threatened communications, but was perhaps justified by the known inefficiency of the Russians and the fact that the Danes were actually fought and defeated with a force no greater than the plan provided. In the end the more conservative course was adopted of settling with Denmark first. Keeping well to the eastern shore, the fleet on March 30 passed into the Sound without injury from the fire of the Kronenburg forts at its entrance, and anchored that evening near Copenhagen.

Three days later, on April 2, 1801, the attack was made as planned, from the southward end of the Middle Ground. Nelson in the *Elephant* commanded the fighting squadron, which consisted of seven 74's, three 64's and two of 50 guns, with 18 bomb vessels, sloops, and fireships. The rest of the ships, under Parker, were anchored at the other end of the shoal and 5 miles north of the city; it seems they were to have coöperated, but the south wind which Nelson needed made attack impossible for them. Against the Danish total of 696 guns on the ships and Trekroner fortification, Nelson's squadron had 1014, but three of his main units grounded during the approach and were of little service. There was no effort at concentration, the British when in position engaging the whole southern part of the Danish line. "Here," in the words of Nelson's later description, "was no maneuvering; it was downright fighting"—a hotly contested action against ships and shore batteries lasting from 10 a. m., when the *Elephant* led into position on the bow of Commodore Fischer's flagship *Dannebroge,* until about one.

In the midst of the engagement, as Nelson restlessly paced the quarterdeck, he caught sight of the signal "Leave off action" flown from Sir Hyde's flagship. Instead of transmitting the signal to the vessels under him, Nelson kept his own for "Close action" hoisted. Colonel Stewart, who was on board at the time, continues the story as follows: "He also observed, I believe to Captain Foley, 'You know, Foley, I have only one eye—I have a right to be blind sometimes'; and then with an archness peculiar to his character, putting the glass to his blind eye, he exclaimed, 'I really do not see the signal.'" It was obeyed, however, by the light vessels under Captain Riou attacking the Trekroner battery, which were suffering severely, and which could also more easily effect a retreat.

Shortly afterward the Danish fire began to slacken and several of the floating batteries surrendered, though before they could be taken they were frequently remanned by fresh

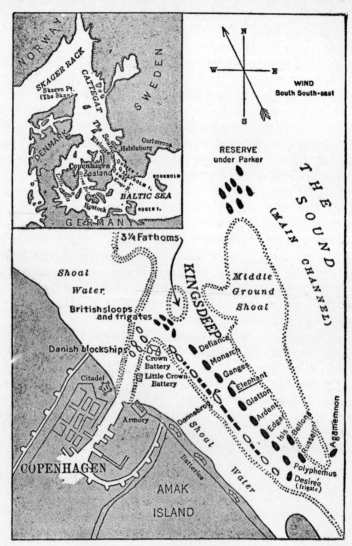

BATTLE OF COPENHAGEN, APRIL 2, 1801

forces from the shore. Enough had been accomplished; and to end a difficult situation—if not to extricate himself from it—Nelson sent the following summons addressed "To the brothers of Englishmen, the Danes": "Lord Nelson has orders to spare Denmark when no longer resisting; if the firing is continued on the part of Denmark, Lord Nelson will be obliged to set fire to the floating batteries he has taken, without having the power of saving the brave Danes who have defended them."

A truce followed, during which Nelson removed his ships. Next day he went ashore to open negotiations, while at the same time he brought bomb vessels into position to bombard the city. The cessation of hostilities was the more readily agreed to by the Danes owing to the fact that on the night before the battle they had received news, which they still kept concealed from the British, of the assassination of the Czar Paul. His successor, they knew, would be forced to adopt a policy more favorable to the true interests of Russian trade. The league in fact was on the verge of collapse. A fourteen weeks' armistice was signed with Denmark. On April 12 the fleet moved into the Baltic, and on May 5, Nelson having succeeded Parker in command, it went on to Revel, whence the Russian squadron had escaped through the ice to Kronstadt ten days before. On June 17 a convention was signed with Russia and later accepted by the other northern states, by which Great Britain conceded that neutrals might engage in trade from one enemy port to another, with the important exception of *colonial* ports, and that naval stores should not be contraband; whereas Russia agreed that enemy goods under certain conditions might be seized in neutral ships, and that vessels under naval escort might be searched by ships-of-war. In the meantime, Nelson, realizing that active operations were over with, resigned his command.

In the opinion of the French naval critic Gravière, the campaign thus ended constitutes in the eyes of seamen Nelson's best title to fame—"*son plus beau titre de gloire.*" [1] Certainly it called forth the most varied talents—grasp of the political and

[1] GUERRES MARITIMES, Vol. II, p. 43.

strategical situation; tact and force of personality in dealing with an inert commander in chief; energy in overcoming not only military obstacles but the doubts and scruples of fellow officers; aggressiveness in battle; and skill in negotiations. In view of the Czar's murder—of which the British Government would seem to have had an inkling beforehand—it may be thought that less strenuous methods would have served. On the contrary, however, hundreds of British merchant vessels had been seized in northern ports, trade had been stopped, and the nation was threatened with a dangerous increment to her foes. Furthermore, after a brief interval of peace, Great Britain had to face ten years more of desperate warfare, during which nothing served her better than that at Copenhagen the northern neutrals had had a sharp taste of British naval power. Force was needed. That it was employed economically is shown by the fact that, when a renewal of peace between France and Russia in 1807 again threatened a northern confederation, Nelson's accomplishment with 12 ships was duplicated, but this time with 25 of the line, 40 frigates, 27,000 troops, the bombardment of Copenhagen, and a regular land campaign.

Upon Nelson's return to England, popular clamor practically forced his appointment to command the Channel defense flotilla against the French armies which were now once more concentrated on the northern coast. This service lasted for only a brief period until the signing of peace preliminaries in October, 1801.

During the eight years of hostilities thus ended Great Britain, it is true, had been fighting largely on the defensive, but on a line of defense carried to the enemy's sea frontiers and comparable to siege lines about a city or fortress, which, when once established, thrust upon the enemy the problem of breaking through. The efforts of France to pierce this barrier, exerted in various directions and by various means, were, as we have seen, defeated by naval engagements, which insured to England the control of the sea. During this period, France lost altogether 55 ships-of-the-line, Holland 18, Spain 10, and Denmark 2, a total of 85, of which at least 50 were captured by the enemy. Great Britain lost 20, but only 5 by capture. The British battle fleet at the close of hostilities had increased to 189 capital ships; that of France had shrunk to 45.

For purposes of commerce warfare the French navy had suffered the withdrawal of many of its smaller fighting vessels and large numbers of its best seamen, attracted into privateering by the better promise of profit and adventure. As a result of this warfare, about 3500 British merchantmen were destroyed, an average of 500 a year, representing an annual loss of 2½ per cent of all the ships of British register. But in the meantime the French merchant marine and commerce had been literally swept off the seas. In 1799 the Directory admitted there was "not a single merchant ship on the seas carrying the French flag." French imports from Asia, Africa, and America in 1800 amounted to only $300,000, and exports to $56,000, whereas England's total export and import trade had nearly doubled, from 44½ million pounds sterling in 1792 to nearly 78 million in 1800. It is true that, owing to the exigencies of war, the amount of British shipping employed in this trade actually fell off slightly, and that of neutrals increased from 13 to 34%. But the profits went chiefly to British merchants. England had become the great storehouse and carrier for the Continent, "Commerce," in the phrase engraved on the elder Pitt's monument, "being united with and made to flourish by war." [1]

REFERENCES

See end of Chapter XII, page 244.

[1] Figures on naval losses from Gravière, GUERRES MARITIMES, Vol. II, ch. VII, and on commerce, from Mahan, FRENCH REVOLUTION AND EMPIRE, Vol. II, ch. XVII.

CHAPTER XII

THE NAPOLEONIC WAR [*Concluded*]: TRAFAL-GAR AND AFTER

THE peace finally ratified at Amiens in March, 1802, failed to accomplish any of the purposes for which England had entered the war. France not only maintained her frontiers on the Scheldt and the Rhine, but still exercised a predominant influence in Holland and western Italy, and excluded British trade from territories under her control. Until French troops were withdrawn from Holland, as called for by the treaty, England refused to evacuate Malta. Bonaparte, who wished further breathing space to build up the French navy, tried vainly to postpone hostilities by threatening to invade England and exclude her from all continental markets. "It will be England," he declared, "that forces us to conquer Europe." The war reopened in May of 1803.

With no immediate danger on the Continent and with all the resources of a regenerated France at his command, Bonaparte now undertook the project of a descent upon England on such a scale as never before. Hazardous as he always realized the operation to be—it was a thousand to one chance, he told the British envoys, that he and his army would end at the bottom of the sea—he was definitely committed to it by his own threats and by the expectation of France that he would now annihilate her hereditary foe.

Napoleon's Plan of Invasion

An army of 130,000 men, with 400 guns and 20 days' supplies, was to embark from four ports close to Boulogne as a center, and cross the 36 miles of Channel to a favorable stretch of coast between Dover and Hastings, distant from London some 70 miles. The transport flotilla, as finally planned, was to consist of 2000 or more small flat-bottomed sailing vessels with auxiliary oar propulsion—*chaloupes* and *bateaux canonnières,* from 60 to 80 feet over all, not over 8 feet in draft, with from two to four guns and a capacity for 100 to 150 men. Large open boats (*péniches*) were also to be used, and all available coast craft for transport of horses and supplies. Shipyards from the Scheldt to the Gironde were soon busy building the special flotilla, and as fast as they were finished they skirted the shores to the points of concentration under protection of coast batteries. Extensive harbor and defense works were undertaken at Boulogne and neighboring ports, and the 120 miles from the Scheldt to the Somme was soon bristling with artillery, in General Marmont's phrase, "a coast of iron and bronze."

The impression was spread abroad that the crossing was to be effected by stealth, in calm, fog, or the darkness of a long winter night, without the protection of a fleet. Almost from the first, however, Bonaparte seems to have had no such intention. The armament of the flotilla itself proved of slight value, and he was resolved to take no uncalled-for risks, on an unfamiliar element, with 100,000 men. An essential condition, which greatly complicated the whole undertaking, became the concentration of naval forces in the Channel sufficient to secure temporary control. "Let us be masters of the Strait for 6 hours," Napoleon wrote to Latouche-Treville in command of the Toulon fleet, "and we shall be masters of the world." In less rhetorical moments he extended the necessary period to from two to fifteen days.

Up to the spring of 1804 neither army nor flotilla was fully ready, and thereafter the crossing was always definitely conditioned upon a naval concentration. But the whole plan called for swift execution. As time lapsed, difficulties multiplied. Harbors silted up, transports were wrecked by storms, British defense measures on land and sea grew more formidable, the Continental situation became more threatening. The Boulogne army thus became more and more—what Napoleon perhaps falsely declared later it had always been—an army concentrated against Austria. To get a fleet into the Channel without a battle was almost impossible, and once in, its position would be dangerous in the extreme. Towards the end, in the opinion of the French student Colonel Desbrière, Napoleon's chief motive in pressing for fleet coöperation was the belief that it would lead to a decisive naval action which, though a defeat, would shift from his own head the odium of failure.

Whether this theory is fully accepted or not, the fact remains that the only sure way of conquering England was by a naval contest. Her first and main defense was the British fleet, which, spread out to the limits of safety to watch French ships wherever harbored, guarded not only against a concentration in the Channel, but against incursions into other fields. The immediate defense of the coasts was intrusted to flotillas of armed boats, over 700 in all, distributed along the coast from Leith south-about to Glasgow, with 100 on the coast of Ireland. Naval men looked upon these as of slight value, a concession, according to Earl St. Vincent, to "the old women in and out" (of both sexes) at home. The distribution of the main battle squadrons varied, but in March, 1805, at the opening of the Trafalgar campaign they were stationed as follows: Boulogne and the Dutch forces were watched by Admiral Keith with 11 of the line and 150 smaller units scattered from the Texel to the Channel Islands. The 21 French ships under Ganteaume at Brest, the strategic center, were closely blockaded by Cornwallis, whose force, by Admiralty orders, was not to fall below 18 of the line. A small squadron had been watching Missiessy's 5 ships at Rochefort and upon his escape in January had followed him to the West Indies. The 5 French and 10 Spanish at Ferrol and the 6 or more ready for sea at Cadiz were held in check by forces barely adequate. In the Gulf of Lyons Nelson with 13 ships had since May, 1803, stood outside the distant but dangerous station of Toulon. Owing to the remoteness from bases, a close and constant blockade was here impossible;

POSITIONS OF BRITISH AND ENEMY SHIPS, MARCH, 1805

moreover, it was the policy to let the enemy get out in the hope of bringing him to action at sea.

To effect a concentration in the Channel in the face of these obstacles was the final aim of all Napoleon's varied naval combinations of 1804 and 1805—combinations which impress one with the truth of Gravière's criticism that the Emperor lacked *"le sentiment exact des difficultés de la marine,"* and especially, one should perhaps add, *de la marine française.* The first plan, the simplest and, therefore, most promising, was that Latouche Tréville with the Toulon fleet should evade Nelson and, after releasing ships on the way, enter the Channel with 16 of the line, while Cornwallis was kept occupied by Ganteaume. This was upset by the death of Latouche, France's ablest and most energetic admiral, in August of 1804, and by the accession, two months later, of Spain and the Spanish navy to the French cause. After many misgivings Napoleon chose Villeneuve to succeed at Toulon. Skilled in his profession, honest, and devoted, he was fatally lacking in self-confidence and energy to conquer difficulties. "It is sad," wrote an officer in the fleet, "to see that force which under Latouche was full of activity, now without faith in either their leader or themselves."

The final plan, though still subject to modifications, was for a concentration on a larger scale in the West Indies. Villeneuve was to go thither, picking up the Cadiz ships on the way, join the Rochefort squadron if it were still there, and wait 40 days for the Brest fleet. Upon its arrival the entire force of 40 ships was to move swiftly back to the Channel. It was assumed that the British squadrons, in alarm for the colonies, would in the meantime be scattered in pursuit.

The Pursuit of Villeneuve

Villeneuve put to sea in a rising gale on January 17, 1805, but was soon back in port with damaged ships, the only effect being to send Nelson clear to Egypt in search of him. A successful start was made on March 30. Refusing to wait for 5 Spanish vessels at Carthagena, Villeneuve with 11 sail reached Cadiz on April 9, picked up one French vessel and two Spanish under Admiral Gravina, and leaving 4 more to follow was off safely on the same night for the West Indies.

From Gibraltar to the Admiralty in London, Villeneuve's appearance in the Atlantic created a profound stir. His departure from Cadiz was known, but not whither he had gone. The five ships on the Cadiz blockade fell back at once to the Channel. A fast frigate from Gibraltar carried the warning to Calder off Ferrol and to the Brest blockade, whence it reached London on April 25. A convoy for Malta and Sicily with 6000 troops under Gen. Craig—a pledge which Russia called for before sending her own forces to southern Italy—was already a week on its way and might fall an easy victim. In consequence of an upheaval at the Admiralty, Lord Barham, a former naval officer now nearly 80 years of age, had just begun his memorable 9 months' administration as First Lord of the Admiralty and director of the naval war. Immediately a whole series of orders went out to the fleets to insure the safety of the troop ships, the maintenance of the Ferrol blockade, an eventual strengthening of forces outside the Channel, and the safety of the Antilles in case Villeneuve had gone there.

Where was Nelson? His scout frigates by bad judgment had lost Villeneuve on the night of March 31 east of Minorca, with no clue to his future course. Nelson took station between Sardinia and the African coast, resolved not to move till he "knew something positive." In the absence of information, the safety of Naples, Sicily, and Egypt was perhaps not merely an obsession on his part, but a proper professional concern; but it is strange that no inkling should have reached him from the Admiralty or elsewhere that a western movement from Toulon was the only one Napoleon now had in mind. It was April 18 before he received further news of the enemy, and not until May 5 was he able to get up to and through the Straits against steady head winds; even then he could not, as he said, "run to the West Indies without something beyond mere surmise." Definite reports from Cadiz that the enemy had gone thither reached him through an Admiral Campbell in the Portuguese service, and were confirmed by the fact that they had been seen nowhere to northward. On the 12th, leaving the *Royal Sovereign* (100) to strengthen the escort of Craig's convoy, which had now appeared, he set out westward with 10 ships in pursuit of the enemy's 18.

He reached Barbados on June 4, only 21 days after Villeneuve's arrival at Martinique. The latter had found that the Rochefort squadron—as a result of faulty transmission of Napoleon's innumerable orders—was already back in Europe, and that the Brest squadron had not come. In fact, held tight in the grip of Cornwallis, it was destined never to leave port. But a reënforcement of 2 ships had reached Villeneuve with orders to wait 35 days longer and in the meantime to harry the British colonies. Disgruntled and despondent, he had scarcely got troops aboard and started north on this mission when he learned that Nelson was hot on his trail. The troops were hastily thrown into frigates to protect the French colonies. Without other provision for their safety, and in disregard of orders, Villeneuve at once turned back for Europe, hoping the Emperor's schemes would still be set forward by his joining the ships at Ferrol.

Nelson followed four days later, on June 13, steering for his old post in the Mediterranean, but at the same time despatching the fast brig *Curieux* to England with news of the French fleet's return. This vessel by great good fortune sighted Villeneuve in mid-ocean, inferred from his northerly position that he was bound for Ferrol, and reached Portsmouth on July 8. Barham at the Admiralty got the news the next morning, angry that he had not been routed out of bed on the arrival of the captain the night before. By 9 o'clock the same morning, orders were off to Calder on the Ferrol station in time so that on the 22d of July he encountered the enemy, still plowing slowly eastward, some 300 miles west of Cape Finisterre.

As a result of admirable communication work and swift administrative action the critic of Nelson at Cape St. Vincent now had a chance to rob the latter of his last victory and end the campaign then and there. His forces were adequate. Though he had only 14 ships to 20, his four three-deckers, according to the estimates of the time, were each worth

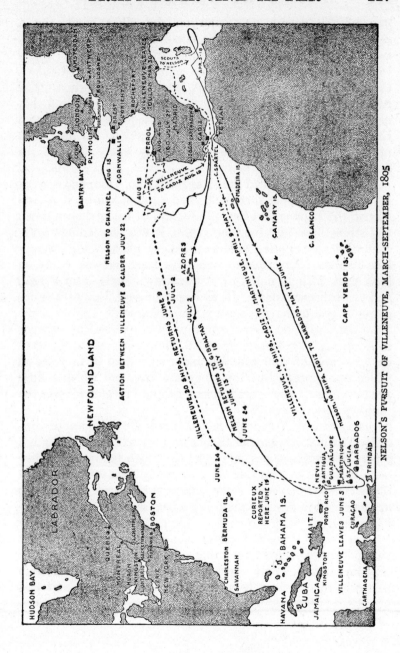

NELSON'S PURSUIT OF VILLENEUVE, MARCH–SEPTEMBER, 1805

two of the enemy 74's, and on the other hand, the 6
Spanish ships with Villeneuve could hardly be counted for
more than three. In the ensuing action, fought in foggy
weather, two of the Spanish were captured and one of Calder's
three-deckers was so injured that it had to be detached. The
two fleets remained in contact for three days following, but
neither took the aggressive. In a subsequent court martial
Calder was reprimanded for "not having done his utmost to
renew the said engagement and destroy every ship of the
enemy."

On July 27 the Allied fleet staggered into Vigo, and a week
later, after dropping three ships and 1200 sick men, it moved
around to Corunna and Ferrol. Instead of being shaken down
and strengthened by the long cruise, it was, according to the
commander's plaintive letters, in worse plight than when it
left Toulon. Nevertheless, ten days later he was ready to
leave port, with 29 units, 14 of them raw vessels from Ferrol,
and 11 of them Spanish. If, as Napoleon said, France was not
going to give up having a navy, something might still be done.
His orders to Villeneuve were to proceed to Brest and thence
to Boulogne. "I count," he ended, "on your zeal in my service, your love of your country, and your hatred of that nation
which has oppressed us for 40 generations, and which a little
preseverance on your part will now cause to reënter forever the
ranks of petty powers." [1]

Such were Villeneuve's instructions, the wisdom or sincerity of which it was scarcely his privilege to question (though
it may be ours). In passing judgment on his failure to execute
them it should be remembered that two months later, to avoid
the personal disgrace of being superseded, he took his fleet out
to more certain disaster than that which it now faced in striking northward from Corunna. *"Un poltron du tête et non de
la cœur"* [2] the French Admiral was handicapped throughout
by a paralyzing sense of the things he could not do.

If he had sailed northward he would have found the British
fleet divided. Nelson, it is true, after returning to Cadiz had

[1] Orders of 26 July, Desbrière, PROJETS, Vol. V, p. 672.
[2] Gravière II. 136.

fallen back from Gibraltar to the Channel, where he left his eleven ships with the Brest squadron in remarkable condition after more than two years at sea. Calder had also joined, bringing Cornwallis' total strength to 39. These stood between the 21 French at Brest and the 29 at Ferrol. But on August 16 Cornwallis divided his forces, keeping 18 (including 10 three-deckers) and sending Calder back to the Spanish coast with the rest. Napoleon called this a disgraceful blunder (*insigne bêtise*), and Mahan adds, "This censure was just." Sir Julian Corbett says it was a "master stroke . . . in all the campaign there is no movement—not even Nelson's chase of Villeneuve—that breathes more deeply the true spirit of war." According to Napoleon, Villeneuve might have "played prisoners' base with Calder's squadron and fallen upon Cornwallis, or with his 30 of the line have beaten Calder's 20 and obtained a decisive superiority."

So perhaps a Napoleonic admiral. Villeneuve left Ferrol on August 13 and sailed northwest on a heavy northeast wind till the 15th. Then, his fixed purpose merely strengthened by false news from a Danish merchantman of 25 British in the vicinity, he turned before the wind for Cadiz. As soon as he was safely inside, the British blockaders again closed around the port.

The Battle of Trafalgar

After twenty-five days in England, Nelson took command off Cadiz on September 28, eager for a final blow that would free England for aggressive war. There was talk of using bomb vessels, Congreve's rockets, and Francis's (Robert Fulton's) torpedoes to destroy the enemy in harbor, but it soon became known that Villeneuve would be forced to put to sea. On October 9, Nelson issued the famous Memorandum, or battle plan, embodying what he called "the Nelson touch," and received by his captains with an enthusiasm which the inspiration of the famous leader no doubt partly explains. This plan, which had been formulating itself in Nelson's mind as far back as the pursuit of the French fleet to the West Indies, may be regarded as the product of his ripest experience and genius; the praise is perhaps not extravagant that "it seems to gather up and coördinate every tactical principle that has ever proved effective." [1]

Though the full text of the Memorandum will repay careful study, its leading principles may be sufficiently indicated by summary. Assuming 40 British ships to 46 of the enemy

NELSON'S VICTORY
Built in 1765. 2162 tons.

(the proportions though not the numbers of the actual engagement), it provides first that "the order of sailing is to be the order of battle, placing the fleet in two lines of 16 ships each, with an advanced squadron of 8 of the fastest sailing two-decked ships." This made for speed and ease in maneuvering, and was based on the expressed belief that so many units could not be formed and controlled in the old-fashioned single line without fatal loss of time. The ships

[1] Corbett, THE CAMPAIGN OF TRAFALGAR, p. 349.

would now come into action practically in cruising formation, which was commonly in two columns. The only noteworthy change contemplated was that the flagships of the first and second in command should shift from first to third place in their respective columns, and even this change was not carried out. Perhaps because the total force was smaller than anticipated, the advance squadron was merged with the two main divisions on the night before the battle, and need not be further regarded. Collingwood, the second in command, was given freedom of initiative by the provision that "after my intentions are made known to him he will have entire direction of his line."

The plan next provides, first for attack from to leeward, and second for attack from to windward. In either case, Collingwood's division was to bring a superior force to bear on 12 ships of the enemy rear, while Nelson would "cut two, three or four ships ahead of their center so far as to ensure getting at their commander in chief." "Something must be left to chance . . . but I look with confidence to a victory before the van of the enemy can succor their rear." And further, "no captain can do very wrong if he places his ship alongside that of an enemy."

Of the attack from the windward a very rough diagram is given, thus:

But aside from this diagram, the lines of which are not precisely straight or parallel in the original, and which can hardly be reconciled with the instructions in the text, there is no clear indication that the attack from the windward (as in the actual battle) was to be delivered in line abreast. What the text says is: "The divisions of the British fleet will be brought nearly within gunshot of the enemy's center. The signal will most probably then be given for the lee line to bear up together, to set all their sails, even steering sails, in order to get as quickly as possible to the enemy's line and to cut through." Thus, if we assume a convergent approach in column, there was to be no slow deployment of the rear or leeward division into line abreast to make the attack of all its ships simultaneous; rather, in the words of a captain describing what really happened, they were simply to "scramble into action" at best speed. Nor is there any suggestion of a preliminary shift from line ahead in the case of Nelson's division. Though endless controversy has raged over the point, the prescribed approach seems to have been followed fairly closely in the battle.

The concentration upon the rear was not new; in fact, it had become almost conventional, and was fully anticipated by the enemy. More originality lay in the manner of "containing" the center and van. For this purpose, in the first place, the approach was to be at utmost speed, not under "battle canvas" but with all sail spread. In the second place, the advance of Nelson's division in column, led by the flagship, left its precise objective not fully disclosed to the enemy until the last moment, and open to change as advantage offered. It could and did threaten the van, and was finally directed upon the center when Villeneuve's presence there was revealed. Finally, the very serious danger of enemy concentration upon the head of the column was mitigated not only by the speed of the approach, but by the concentration there of three heavy three-deckers. The plan in general had in view a particular enemy, superior in numbers but weak in gunnery, slow in maneuver, and likely to avoid decisive action. It aimed primarily at rapidity of movement, but combined also the merits of concentration, simplicity, flexibility, and surprise.

In this discussion of the scheme of the battle, around which interest chiefly centers, the actual events of the engagement have been in some measure anticipated, and may now be told more briefly. Driven to desperation by the goadings of Napoleon and the news that Admiral Rosily was approaching to supersede him, Villeneuve at last resolved to put to sea. "The intention of His Majesty," so the Minister of Marine had written, "is to seek in the ranks, wherever they may be found,

officers best suited for superior command, requiring above all
a noble ambition, love of glory, decision of character, and un-
bounded courage. His Majesty wishes to destroy that circumspection which is the reproach of the navy; that defensive
system which paralyzes our fleet and doubles the enemy's.
He counts the loss of vessels nothing if lost with honor; he
does not wish his fleet blockaded by an enemy inferior in
strength; and if that is the situation at Cadiz he advises and
orders you to attack."

The Allied fleet worked out of Cadiz on the 19th of October and on the 20th tacked southward under squally westerly
winds. On the 21st, the day of the battle, the wind was still
from the west, light and flawy, with a heavy swell and signs
of approaching storm. At dawn the two fleets were visible to
each other, Villeneuve about 9 miles northeast and to leeward
of the British and standing southward from Cape Trafalgar.
The French Admiral had formed his main battle line of 21
ships, French and Spanish intermingled, with the *Santisima
Trinidad* (128) in the center and his flagship *Bucentaure* next;
the remaining 12 under the Spanish Admiral Gravina constituted a separate squadron stationed to windward to counter
an enemy concentration, which was especially expected upon
the rear.

As the British advance already appeared to threaten this
end of their line, the Allied fleet wore together about 9 o'clock,
thus reversing their order, shifting their course northward,
and opening Cadiz as a refuge. The maneuver, not completed
until an hour later, left their line bowed in at the center, with
a number of ships slightly to leeward, while Gravina's squadron mingled with and prolonged the rear in the new order.

The change, though it aroused Nelson's fear lest his quarry
should escape, facilitated his attack as planned, by exposing
the enemy rear to Collingwood's division. As rapidly as the
light airs permitted, the two British columns bore down, Nelson
in the *Victory* (100) leading the windward division of 12
ships, closely followed by the heavy *Neptune* and *Téméraire*,
while Collingwood in the freshly coppered and refitted *Royal
Sovereign* set a sharp pace for the 15 sail to leeward. Of the

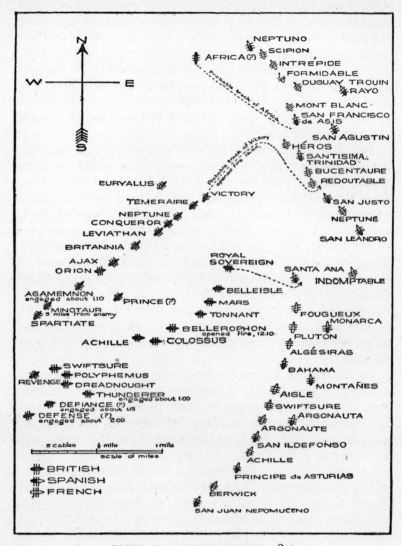

BATTLE OF TRAFALGAR, OCT. 21, 1805

Position of ships about noon, when *Royal Sovereign* opened fire.
(From plan by Capt. T. H. Tizard, R.N., British Admiralty Report, 1913.)

forty ships Nelson had once counted on, some had not come from England, and a half dozen others were inside the straits for water. While the enemy were changing course, Collingwood had signaled his division to shift into a line of bearing, an order which, though rendered almost ineffective by his failure to slow down, served to throw the column off slightly and bring it more nearly parallel to the enemy rear. (See plan.) Both commanders clung to the lead and pushed ahead as if racing into the fray, thus effectually preventing deployment and leaving trailers far behind. Nelson went so far as to try to jockey his old friend out of first place by ordering the *Mars* to pass him, but Collingwood set his studding sails and kept his lead. Possibly it was then he made the remark that he wished Nelson would make no more signals, as they all knew what they had to do, rather than after Nelson's famous final message: "England expects that every man will do his duty."

Nelson, uncertain of Villeneuve's place in the line and anxious to prevent escape northward, steered for a gap ahead of the *Santisima Trinidad,* as if to threaten the van. But at 12:00 noon, as the first shots were fired at the *Royal Sovereign,* flags were broken from all ships, and Villeneuve's location revealed. Swinging to southward under heavy fire, the *Victory* passed under the stern of the *Bucentaure* and then crashed into the *Redoutable,* which had pushed close up to the flagship. The relative effectiveness of the gunnery in the two fleets is suggested by the fact that the *Victory* while coming in under the enemy's concentrated fire had only 50 killed and wounded, whereas the raking broadside she finally poured into the *Bucentaure's* stern is said to have swept down 400 men. Almost simultaneously with the leader, the *Téméraire* and *Neptune* plunged into the line, the former closing with the *Bucentaure* and the latter with the *Santisima Trinidad* ahead. Other ships soon thrust into the terrific artillery combat which centered around the leaders in a confused mingling of friend and foe.

At about 12:10, nearly half an hour before the *Victory* penetrated the Allied line, the *Royal Sovereign* brought up on the leeward side of the *Santa Ana,* flagship of the Spanish

Admiral Alava, after raking both her and the *Fougueux* astern. The *Santa Ana* was thirteenth in the actual line, but, as Collingwood knew, there were 16, counting those to leeward, among the ships he had thus cut off for his division to subdue. As a combined effect of the light breeze and the manner of attack, it was an hour or more before the action was made general by the advent of British ships in the rear. All these suffered as they closed, but far less than those near the head of the line. Of the total British casualties fully a third fell upon the four leading ships—*Victory, Téméraire, Royal Sovereign* and *Belleisle.*

Not until about three o'clock were the shattered but victorious British in the center threatened by the return of the ten ships in the Allied van. Culpably slow, however hindered by lack of wind, several of these joined stragglers from Gravina's division to leeward; the *Intrépide,* under her brave skipper Infernet, set an example all might well have followed by steering straight for the *Bucentaure,* and surrendered only to overwhelming odds; five others under Rear Admiral Dumanoir skirted to windward and escaped with the loss of one of their number, cut off by two British late-comers, *Spartiate* and *Minotaur.*

"Partial firing continued until 4:30, when a victory having been reported to the Right Honorable Lord Viscount Nelson, he died of his wound." So reads the *Victory's* log. The flagship had been in deadly grapple with the *Redoutable,* whose complement, like that of many another French and Spanish ship in the action, showed that the decadence of their navies was not due to lack of fighting spirit in the rank and file. Nelson was mortally wounded by a musket shot from the mizzen-top soon after the ships closed. In his hour of supreme achievement death came not ungraciously, giving final assurance of the glory which no man ever faced death more eagerly to win.

Of the Allied fleet, four fled with Dumanoir, but were later engaged and captured by a British squadron near Corunna. Eleven badly battered survivors escaped into Cadiz. Of the 18 captured, 11 were wrecked or destroyed in the gales

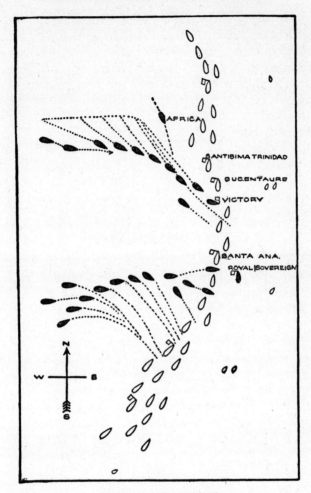

TRAFALGAR, ABOUT 12:30

From plan attached to report of Capt. Prigny, Villeneuve's Chief of Staff (Desbrière, *Trafalgar*, App. p. 128.)

that swept the coast for several days after the battle; three were recaptured or turned back to their crews by the prize-masters, and only four eventually reached Gibraltar.

The Trafalgar victory did not indeed reduce France to terms, and it thus illustrates the limitations of naval power against an enemy not primarily dependent upon the sea. But it freed England from further threat of invasion, clinched her naval predominance, and opened to her the prospect of taking a more aggressive part in the land war. Even this prospect was soon temporarily thrust into the background. On the very day of Trafalgar Napoleon's bulletins announced the surrender of 60,000 Austrians at Ulm, and the Battle of Austerlitz a month later crushed the Third Coalition. The small British contingents in Germany and southern Italy hastened back to their transports. It was only later, when France was approaching exhaustion, that British forces in the Spanish peninsula and elsewhere took a conspicuous part in the Continental war.

The Continental System

England's real offensive strength lay not in her armies but in her grip on Europe's intercourse with the rest of the world. And on the other hand, the only blow that Napoleon could still strike at his chief enemy was to shut her from the markets of Europe—to "defeat the sea by the land." This was the aim of his Continental System. It meant a test of endurance—whether he could force France and the rest of Europe to undergo the tremendous strain of commercial isolation for a sufficient period to reduce England to ruin.

The Continental System came into being with Napoleon's famous Berlin Decree of November, 1806, which, declaring a "paper" blockade of the British Isles, put all trade with England under the ban. Under this decree and later supplementary measures, goods of British origin, whatever their subsequent ownership, were confiscated or destroyed wherever French agents could lay hands on them; and neutral vessels were seized and condemned for entering British ports, accepting British convoy, or even submitting to British search.

England's chief retaliatory measure was the Orders in Council of November, 1807. Her object in these orders and later modifications was not to cut off trade with the Continent, but to control it to her own profit and the injury of the enemy— in short, "no trade except through England." The orders aimed to compel the aid of neutrals by excluding neutral ships from the Continent unless they should first enter British ports, pay British dues, and (as would be an inevitable consequence) give covert assistance in carrying on British trade.

The Continental System reached its greatest efficiency during the apogée of Napoleon's power in 1809 and 1810. To check forbidden traffic, which continued on an enormous scale, he annexed Holland to his empire, and threw a triple cordon of French troops along Germany's sea frontier. As a result, in the critical year of 1811 goods piled up in British warehouses, factories closed, bankruptcies doubled, and her financial system tottered.[1] But to bar the tide of commerce at every port from Trieste to Riga was like trying to stem the sea. At each leak in the barrier, sugar, coffee, and British manufactures poured in, and were paid for at triple or tenfold prices, not in exports, but in coin. Malta, the Channel Islands, and Heligoland (seized by England from Denmark in 1807) became centers of smuggling. The beginning of the end came when the Czar, tired of French dictation and a policy ruinous to his country, opened his ports, first to colonial products (December, 1810), and a year later to all British wares. Six hundred vessels, brought under British convoy into the Baltic, docked at Libau, and caravans of wagons filled the roads leading east and south.

In June of 1812 Napoleon gathered his "army of twenty nations" for the fatal Russian campaign. Now that they had served their purpose, England on June 23 revoked her Orders in Council. The Continental System had failed.

The War of 1812

In the same month, on June 18, the United States declared war on Great Britain. Up to 1807 her commerce and shipping, in the words of President Monroe, had "flourished beyond

---

[1] In spite of this crisis, British trade showed progressive increase in each half decade from 1800 to 1815, and did not fall off again until the five years after the war. The figures (in millions of pounds sterling) follow: 1801-05, 61 million; 1806-10, 67 million; 1811-15, 74 million; 1816-20, 60 million.—Day, HISTORY OF COMMERCE, p. 355.

example," as shown by the single fact that her re-export trade
(in West Indies products) was greater in that year than ever
again until 1915.[1]   Later they had suffered from the coer-
cion of both belligerents, and from her own futile counter-
measures of embargo and non-intercourse. Her final declaration came tardily, if not indeed unwisely as a matter of practical policy, however abundantly justified by England's commercial restrictions and her seizure of American as well as
British seamen on American ships.   An additional motive,
which had decisive weight with the dominant western faction
in Congress, was the hope of gaining Canada or at least extending the northern frontier.

A subordinate episode in the world conflict, the War of 1812
cannot be neglected in naval annals. The tiny American navy
retrieved the failures of American land forces, and shook the
British navy out of a notorious slackness in gunnery and discipline engendered by its easy victories against France and
Spain.

In size the British Navy in 1812 was more formidable than
at any earlier period of the general war. Transport work
with expeditionary forces, blockade and patrol in European
waters, and commerce protection from the China Sea to the
Baltic had in September, 1812, increased the fleet to 686 vessels in active service, including 120 of the line and 145 frigates.
There were 75 in all on American stations, against the total
American Navy of 16, of which the best were the fine 44-gun
frigates *Constitution, President* and *United States*. In the
face of such odds, and especially as England's European preoccupations relaxed, the result was inevitable. After the first
year of war, while a swarm of privateers and smaller war vessels still took heavy toll of British commerce, the frigates were
blockaded in American ports and American commerce was
destroyed.

But before the blockade closed down, four frigate actions
had been fought, three of them American victories. In each

[1] United States exports rose from a value of 56 million dollars in 1803
to 108 million in 1807; then fell to 22 million in 1808, and after rising
to about 50 million before the war, went down to 6 million in 1814.—
Ibid., p 480.

Ship[1]	Commander	Guns	Wt of broad-side	Crew	Casu-alties	Place and date
Constitution[2].....	Hull	54	684	456	14	750 miles east of Boston, Aug. 19, 1812.
Guerrière (Brit.)...	Dacres	49	556	272	79	
United States[2]....	Decatur	54	786	478	12	Off Canary Islands, Oct. 25, 1812.
Macedonian (Brit.)	Carden	49	547	301	104	
Constitution[2].....	Bainbridge	52	654	475	34	Near Bahia, Dec. 29, 1812.
Java (Brit.).......	Lambert	49	576	426	150	
Chesapeake.......	Lawrence	50	542	379	148	Off Boston, June 1, 1813.
Shannon (Brit.)[2]..	Broke	52	550	330	83	

[1] The figures are from Roosevelt's NAVAL WAR OF 1812, in which 7% is deducted for the short weight of American shot.
[2] Victorious.

instance, as will be seen from the accompanying table, the advantage in weight of broadside was with the victor. The American frigates were in fact triumphs of American shipbuilding, finer in lines, more strongly timbered, and more heavily gunned than British ships of their class. But that good gunnery and seamanship figured in the results is borne out by the fact that of the eight sloop actions fought during the war, with a closer approach to equality of strength, seven were American victories. The British carronades that had pounded French ships at close range proved useless against opponents that knew how to choose and hold their distance and could shoot straight with long 24's.

"It seems," said a writer in the London *Times,* "that the Americans have some superior mode of firing." But when Broke with his crack crew in the *Shannon* beat the *Chesapeake* fresh out of port, he demonstrated, as had the Americans in other actions, that the superiority was primarily a matter of training and skill.

On the Great Lakes America's naval efforts should have

centered, for here was her main objective and here she was on equal terms. Both sides were tremendously hampered in communications with their main sources of supply. But with an approach from the sea to Montreal, the British faced no more serious obstacle in the rapids of the St. Lawrence above than did the Americans on the long route up the Mohawk, over portages into Oneida Lake, and thence down the Oswego to Ontario, or else from eastern Pennsylvania over the mountains to Lake Erie. The wilderness waterways on both sides soon saw the strange spectacle of immense anchors, cables, cannon, and ship tackle of all kinds, as well as armies of sailors, shipwrights, and riggers, making their way to the new rival bases at Sackett's Harbor and Kingston, both near the foot of Lake Ontario.

Of the whole lake and river frontier, Ontario was of the most vital importance. A decisive American victory here, including the capture of Kingston, would cut enemy communications and settle the control of all western Canada. Kingston as an objective had the advantage over Montreal that it was beyond the direct reach of the British navy. The British, fully realizing the situation, made every effort to build up their naval forces on this lake, and gave Commodore Yeo, who was in command, strict orders to avoid action unless certain of success. On the other hand, the American commander, Chauncey, though an energetic organizer, made the mistake of assuming that his mission was also defensive. Hence when one fleet was strengthened by a new ship it went out and chased the other off the lake, but there was little fighting, both sides engaging in a grand shipbuilding rivalry and playing for a sure thing. Naval control remained unsettled and shifting throughout the war. It was fortunate, indeed, says the British historian, James, that the war ended when it did, or there would not have been room on the lake to maneuver the two fleets. The *St. Lawrence,* a 112-gun three-decker completed at Kingston in 1814, was at the time the largest man-of-war in the world.

Possibly a growing lukewarmness about the war, manifested on both sides, prevented more aggressive action. But it did not prevent two brilliant American victories in the lesser theaters of Lake Erie and Lake Champlain. Perry's achievement on Lake Erie in building a superior flotilla in the face of all manner of obstacles was even greater than that of the victory itself. The result of the latter, won on September 10, 1813, is summed up in his despatch: "We have met the enemy and they are ours—2 ships, 2 brigs, 1 schooner, and 1 sloop." It assured the safety of the northwestern frontier.

On Lake Champlain Macdonough's successful defense just a year later held up an invasion which, though it would not have been pushed very strenuously in any case, might have made our position less favorable for the peace negotiations then already under way. In this action, as in the one on Lake Erie, the total strength of each of the opposing flotillas, measured in weight of broadsides (1192 pounds for the British against 1194 for the Americans), was about that of a single ship-of-the-line. But the number of units employed raised all the problems of a squadron engagement. Macdonough's shrewd choice of position in Plattsburg Bay, imposing upon the enemy a difficult approach under a raking fire, and his excellent handling of his ships in action, justify his selection as the ablest American naval leader developed by the war.

At the outbreak of the American War, France and England had been engaged in a death grapple in which the rights of neutrals were trampled under foot. Napoleon, by his paper blockade and confiscations on any pretext, had been a more glaring offender. But America's quarrel was after all not with France, who needed American trade, but with England, a commercial rival, who could back her restrictions by naval power. Once France was out of the war, the United States found it easy to come to terms with England, whose commerce was suffering severely from American privateers.[1] At the close of the war the questions at issue when it began had

[1] According to figures cited in Mahan's WAR OF 1812, (Vol. II, p. 224), 22 American naval vessels took 165 British prizes, and 526 privateers took 1344 prizes. In the absence of adequate motives on either side for prolonging the war, these losses, though not more severe than those inflicted by French cruisers, were decisive factors for peace.

dropped into abeyance, and were not mentioned in the treaty terms.

The view taken of the aggressions of sea power in the Napoleonic Wars will depend largely on the view taken regarding the justice of the cause in which it fought. It saved the Continent from military conquest. It preserved the European balance of power, a balance which statesmen of that age deemed essential to the safety of Europe and the best interests of America and the rest of the world. On the other hand, but for the sacrifices of England's land allies, the Continental System would have forced her to make peace, though still undefeated at sea. Even if her territorial accessions were slight, England came out of the war undisputed "mistress of the seas" as she had never been before, and for nearly a century to come was without a dangerous rival in naval power and world commerce.

REFERENCES

For general history of the period see: HISTORIES OF THE BRITISH NAVY by Clowes (Vols. V, VI, 1900) and Hannay (1909), Mahan's INFLUENCE OF SEA POWER UPON THE FRENCH REVOLUTION AND EMPIRE (1892) and WAR OF 1812 (1905), Chevalier's HISTOIRE DE LA MARINE FRANÇAISE SOUS LA PREMIÈRE RÉPUBLIQUE (1886), Gravière's GUERRES MARITIMES (1885), Callender's SEA KINGS OF BRITAIN (Vol. III, 1911), and Maltzahn's NAVAL WARFARE (tr. Miller, 1908).

Among biographies: Mahan's and Laughton's lives of Nelson, Anson's LIFE OF JERVIS (1913), Clark Russell's LIFE OF COLLINGWOOD (1892), and briefer sketches in FROM HOWARD TO NELSON, ed. Laughton (1899).

For the Trafalgar campaign see:
British Admiralty blue-book on THE TACTICS OF TRAFALGAR (with bibliography, 1913), Corbett's CAMPAIGN OF TRAFALGAR (1910), Col. Desbrière's PROJETS ET TENTATIVES DE DÉBARQUEMENT AUX ILES BRITANNIQUES (1902) and CAMPAGNE MARITIME DE TRAFALGAR (1907).

See also Col. C. E. Callwell's MILITARY OPERATIONS AND MARITIME PREPONDERANCE (1913), and Professor Clive Day's HISTORY OF COMMERCE (revised edition, 1911, with bibliography).

CHAPTER XIII

REVOLUTION IN NAVAL WARFARE: HAMPTON ROADS AND LISSA.

DURING the 19th century, from 1815 to 1898, naval power, though always an important factor in international relations, played in general a passive rôle. The wars which marked the unification of Germany and Italy and the thrusting back of Turkey from the Balkans were fought chiefly on land. The navy of England, though never more constantly busy in protecting her far-flung empire, was not challenged to a genuine contest for mastery of the seas. In the Greek struggle for independence there were two naval engagements of some consequence—Chios (1822), where the Greeks with fireships destroyed a Turkish squadron and gained temporary control of the Ægean, and Navarino (1827), in which a Turkish force consisting principally of frigates was wiped out by a fleet of the western powers. But both of these actions were one-sided, and showed nothing new in types or tactics. In the American Civil War control of the sea was important and even decisive, but was overwhelmingly in the hands of the North. Hence the chief naval interest of the period lies not so much in the fighting as in the revolutionary changes in ships, weapons, and tactics—changes which parallel the extraordinary scientific progress of the century; and the engagements may be studied now, as they were studied then, as testing and illustrating the new methods and materials of naval war.

Changes in Ships and Weapons

Down to the middle of the 19th century there had been only a slow and slight development in ships and weapons for a period of nearly 300 years. A sailor of the Armada would soon have felt at home in a three-decker of 1815. But he would have been helpless as a child in the fire-driven iron monsters that fought at Hampton Roads. The shift from sail to steam, from oak to iron, from shot to shell, and from muzzle-loading smoothbore to breech-loading rifle began about 1850; and progress thereafter was so swift that an up-to-date ship of each succeeding decade was capable of defeating a whole squadron of ten years before. Success came to depend on the adaptability and mechanical skill of personnel, as well as their courage and discipline, and also upon the progressive spirit of constructors and naval experts, faced with the most difficult problems, the wrong solution of which would mean the waste of millions of dollars and possible defeat in war. Every change had to overcome the spirit of conservatism inherent in military organizations, where seniority rules, errors are sanctified by age, and every innovation upsets cherished routine. Thus in the contract for Ericsson's *Monitor* it was stipulated, that she should have masts, spars, and sails!

The first successful steamboat for commerce was, as is well known, Robert Fulton's flat-bottomed side-wheeler *Clermont,* which in August, 1807, made the 150 miles from New York to Albany in 32 hours. During the war of 1812 Fulton designed for coast defense a heavily timbered, double-ender floating battery, with a single paddle-wheel located inside amidships. On her trial trip in 1815 this first steam man-of-war, the U. S. S. *Fulton,* carried 26 guns and made over 6 knots, but she was then laid up and was destroyed a few years later by fire. Ericsson's successful application of the screw propeller in 1837 made steam propulsion more feasible for battleships by clearing the decks and eliminating the clumsy and exposed side-wheels. The first American screw warship was the U. S. S. *Princeton,* of 1843, but every ship in the American Navy at the outbreak of the Civil War had at least auxiliary sail rig. Though by 1850 England had 30 vessels with auxiliary steam, the *Devastation* of 1869 was the first in the British service to use steam exclusively. Long after this time old "floating museums" with sail rig and smoothbores were re‹

tained in most navies for motives of economy, and even the first ships of the American "White Squadron" were encumbered with sails and spars.

Progress in ordnance began about 1822, when explosive shells, hitherto used only in mortars, were first adopted for ordinary cannon with horizontal fire. At the time of the Crimean War shells were the usual ammunition for lower

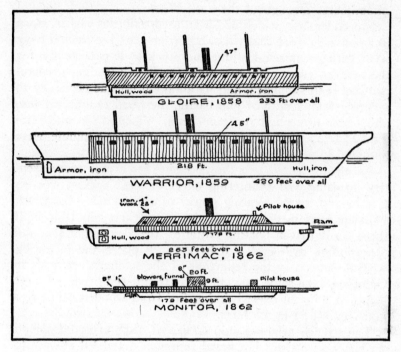

EARLY IRONCLADS

tier guns, and at Sinope in 1853 their smashing effect against wooden hulls was demonstrated when a Russian squadron destroyed some Turkish vessels which fired only solid shot. The great professional cry of the time, we are told, became "For God's sake, keep out the shell." [1]

In 1851 Minié rifles supplanted in the British army the old

[1] Custance, THE SHIP OF THE LINE IN BATTLE, p. 9.

smoothbore musket or "Brown Bess," with which at ranges above 200 yards it was difficult to hit a target 11 feet square. This change led quickly to the rifling of heavy ordnance as well. The first Armstrong rifles of 1858—named after their inventor, Sir William Armstrong, head of the Royal Gun Factory at Woolwich—included guns up to 7-inch diameter of bore. The American navy, however, depended chiefly on smoothbores throughout the Civil War.

Breech-loading, which had been used centuries earlier, came in again with these first rifles, but after 1865 the British navy went back to muzzle-loading and stuck to it persistently for the next 15 years. By that time the breech-loading mechanism had been simplified, and its adoption became necessary to secure greater length of gun barrel, increased rapidity of fire, and better protection for gun-crews. About 1880 quick-fire guns of from 3 to 6 inches, firing 12 or 15 shots a minute, were mounted in secondary batteries.

As already suggested, the necessity for armor arose from the smashing and splintering effect of shell against wooden targets and the penetrating power of rifled guns. To attack Russian forts in the Crimea, the French navy in 1855 built three steam-driven floating batteries, the *Tonnant, Lave,* and *Dévastation,* each protected by 4.3-inch plates and mounting 8 56-lb. guns. In the reduction of the Kinburn batteries, in October of the same year, these boats suffered little, but were helped out by an overwhelming fire from wooden ships, 630 guns against 81 in the forts.

The French armored ship *Gloire* of 1859 caused England serious worry about her naval supremacy, and led at once to H. M. S. *Warrior,* like the *Gloire,* full rigged with auxiliary steam. The *Warrior's* 4.5-inch armor, extending from 6 feet below the waterline to 16 feet above and covering about 42 per cent of the visible target, was proof against the weapons of the time. At this initial stage in armored construction, naval experts turned with intense interest to watch the work of ironclads against ships and forts in the American Civil War.

The American Civil War

The naval activities of this war are too manifold to follow in detail. For four years the Union navy was kept constantly occupied with the tasks of blockading over 3000 miles of coast-line, running down enemy commerce destroyers, co-operating with the army in the capture of coast strongholds, and opening the Mississippi and other waterways leading into the heart of the Confederacy. To make the blockade effective and cut off the South from the rest of the world, the Federal Government unhesitatingly applied the doctrine of "continuous voyage," seizing and condemning neutral ships even when bound from England to Bermuda or the Bahamas, if their cargo was ultimately destined for Southern ports. The doctrine was declared inapplicable when the last leg of the journey was by land,[1] doubtless because there was little danger of heavy traffic across the Mexican frontier. Blockade runners continued to pour goods into the South until the fall of Fort Fisher in 1865; but as the blockade became more stringent, it crippled the finances of the Confederacy, shut out foodstuffs and munitions, and shortened, if it did not even have a decisive effect in winning the war.

To meet these measures the South was at first practically without naval resources, and had to turn at once to new methods of war. Its first move was to convert the steam frigate *Merrimac,* captured half-burned with the Norfolk Navy Yard, into an ironclad ram. A casemate of 4 inches of iron over 22 inches of wood, sloping 35 degrees from the vertical, was extended over 178 feet, or about two-thirds of her hull. Beyond this structure the decks were awash. The *Merrimac* had an armament of 6 smoothbores and 4 rifles, two of the latter being pivot-guns at bow and stern, and a 1500-lb. cast-iron beak or ram. With her heavy load of guns and armor she drew 22 feet aft and could work up a speed of barely 5 knots.

Faced with this danger, the North hurriedly adopted Ericsson's plan for the *Monitor,*[2] which was contracted for on October 4, 1861, and launched after 100 days. Old marlin-spike

---

[1] Peterhoff Case, 1866 (5 Wall, 28).

[2] So called by Ericsson because it would "admonish" the South, and

seamen pooh-poohed this "cheesebox on a raft." As a naval officer said, it might properly be worshiped by its designer, for it was an image of nothing in the heavens above, or the earth beneath, or the waters under the earth. It consisted of a revolving turret with 8-inch armor and two 11-inch smooth-bore guns, set on a raft-like structure 142 feet in length by 41½ feet in beam, projecting at bow, stern, and sides beyond a flat-bottomed lower hull. Though unseaworthy, the *Monitor* maneuvered quickly and drew only 10½ feet. She was first ordered to the Gulf, but on March 6 this destination was suddenly changed to the Chesapeake.

The South in fact won the race in construction and got its ship first into action by a margin of just half a day. At noon on March 8, with the iron-workers still driving her last rivets, the *Merrimac* steamed out of Norfolk and advanced ponderously upon the three sail and two steam vessels then anchored in Hampton Roads.

In the Northern navy there had been much skepticism about the ironclad and no concerted plan to meet her attack. Under a rain of fire from the Union ships, and from shore fortifications too distant to be effective, the *Merrimac* rammed and sank the sloop-of-war *Cumberland,* and then, after driving the frigate *Congress* aground, riddled her with shells. Towards nightfall the Confederate vessel moved down stream, to continue the slaughter next day.

About 12 o'clock that night, after two days of terrible buffeting on the voyage down the coast, the little *Monitor* anchored on the scene lighted up by the burning wreck of the *Congress.* The first battle of ironclads began next morning at 8:30 and continued with slight intermission till noon. It ended in a triumph, not for either ship, but for armor over guns. The *Monitor* fired 41 solid shot, 20 of which struck home, but merely cracked some of the *Merrimac's* outer plates. The *Monitor* was hit 22 times by enemy shells. Neither craft was seriously harmed and not a man was killed on either side, though several were stunned or otherwise injured. Lieut.

also suggest to England "doubts as to the propriety of completing four steel-clad ships at three and one-half millions apiece."

Worden, in command of the *Monitor,* was nearly blinded by a shell that smashed in the pilot house, a square iron structure then located not above the turret but on the forward deck.

The drawn battle was hailed as a Northern victory. Imagination had been drawing dire pictures of what the *Merrimac* might do. At a Cabinet meeting in Washington Sunday morning, March 9, Secretary of War Stanton declared: "The *Merrimac* will change the course of the war; she will destroy *seriatim* every naval vessel; she will lay all the cities on the seaboard under contribution. I have no doubt that the enemy is at this minute on the way to Washington, and that we shall have a shell from one of her guns in the White House before we leave this room." The menace was somewhat exaggerated. With her submerged decks, feeble engines, and general awkwardness, the *Merrimac* could scarcely navigate in Hampton Roads. In the first day's fighting her beak was wrenched off and a leak started, two guns were put out of action, and her funnel and all other top-hamper were riddled. As was shown by Farragut in Mobile Bay, and again by Tegetthoff at Lissa, even wooden vessels, if in superior numbers, might do something against an ironclad in an aggressive mêlée.

Both the antagonists at Hampton Roads ended their careers before the close of 1862; the *Merrimac* was burned by her crew at the evacuation of Norfolk, and the *Monitor* was sunk under tow in a gale off Hatteras. But turret ships, monitors, and armored gunboats soon multiplied in the Union navy and did effective service against the defenses of Southern harbors and rivers. Under Farragut's energetic leadership, vessels both armored and unarmored passed with relatively slight injury the forts below New Orleans, at Vicksburg, and at the entrance to Mobile Bay. Even granting that the shore artillery was out of date and not very expertly served, it is well to realize that similar conditions may conceivably recur, and that the superiority of forts over ships is qualified by conditions of equipment and personnel.

Actually to destroy or capture shore batteries by naval force is another matter. As Ericsson said, "A single shot will sink

a ship, while 100 rounds cannot silence a fort." [1]   Attacks of
this kind against Fort McAllister and Charleston failed.   At
Charleston, April 7, 1863, the ironclads faced a cross-fire from
several forts, 47 smoothbores and 17 rifles against 29 smoothbores and 4 rifles in the ships, and in waters full of obstructions
and mines.

The capture of Fort Fisher, commanding the main entrance
to Wilmington, North Carolina, was accomplished in January,
1865, by the combined efforts of the army and navy.   The
fort, situated on a narrow neck of land between the Cape Fear
River and the sea, had 20 guns on its land face and 24 on its
sea face, 15 of them rifled.   Against it were brought 5 ironclads with 18 guns, backed up by over 200 guns in the rest of
the fleet.   After a storm of shot and shell for three successive
days, rising at times to "drum-fire," the barrage was lifted at
a signal and troops and sailors dashed forward from their
positions on shore.   Even after this preparation the capture
cost 1000 men.   As at Kinburn in the Crimean War, the effectiveness of the naval forces was due less to protective armor
than to volume of fire.

Submarines and Torpedoes

In the defense of Southern harbors, mines and torpedoes for
the first time came into general use, and the submarine scored
its first victim.   Experiments with these devices had been going on for centuries, but were first brought close to practical
success by David Bushnell, a Connecticut Yankee of the American Revolution.   His tiny submarine, resembling a mud-turtle
standing on its tail, embodied many features of modern under-
water boats, including a primitive conning tower, screw propulsion (by foot power), a vertical screw to drive the craft
down, and a detachable magazine with 150 pounds of gunpowder.   The *Turtle* paddled around and even under British
men-of-war off New York and New London, but could not
drive a spike through their copper bottoms to attach its mine.

Robert Fulton, probably the greatest genius in nautical in-

[1] Wilson, IRONCLADS IN ACTION, Vol. I, p. 91.

vention, carried the development of both mines and sub-marines much further. His *Nautilus,* so-called because its col-lapsible sail resembled that of the familiar chambered nautilus, was surprisingly ahead of its time; it had a fish-like shape, screw propulsion (by a two-man hand winch), horizontal div-ing rudder, compressed air tank, water tank filled or emptied by a pump, and a torpedo [1] consisting of a detachable case of gunpowder. A lanyard ran from the torpedo through an eye in a spike, to be driven in the enemy hull, and thence to the submarine, which as it moved away brought the torpedo up taut

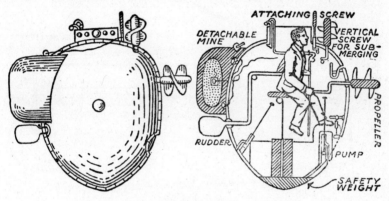

BUSHNELL'S TURTLE

against the spike and caused its explosion. Fulton interested Napoleon in his project, submerged frequently for an hour or more, and blew up a hulk in Brest harbor. But the greybeards in the French navy frowned on these novel methods, declar-ing them "immoral" and "contrary to the laws of war."

Later the British Government entered into negotiations with the inventor, and in October, 1804, used his mines in an un-successful attack on the French flotilla of invasion at Bou-logne. Only one pinnace was sunk. Fulton still maintained that he could "sweep all military marines off the ocean." [2] But Trafalgar ended his chances. As the old Admiral Earl St.

[1] This name, coined by Fulton, was from the *torpedo electricus,* or cramp fish, which kills its victim by electric shock.
[2] Letter to Pitt, Jan. 6, 1806.

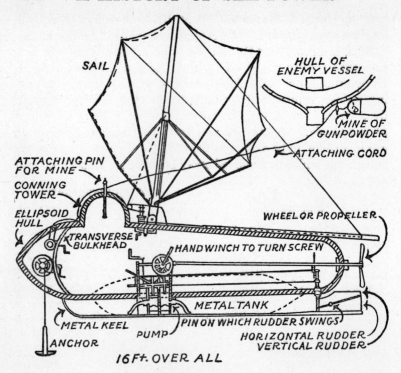

FULTON'S NAUTILUS

Vincent remarked, "Pitt [the Prime Minister] would be the greatest fool that ever existed to encourage a mode of war which they who command the sea do not want and which if successful would deprive them of it." So Fulton took £15,000 and dropped his schemes.

Much cruder than the *Nautilus,* owing to their hurried construction, were the Confederate "Davids" of the Civil War. One of these launches, which ran only semi-submerged, drove a spar torpedo against the U. S. S. *New Ironsides* off Charleston, but it exploded on the rebound, too far away. The C. S. S. *Hunley* was a real submarine, and went down readily, but on five occasions it failed to emerge properly, and drowned in these experiments about 35 men. In August, 1864, running on the surface, it sank by torpedo the U. S. Corvette *Housa-*

tonic off Charleston, but went down in the suction of the larger vessel, carrying to death its last heroic crew.

By the end of the century, chiefly owing to the genius and patient efforts of two American inventors, John P. Holland and Simon Lake, the submarine was passing from the experimental to the practical stage. Its possibilities were increased by the Whitehead torpedo (named after its inventor, a British engineer established in Fiume, Austria), which came out in 1868 and was soon adopted in European navies. With gyroscopic stabilizing devices and a "warmer" for the compressed air of its engine, the torpedo attained before 1900 a speed of 28 knots and a possible range of 1000 yards. Its first victim was the Chilean warship *Blanco,* sunk in 1891 at 50 yards after two misses. Thornycroft in England first achieved speed for small vessels, and in 1873 began turning out torpedo boats. Destroyers came in twenty years later, and by the end of the century were making over 30 knots.

Long before this time the lessons of the Civil War had hastened the adoption of armor, the new ships ranging from high-sided vessels with guns in broadside, as in the past, to low freeboard craft influenced by the *Monitor* design, with a few large guns protected by revolving turrets or fixed barbettes, and with better provision for all-around fire. Ordnance improved in penetrating power, until the old wrought-iron armor had to be 20 inches thick and confined to waterline and batteries. Steel "facing" and the later plates of Krupp or Harveyized steel made it possible again to lighten and spread out the armor, and during the last decade of the century it steadily increased its ascendancy over the gun.

The Battle of Lissa

The adoption of armor meant sacrifice of armament, and a departure from Farragut's well-tried maxim, "The best protection against the enemy's fire is a well-sustained fire from your own guns." Thus the British *Dreadnought* of 1872 gave 35% of its displacement to armor and only 5% to armament. Invulnerability was secured at the expense of offensive power.

That aggressive tactics and weapons retained all their old value in warfare was to receive timely illustration in the Battle of Lissa, fought in the year after the American war. The engagement illustrated also another of Farragut's pungent maxims to the effect that iron in the ships is less important than "iron in the men"—a saying especially true when, as with the Austrians at Lissa, the iron is in the chief in command.

In 1866 Italy and Prussia attacked Austria in concert, Italy having secured from Bismarck a pledge of Venetia in the event of victory. Though beaten at Custozza on June 24, the Italians did their part by keeping busy an Austrian army of 80,000. Moltke crushed the northern forces of the enemy at Sadowa on July 3, and within three weeks had reached the environs of Vienna and practically won the war. Lissa was fought on July 20, just 6 days before the armistice. This general political and military situation should be borne in mind as throwing some light on the peculiar Italian strategy in the Lissa campaign.

Struggling Italy, her unification under the House of Piedmont as yet only partly achieved, had shown both foresight and energy in building up a fleet. Her available force on the day of Lissa consisted of 12 armored ships and 16 wooden steam vessels of some fighting value. The ironclads included 7 armored frigates, the best of which were the two "kings," *Re d'Italia* and *Re di Portogallo*, built the year before in New York (rather badly, it is said), each armed with about 30 heavy rifles. Then there was the new single-turret ram *Affondatore*, or "Sinker," with two 300-pounder 10-inch rifles, which came in from England only the day before the battle. Some of the small protected corvettes and gunboats were of much less value, the *Palestro*, for instance, which suffered severely in the fight, having a thin sheet of armor over only two-fifths of her exposed hull.

The Austrian fleet had the benefit of some war experience against Denmark in the North Sea two years before, but it was far inferior and less up-to-date, its armored ships consisting of 7 screw frigates armed chiefly with smoothbores. Of the wooden ships, there were 7 screw frigates and corvettes, 9 gunboats and schooners, and 3 little side-wheelers—a total of 19. The following table indicates the relative strength:

	Armored		Wooden		Small craft		Total		Rifles		Total w't of metal
	No.	Guns	No.	Guns	No.	Guns	No.	Guns	No.	Weight	
Austria	7	176	7	304	12	52	22	532	121	7,130	23,538
Italy..	12	243	11	382	5	16	28	641	276	28,700	53,236

Thus in general terms the Italians were nearly twice as strong in main units, could fire twice as heavy a weight of metal from all their guns, and four times as heavy from their rifles. Even without the *Affondatore,* their advantage was practically as great as this from the beginning of the war.

With such a preponderance, it would seem as if Persano, the Italian commander in chief, could easily have executed his savage-sounding orders to "sweep the enemy from the Adriatic, and to attack and blockade them wherever found." He was dilatory, however, in assembling his fleet, negligent in practice and gun drill, and passive in his whole policy to a degree absolutely ruinous to morale. War was declared June 20, and had long been foreseen; yet it was June 25 before he moved the bulk of his fleet from Taranto to Ancona in the Adriatic. Here on the 27th they were challenged by 13 Austrian ships, which lay off the port cleared for action for two hours, while Persano made no real move to fight. It is said that the Italian defeat at Custozza three days before had taken the heart out of him. On July 8 he put to sea for a brief three days' cruise and went through some maneuvers and signaling but no firing, though many of the guns were newly mounted and had never been tried by their crews.

At this time Napoleon III of France had already undertaken mediation between the hostile powers. In spite of the orders of June 8, quoted above, which seem sufficiently definite, and urgent orders to the same effect later, Persano was unwilling to take the offensive, and kept complaining of lack of clear instructions as to what he should do. He was later convicted of cowardice and negligence; but the campaign he finally undertook against Lissa was dangerous enough, and it seems possible that some secret political maneuvering was partly responsible for his earlier delay.[1]

It is significant at least that the final proposal to make a descent upon the fortified island of Lissa came not from Persano but from the Minister of Marine. On July 15 the latter took up the project with the fleet chief of staff, d'Amico, and with Rear Admiral Vacca, but not until later with Persano. All agreed that the prospect of a truce allowed no time for a movement against Venice or the Austrian base at Pola, but that they should strike a swift stroke elsewhere. Lissa commanded the Dalmatian coast, was essential to naval control in the Adriatic, and was coveted by Italy then as in later times. It would be better than trying to crush the enemy fleet at the risk of her own if she could enter the peace conference with possession of Lissa a *fait accompli*.

Undertaken in the face of an undefeated enemy fleet, this move has been justly condemned by naval strategists. But with a less alert opponent the coup might have succeeded. Tegetthoff, the Austrian commander, was not yet 41 years of age, but had been in active naval service since he was 18, and had led a squadron bravely in a fight with the Danes two years before off Heligoland. He had his heterogeneous array of fighting craft assembled at Pola at the outbreak of war. "Give me everything you have," he told the Admiralty when they asked him what ships he wanted; "I'll find some use for them." His crews were partly men of Slav and Italian stock from the Adriatic coast, including 600 from Venice; there is no reason for supposing them better than those of Persano. The influ-

---

[1] In July Persano wrote to the Deputy Boggio: "Leave the care of my reputation to me; I would rather be wrongly dishonored than rightly condemned. Patience will bring peace; I shall be called a traitor, but nevertheless Italy will have her fleet intact, and that of Austria will be rendered useless." Quoted in Bernotti, IL POTERE MARITTIMO NELLA GRANDE GUERRA, p. 177.

ence of their leader, however, inspired them with loyalty and fighting spirit, and their defiance of the Italians at Ancona on June 27 increased their confidence. When successive cable messages from Lissa satisfied him that the Italian fleet was not attempting a diversion but was actually committed to an attack on the island, Tegetthoff set out thither on July 19 with his entire fighting force. His order of sailing was the order of battle. "Every captain knew the admiral's intention as well as the admiral himself did; every officer knew what had to be done, and every man had some idea of it, and above all knew that he had to fight." [1]

In the meantime the Italian drive on Lissa had gone ahead slowly. The island batteries were on commanding heights and manned by marines and artillerymen resolved to fight to the last ditch. During the second day's bombardment the *Affondatore* appeared, and also some additional troops needed to complete the landing force. Two-thirds of the guns on shore were silenced that day, and if the landing operations had been pushed, the island captured, and the fleet taken into the protected harbor of St. Giorgio, Tegetthoff would have had a harder problem to solve. But as the mist blew away with a southerly wind at 10 o'clock on the next day, July 20, the weary garrison on the heights of the island gave cheer after cheer as they saw the Austrian squadron plunging through the head seas at full speed from the northeastward, while the Italian ships hurriedly drew together north of the island to meet the blow.

The Austrians advanced in three successive divisions, ironclads, wooden frigates, and finally the smaller vessels, each in a wedge-shaped formation (shown by the diagram), with the apex toward the enemy. The object was to drive through the Italian line if possible near the van and bring on a close scrimmage in which all ships could take part, ramming tactics could be employed, and the enemy would profit less by their superiority in armor and guns. Like Nelson's at Trafalgar, Tegetthoff's formation was one not likely to be imitated, but it was

[1] Laughton, STUDIES IN NAVAL HISTORY, Tegetthoff, p. 164.

at least simple and well understood, and against a passive resistance it gave the results planned.

"Ecco i pescatori!" (Here come the fishermen), cried Persano, with a scorn he was far from actually feeling. The Italians were in fact caught at a disadvantage. One of their best

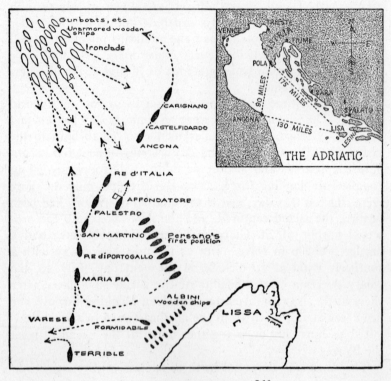

BATTLE OF LISSA, JULY 20, 1866

ships, the *Formidabile,* had been put *hors de combat* by the
batteries on the day before. Another, coming in late from the
west end of the island, took no part in the action. The wooden
ships, owing to the cowardice of their commander, Albini, also
kept out of the fight, though Persano signaled desperately to
them to enter the engagement and "surround the enemy rear."
With his remaining ironclads Persano formed three divisions

of three ships each and swung across the enemy's bows in line ahead. Just at the critical moment, and for no very explicable motive, he shifted his flag from the *Re d'Italia* in the center to the *Affondatore*, which was steaming alone on the starboard side of the line. The change was not noted by all his ships, and thus caused confusion of orders. The delay involved also left a wider gap between van and center, and through this the Austrians plunged, Tegetthoff in his flagship *Erzherzog Ferdinand Max* leading the way.

Here orderly formation ended, and only the more striking episodes stand out in a desperate close combat, during which the black ships of Austria and the gray of Italy rammed or fired into each other amid a smother of smoke and spray. The Austrian left flank and rear held up the Italian van; the Austrian ironclads engaged the Italian center; and the wooden ships of the Austrian middle division, led by the 92-gun *Kaiser*, smashed into the Italian rear. Of all the Austrian ships, the big *Kaiser*, a relic of other days, saw the hardest fighting. Twice she avoided the *Affondatore's* ram, and she was struck by one of her 300-pound projectiles. Then the *Re di Portogallo* bore down, but Petz, the *Kaiser's* captain, rang for full speed ahead and steered for the ironclad, striking a glancing blow and scraping past her, while both ships poured in a heavy fire. The *Kaiser* soon afterward drew out of the action, her foremast and funnel down, and a bad blaze burning amidships. Altogether she fired 850 rounds in the action, or about one-fifth of the total fired by the Austrians, and she received 80 hits, again one-fifth of the total. Of the 38 Austrians killed and 138 wounded in the battle, she lost respectively 24 and 75.

The *Kaiser's* combat, though more severe, was typical of what was going on elsewhere. The Italian gunboat *Palestro* was forced to withdraw to fight a fire that threatened her magazines. The *Re d'Italia*, which was at first supposed by the Austrians to be Persano's flagship, was a center of attack and had her steering gear disabled. As she could go only straight ahead or astern, the Austrian flagship seized the chance and rammed her squarely amidships at full speed, crashing through her armor and opening an immense hole. The Italian gunboat heeled over to starboard, then back again, and in a few seconds went down, with a loss of 381 men.

This spectacular incident practically decided the battle. After an hour's fighting the two squadrons drew apart about noon, the Austrians finally entering St. Giorgio harbor and the Italians withdrawing to westward. During the retreat the fire on the *Palestro* reached her ammunition and she blew up with a loss of 231 of her crew. Except in the two vessels destroyed, the Italian losses were slight—8 killed and 40 wounded. But the armored ships were badly battered, and less than a month later the *Affondatore* sank in a squall in Ancona harbor, partly, it was thought, owing to injuries received at Lissa.

For a long time after this fight, an exaggerated view was held regarding the value of ramming, line abreast formation, and bow fire. Weapons condition tactics, and these tactics of Tegetthoff were suited to the means he had to work with. But they were not those which should have been adopted by his opponents; nor would they have been successful had the Italians brought their broadsides to bear on a parallel course and avoided a mêlée. What the whole campaign best illustrates—and the lesson has permanent interest—is how a passive and defensive policy, forced upon the Italian fleet by the incompetence of its admiral or otherwise, led to its demoralization and ultimate destruction. After a long period of inactivity, Persano weakened his force against shore defenses before he had disposed of the enemy fleet, and was then taken at a disadvantage. His passive strategy was reflected in his tactics. He engaged with only a part of his force, and without a definite plan; "A storm of signals swept over his squadron" as it went into action. What really decided the battle was not the difference in ships, crews, or weapons, but the difference in aggressiveness and ability of the two admirals in command.

The Battle of the Yalu

Twenty-eight years elapsed after Lissa before the next significant naval action, the Battle of the Yalu, between fleets of China and Japan. Yet the two engagements may well be taken together, since at the Yalu types and tactics were still transitional, and the initial situation at Lissa was duplicated— line abreast against line ahead. The result, however, was reversed, for the Japanese in line ahead took the initiative, used their superior speed to conduct the battle on their own terms, and won the day.

Trouble arose in the Far East over the dissolution of the decrepit monarchy of Korea, upon which both Japan and China cast covetous eyes. As nominal suzerain, China in the spring of 1894 sent 2000 troops to Korea to suppress an insurrection. Japan countered by despatching 5000 troops, and on July 20 demanded that China renounce all claim to suzerainty. With no formal war declaration, hostilities broke out on July 25, when four fast Japanese cruisers, including the *Naniwa Kan* under the future Admiral Togo, fell upon the Chinese cruiser *Tsi-yuen* and two smaller vessels, captured the latter and battered the cruiser badly before she got away, and then to complete the day's work sank a Chinese troop transport, saving only the European officers on board.

After this affair the Chinese Admiral Ting, a former cavalry officer but with some naval experience, favored taking the offensive, since control of the sea by China would at once decide the war. But the Chinese Foreign Council gave him orders not to cruise east of a line from Shantung to the mouth of the Yalu. Reverses on land soon forced him to give all his time to troop transportation, and this occupied both navies throughout the summer.

On September 16, the day before the Battle of the Yalu, the Chinese battleships escorted transports with 5000 troops to the mouth of the Yalu, and on the following morning they were anchored quietly outside the river. "For weeks," writes an American naval officer who was in command of one of the Chinese battleships, "we had anticipated an engagement, and had had daily exercise at general quarters, etc., and little remained to be done. . . . The fleet went into action as well prepared as it was humanly possible for it to be with the same officers and men, handicapped as they were by official corruption and treachery ashore." [1]   As the midday meal was in preparation, columns of black smoke appeared to southwestward.   The squadron at once weighed anchor, cleared for action, and put on forced draft, while "dark-skinned men, with queues tightly coiled around their heads, and with arms bare to the elbow, clustered along the decks in groups at the guns, waiting to kill or be killed."   Out of the smoke soon emerged 12 enemy cruisers which, with information of the Chinese movements, had entered the Gulf intent on battle.

The forces about to engage included the best ships of both nations.   There were 12 on each side, excluding 4 Chinese torpedo boats, and 10 actually in each battle line.   The main strength of the Chinese was concentrated in two second-class battleships, the *Ting-yuen* and the *Chen-yuen,* Stettin-built in 1882, each of 7430 tons, with 14-inch armor over half its length, four 12-inch Krupp guns in two barbettes, and 6-inch rifles at bow and stern.   The two barbettes were *en echelon* (the starboard just ahead of the port), in such a way that while all four guns could fire dead ahead only two could bear on the port quarter or the starboard bow.   These ships were designed for fighting head-on; and hence to use them to best advantage Admiral Ting formed his squadron in line abreast, with the *Ting-yuen* and *Chen-yuen* in the center.   The rest of the line were a "scratch lot" of much smaller vessels—two armored cruisers (*Lai-yuen* and *King-yuen*) with 8 to 9-inch armored belts; three protected cruisers (*Tsi-yuen, Chi-yuen,* and *Kwang-ping*) with 2 to 4-inch armored decks; on the left flank the old corvette *Kwang-chia;* and opposite her two other "lame ducks" of only 1300 tons, the *Chao-yung* and *Yang-wei.* Ting had properly strengthened his center, but had left his flanks fatally weak.   On board the flagship *Ting-yuen* was Major von Hannekin, China's military adviser, and an ex-

[1] Commander P. N. McGiffin, THE BATTLE OF THE YALU, *Century Magazine.* August, 1895, pp. 585-604.

petty officer of the British navy named Nichols. Philo N. Mc-Giffin, a graduate of the United States Naval Academy, commanded the *Chen-yuen.*

The Japanese advanced in column, or line ahead, in two divisions. The first, or "flying squadron," was led by Rear Admiral Tsuboi in the *Yoshino,* and consisted of four fast protected cruisers. Four similar ships, headed by Vice Admiral Ito in the *Matsushima,* formed the chief units of the main squadron, followed by the older and slower ironclads, *Fuso* and *Hiyei.* The little gunboat *Akagi* and the converted steamer *Saikio Maru* had orders not to engage, but nevertheless pushed in on the left of the line. Aside from their two battleships, the Chinese had nothing to compare with these eight new and well-armed cruisers, the slowest of which could make 17½ knots.

In armament the Japanese also had a marked advantage, as the following table, from Wilson's *Ironclads in Action,* will show:

SHIPS	GUNS			SHOTS IN 10 MINUTES	
Number	6-inch	Large quick fire	Small q. f. and machine	Number	Weight of metal
China....... 12	40	2	130	33	4,885
Japan....... 10	34	66	154	185	11,706

The smaller quick-fire and machine guns proved of slight value on either side, but the large Japanese quick-firers searched all unprotected parts of the enemy ships with a terrific storm of shells. After the experience of July 25, the Chinese had discarded much of their woodwork and top hamper, including boats, thin steel gun-shields, rails, needless rigging, etc., and used coal and sand bags on the upper decks; but the unarmored ships nevertheless suffered severely. From the table it is evident that the Japanese could pour in six times as great a volume of fire. The Chinese had a slight advantage in heavier guns, and their marksmanship, it is claimed, was equally accurate (possibly 10% hits on each side), but their ammunition was defective and consisted mostly of non-bursting projectiles. They had only 15 rounds of shell for each gun.

During the approach the Japanese steered at first for the enemy center, thus concealing their precise objective, and then swung to port, with the aim of attacking on the weaker side of the Chinese battleships (owing to their barbette arrangement) and on the weaker flank of the line. In the meantime the Chinese steamed forward at about 6 knots and turned somewhat to keep head-on, thus forcing the Japanese to file across their bows. At 12.20 p.m. the *Chen-yuen* and *Ting-yuen* opened at 5800 yards on Tsuboi's squadron, which held its fire until at 3000 yards or closer it swung around the Chinese right wing.

The main squadron followed. Admiral Ito has been criticized for thus drawing his line across the enemy's advance, instead of attacking their left flank. But he was previously committed to the movement, and executed it rapidly and for the most part at long range. Had the Chinese pressed forward at best speed, Lissa might have been repeated. As it was, they cut off only the *Hiyei*. To avoid ramming, this old ironclad plunged boldly between the *Chen-yuen* and *Ting-yuen*. She was hit 22 times and had 56 killed and wounded, but managed to pull through.

Before this time the *Chao-yung* and *Yang-wei* on the right flank of the Chinese line had crumpled under a heavy cross-fire from the flying squadron. These ships had wooden cabins on deck outboard, and the whole superstructure soon became roaring masses of flames. Both dropped out of line and burned to the water's edge. The two ships on the opposite flank had seized an early opportunity to withdraw astern of the line, and were now off for Port Arthur under full steam, "followed," writes McGiffin, "by a string of Chinese anathemas from our men at the guns."

The Japanese van turned to port and was thus for some

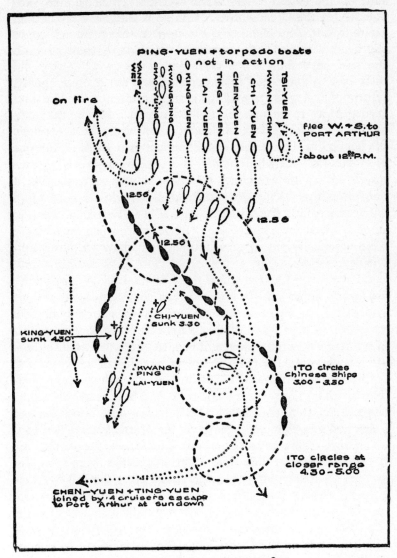

BATTLE OF THE YALU, SEPT. 17, 1894

time out of action. The main division turned to starboard
and circled the Chinese rear. Of the 6 Chinese ships left in
the line, the four smaller seem now to have moved on to
southward, while both Japanese divisions concentrated on
the two battleships *Chen-yuen* and *Ting-yuen*. These did
their best to keep head to the enemy, and stood up doggedly,
returning slowly the fire of the circling cruisers. Tsuboi soon
turned away to engage the lighter vessels. Finally, at 3.26,
as the *Matsushima* closed to about 2000 yards, the *Chen-yuen*
hit her fairly with a last remaining 12-inch shell. This one
blow put Ito's flagship out of action, exploding some ammunition, killing or wounding 50 or more men, and starting a
dangerous fire. The Japanese hauled off, while according to
Chinese accounts the battleships actually followed, but at 4.30
came again under a severe fire. About 5.30, when the Chinese
were practically out of ammunition, Ito finally withdrew and
recalled his van.

Of the other Chinese ships, the *Chi-yuen* made a desperate
attempt to approach the Japanese van and went down at 3.30
with screws racing in the air. The *King-yuen,* already on fire,
was shot to pieces and sunk an hour later by the *Yoshino's*
quick-firers. As the sun went down, the *Lai-yuen* and *Kwang-
ping,* with two ships from the river mouth, fell in behind the
battleships and staggered off towards Port Arthur, unpursued.
The losses on the two armored ships had been relatively slight
—56 killed and wounded. The Japanese lost altogether 90
killed and 204 wounded, chiefly on the *Matsushima* and *Hiyei*.

Though China saved her best ships from the battle, her
fighting spirit was done for. The battleships were later destroyed by Japanese torpedo operations after the fall of Wei-
hai-wei. Her crews had on the whole fought bravely, handicapped as they were by their poor materials and lack of skill.
For instance, when McGiffin called for volunteers to ex-
tinguish a fire on the *Chen-yuen's* forecastle, swept by enemy
shells, "men responded heartily and went to what seemed
to them certain death." It was at this time that the commander himself, leading the party, was knocked over by a

shell explosion and then barely escaped the blast of one of his own 12-inch guns by rolling through an open hatch and falling 8 feet to a pile of débris below.

In the way of lessons, aside from the obvious ones as to the value of training and expert leadership and the necessity of eliminating inflammables in ship construction, the battle revealed on the one hand the great resisting qualities of the armored ship, and on the other hand the offensive value of superior gunfire. Admiral Mahan said at the time, "The rapid fire gun has just now fairly established its position as the greatest offensive weapon in naval warfare." [1] Another authority has noted that, both at Lissa and the Yalu, "The winning fleet was worked in divisions, as was the British fleet in the Dutch wars and at Trafalgar, and the Japanese fleet afterwards at Tsushima." Remarking that experiments with this method were made by the British Channel Fleet in 1904, the writer continues: "The conception grew out of a study of Nelson's Memorandum. Its essence was to make the fleet flexible in the hands of the admiral, and to enable any part to be moved by the shortest line to the position where it was most required." [2]

By the Treaty of Shimonoseki (April 17, 1895) which closed the war, Japan won Port Arthur and the Liao-tung Peninsula, the Pescadores Islands and Formosa, and China's withdrawal from Korea. But just as she was about to lay hands on these generous fruits of victory, they were snatched out of her grasp by the European powers, which began exploiting China for themselves. Japan had to acquiesce and bide her time, using her war indemnity and foreign loans to build up her fleet. The Yalu thus not only marks the rise of Japan as a formidable force in international affairs, but brings us to a period of intensified colonial and commercial rivalry in the Far East and elsewhere which gave added significance to naval power and led to the war of 1914.

[1] LESSONS FROM THE YALU FIGHT, *Century Magazine*, August, 1895, p. 630.
[2] Custance, THE SHIP OF THE LINE IN BATTLE, p. 103.

REFERENCES

Aside from those already cited see:
ROBERT FULTON, ENGINEER AND ARTIST, H. W. Dickinson, 1913.
THE STORY OF THE GUNS, J. E. Tennant, 1864.
THE BRITISH NAVY, Sir Thomas Brassey, 1884.
CLOWES' HISTORY OF THE ROYAL NAVY, Vol. VII (p. 20, bibliography).
NAVAL DEVELOPMENT OF THE 19TH CENTURY, N. Barnaby, 1904.
THE TORPEDO IN PEACE AND WAR, F. T. Jane, 1898.
SUBMARINE WARFARE, H. C. Fyfe, 1902.
THE SUBMARINE IN WAR AND PEACE, Simon Lake, 1918.
FOUR MODERN NAVAL CAMPAIGNS, Lissa, W. L. Clowes, 1902.
THE AUSTRO-ITALIAN NAVAL WAR, Journal of the United Service
    Institution, Vol. XI, pp. 104ff.

CHAPTER XIV

RIVALRY FOR WORLD POWER

EVEN more significant in its relation to sea power than the revolution in armaments during the 19th century was the extraordinary growth of ocean commerce. The total value of the world's import and export trade in 1800 amounted in round numbers to 1½ billion dollars, in 1850 to 4 billion, and in 1900 to nearly 24 billion. In other words, during a period in which the population of the world was not more than tripled, its international exchange of commodities was increased 16-fold. This growth was of course made possible largely by progress in manufacturing, increased use of steam navigation, and vastly greater output of coal and iron.[1] At the end of the Napoleonic wars England was the only great commercial and industrial state. At the close of the century, though with her colonies she still controlled one-fourth of the world's foreign trade, she faced aggressive rivals in the field. The United States after her Civil War, and Germany after her unification and the Franco-Prussian War, had achieved an immense industrial development, opening up resources in coal and iron that made them formidable competitors. Germany in particular, a late comer in the colonial field, felt that her future lay upon the seas, as a means of securing access on favorable terms to world markets and raw materials. Other nations also realized that their continued growth and prosperity would depend upon commercial expansion. This might be accomplished in a measure by cheaper production and superior business organization, but could be greatly aided by political means—by colonial activity, by securing control

---

[1] Coal production increased during the century from 11.6 million tons to 610 million, and pig iron from half a million tons to 37 million. Figures from Day, HISTORY OF COMMERCE, Ch. XXVIII.

or special privileges in unexploited areas and backward states, by building up a merchant fleet under the national flag. Obviously, since the seas join the continents and form the great highways of trade, this commercial and political expansion would give increased importance to naval power.

Admiral Mahan, an acute political observer as well as strategist, summed up the international situation in 1895 and again in 1897 as "an equilibrium on the [European] Continent, and, in connection with the calm thus resulting, an immense colonizing movement in which all the great powers were concerned." [1] Later, in 1911, he noted that colonial rivalries had again been superseded by rivalries within Europe, but pointed out that the European tension was itself largely the product of activities and ambitions in more distant spheres. In fact the international developments of recent times, whether in the form of colonial enterprises, armament competition, or actual warfare, find a common origin in economic and commercial interests. Commerce and quick communications have drawn the world into closer unity, yet by a kind of paradox have increased the possibilities of conflict. Both by their common origin and by their far-reaching consequences, it is thus possible to connect the story of naval events from the Spanish-American to the World War, and to gather them up under the general title, "rivalry for world power."

I.   THE SPANISH-AMERICAN WAR

To this rivalry the United States could hardly hope or desire to remain always a passive spectator, yet, aside from trying to stabilize the western hemisphere by the Monroe Doctrine, she cherished down to the year 1898 a policy of isolation from world affairs. During the first half of the 19th century, it is true, her interests were directed outward by a flourishing merchant marine. In 1860 the American merchant fleet of 2,500,000 tons was second only to Great Britain's and nearly equal to that of all other nations combined. But its decay had already begun, and continued rap-

[1] NAVAL STRATEGY, p. 104.

idly. The change from wood to iron construction enabled England to build cheaper ships; and American shipping suffered also from lack of government patronage, diversion of capital into more profitable projects of Western development, and loss of a third of its tonnage by destruction or shift to foreign register during the Civil War. At the outbreak of that war 72 per cent of American exports were carried in American bottoms; only 9 per cent in 1913. Thus the United States had reached the unsatisfactory condition of a nation with a large and rapidly growing foreign commerce and an almost non-existent merchant marine.

This was the situation when the nation was thrust suddenly and half unwillingly into the main stream of international events by the Spanish-American War. Though this war made the United States a world power, commercial or political aggrandizement played no part in her entry into the struggle. It arose solely from the intolerable conditions created by Spanish misrule in Cuba, and intensified by armed rebellion since 1895. Whatever slight hope or justification for non-intervention remained was destroyed by the blowing up of the *U. S. S. Maine* in Havana harbor, February 15, 1898, with the loss of 260 of her complement of 354 officers and men. Thereafter the United States pushed her preparations for war; but the resolution of Congress, April 19, 1898, authorizing the President to begin hostilities expressly stated that the United States disclaimed any intention to exercise sovereignty over Cuba, and after its pacification would "leave the government and control of the island to its people."

It was at once recognized that the conflict would be primarily naval, and would be won by the nation that secured control of the sea. The paper strength of the two navies left little to choose, and led even competent critics like Admiral Colomb in England to prophesy a stalemate—a "desultory war." Against five new American battleships, the *Iowa, Indiana, Massachusetts, Oregon* and *Texas,* the first four of 10,000 tons, and the armored cruisers *Brooklyn* and *New York* of 9000 and 8000 tons, Spain could oppose the battleship *Pelayo,* a little better than the *Texas,* and five armored cruisers, the

Carlos V, Infanta Maria Teresa, Almirante Oquendo, and *Vizcaya,* each of about 7000 tons, and the somewhat larger and very able former Italian cruiser *Cristobal Colon.* Figures and statistics, however, give no idea of the actual weakness of the Spanish navy, handicapped by shiftless naval administration, by dependence on foreign sources of supply, and by the incompetence and lack of training of personnel. Of the squadron that came to Cuba under Admiral Cervera, the *Colon* lacked two 10-inch guns for her barbettes, and the *Vizcaya* was so foul under water that with a trial speed of 18½ knots she never made above 13—Cervera called her a "buoy." There was no settled plan of campaign; to Cervera's requests for instructions came the ministerial reply that "in these moments of international crisis no definite plans can be formulated." [1] The despairing letters of the Spanish Admiral and his subordinates reveal how feeble was the reed upon which Spain had to depend for the preservation of her colonial empire. The four cruisers and two destroyers that sailed from the Cape Verde Islands on April 29 were Spain's total force available. The *Pelayo* and the *Carlos V,* not yet ready, were the only ships of value left behind.

On the American naval list, in addition to the main units already mentioned, there were six monitors of heavy armament but indifferent fighting value, a considerable force of small cruisers, four converted liners for scouts, and a large number of gunboats, converted yachts, etc., which proved useful in the Cuban blockade. Of these forces the majority were assembled in the Atlantic theater of war. The *Oregon* was on the West Coast, and made her famous voyage of 14,700 miles around Cape Horn in 79 days, at an average speed of 11.6 knots, leaving Puget Sound on March 6 and touching at Barbados in the West Indies on May 18, just as the Spanish fleet was steaming across the Caribbean. The cruise effectively demonstrated the danger of a divided navy and the need of an Isthmian canal. Under Commodore Dewey in the Far East were two gunboats and four small cruisers, the

[1] Bermejo to Cervera, April 4, 1898.

best of them the fast and heavily armed flagship *Olympia*, of 5800 tons.

The Battle of Manila Bay

With this latter force the first blow of the war was struck on May 1 in Manila Bay. Dewey, largely through the influence of Assistant Secretary of the Navy Roosevelt, had

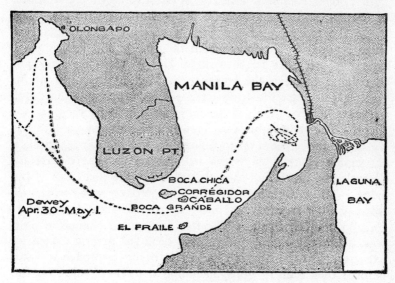

APPROACHES TO MANILA

been appointed to the eastern command the autumn before. On reaching his station in January, he took his squadron to Hong Kong to be close to the scene of possible hostilities. On February 25 he received a despatch from Roosevelt, then Acting Secretary: "Keep full of coal. In the event of declaration of war Spain, your duty will be to see that Spanish squadron does not leave the Asiatic coast, and then offensive operations in the Philippine Islands." On April 25 came the inspiring order: "Proceed at once to Philippine Islands. Commence operations particularly against the Spanish fleet. You must capture vessels or destroy. Use utmost endeavor." The

Commodore had already purchased a collier and a supply ship for use in addition to the revenue cutter *McCulloch,* overhauled his vessels and given them a war coat of slate-gray, and made plans for a base at Mirs Bay, 30 miles distant in Chinese waters, where he would be less troubled by neutrality rules in time of war. On April 22 the *Baltimore* arrived from San Francisco with much-needed ammunition. On the 27th Consul Williams joined with latest news of preparations at Manila, and that afternoon the squadron put to sea.

On the morning of the 30th it was off Luzon, and two ships scouted Subig Bay, which the enemy had left only 24 hours before. At 12 that night Dewey took his squadron in column through the entrance to Manila Bay, just as he had steamed past the forts on the Mississippi with Farragut 35 years before. Only three shots were fired by the guns on shore. The thoroughness of Dewey's preparations, the rapidity of his movements up to this point, and his daring passage through a channel which he had reason to believe strongly defended by mines and shore batteries are the just titles of his fame. The entrance to Manila is indeed 10 miles wide and divided into separate channels by the islands Corregidor, Caballo, and El Fraile. The less frequented channel chosen was, as Dewey rightly judged, too deep for mining except by experts. Yet the Spanish had news of his approach the day before; they had 17 guns, including 6 modern rifles, on the islands guarding the entrance; they had plenty of gunboats that might have been fitted out as torpedo launches for night attack. It does not detract from the American officer's accomplishment that he drew no false picture of the obstacles with which he had to deal.

At daybreak next morning, having covered slowly the 24 miles from the mouth of the bay up to Manila, the American ships advanced past the city to attack the Spanish flotilla drawn up under the Cavite batteries 6 miles beyond. Here was what an American officer described as "a collection of old tubs scarcely fit to be called men-of-war." The most serviceable was Admiral Montojo's flagship *Reina Cristina,* an unarmored cruiser of 3500 tons; the remaining half dozen were

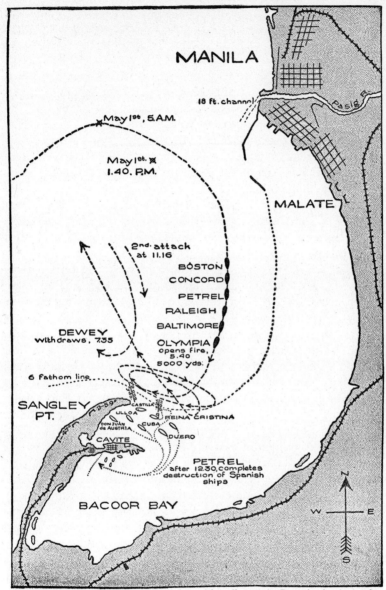

MANILA

18 ft. channel

May 1st, 5.A.M.

May 1st. 1.40. P.M.

MALATE

2nd. attack at 11.16

BOSTON
CONCORD
PETREL
RALEIGH
BALTIMORE
OLYMPIA
opens fire,
5.40
5000 yds.

DEWEY
withdraws, 7.35

6 fathom line

SANGLEY
PT.

CASTILLA
ULLOA
DON JUAN
de AUSTRIA
REINA CRISTINA
CUBA
DUERO
CAVITE

PETREL
after 12.30, completes
destruction of Spanish
ships

BACOOR BAY

N
W — E
S

After diagram in Dewey's *Autobiography.*

BATTLE OF MANILA, MAY 1, 1898

older ships of both wood and iron, some of them not able to get under way. They mounted 31 guns above 4-inch to the Americans' 53. More serious in prospect, though not in reality, was the danger from shore batteries and mines. The United States vessels approached in column, led by the *Olympia*, which opened fire at 5.40. In the words of Admiral Dewey's report. "The squadron maintained a continuous and precise fire at ranges varying from 5000 to 2000 yards, countermarching in a line approximately parallel to that of the Spanish fleet. The enemy's fire was vigorous, but generally ineffective. Three runs were made from the eastward and three from the westward, so that both broadsides were brought to bear." One torpedo launch which dashed out was sunk and another driven ashore. The *Cristina* moved out as if to ram, but staggered back under the *Olympia's* concentrated fire. At 7.35, owing to a mistaken report that only 15 rounds of ammunition were left for the 5-inch guns, the American squadron retired temporarily, but renewed action at 11.16 and ended it an hour later, when the batteries were silenced and "every enemy ship sunk, burned or deserted."

As reported by Admiral Montojo, the Spanish lost 381 men. The American ships were hit only 15 times and had 7 men slightly injured. Volume and accuracy of gunfire won the day. Somewhat extravagant language has been used in describing the battle, which, whatever the perils that might naturally have been expected, was a most one-sided affair. But it is less easy to overpraise Admiral Dewey's energetic and aggressive handling of the entire campaign.

Manila thereafter lay helpless under the guns of the squadron, and upon the arrival and landing of troops surrendered on August 13, after a merely formal defense. In the interim, Spain sent out a relief force under Admiral Camara consisting of the *Pelaya, Carlos V* and other smaller units, before encountering which Dewey planned to leave Manila and await the arrival of two monitors then on their way from San Francisco. After getting through the Suez Canal, Camara was brought back (July 8) by an American threat against the coast of Spain.

Soon after the battle a number of foreign warships congregated at Manila, including 5 German ships under Admiral von Diedrichs, a force superior to Dewey's, and apparently bent on learning by persistent contravention all the rules of a blockaded port. The message finally sent to the German Admiral is reticently described by Dewey himself, but is said to have been to the effect that, if the German admiral wanted a fight, "he could have it right now." On the day of the surrender of Manila the British and the Japanese ships in the harbor took a position between the American and the German squadrons. This was just after the seizure of Kiao-chau, at a time when Germany was vigorously pushing out for "a place in the sun." But for the American commander's quiet yet firm stand, with British support, the United States might have encountered more serious complications in taking over 127,000 square miles of archipelago in the eastern world, with important trade interests, a lively insurrection, and a population of 7 million.

The Santiago Campaign

In the Atlantic, where it was the American policy not to carry their offensive beyond Spain's West Indies possessions, events moved more slowly. Rear Admiral Sicard, in command of the North Atlantic squadron based on Key West, was retired in March for physical disability and succeeded by William T. Sampson, who stepped up naturally from senior captain in the squadron and was already distinguished for executive ability and knowledge of ordnance. Sampson's first proposal was, in the event of hostilities, a bombardment of Havana, a plan approved by all his captains and showing a confidence inspired perhaps by coastal operations in the Civil War; but this was properly vetoed by the Department on the ground that no ships should be risked against shore defenses until they had struck at the enemy's naval force and secured control of the sea. An earlier memorandum from Secretary Long, outlining plans for a blockade of Cuba, had been based on suggestions from Rear Admiral (then Captain) Mahan,[1] and his strategic insight may have guided this decision. On April 22, Sampson, now acting rear admiral, placed his force off Havana and established a close blockade over 100 miles on the northern coast.

The problem for American strategy was now Cervera's "fleet in being,"—inferior in force but a menace until destroyed or put out of action—which, as before stated, left the Cape Verde Islands on April 29, for a destination unknown. A bombardment of cities on the American coast or a raid on the North Atlantic trade routes was within the realm of possibilities. Difficulties of coaling and an inveterate tendency to leave the initiative to the enemy decided the Spanish against such a project. But its bare possibility set the whole east coast in a panic, which has been much ridiculed, but which arose naturally enough from a complete lack of instruction in naval matters and from lack of a sensible control of the press. The result was an unfortunate division of the fleet. A so-called Flying squadron under Commodore Schley, consisting of the *Brooklyn, Massachusetts, Texas,* and 3 small cruisers, was held at Hampton Roads; whereas, if not thus employed, these ships might have blockaded the south side of Cuba from the beginning of the war. A northern patrol squadron, of vessels not of much use for this or any other purpose, was also organized to guard the coast from Hampton Roads north.

On May 4, with Cervera still at large, Sampson lifted his guard of Havana—unwisely in the opinion of Mahan—and took his best ships, the *New York, Indiana, Iowa,* and two monitors, to reconnoiter San Juan, Porto Rico, where it was thought the missing fleet might first appear. Just as he was bombarding San Juan, on the morning of May 12, the Navy Department received a cable from Martinique announcing Cervera's arrival there. Havana and Cienfuegos (on the south side of Cuba and connected with Havana by rail) were considered the only two ports where the Spanish fleet could be of value to the forces on the island; and from these two

[1] Goode, WITH SAMPSON THROUGH THE WAR, p. 19.

ports both American squadrons were at this time a thousand miles away. Schley hastened southward, left Key West on the 19th, and was off Cienfuegos by daylight on the 21st. It was fairly quick work; but had the Spanish fleet moved thither at its usual speed of 6 knots from its last stopping-place, it would have got there first by at least 12 hours. The Spanish admiral, finding no coal at Martinique, had left a crippled destroyer there and moved on to the Dutch island of Curaçao, where on the 14th and 15th he secured with difficulty about 500 tons of fuel. Thence, in all anxiety, he made straight for the nearest possible refuge, Santiago, where he put in at daybreak on the 19th and was soon receiving congratulations on the completion of a successful cruise.

By the next day Sampson, having hurried back from San Juan and coaled, was again in force off Havana. There he received news of Cervera's arrival in Santiago. Since Havana could not be uncovered, he sent instructions to Schley—at first discretionary, and then, as the reports were confirmed, more imperative—to blockade the eastern port. Though the commander of the Flying Squadron received the latter orders on the 23d, he had seen smoke in Cienfuegos harbor and still believed he had Cervera cornered there. Accordingly he delayed until evening of the next day. Then, after reaching Santiago, he cabled on the 27th that he was returning to Key West to coal, though he had a collier with him and stringent orders to the contrary; and it was not until the 29th that he actually established the Santiago Blockade. Sampson, his superior in command (though not his senior in the captains' list), later declared his conduct at this time "reprehensible" [1]—possibly too harsh a term, for the circumstances tried judgment and leadership in the extreme. Cervera found Santiago destitute of facilities for refitting. Yet the fact

---

[1] Letter to Secretary, July 10, 1898, SAMPSON-SCHLEY DOCUMENTS, p. 136: "Had the commodore left his station at that time he probably would have been court-martialed, so plain was his duty. . . . This reprehensible conduct I cannot separate from his subsequent conduct, and for this reason I ask you to do him ample justice on this occasion." A court of inquiry later decided that Commodore Schley's service up to June 1 was characterized by "vacillation, dilatoriness, and lack of enterprise."

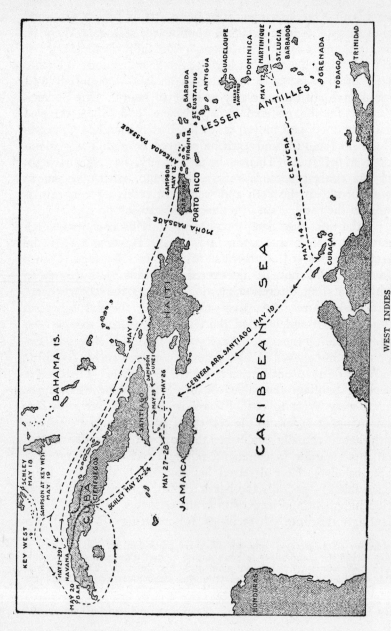

WEST INDIES

Movements in Santiago campaign.

remains that he had 10 days in which to coal and get away. "We cannot," writes Admiral Mahan, "expect ever again to have an enemy so inept as Spain showed herself to be."[1]

The "bottling up" of Cervera cleared the situation, and the navy could now concentrate on a task still difficult but well defined. Sampson brought his force to Santiago on June 1, and assumed immediate command. A close blockade was instituted such as against adequate torpedo and mine defenses would have been highly dangerous even at that day. Three picket launches were placed about a mile off shore, three small vessels a mile further out, and beyond these the 5 or 6 major units, under steam and headed toward the entrance in a carefully planned disposition to meet any attempt at escape. At night a battleship stood in and played its searchlight directly on the mouth of the channel. The latter was six miles in length, with difficult turns, and at the narrowest point only 300 feet wide. Lieut. Hobson's gallant effort on June 3 to sink the collier *Merrimac* across the channel had made its navigation even more difficult, though the vessel did not lie athwart-stream. Mine barriers and batteries on the high hills at the harbor mouth prevented forcing the channel, but the guns were mostly of ancient type and failed to keep the ships at a distance. On the other hand, bombardments from the latter did little more than to afford useful target practice.

The despatch of troops to Santiago was at once decided upon, and the subsequent campaign, if it could be fully studied, would afford interesting lessons in combined operations. On June 22, 16,000 men under General Shafter landed at Dai-quiri, 15 miles east of Santiago, in 52 boats provided by the fleet, though the War Department had previously stated that the general would "land his own troops."[2] "It was done in a scramble," writes Col. Roosevelt; and there was great difficulty in getting the skippers of army transports to bring their vessels within reasonable distance of the shore. Since the sole object of the campaign was to get at and destroy the enemy fleet, the navy fully expected and understood that the

[1] LESSONS OF THE WAR WITH SPAIN, p. 157.
[2] Goode, WITH SAMPSON THROUGH THE WAR, p. 182.

army would make its first aim to advance along the coast and
capture the batteries at the entrance, so that the mines could
be lifted and the harbor forced.   Army authorities declare
this would have involved division of forces on both sides of
the channel and impossibilities of transportation due to lack
of roads.   But these difficulties applied also in a measure to
the defenders, and might perhaps have been surmounted by
full use of naval aid.

Instead, the army set out with some confidence to capture
the city itself.   El Caney and San Juan Hill were seized on July
2 after a bloody struggle in which the Spanish stuck to their
defenses heroically and inflicted 1600 casualties.   By their own
figures the Spanish on this day had only 1700 men engaged,
though there were 36,500 Spanish troops in the province and
12,000 near at hand.   In considerable discouragement, Shafter
now spoke of withdrawal, and urged Sampson "immediately
to force the entrance" [1]—in spite of the fact that the main
purpose in sending troops had been to avoid this very measure.
In view of threatening foreign complications and the impossibility of replacing battleships, it was imperative not to risk
them against mines.

Food conditions were serious in Santiago, but Cervera
was absolutely determined not to assume responsibility for
taking his fleet out to what he regarded as certain slaughter.
A night sortie, with ships issuing one by one out of an intricate
channel into the glare of searchlights, he declared more difficult than one by day.   Fortunately for the Americans, in
view of the situation ashore, the decision was taken out of
his hands, and Governor General Blanco from Havana perem-
torily ordered him to put to sea.   The time of his exit, Sunday morning, July 3, was luckily chosen, for Sampson, in the
New York, was 10 miles to eastward on his way to a conference with Shafter, and the *Massachusetts* was at Guantanamo
for coal.   The flagship *Maria Teresa* led out at 9.35, followed
10 minutes later by the *Vizcaya,* and then by the *Colon,
Oquendo,* and the destroyers *Furor* and *Pluton,* each turning
westward at top speed.

[1] *Ibid.,* p. 190.

Simultaneously the big blockaders crowded toward them and opened a heavy fire, while stokers shoveled desperately below to get up steam. To the surprise of other vessels, Schley's ship, the *Brooklyn,* after heading towards the entrance, swung round, not with the enemy, but to starboard, just sliding past the *Texas'* bow. This much discussed maneuver Schley afterward explained as made to avoid blanketing the fire of the rest of the squadron. The *Oregon,* which throughout the blockade had kept plenty of steam, "rushed past

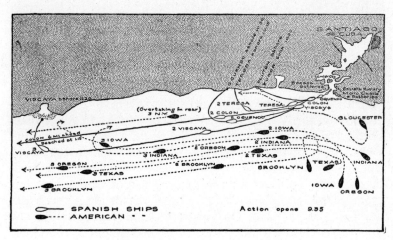

BATTLE OF SANTIAGO, JULY 3, 1898

the *Iowa,"* in the words of Captain Robley Evans, "like an express train," in a cloud of smoke lighted by vicious flashes from her guns. In ten minutes the *Maria Teresa* turned for shore, hit by 30 projectiles, her decks, encumbered with woodwork, bursting into masses of flame. The concentration upon her at the beginning had shifted to the *Oquendo* in the rear, which ran ashore with guns silenced 5 minutes after the leader.

Shortly before 11, the *Vizcaya,* with a torpedo ready in one of her bow tubes, turned towards the *Brooklyn,* which had kept in the lead of the American ships. A shell hitting squarely in the *Vizcaya's* bow caused a heavy explosion and she sheered away, the guns of the *Brooklyn, Oregon,* and

Iowa bearing on her as she ran towards the beach. The *Colon,* with a trial speed of 20 knots, and 6 miles ahead of the *Brooklyn* and *Oregon,* appeared to stand a good chance of getting finally away. The *New York,* rushing back toward the battle, was still well astern. But the *Colon's* speed, which had averaged 13.7 knots, slackened as her fire-room force played out; and shortly after 1 p.m. she ran shoreward, opened her Kingston valves, and went down after surrender. She had been hit only 6 times.

In the first stage of the fight the little yacht *Gloucester,* under Lieutenant Commander Wainwright, had dashed pluckily upon the two destroyers, which were also under fire from the secondary batteries of the big ships. The *Furor* was sunk and the *Plutón* driven ashore.

There is hardly a record in naval history of such complete destruction. Of 2300 Spaniards, 1800 were rescued as prisoners from the burning wrecks or from the Cuban guerillas on shore, 350 met their death, and the rest escaped towards Santiago. The American loss consisted of one man killed and one wounded on the *Brooklyn.* This ship, which owing to its leading position had been the chief enemy target, received 20 hits from shells or fragments, and the other vessels altogether about as many more. An examination of the half-sunken and fire-scarred Spanish hulks showed 42 hits out of 1300 rounds from the American main batteries, or 3.2 per cent, and 73 from secondary batteries. Probably these figures should be doubled to give the actual number, but even so they revealed the need of improvement in gunnery.

Sampson was right when he stated earlier in the campaign that the destruction of the Spanish fleet would end the war. Santiago surrendered a fortnight later without further fighting. An expeditionary force under General Miles made an easy conquest of Puerto Rico. On August 12, a protocol of peace was signed, by the terms of which the United States took over Puerto Rico, Guam, and the Philippines (upon payment of 20 million dollars), and Cuba became independent under American protection. The war greatly strengthened the position of the United States in the Caribbean, and gave her new interests and responsibilities in the Pacific. In the possession of distant dependencies the nation found a new motive for increased naval protection and for more active concern in international affairs.

2. THE RUSSO-JAPANESE WAR

At the time when the United States acquired the Philippines, the Far East was a storm center of international disturbance. Russia, with the support of Germany and France, had, as already noted, combined to prevent Japan from fully exploiting her victory over China. The latter country, however, had every appearance of a melon ripe for cutting; and under guise of security for loans, indemnity for injuries, railroad and treaty-port concessions, and special spheres of influence, each European nation endeavored to mark out its prospective share. Russia, in return for protecting China against Japan, gained a short-cut for her Siberian Railway across Northern Manchuria, with rail and mining concessions in that province and prospects of getting hold of both Port Arthur and Kiao-chau. But, at an opportune moment for Germany, two German missionaries were murdered in 1897 by Chinese bandits. Germany at once seized Kiao-chau, and in March, 1898, extorted a 99-year lease of the port, with exclusive development privileges throughout the peninsula of Shantung. "The German Michael," as Kaiser Wilhelm said at a banquet on the departure of his fleet to the East, had "firmly planted his shield upon Chinese soil"; and "the gospel of His Majesty's hallowed person," as Admiral Prince Heinrich asserted in reply, "was to be preached to every one who will hear it and also to those who do not wish to hear." "Our establishment on the coast of China," writes ex-Chancellor von Bülow, "was in direct and immediate connection with the progress of the fleet, and a first step into the field of world politics . . . giving us *a place in the sun* in Eastern Asia." [1]

Thus forestalled at Kiao-chau, Russia at once pushed

[1] From London *Spectator,* Dec. 26, 1897, quoted in Morse, INTERNATIONAL RELATIONS OF THE CHINESE EMPIRE, Vol. III, p. 108.

through a 25-year lease of Port Arthur, and proceeded to strengthen it as a fortified port and naval base. England, though preoccupied with the Boer War, took Wei-hai-wai as a precautionary measure, "for as long a time as Port Arthur

THEATER OF OPERATIONS, RUSSO-JAPANESE WAR

shall remain a possession of Russia."[1]   France secured a new base in southern China on Kwang-chau Bay, and Italy tried likewise but failed.   Aroused by the foreign menace, the feeling of the Chinese masses burst forth in the summer of 1900 in the massacres and uprisings known as the Boxer Rebellion.   In the combined expedition to relieve the legations at

[1] *Ibid.*, III, 118.

Peking Japanese troops displayed superior deftness, discipline, and endurance, and gained confidence in their ability to cope with the armies of European powers.

In the period following, Germany in Shantung and Russia in Manchuria pursued steadily their policy of exploitation. Against it, the American Secretary of State John Hay advanced the policy of the *Open Door,* "to preserve Chinese territorial and administrative entity . . . and safeguard for the world the principle of equal and impartial trade with all parts of the Chinese Empire." [1] To this the powers gave merely lip-service, realizing that her fixed policy of isolation would restrain the United States from either diplomatic combinations or force. "The open hand," wrote Hay in discouragement, "will not be so convincing to the poor devils of Chinese as the raised club," [2] nor was it so efficacious in dealing with other nations concerned. Japan, however, had strained every energy to build up her army and navy for a conflict that seemed inevitable, and was ready to back her opposition to European advances by force if need be. In 1902 she protected herself against a combination of foes by defensive alliance with England. She demanded that Russia take her troops out of Manchuria and recognize Japanese predominance in Korea. Russia hoped to forestall hostilities until she could further strengthen her army and fleet in the East, but when the transfer of ships reached the danger point, Japan struck viciously on the night of February 8, 1904, and two days later formally declared war.

As in the Spanish-American War, control of the sea was vital, since Japan must depend upon it to move her troops to the continental theater of war. Nor could she hold her army passive while awaiting the issue of a struggle for sea control. Delay would put a greater relative strain on her finances, and give Russia, handicapped by long communications over the single-track Siberian Railway, a better chance to mass in the East her troops and supplies. Japan's plan was therefore to strike hard for naval advantage, but to begin at once, in any

[1] Note to the European Powers, July 3, 1900.
[2] Thayer, Life of Hay, II, 369.

event, the movement of troops overseas.   At the outbreak of war her fleet of 6 battleships and 6 armored cruisers, with light cruiser and destroyer flotillas, was assembled at Sasebo near the Straits of Tsushima, thoroughly organized for fighting and imbued with the spirit of war.   Japan had an appreciable naval superiority, but was handicapped by the task of protecting her transports and by the necessity—which she felt keenly—of avoiding losses in battle which would leave her helpless upon the possible advent of Russia's Baltic reserves.

Russia's main naval strength in the East consisted of 7 battleships and 3 armored cruisers, presenting a combined broadside of 100 guns against Japan's 124.   The support of the Black Sea fleet was denied by the attitude of England, which would prevent violation of the agreement restricting it from passing the Dardanelles.   The Baltic fleet, however, was an important though distant reserve force, a detachment from which was actually in the Red Sea on its way east at the outbreak of war.

Just as clearly as it was Japan's policy to force the fighting on land, so it should have been Russia's to prevent Japan's movement of troops by aggressive action at sea.   This called for concentration of force and concentration of purpose.   But neither was evident in the Russian plan of campaign, which betrayed confusion of thought and a traditional leaning toward the defensive—acceptance on the one hand of what has been called "fortress fleet" doctrine, that fleets exist to protect bases and can serve this purpose by being shut up in them; and on the other hand of exaggerated "fleet in being" theory, that the mere presence of the Russian fleet, though inactive, would prevent Japan's use of the sea.   Thus in October, 1903, Witjeft, chief of the Port Arthur naval staff, declared that a landing of Japanese troops either in the Liaotung or the Korean Gulf was "impossible so long as our fleet is not destroyed."   Just as Russia's total force was divided between east and west, so her eastern force was divided between Vladivostok and Port Arthur, with the Japanese in central position between.   **Three armored cruisers were in** the northern port, and 7 battleships in the other; and all Russia's efforts after war broke out were vainly directed toward remedying this faulty disposition before it began. The whole Russian fleet in the East, moreover, was, it is said, badly demoralized and unready for war, owing chiefly to bureaucratic corruption and to the fact that not merely its strategical direction but its actual command was vested in the Viceroy, Alexieff, with headquarters on shore.

Operations Around Port Arthur

On January 3, 1904, Japan presented practically an ultimatum; on February 6 broke off diplomatic relations; on February 8 declared war; and on the same night—just as the Czar was discussing with his council what should be done—she delivered her first blow. By extraordinary laxity, though the diplomatic rupture was known, the Port Arthur squadron remained in the outer anchorage, "with all lights burning, without torpedo nets out, and without any guard vessels." [1] Ten Japanese destroyers attacked at close quarters, fired 18 torpedoes, and put the battleship *Tsarevitch* and two cruisers out of action for two months. It was only poor torpedo work, apparently, that saved the whole fleet from destruction. A Russian light cruiser left isolated at Chemulpo was destroyed the next day. The transportation of troops to Korea and Southern Manchuria was at once begun. Though not locked in by close blockade, and not seriously injured by the frequent Japanese raids, bombardments, and efforts to block the harbor entrance, the Port Arthur squadron made no move to interfere.

Both fleets suffered from mines. Vice Admiral Makaroff, Russia's foremost naval leader, who took command at Port Arthur in March, went down with the *Petropavlosk* on April 13, when his ship struck a mine laid by the Japanese. On May 14, on the other hand, the Russian mine-layer *Amur* slipped out in a fog, spread her mines in the usual path of Japanese vessels off the port, and thus on the same day sank

[1] Semenoff, RASPLATA, p. 45.

two of their best ships, the *Hatsuse* and *Yashima*. Mining, mine-sweeping, an uneventful Russian sortie on June 23, progress of Japanese land forces down the peninsula and close investment of Port Arthur—this was the course of events down to the final effort of the Russian squadron on August 10.

By this time Japanese siege guns were actually reaching

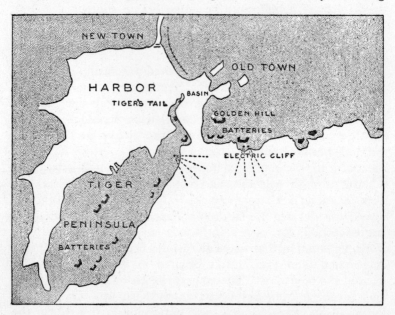

HARBOR OF PORT ARTHUR

ships in the harbor. Action of any kind, especially if it involved some injury to the enemy navy, was better than staying to be shot to pieces from the shore. Yet Makaroff's successor, Witjeft, painfully and consciously unequal to his responsibilities, still opposed an exit, and left port only upon imperative orders from above. Scarcely was the fleet an hour outside when Togo appeared on the scene. The forces in the Battle of August 10 consisted of 6 Russian battleships and 4 cruisers, against 6 Japanese armored vessels and 9 cruisers; the combined large-caliber broadsides of the armored ships being 73 to 5z, and of the cruisers 55 to 21, in favor of Togo's squadron. In spite of this superiority in armament, and of fully a knot in speed, Togo hesitated to close to decisive range. Five hours or more of complicated maneuvering ensued, during which both squadrons kept at "long bowls," now passing each other, now defiling across van or rear, without marked advantage for either side.

At last, at 5.40 p.m., the Japanese got in a lucky blow. Two 12-inch shells struck the flagship *Tsarevitch*, killing Admiral Witjeft, jamming the helm to starboard, and thus serving to throw the whole Russian line into confusion. Togo now closed to 3000 yards, but growing darkness enabled his quarry to escape. The battle in fact was less one-sided than the later engagement at Tsushima. On both sides the percentage of hits was low, about 1% for the Russians and 6 or 7% for their opponents. Togo's flagship *Mikasa* was hit 30 times and lost 125 men; the total Japanese loss was about half that of the enemy—236 to 478.

Much might still have been gained, in view of the future coming of the Baltic fleet, had the Russians still persisted in pressing onward for Vladivostok; but owing to loss of their leader and ignorance of the general plan, they scattered. The cruiser *Novik* was caught and sunk, another cruiser was interned at Shanghai, a third at Saigon, and the *Tsarevitch* at Kiao-chau. The rest, including 5 of the 6 battleships, fled back into the Port Arthur death-trap. Largely in order to complete their destruction, the Japanese sacrificed 60,000 men in desperate assaults on the fortress, which surrendered January 2, 1905. As at Santiago, the necessity of saving battleships, less easily replaced, led the Japanese to the cheaper expenditure of men.

On news of the Port Arthur sortie, the Vladivostok squadron, which hitherto had made only a few more or less futile raids on Japanese shipping, advanced toward Tsushima Straits, and met there at dawn of August 14 a slightly superior force of 4 cruisers under Kamimura. The better shooting of the Japanese soon drove the slowest Russian ship, the *Rurik*, out of line; the other two, after a plucky fight, managed to get away, with hulls and funnels riddled by enemy shells.

The complete annulment of Russia's eastern fleet in this first stage of hostilities had enabled Japan to profit fully by her easier communications to the scene of war. Its final destruction with the fall of Port Arthur gave assurance of victory. The decisive battle of Mukden was fought in March, 1905. Close to their bases, trained to the last degree, inspired by success, the Japanese navy could now face with confidence the approach of Russia's last fleet.

Rojdestvensky's Cruise

After a series of accidents and delays, the Baltic fleet under Admiral Rojdestvensky—8 battleships, 5 cruisers, 8 destroyers, and numerous auxiliaries—left Libau Oct. 18, 1904, on its 18,000-mile cruise. Off the Dogger Bank in the North Sea, the ships fired into English trawlers under the impression that they were enemy torpedo craft, and thus nearly stirred England to war. Off Tangier some of the lighter vessels separated to pass by way of Suez, and a third division from Russia followed a little later by the same route. Hamburg-American colliers helped Rojdestvensky solve his logistical problem on the long voyage round Africa, and German authorities stretched neutrality rules upon his arrival in Wahl-fish Bay, for the engrossment of Russia in eastern adventures was cheerfully encouraged by the neighbor on her southern frontier. France also did her best to be of service to the fleet of her ally, though she had "paired off" with England to remain neutral in the war.

With the reunion of the Russian divisions at Nossi Bé, Madagascar, January 9, 1905, came news of the fall of Port Arthur. The home government now concluded to despatch the fag-ends of its navy, though Rojdestvensky would have preferred to push ahead without waiting for such "superfluous encumbrances" to join. Ships, as his staff officer Semenoff afterward wrote, were needed, but not "old flatirons and

galoshes"; guns, but not "holes surrounded by iron." [1] After
a tedious 10 weeks' delay in tropical waters, the fleet moved on
to French Indo-China, where, after another month of waiting,
the last division under Nebogatoff finally joined—a slow old
battleship, 3 coast defense ironclads, and a cruiser. Upon these,
Rojdestvensky's officers vented their vocabulary of invective,
in which "war junk" and "auto-sinkers" were favorite terms.

Having already accomplished almost the impossible, the armada of 50 units on May 14 set forth on the last stage of its
extraordinary cruise. Of three possible routes to Vladivostok
—through the Tsugaru Strait between Nippon and Yezo,
through the Strait of La Perouse north of Yezo, or through
the Straits of Tsushima—the first was ruled out as too difficult of navigation; the second, because it would involve coaling off the coast of Japan. Tsushima remained. To avoid
torpedo attack, the Russian admiral planned to pass the straits
by day, and fully expected battle. But the hope lingered in
his mind that fog or heavy weather might enable him to pass
unscathed. He had been informed that owing to traffic conditions on the Siberian railway, he could get nothing at Vladivostok in the way of supplies. Hence, as a compromise measure which weakened fighting efficiency, he took along 3 auxiliary steamers, a repair ship, 2 tugs, and 2 hospital ships, the
rest of the train on May 25 entering Shanghai; and he so filled
the bunkers and piled even the decks with fuel, according to
Nebogatoff's later testimony, that they went into action burdened with coal for 3,000 miles. [2]

The main Russian fighting force entered the battle in three
divisions of 4 ships each: (1) the *Suvaroff* (flagship), *Alexander III, Borodino* and *Orel,* each a new battleship of about
13,600 tons; (2) the *Ossliabya,* a slightly smaller battleship,
and three armored cruisers; (3) Nebogatoff's division as
given above, with the exception of the cruiser. Then there
was a squadron of 4 smaller cruisers, 4 other cruisers as scouts,
and 9 destroyers. The Japanese engaged in two main divisions
of 6 ships each (4 battleships and 8 armored cruisers), backed

[1] Rasplata, p. 426.
[2] Mahan, Naval Strategy, p. 412.

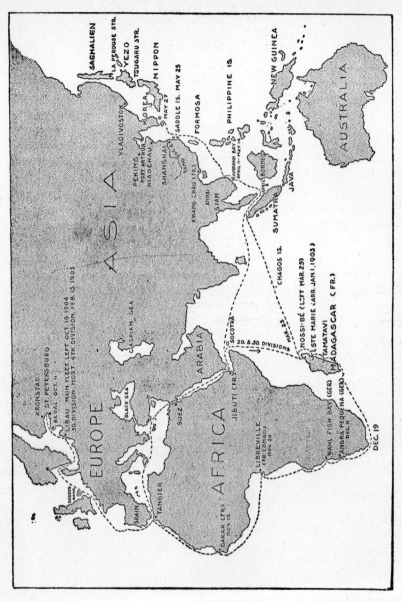

ROJDESTVENSKY'S CRUISE, OCT. 18, 1904-MAY 27, 1905

by four light cruiser divisions of 4 ships each. The Russian line had the advantage in heavy ordnance, as will appear from the following table, but this was more than compensated for by the enemy's superiority in 8-inch guns and quick-firers, which covered the Russians with an overwhelming rain of shells. Of guns in broadside, the Japanese ships-of-the-line had 127 to 98; and the cruisers 89 to 43.

	Ships	MAIN BATTERIES				Q. F.	
		12"	10"	9"	8"	6"	4.7"
Japan.............	12	16	1		30	160	
Russia...........	12	26	15	4	3	90	20

On the basis of these figures, and the 50% superiority of the Japanese in speed, the issue could hardly be in doubt. Admiral Togo, moreover, had commanded his fleet in peace and war for 8 years, and had veteran subordinates on whom he could depend to lead their divisions independently yet in coordination with the general plan. Constant training and target practice had brought his crews to a high degree of skill. The Japanese shells were also superior, with fuses that detonated their charges on the slightest contact with an explosive force like that of mines. Between the enemy and their base, the Japanese could wait quietly in home waters, while the Russian fleet was worn out by its eight months' cruise. At best, the latter was a heterogeneous assemblage of new ships hastily completed and old ships indifferently put in repair, which since Nebogatoff joined had had but one opportunity for maneuvers and had operated as a unit for only 13 days.

On the night of May 26-27, as the Russian ships approached Tsushima through mist and darkness, half the officers and men were at their posts, while the rest slept beside the guns. Fragments of wireless messages—"Last night" . . . "nothing" . . . "eleven lights" . . . "but not in line"—revealed enemy patrols in the waters beyond. Semen off on the *Suvaroff* describes vividly "the tall, somewhat bent figure of the Admiral on the side of the bridge, the wrinkled face of the man at the wheel stooping over the compass, the guns' crews chilled at their posts." In the brightly lighted engine-rooms, "life and movement was visible on all sides; men were nimbly running up and down ladders; there was a tinkling of bells and buzzing of voices; orders were being transmitted loudly; but, on looking more intently, the tension and anxiety—that same peculiar frame of mind so noticeable on deck—could also be observed." [1]

The Battle of Tsushima

At dawn (4.45) the Japanese scout *Sinano Maru*, which for an hour or more had been following in the darkness, made them out clearly and communicated the intelligence at once to Togo in his base at Masampho Bay, on the Korean side of the straits, and to the cruiser divisions off the Tsushima Islands. This was apparently the first definite news that Togo had received for several days, and the fact suggests that his scouting arrangements were not above criticism, for it took fast steaming to get to the straits by noon. Cruiser divisions were soon circling towards the Russians through the mist and darting as swiftly away, first the 5th and 6th under Takeomi and Togo (son of the admiral), then the 3d under Dewa, all reporting the movements of the enemy fleet and shepherding it till the final action began. Troubled by their activity, Rojdestvensky made several shifts of formation, first placing his 1st and 2d divisions in one long column ahead of the 3d, then at 11.20 throwing the 1st division again to starboard, while the cruisers protected the auxiliaries which were steaming between the lines in the rear.

This was the disposition when, shortly after one o'clock, the Japanese main divisions appeared to northward about 7 miles distant, steaming on a westerly course across the enemy's bows. Since morning Togo had covered a distance of 90 miles. From

[1] THE BATTLE OF TSUSHIMA, p. 28.

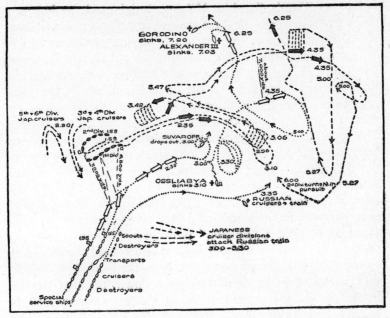

BATTLE OF TSUSHIMA, MAY 27, 1905

Japanese
  I Division (Togo)
    Mikasa, B.S.
    Shikishima, B.S.
    Asahi, B.S.
    Fuji, B.S.
    Nisshin, A.C.
    Kasuga

  II Division (Kamimura)
    Idzumo
    Iwate
    Adzumo
    Asama
    Tokiwa
    Yakumo

Russians
  I Division
    Suvaroff
    Alexander III
    Borodino
    Orel

  II Division
    Ossliabya (flag)

  III Division

his signal yards fluttered the stirring message: "The fate of the empire depends upon to-day's battle. Let every man do his utmost." Ordering all his cruisers to circle to the Russian rear, and striking himself for their left flank, which at the moment was the weaker, Togo first turned southward as if to pass on opposite courses, and then at about two o'clock led his two divisions around to east-northeast, so as to "cross the T" upon the head of the enemy line.

Just as Togo's flagship *Mikasa* straightened on her new course, nearly north of the *Suvaroff,* and 6400 yards distant, the *Suvaroff* opened fire. It has been suggested that at this critical moment the Russian admiral should have closed with the enemy, or, leading his ships on a northwesterly course, laid his starboard broadsides on the knuckle formed by the Japanese turn. But the position of the enemy cruisers and destroyers, and worry over his transports, guided his movements. Moreover, he had not yet completed an awkardly executed maneuver to get his ships back into single column with the 1st division ahead. The *Ossliabya* and other ships of the 2d division were thrown into confusion, and forced to slow down and even stop engines. Under these difficulties, the *Suvaroff* sheered more to eastward. As they completed their turn the Japanese secured a "capping" position and could concentrate on the leading ships of both the 1st and the 2d Russian divisions, 4 ships on the *Suvaroff* and 7 on the *Ossliabya.* Under this terrible fire the *Ossliabya* went down, the first modern battleship (in the narrow sense of the word) ever sunk by gunfire, and the *Suvaroff* a few moments later fell out of line, torn by shells, her forward funnel down, and steering gear jammed. "She was so battered," wrote a Japanese observer, "that scarcely any one would have taken her for a ship."

With an advantage in speed of 15 knots to 9, the Japanese drew ahead. The *Alexander,* followed by other Russian ships in much confusion, about three o'clock made an effort to pass northward across the enemy rear, but they were countered by the Japanese first division turning west together and the 2d division in succession at 3.10. The first and decisive phase of the action thus ended. Both fleets eventually resumed easterly and then southerly courses, for considerable periods completely lost to each other in smoke and haze.

Plunging through heavy seas from the southwest, the Japanese cruisers had in the meantime punished the Russian rear less severely than might have been expected. Two transports went down in flames, two cruisers were badly damaged, and the high-sided ex-German liner *Ural* was punctured with shells. On the other hand, Dewa's flagship *Kasagi* was driven to port with a bad hole under water, and Togo's old ship *Naniwa Kan* had to cease action for repairs. Hits and losses in fact were considerable in both the main and the cruiser divisions of the Japanese, their total casualties numbering 465. Late in the afternoon the Russian destroyer *Buiny* came up to the wreck of the *Suvaroff,* and lurched alongside long enough for Rojdestvensky, wounded and almost unconscious, to be practically thrown on board. He was captured with the destroyer next day. In spite of her injuries, the *Suvaroff* held off a swarm of cruisers and destroyers until at last torpedoed at 7.20 p. m.

The Russian battleships had meanwhile described a large circle to southward, and at 5 p. m. were again steaming north, accompanied by some of their cruisers and train. Attacked once more between 6 and 7 o'clock, and almost incapable of defense, the *Alexander III* and *Borodino* went down, making 4 ships lost out of the 5 new vessels that had formed the backbone of Rojdestvensky's forces. In the gathering darkness Nebogatoff collected the survivors and staggered northward.

Of slight value in the day engagement, 21 Japanese destroyers, with about 40 torpedo boats which had sheltered under Tsushima Island, now darted after the fleeing foe. In the fog and heavy weather they were almost as great a menace to each other as to the enemy. Russian ships without searchlights escaped harm. Of three or perhaps four Russian vessels struck, all but the *Navarin* stayed afloat until the next day. Admiral Custance estimates 8 hits, or 9% of the torpedoes fired. There were at least 6 collisions among the flotillas, and 4 boats destroyed.

On the morning of the 28th the remains of the Russian fleet were scattered over the sea. Nebogatoff with 4 battleships and 2 cruisers surrendered at 10.30. Of the 37 ships all told that entered Tsushima Straits, only the following escaped: the cruisers *Oleg, Aurora,* and *Jemschug* reached Manila on June 3; a tug and a supply ship entered Shanghai, and another transport with plenty of coal went clear to Madagascar; only the fast cruiser *Almaz* and two destroyers made Vladivostok.

Among the lessons to be drawn from Tsushima, one of the

clearest is the weakening effect of divided purpose. With all honor to Admiral Rojdestvensky for his courage and persistence during his cruise, it is evident that at the end he allowed the supply problem to interfere with his preparations for battle, and that he fought "with one eye on Vladivostok." It is evident also that only by a long period of training and operating as a unit can a collection of ships and men be welded into an effective fighting force. Torpedo results throughout the war, whether due to faulty materials or unskilled employment, were not such as to increase the reliance upon this weapon. The gun retained its supremacy; and the demonstrated advantage conferred by speed and heavy armament in long range fighting was reflected in the "all-big-gun" *Dreadnought* of 1906 and the battle cruisers of 1908.

Immediately after the Russian navy had been swept out of existence, President Roosevelt offered to mediate, and received favorable replies from the warring nations. By the treaty signed at Portsmouth, New Hampshire, on September 5, 1905, Russia withdrew from Manchuria in favor of China, recognized Japan's paramount position in Korea (annexed by Japan in 1910), and surrendered to Japan her privileges in Port Arthur and the Liao-tung Peninsula. In lieu of indemnity, Japan after a long deadlock was induced by pressure on the part of England and the United States to accept that portion of the island of Saghalien south of the parallel of 50°. Thus the war thwarted Russia's policy of aggressive imperialism in the East, and established Japan firmly on the mainland at China's front door. At the same time, by the military débâcle of Russia, it dangerously disturbed the balance of power in Europe, upon which the safety of that continent had long been made precariously to depend.

REFERENCES

Spanish-American War

Notes on the Spanish American War (a series of publications issued by the Office of Naval Intelligence, U. S. Navy Department, 1900).

Sampson-Schley Official Communications to the U. S. Senate, Gov't Printing Office, 1899.
The Downfall of Spain, H. W. Wilson, 1900.
With Sampson Through the War, W. A. M. Goode, 1899.
A History of the Spanish-American War, R. H. Tetherington, 1900.

Russo-Japanese War

International Relations of the Chinese Empire, 3 vols., H. B. Morse, 1918.
The Battle of Tsushima (1906), Rasplata (1910), Captain Vladimir Semenoff.
Japanese Official History, translated in U. S. Naval Institute Proceedings, July-August, September-October, 1914.
The Ship of the Line in Battle, Admiral Reginald Custance, 1912.
The Russian Navy in the Russo-Japanese War, Captain N. Klado, 1905.
Official British History of the Russo-Japanese War, 3 vols., 1910.
The American Merchant Marine, Debaters' Handbook Series, N. Y., 1916 (with bibliography).

CHAPTER XV

THE WORLD WAR: THE FIRST YEAR (1914-1915)

THE Russo-Japanese war greatly weakened Russia's posi·
tion in Europe, and left the Dual Alliance of France and Russia
overweighted by the military strength of the Teutonic Empires,
Germany and Austria, whether or not Italy should adhere to
the Triple Alliance with these nations. To Great Britain, such
a disturbance of the European balance was ever a matter of
grave concern, and an abandonment of her policy of isolation
was in this instance virtually forced upon her by Germany's
rivalry in her own special sphere of commerce and sea power.

The disturbing effect of Germany's naval growth during
the two decades prior to 1914 affords in fact an excellent illustration of the influence of naval strength in peace as well as
in war. Under Bismarck Germany had pushed vigorously
though tardily into the colonial field, securing vast areas of
rather doubtful value in East and West Africa, and the
Bismarck Archipelago, Marshall Islands, and part of New
Guinea in the Pacific. With the accession of William II in
1888 and the dropping of the pilot, Bismarck, two years later,
she embarked definitely upon her quest for world power. The
young Kaiser read eagerly Mahan's *Influence of Sea Power
Upon History* (1890), distributed it among the ships of his
still embryonic navy, and fed his ambition on the doctrines of
this epoch-making work.

Naval development found further stimulus and justification
in the rapid economic growth of Germany. In 1912 her industrial production attained a value of three billion dollars, as
compared with slightly over four billion for England and
seven billion for the United States. Since 1893 her merchant
marine had tripled in size and taken second place to that of
England with a total of over five million tons. During the same

period she surpassed France and the United States in volume of foreign commerce, and in this respect also reached a position second to Great Britain, with a more rapid rate of increase. An emigration of 220,000 a year in the early eighties was cut down to 22,000 in 1900.[1] To assure markets for her manufactures, and continued growth in population and industry, Germany felt that she must strive to extend her political power.

Though Germany's commercial expansion met slight opposition even in areas under British control, it undoubtedly justified measures of political and naval protection; and it was this motive that was advanced in the preface to the German Naval Bill of 1900, which declared that, "To protect her sea trade and colonies . . . Germany must have a fleet so strong that a war, even with the greatest naval power, would involve such risks as to jeopardize the position of that power."[2] Furthermore, Germany's quest for colonies and points of vantage such as Kiao-chau, her scheme for a Berlin-Bagdad railroad with domination of the territories on the route, had parallel in the activities of other nations. Unfortunately, however, Germany's ambitions grew even more rapidly than her commerce, until her true aim appeared to be destruction of rivals and domination of the world.

The seizure of Kiao-chau in 1897-98 coincided with the appointment of Admiral von Tirpitz as Imperial Minister of Marine. Under his administration, the Naval Bill of 1900, passed in a heat of anglophobia aroused by the Boer War, doubled the program of 1898, and contained ingenious provisions by which the Reichstag was bound to steady increases covering a long period of years, and by which the Navy Department was empowered to replace worthless old craft, after 20 or 25 years' service, with new ships of the largest size. As the armament race grew keener, this act was amended in the direction of further increases, but its program was never cut down.

International crises and realignments marked the growing tension of these years. In 1905 England extended for ten

---

[1] Figures from Priest, GERMANY SINCE 1840, p. 150 ff.
[2] Hurd and Castle, GERMAN SEA POWER, Appendix II.

years her understanding with Japan. By the *Entente Cordiale* with France in 1904 and a later settlement of outstanding difficulties with Russia, she also practically changed the Dual Alliance into a Triple Entente, though without positively binding herself to assistance in war. To the agreement of 1904 by which England and France assured each other a free hand in Egypt and Morocco, respectively, the Kaiser raised strenuous objections, and forced the resignation of the anglophile French Foreign Minister, Delcassé; but at the Algeciras Convention of 1906, assembled to settle the Morocco question, Germany and Austria stood virtually alone. Even the American delegates, sent by President Roosevelt at the Kaiser's invitation, voted generally with the Western Powers. When Austria annexed Bosnia and Herzegovina in 1909, the Kaiser shook the mailed fist to better effect than at Algeciras, with the result that Russia had to accept this extension of Austro-German influence in the Balkan sphere. Still again two years later, when the German cruiser *Panther* made moves to establish a base at Agadir on the Atlantic coast of Morocco, Europe approached the verge of war; but Germany found the financial situation against her, backed down, and eventually took a strip of land on the Congo in liquidation of her Morocco claims.

For all her resolute saber-rattling in these years, Germany found herself checkmated in almost every move. The Monroe Doctrine, for which the United States showed willingness to fight in the Venezuela affair of 1902, balked her schemes in the New World. In the Far East she faced Japan; in Africa, British sea power. A *"Drang nach Osten,"* through the Balkans and Turkey toward Asia Minor, offered on the whole the best promise; and it was in this quarter that Austria's violent demands upon Serbia aroused Russia and precipitated the World War.

Great Britain's foreign agreements, already noted, had as a primary aim the concentration of her fleet in home waters. Naval predominance in the Far East she turned over to Japan; in the western Atlantic, to the United States (at least by acceptance of the Monroe Doctrine and surrender of treaty rights to share in the construction of the Panama Canal) ; and in the Mediterranean, to France, though England still kept a strong cruiser force in this field. The old policy of showing the flag all over the world was abandoned, 160 old ships were sent to the scrap heap as unable "either to fight or to run away," and 88% of the fleet was concentrated at home, so quietly that it "was found out only by accident by Admiral Mahan." [1]

These and other changes were carried out under the energetic régime of Admiral Fisher, First Sea Lord from 1904 to 1910. The British *Dreadnought* of 1906, completed in 10 months, and the battle cruisers of 1908—*Indefatigable, Invincible* and *Indomitable*—came as an unpleasant surprise to Germany, necessitating construction of similar types and enlargement of the Kiel Canal. Reforms in naval gunnery urged by Admiral Sir Percy Scott were taken up, and plans were made for new bases in the Humber, in the Forth at Rosyth, and in the Orkneys, necessitated by the shift of front from the Channel to the North Sea. But against the technical skill, painstaking organization, and definitely aggressive purpose of Germany, even more radical measures were needed to put the tradition-ridden British navy in readiness for war.

Naval preparedness was vital, for the conflict was fundamentally, like the Napoleonic Wars, a struggle between land power predominant on the Continent and naval power supreme on the seas. As compared with France in the earlier struggle, Germany was more dependent on foreign commerce, and in a long war would feel more keenly the pressure of blockade. On the other hand, while the naval preponderance of England and her allies was probably greater than 100 years before, England had to throw larger armies into the field and more of her shipping into naval service, and found her commerce not augmented but cut down.

Indeed, Germany was not without advantage in the naval war. As she fully expected, her direct sea trade was soon shut off, and her shipping was driven to cover or destroyed. But Germany was perhaps 80% self-supporting, was well sup-

[1] Admiral Fisher, MEMORIES, p. 185.

plied with minerals and munitions, and could count on trade through neutral states on her frontiers. Her shallow, well-protected North Sea coast-line gave her immunity from naval attack and opportunity to choose the moment in which to throw her utmost strength into a sortie. So long as her fleet remained intact, it controlled the Baltic by virtue of an interior line through the Kiel Canal, thus providing a strangle hold on Russia and free access to northern neutrals. Only by dangerous division of forces, or by leaving the road to England and the Atlantic open, could the British fleet enter the Baltic Sea. England it is true had a superior navy (perhaps less superior than was commonly thought), and a position of singular advantage between Germany and the overseas world. But for her the maintenance of naval superiority was absolutely essential. An effective interference with her sea communications would quickly put her out of the war.

The importance (for Germany as well as for England) of preserving their main fighting fleets, may explain the wariness with which they were employed. Instead of risking them desperately, both sides turned to commerce warfare—the Western Powers resorting to blockade and the Germans to submarines. Each of these forms of warfare played a highly important part in the war, and the submarine campaign in particular, calling for new methods and new instruments, seems almost to have monopolized the naval genius and energies of the two groups of belligerents. It may be noted, however, that but for the cover given by the High Seas Fleet, the submarine campaign could hardly have been undertaken; and but for the Grand Fleet, it would have been unnecessary.

The naval strength of the various belligerents in July, 1914, appears in the table on the following page.[1]

Owing to new construction, these figures underwent rapid change. Thus England added 4 dreadnoughts (2 built for Turkey) in August, 1914; the battle cruiser *Tiger* in November; the dreadnought *Canada* and 5 *Queen Elizabeths* in 1915; and 5 *Royal Sovereigns* in 1915-1916. In comparisons, full account is not always taken of the naval support of England's

[1] From table prepared by U. S. Office of Naval Intelligence, July 1, 1916.

	Great Britain	Germany	U. S. (1916)	France	Japan	Russia	Italy	Austria
Dreadnoughts...	20	13	12	4	2	..	3	3
Pre-dreadn'ts...	40	20	21	18	13	7	8	6
Battle Cruisers..	9	4	..	..	2	..	..	..
Armored Cr's...	34	9	10	20	13	6	9	2
Cruisers........	74	41	14	9	13	9	6	5
Destroyers......	167	130	54	84	50	91	36	18
Submarines.....	78	30	44	64	13	30	19	6

allies; it is true, however, that the necessity of protecting coasts, troop convoys, and commerce prevented her from throwing her full strength into the North Sea. Her capital ships were in two main divisions—the 1st or Grand Fleet in the Orkneys, and the 2d fleet, consisting at first of 16 pre-dreadnoughts, in the Channel. Admiral Jellicoe[1] gives the strength of the Grand Fleet and the German High Seas Fleet, on August 4, 1914, as follows:

	Dreadnoughts	Pre-Dreadnoughts	Battle cruisers	Light cruisers	Destroyers	Airships	Cruisers
British..	20	8	4	12	42	..	9
German.	13	16	3	15	88	1	2

Of submarines, according to the same authority, England had 17 of the D and E classes fit for distant operations, and 37 fit only for coast defense, while Germany had 28 U boats, all but two or three of which were able to cruise overseas. The British admiral's account of the inferiority of the British navy in submarines, aircraft, mines, destroyers, director firing (installed in only 8 ships in 1914), armor-piercing shells, and

[1] THE GRAND FLEET, p. 31.

protection of bases, seems to justify the caution of British operations, but is a severe indictment of the manner in which money appropriated for the navy was used.

To open a war with England by surprise naval attack was no doubt an element in German plans; but in 1914 this was negatived by the forewarning of events on the Continent, by Germany's persistent delusion that England would stay neutral, and by the timely mobilization of the British fleet. This had been announced the winter before as a practical exercise, was carried out according to schedule from July 16 to July 23 (the date of Austria's ultimatum to Serbia), and was then extended until July 29, at which date the Grand Fleet sailed for Scapa Flow.

At midnight of August 4 the British ultimatum to Germany expired and hostilities began. During the same night the Grand Fleet swept the northern exit of the North Sea to prevent the escape of enemy raiders, only one of which, the *Kaiser Wilhelm der Grosse,* actually reached the Atlantic in this first stage of the war. On a similar sweep further south, the Harwich light cruiser and destroyer force under Commodore Tyrwhitt sank by gunfire the mine layer *Königin Luise,* which a trawler had reported "throwing things overboard"; but the next morning, August 6, the cruiser *Amphion,* returning near the same position, was destroyed by two mines laid by her victim of the day before. On the same date five cables were cut leading from Germany overseas. From August 10 to 23 all British forces were busy covering the transit of the first troops sent to the Continent. Such, in brief summary, and omitting more distant activities for the present, were the opening naval events of the war.

The Heligoland Bight Action

On the morning of August 28 occurred a lively action in Heligoland Bight, which cost Germany 3 light cruisers and a destroyer, and seemed to promise further aggressive action off the German shores. The British plan called for a destroyer and light cruiser sweep southward to a point about 12 miles

west of Heligoland, and thence westward, with submarines
disposed off Heligoland as decoys, the object being to cut off
German destroyers and patrols. Commodore Tyrwhitt's force
.which was to execute the raid consisted of the 1st and 3rd
flotillas of 16 destroyers each, led by the new light cruiser
Arethusa, flagship (28.5 knots, two 6″, six 4″ guns), and the
Fearless (25.4 knots, ten 4″ guns). These were to be supported about 50 miles to westward by two battle cruisers from
the Humber. This supporting force was at the last moment

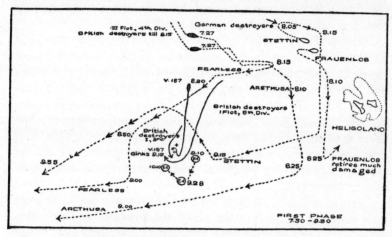

HELIGOLAND BIGHT ACTION, AUG. 28, 1914

joined by three battle cruisers under Admiral Beatty and 6
cruisers under Commodore Goodenough from the Grand Fleet;
but news of the accession never reached Commodore Keyes of
the British submarines, who was hence puzzled later by the
appearance of Goodenough's cruisers on the scene.

The Germans, it appears, had got wind of the enemy plan,
and arranged a somewhat similar counter-stroke. As Commodore Tyrwhitt's flotillas swept southward, they engaged
and chased 10 German destroyers straight down upon Heligoland. Here the *Arethusa* and the *Fearless* were sharply engaged with two German light cruisers, the *Stettin* and the
Frauenlob (ten 4.1″ guns each), until actually in sight of the

island. Both sides suffered, the *Frauenlob* withdrawing to Wilhelmshaven with 50 casualties, and the *Arethusa* having her speed cut down and nearly every gun put temporarily out of commission.

Whipping around to westward, the flotillas caught the German destroyer *V 187*, which at 9.10, after an obstinate resistance, was reduced to a complete wreck enveloped in smoke and steam. As British destroyers picked up survivors, they were driven off by the *Stettin;* but two boats with British crews and German prisoners were rescued later by the British submarine *E 4*, which had been lurking nearby.

Extraordinary confusion now developed from the fact that Commodore Keyes in his submarine flotilla leader *Lurcher* sighted through the mist two of Goodenough's cruisers (which had chased a destroyer eastward), and reported them as enemies. The call was picked up by Goodenough himself, who brought his remaining four ships to Keyes' assistance; but when these appeared, Keyes thought that he had to deal with four enemies more! Tyrwhitt was also drawn backward by the alarm. Luckily the situation was cleared up without serious consequences.

German cruisers, darting out of the Ems and the Jade, were now entering the fray. At 10.55 the *Fearless* and the *Arethusa* with their flotillas were attacked by the *Stralsund*, which under a heavy fire made off toward Heligoland. Then at 11.15 the *Stettin* engaged once more, and five minutes later the *Mainz*. Just as this last ship was being finished up by destroyer attack, and the *Stettin* and two fresh cruisers, *Köln* and *Ariadne*, were rushing to her assistance, Beatty's five battle cruisers appeared to westward and rose swiftly out of the haze.

Admiral Beatty's opportune dash into action at this time, from his position 40 miles away, was in response to an urgent call from Tyrwhitt at 11.15, coupled with the fact that, as the Admiral states in his report, "The flotillas had advanced only 2 miles since 8 a.m., and were only about 25 miles from two enemy bases." "Our high speed," the report continues, "made submarine attack difficult, and the smoothness of the sea made their detection fairly easy. I considered that we were powerful enough to deal with any sortie except by a battle squadron, which was unlikely to come out in time, provided our stroke was sufficiently rapid."

The *Stettin* broke backward just in the nick of time. The *Köln,* flagship of the German commodore, was soon staggering off in a blaze, and was later sunk with her total complement of 380 officers and men. The *Ariadne,* steaming at

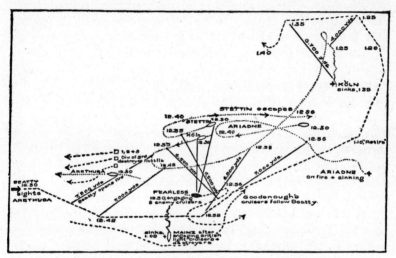

HELIGOLAND BIGHT ACTION, FINAL PHASE, 12:30–1:40
From 20 to 40 miles slightly S. of W. from Heligoland.

high speed across the bows of the British flagship *Lion,* was put out of action by two well-placed salvos. At 1.10 the *Lion* gave the general signal "Retire."

Though the German cruisers had fought hard and with remarkable accuracy of fire, their movements had been tardy and not well concerted. The British losses amounted altogether to only 33 killed and 40 wounded; while the enemy lost in killed, wounded, and prisoners over 1000 men. Very satisfactory, from the British standpoint, was the effect of the victory upon their own and upon enemy morale.

Encouragement of this kind was desirable, for German submarines and mines were already beginning to take their toll. Off the Forth on September 5, a single torpedo sank the light cruiser *Pathfinder* with nearly all hands. This loss was avenged when a week later the *E 9,* under Lieut. Commander Max Horton, struck down the German cruiser *Hela* within 6 miles of Heligoland. But on September 22, at 6.30 a.m., a single old-type German craft, the *U 9,* dealt a staggering blow. With a total of 6 torpedoes Commander Weddigen sank first the *Aboukir,* and then in quick succession the *Hogue* and the *Cressy,* both dead in the water at the work of rescue. The loss of these rather antiquated vessels was less serious than that of over 1400 trained officers and men. A shock to British traditions came with the new order that ships must abandon injured consorts and make all speed away.

In the bases at Rosyth and Scapa Flow, which at the outbreak of war were totally unprotected against submarines and thought to be beyond their reach, the Grand Fleet felt less secure than when cruising on the open sea. Safer refuges were sought temporarily on the west coast of Scotland and at Lough Swilly in the north of Ireland, but even off this latter base on October 27, the big dreadnought *Audacious* was sunk by mines laid by the German auxiliary cruiser *Berlin.* In view of the impending Turkish crisis, the loss was not admitted by the Admiralty, though since pictures of the sinking ship had actually been taken by passengers on the White Star liner *Olympic,* it could not long remain concealed. Mines and submarines had seemingly put the British navy on the defensive, even if consolation could be drawn from the fact that troops and supplies were crossing safely to France, the enemy had been held up at the Marne, the German surface fleet was passive, and the blockade was closing down.

Escape of the "Göben" and the "Breslau"

In distant waters Germany at the outbreak of the war had only ten cruisers—*Scharnhorst, Gneisenau, Emden, Nürnberg,* and *Leipzig* in the Pacific, *Königsberg* on the east coast of Africa, *Karlsruhe* and *Dresden* in the West Indies, and

Göben and *Breslau* in the Mediterranean. Within six months'
time, these, together with a few auxiliary cruisers fitted out
abroad, were either destroyed or forced to intern in neutral
ports. Modern wireless communication, difficulties of coaling and supply, and the overwhelming naval strength of the
Allies made the task of surface raiders far more difficult than
in previous wars. They were nevertheless skillfully handled,
and, operating in the wide ocean areas, created a troublesome
problem for the Western Powers.

The battle cruiser *Göben* and the light cruiser *Breslau* alone,
operating under Admiral Souchon in Mediterranean waters,
accomplished ultimate results which would have easily justified the sacrifice of ten times the number of ships lost by
Germany in distant seas. To hunt down these two vessels,
and at the same time contain the Austrian Navy, the Entente
had in the Mediterranean not only the bulk of the French
fleet but also 3 battle cruisers, 4 armored cruisers, and 4
light cruisers of Great Britain. Early on August 4, as he
was about to bombard the French bases of Bona and Philippe-
ville in Algiers, Admiral Souchon received wireless orders
to make for the Dardanelles. Germany and England were then
on the very verge of war. Knowing the British ships to be
concentrated near Malta, and actually passing the *Indomitable*
and the *Invincible* in sullen silence as he turned eastward,
the German commander decided to put in at Messina, Sicily.

At the end of the 24 hours granted in this port, the prospects for the German ships appeared so desperate that the
officers, it is said, made their final testaments before again
putting to sea. Slipping eastward through the Straits of
Messina at twilight of the 6th, they were sighted by the
British scout *Gloucester,* which stuck close at their heels all
that night and until 4.40 p.m. the next day. Then, under orders to turn back, and after boldly engaging the *Breslau* to
check the flight, Captain Kelly of the *Gloucester* gave up the
pursuit as the enemy rounded the Morea and entered the Greek
Archipelago.

The escape thus apparently so easy was the outcome of lack
of coördination between French and British, slow and poor in-

formation from the British Admiralty, and questionable disposition of the British forces on the basis of information actually at hand. Prior to hostilities, it was perhaps unavoidable that the British commander, Admiral Milne, should be ignorant of French plans; but even on August 5 and 6 he still kept all his battle cruisers west and north of Sicily to protect the French troop transports, though by this time he might have felt assured that the French fleet was at sea. At the time of the escape Admiral Troubridge with 4 armored cruisers and a destroyer force barred the Adriatic; though he caught the *Gloucester's* calls, he was justified in not moving far from his station without orders, in view of his inferior strength and speed. Not until August 10 did British forces enter the Ægean; and at 5 p.m. that day the two German ships steamed uninvited up the Dardanelles. Since the Turkish situation was still somewhat dubious, Admiral Souchon had been ordered to delay his entrance; but on the 10th, hearing British wireless signals steadily approaching his position in the Greek islands, he took the decision into his own hands. Germany had "captured Turkey," as an Allied diplomat remarked upon seeing the ships in the Golden Horn.

In this affair the British, it is true, had many preoccupations—the hostile Austrian fleet, the doubtful neutrality of Italy, the French troop movement, the safety of Egypt and Suez. Yet the Admiralty were well aware that the German Ambassador von Wangenheim was dominant in Turkish councils and that the Turkish army was mobilized under German officers. It seems strange, therefore, that an escape into Constantinople was, in the words of the British Official History, "the only one that had not entered into our calculations." The whole affair illustrates the immense value political information may have in guiding naval strategy. The German ships, though ostensibly "sold" to the Turks, retained their German personnel. Admiral Souchon assumed command of the Turkish Navy, and by an attack on Russian ships in the Black Sea later succeeded in precipitating Turkey's entrance into the war, with its long train of evil consequences for the Western Powers.

Coronel and the Falkland Islands

In the Pacific the German cruisers were at first widely scattered, the *Emden* at Kiao-chau, the *Leipzig* on the west coast of Mexico, the *Nürnberg* at San Francisco, and the armored cruisers *Gneisenau* and *Scharnhorst* under Admiral von Spee in the Caroline Islands. The two ships at the latter point, after being joined by the *Nürnberg,* set out on a leisurely cruise for South America, where, in view of Japan's entry into the war, the German Admiral may have felt that he would secure a clearer field of operations and, with the aid of German-Americans, better facilities for supplies. After wrecking on their way the British wireless and cable station at Fanning Island, and looking into Samoa for stray British cruisers, the trio of ships were joined at Easter Island on October 14 by the *Leipzig* and also by the *Dresden,* which had fled thither from the West Indies.

The concentration thus resulting seems of doubtful wisdom, for, scattered over the trade routes, the cruisers would have brought about greater enemy dispersion and greater injury to commerce; and, as the later course of the war was to show, the loss of merchant tonnage was even more serious for the Entente than loss of fighting ships. It seems evident, however, that Admiral von Spee was not attracted by the tame task of commerce destroying, but wished to try his gunnery, highly developed in the calm waters of the Far East, against enemy men-of-war.

In its present strength and position, the German "fleet in being" constituted a serious menace, for to assemble an adequate force against it on either side of Cape Horn would mean to leave the other side dangerously exposed. It was with a keen realization of this dilemma that Admiral Cradock in the British armored cruiser *Good Hope* left the Falklands on October 22 to join the *Monmouth, Glasgow,* and auxiliary cruiser *Otranto* in a sweep along the west coast. The old battleship *Canopus,* with 12-inch guns, but only 12 knots cruising speed, was properly judged too slow to keep with the squadron. It is difficult to say whether the failure to send

Cradock reënforcements at this time from either the Atlantic or the Pacific was justified by the preoccupations in those fields. Needless to say, there was no hesitation, *after* Coronel, in hurrying ships to the scene. On November 1, when the Admiralty Board was reorganized with Admiral Fisher in his old place as First Sea Lord, orders at once went out sending the *Defense* to Cradock and enjoining him not to fight without the *Canopus*. But these orders he never received.

The composition of the two squadrons now approaching each other off the Chilean coast was as follows:

Name	Type	Displacement	Belt armor	Guns	Speed
Scharnhorst...	Armored cruiser	11,600	6-inch	8–8.2″, 6–6″	23.5
Gneisenau....	Armored cruiser	11,600	6-inch	8–8.2″, 6.6″	23.5
Leipzig.......	Protected cruiser	3,250	none	10–4″	23
Nürnberg.....	Light cruiser	3,450	none	10–4″	24
Dresden......	Light cruiser	3,600	none	10–4″	24
Good Hope...	Armored cruiser	14,000	6-inch	2–9.2″, 16–6″, 14–3″	24
Monmouth...	Armored cruiser	9,800	4-inch	14–6″, 8–3″	24
Glasgow......	Light cruiser	4,800	none	2–6″, 10–4″	26.5
Canopus (not engaged)	Coast defense	12,950	6-inch	4–35 cal. 12″, 12–6″	16.5

Without the *Canopus,* the British had perhaps a slight advantage in squadron speed, but only the two 9.2-inch guns of the *Good Hope* could match the sixteen 8.2-inch guns of the Germans. Each side had information of the other's strength; but on the afternoon of November 1, the date of the Battle of Coronel, each supposed that only one enemy cruiser was in the immediate vicinity. Hence there was mutual surprise when the two squadrons, spread widely on opposite courses, came in contact at 4.40 p. m.

While concentrating and forming his squadron, Admiral Cradock must have pondered whether he should fight or retreat. The *Canopus* he knew was laboring northward 250 miles away. It was highly doubtful whether he could bring the enemy into action later with his slow battleship in line. His orders were to "search and protect trade." "Safety," we are told, "was a word he hardly knew." But his best justification lay in the enemy's menace to commerce and in the comment of Nelson upon a similar situation, "By the time the enemy has beat our fleet soundly, they will do us no more harm that year." It was perhaps with this thought that Admiral Cradock signaled to the *Canopus,* "I am going to fight the enemy now."

At about 6 p.m. the two columns were 18,000 yards distant on southerly converging courses. The British, to westward and slightly ahead, tried to force the action before sunset, when they would be silhouetted against the afterglow. Their speed at this time, however, seems to have been held up by the auxiliary cruiser *Otranto,* which later retreated southwestward, and their efforts to close were thwarted by the enemy's turning slightly away. Admiral von Spee in fact secured every advantage of position, between the British and the neutral coast, on the side away from the sun, and on such a course that the heavy seas from east of south struck the British ships on their engaged bows, showering the batteries with spray and rendering useless the lower deck guns.

At 7 o'clock the German ships opened fire at 11,260 yards. The third salvo from the *Scharnhorst* disabled the *Good Hope's* forward 9.2-inch gun. The *Monmouth's* forecastle was soon on fire. It seems probable indeed that most of the injury to the British was inflicted by accurate shooting in this first stage of the action. On account of the gathering darkness, Admiral von Spee allowed the range to be closed to about 5500 yards, guiding his aim at first by the blaze on the Monmouth, and then for a time ceasing fire. Shortly before 8 o'clock a huge column of flame shooting up between the stacks of the *Good Hope* marked her end. The *Monmouth* sheered away to westward and then northward with a heavy list that prevented the use of her port guns. An hour later, at 9.25, with her flag still flying defiantly, she was sunk by the *Nürnberg* at point blank range. The *Glasgow,* which had fought throughout the action, but had suffered little from the fire of the German light cruisers, escaped in the darkness.

"It is difficult," writes an American officer, "to find fault

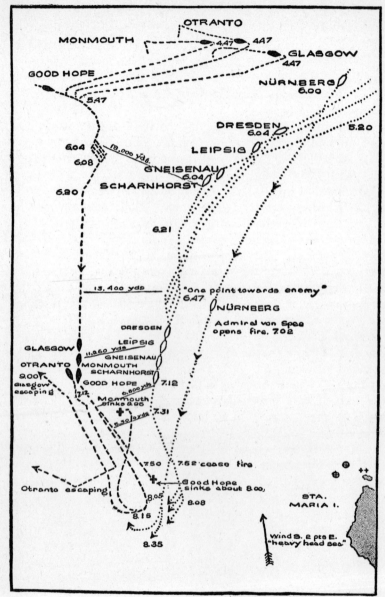

From *Official British Naval History*, Vol. I.

BATTLE OF CORONEL, NOV. I, 1914

with the tactics of Admiral von Spee; he appears to have maneuvered so as to secure the advantage of light, wind, and sea, and to have suited himself as regards the range." [1] The *Scharnhorst* was hit twice, the *Gneisenau* four times, and the German casualties were only two men wounded.

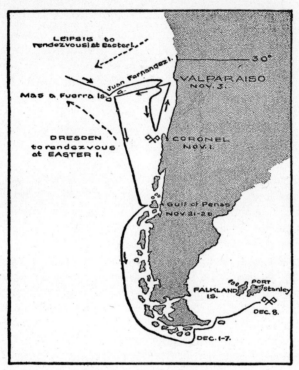

ADMIRAL VON SPEE'S MOVEMENTS

This stinging blow and the resultant danger aroused the new Board of Admiralty to energetic moves. Entering the Atlantic, the German squadron might scatter upon the trade routes or support the rebellion in South Africa. Again, it might double westward or northward in the Pacific, or pass in groups of three, as permitted by American rules, through the Panama Canal into the West Indies. Concerted measures

[1] Commander C. C. Gill, NAVAL POWER IN THE WAR, p. 51.

were taken against these possibilities. Despite the weakening of the Grand Fleet, the battle cruisers *Invincible* and *Inflexible* under Admiral Sturdee, former Chief of Admiralty Staff, sailed on November 11 for the Falkland Islands. Their destination was kept a close secret, for had the slightest inkling of their mission reached German ears it would at once have been communicated to von Spee.

After the battle, the German admiral moved slowly southward, coaling from chartered vessels and prizes; and it was not until December 1 that he rounded the Horn. Even now, had he moved directly upon the Falklands, he would have encountered only the *Canopus,* but he again delayed several days to take coal from a prize. On December 7 the British battle cruisers and other ships picked up in passage arrived at the island base and at once began to coal.

Their coming was not a moment too soon. At 7.30 the next morning, while coaling was still in progress and fires were drawn in the *Bristol,* the signal station on the neck of land south of the harbor reported two strange vessels, which proved to be the *Gneisenau* and the *Nürnberg,* approaching from the southward. As they eased down to demolish the wireless station, the *Canopus* opened on them at about 11,000 yards by indirect fire. The two ships swerved off, and at 9.40, perceiving the dense clouds of smoke over the harbor and what appeared to be tripod masts, they fell back on their main force.

Hull down, and with about 15 miles' start, the Germans, had they scattered at this time might, most of them at least, have escaped, as they certainly would have if their approach had been made more cautiously and at a later period in the day. The British ships were now out, with the fast *Glasgow* well in the lead. In the chase that followed, Admiral von Spee checked speed somewhat to keep his squadron together. Though Admiral Sturdee for a time did the same, he was able at 12.50 to open on the rear ship *Leipzig* at 16,000 yards. At 1.20 the German light cruisers scattered to southwestward, followed by the *Cornwall, Kent,* and *Glasgow.* The 26-knot *Bristol,* had she been able to work up steam in time, would have been invaluable in this pursuit; she was sent instead to destroy three enemy colliers or transports reported off the islands.

Between the larger ships the action continued at long range, for the superior speed of the battle cruisers enabled Admiral Sturdee to choose his distance, and his proper concern was to demolish the enemy with his own ships unscathed. At 2.05 he turned 8 points to starboard to clear the smoke blown down from the northwest and reduce the range, which had increased to 16,000 yards. Admiral von Spee also turned southward, and the stern chase was renewed without firing until 2.45. At this point both sides turned to port, the Germans now slightly in the rear and working in to 12,500 yards to use their 5.9-inch guns.

At 3.15 the British came completely about to avoid the smoke, and the Germans also turned, a little later, as if to cross their bows. (See diagram.) The *Gneisenau* and *Scharnhorst*, though fighting gamely, were now beaten ships, the latter with upper works a "shambles of torn and twisted iron," and holes in her sides through which could be seen the red glow of flames. She turned on her beam-ends at 4.17 and sank with every man on board. At 6 o'clock, after a fight of extraordinary persistence, the *Gneisenau* opened her sea-cocks and went down. All her 8-inch ammunition had been expended, and 600 of her 850 men were disabled or killed. Some 200 were saved.

Against ships with 12-inch guns and four times their weight of broadside the *Gneisenau* and *Scharnhorst* made a creditable record of over 20 hits. The British, however, suffered no casualties or material injury. While Admiral Sturdee's tactics are thus justified, the prolongation of the battle left him no time to join in the light cruiser chase, and even opened the possibility, in the rain squalls of the late afternoon, that one of the armored cruisers might get away. In spite of a calm sea and excellent visibility during most of the action, the gunnery of the battle cruisers appears to have been less accurate at long range than in the later engagement off the Dogger Bank.

Following similar tactics, the *Glasgow* and *Cornwall* over-

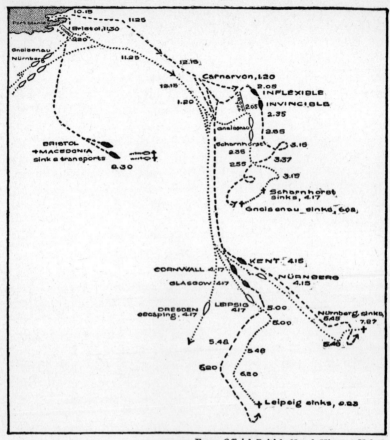

From *Official British Naval History*, Vol. I.

BATTLE OF THE FALKLAND ISLANDS, DEC. 8, 1914

British Squadron

Name	Type	Guns	Speed
Invincible	Battle Cruiser	8—12", 16—4"	26.5
Inflexible	Battle Cruiser	8—12", 16—4"	26.5
Carnarvon	Armored Cruiser	4—7.5", 6—6"	23.0
Cornwall	Armored Cruiser	14—6"	23.5
Kent	Armored Cruiser	14—6"	23.0
Bristol	Scout Cruiser	2—6", 10—4"	26.5
Glasgow	Scout Cruiser	2—6", 10—4"	26.5
Canopus	Coast Defense	4—12", 12—6"	16.5

German Squadron

Name	Type	Guns	Speed
Scharnhorst	Armored Cruiser	8—8.2", 6—6"	23.5
Gneisenau	Armored Cruiser	8—8.2", 6—6"	23.5
Leipzig	Protected Cruiser	10—4"	23.0
Nürnberg	Scout Cruiser	10—4"	24.0
Dresden	Scout Cruiser	10—4"	24.0

took and finally silenced the *Leipzig* at 7 p.m., four hours after the *Glasgow* had first opened fire. Defiant to the last, like the *Monmouth* at Coronel, and with her ammunition gone, she sank at 9.25, carrying down all but 18 of her officers and crew. The *Kent,* stoking all her woodwork to increase steam, attained at 5 o'clock a position 12,000 yards from the *Nürnberg,* when the latter opened fire. At this late hour a long range action was out of the question. As the *Nürnberg* slowed down with two of her boilers burst, the *Kent* closed to 3000 yards and at 7.30 finished off her smaller opponent. The *Dresden,* making well above her schedule speed of 24 knots, had disappeared to southwestward early in the afternoon. Her escape entailed a long search, until, on March 14, 1915, she was destroyed by the *Kent* and *Glasgow* off Juan Fernandez, where she had taken refuge for repairs.

Cruise of the "Emden"

Among the German cruisers other than those of Admiral von Spee's squadron, the exploits of the *Emden* are best known, and reminiscent of the *Alabama's* famous cruise in the American Civil War. It may be noted, however, as indicative of changed conditions, that the *Emden's* depredations covered only two months instead of two years. A 3600 ton ship with a speed of 25 knots, the *Emden* left Kiao-chau on August 6, met von Spee's cruisers in the Ladrones on the 12th, and on September 10 appeared most unexpectedly on the west side of the Bay of Bengal. Here she sank five British merchantmen, all following the customary route with lights aglow. On the 18th she was off the Rangoon River, and 6 days later across the bay at Madras, where she set ablaze two tanks of the Burma Oil Company with half a million gallons of kerosene. From September 26 to 29 she was at the junction of trade routes west of Ceylon, and again, after an overhaul in the Chagos Archipelago to southward, spent October 16-19 in the same profitable field. Like most raiders, she planned to operate in one locality not more than three or four days, and then, avoiding all vessels on her course, strike suddenly elsewhere. During this period, British, Japanese, French, and Russian crusiers—the Germans assert there were 19 at one time—followed her trail.

The most daring adventure of Captain von Müller, the *Emden's* skipper, was now carried out in the harbor of Penang, on the west side of the Malay Peninsula. With an additional false funnel to imitate British county-class cruisers, the *Emden* at daybreak of October 28 passed the picket-boat off the harbor unchallenged, destroyed the Russian cruiser *Jemtchug* by gunfire and two torpedoes, and, after sinking the French destroyer *Mousquet* outside, got safely away. The Russian commander was afterward condemned for letting his ship lie at anchor with open lights, with only an anchor watch, and with strangers at liberty to visit her.

Steaming southward, the raider made her next and last appearance on the morning of November 9 off the British cable and wireless station on the Cocos Islands. As she approached, word was promptly cabled to London, Adelaide, and Singapore, and—more profitably—was wirelessed to an Australian troop convoy then only 45 miles away. The *Emden* caught the message, but nevertheless sent a party ashore, and was standing outside when the armored cruiser *Sydney* came charging up. Against the *Emden's* ten 4.1-inch guns, the *Sydney* had eight 6-inch guns, and she was at least 4 knots faster. Outranged and outdone in speed, the German ship was soon driven ashore in a sinking condition, with a funnel down and steering gear disabled. During her two months' activity thus ended, the *Emden* had made 21 captures, destroying ships and cargoes to the value of over $10,000,000.

The other German cruisers were also short-lived. The *Karlsrühe,* after arming the liner *Kronprinz Wilhelm* off the Bahamas (August 6) and narrowly escaping the *Suffolk* and the *Bristol* by superior speed, operated with great success on the South American trade routes. Her disappearance—long a mystery to the Allies—was due to an internal explosion, just as she was about to crown her exploits by a raid on the island of Barbados. The *Königsberg,* on the east coast of Africa, surprised and sank the British light cruiser *Pegasus*

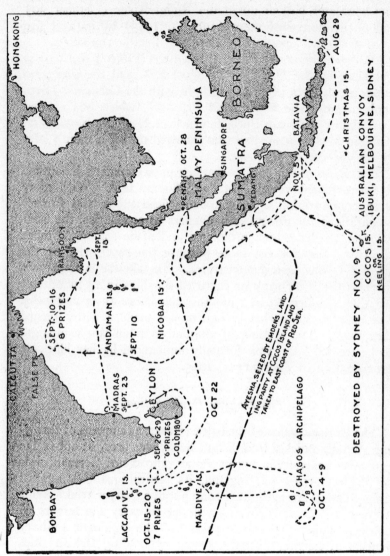

THE CRUISE OF THE EMDEN, SEPT. 1-NOV. 9, 1914

while the latter lay at Mombasa, Zanzibar, making repairs. She was later bottled up in the Rufigi River (October 30) and finally destroyed there (July 11, 1915) by indirect fire from monitors, "spotted" by airplanes.

Of the auxiliary cruisers, the *Kaiser Wilhelm der Grosse* was sunk by the *Highflyer* (August 26), and the *Cap Trafalgar* went down after a hard fight with the *Carmania* (September 14). The *Prinz Eitel Friedrich,* which had entered the Atlantic with von Spee, interned at Newport News, Virginia, in March, 1915, and was followed thither a month later by the *Kronprinz Wilhelm.*

The results of this surface warfare upon commerce amounted to 69 merchant vessels, totaling 280,000 tons. With more strict concentration upon commerce destruction, and further preparations for using German liners as auxiliaries, the campaign might have been prolonged and made somewhat more effective. But for the same purpose the superiority of the submarine was soon demonstrated. To take the later surface raiders: the *Wolf* sank or captured 20 ships in 15 months at sea; the *Seeadler,* 23 in 7 months; the *Möwe* 15 in 2 months. But many a submarine in one month made a better record than these. The opening of Germany's submarine campaign, to be treated later, was formally announced by her blockade proclamation of February 4, 1915.

The Dogger Bank Action

The strategic value of the battle cruiser, as a means of throwing strength quickly into distant fields, was brought out in the campaign against von Spee. As an outcome of German raids on the east coast of England, its tactical qualities, against units of equal strength, were soon put to a sharper trial. Aside from mere *Schrecklichkeit*—a desire to carry the terrors of war to English soil—these raids had the legitimate military objects of helping distant cruisers by holding British ships in home waters, of delaying troop movements to France, and of creating a popular clamor that might force a dislocation or division of the Grand Fleet. The first incursion, on No-

vember 5, 1914, inflicted only trifling damage.   The second, on
December 16, was marked by the bombardment of Scarborough,
Hartlepool, and Whitby, in which about 100 non-combatants
were killed and 500 injured.

This time, however, the British had definite forewarning of
the enemy sortie.   At the wreck of the German cruiser *Magde-
burg* in the Baltic, in the first month of the war, the Russians
had picked from the water a German code book together with a
chart of the North Sea marked off into numbered squares.
This they turned over to the British.   Subsequent neglect of
the Germans to shift their code, combined with skillful use of
directional wireless stations by the British and the generally
excellent work of the Admiralty intelligence service, gave the
latter an almost uncanny accuracy in forecasting enemy moves.

Thus it happened that after the raid of December 16 the retreat of Admiral Hipper, who commanded the German battle
cruiser force, was blocked by four battle cruisers under Admiral
Beatty and a division of six battleships from the Grand Fleet.
There were several contacts, but in the heavy weather and driving mist Hipper slipped past both opposing forces by a course
to northward, and got safely away.

A third sortie, January 24, 1915, brought on the Dogger
Bank action, the first actual engagement between battle cruisers
and one of the two capital ship actions of the war.   At dawn on
this date the *Seydlitz* (flagship of Admiral Hipper), *Moltke,
Derfflinger,* and armored cruiser *Blücher,* with a division of destroyers, were moving westward for a sweep toward the English
coast.   Again with accurate foreknowledge of their strength
and course, the Admiralty had ordered Beatty's battle cruisers
and the Harwich cruiser and destroyer force to a meeting point
on the enemy's projected line of advance.   The Harwich force
first made contact with the enemy about 7 a.m.   Fortunately
for the Germans, they had already been warned of Beatty's approach by one of their scouts, and had just turned back when
the British battle cruisers made them out to southeastward 14
miles away.   The forces opposed are tabulated on the following page.

British	Dis-place-ment	Ar-mor	Guns	Best re-cent speed	German	Dis-place-ment	Ar-mor	Guns	Best re-cent speed
Lion.........	26,350	9″	8 13.5″	31.7	Derfflinger	26,180	13″	8 12″	30
Tiger........	28,500	9″	8 13.5″	32	Seydlitz...	24,610	11″	10 11″	29
Princess Royal	28,350	9″	8 13.5″	31.7	Moltke...	22,640	11″	10 11″	28.4
New Zealand..	18,800	8″	8 12″	29	Blücher...	15,550	6″	12 8.2″	25.3
Indomitable...	17,250	7″	8 12″	28.7					

Settling at once to a stern chase, the British leaders gradually worked up to 28.5 knots, while the Germans, handicapped by the slower *Blücher,* were held down to about 25. At 8.52 the *Lion* (flagship) was within 20,000 yards of the *Blücher,* and after deliberate ranging shots scored her first hit at 9.09. The enemy opened fire at 9.14. Thus the action continued, both squadrons on a south-southeasterly course in lines of bearing, the Germans concentrating on the two leading enemy ships, and the British, as the range decreased, firing on their opposites, though, owing to faulty distribution, the *Tiger* fired for a time on the *Seydlitz* and then on the *Blücher,* leaving the *Moltke* free from attack. The *Seydlitz* was hit only three times during the battle, but one of these shells, at 9.43, put both her after turrets out of action and annihilated their entire guncrews, a total of 159 men. Only quick action prevented the flames from reaching the magazines. The Germans subsequently took strong protective measures against turret fires and their communication downward, though a similar near-disaster in the A turret of the *Lion* was apparently not turned to similar profit.

At about this same time the *Blücher,* under heavy fire, dropped out of the line. Badly crippled, she was assigned by Beatty to the *Indomitable* and was sunk at 12.37. After the injury to the *Seydlitz* the Germans opened the range for a time, and British also turned somewhat away either because of German destroyer threats or in order to utilize the advantage of their longer range guns.

The *Lion* had also suffered severely from the enemy's concentrated fire. During the action she was hit fifteen times. A hit forward under water at 10.18 burst a feed tank and stopped the

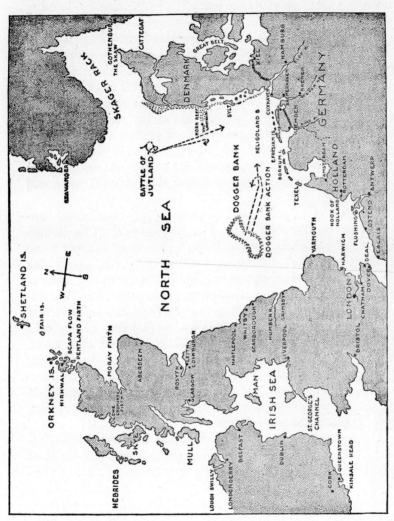

THEATER OF OPERATIONS IN THE NORTH SEA

port engine.   By 10.51, according to Beatty's report, "all lights were out, she was making water rapidly, listing heavily to port, and was unable to maintain her place in the line."   Turning over the command temporarily to Admiral Moore in the *Tiger,* Beatty signaled to "attack the enemy rear" and "keep closer to the enemy", but in the ensuing confusion these orders either were not seen or were misinterpreted.   Just before dropping out the *Lion* had made an abrupt shift to northward on a false alarm of submarines.   This northerly course was continued by the squadron, and after circling about the stricken *Blücher* Admiral Moore about noon broke off the action and turned back.   At this time the *Tiger* had been hit eight times and the *Princess Royal* and *New Zealand* not at all.   At 12.20, when Beatty shifted to the *Princess Royal,* the Germans were well out of range.

"The injury to the *Lion,*" to quote Beatty once more, "undoubtedly deprived us of a greater victory."   The British radios had picked up calls to Hipper promising support from the High Sea Fleet, though as a matter of fact this body was not at sea and its best squadron (Sq. III) was beyond reach at Kiel.   Admiral Moore's decision to give up the chase was influenced, however, by the danger to the *Lion* in case of retreat before superior forces, as well as by the fear that he might be drawn into submarine traps or mine fields.   On the other hand, the distance to Heligoland was still at least 70 miles, the German ships had been slowed down by injuries, and the Grand Fleet was rapidly approaching.   The element of caution, seen again at Jutland fifteen months later, seems to have prevented pressing the engagement to more decisive results.

Among the lessons of the battle, aside from the dangers resulting from turret hits, the most obvious was the folly of including the slower *Blücher* in the German line.   Any encounter that developed on such a raid was almost certain to be with superior forces, against which the armored cruiser would be of slight value.   And in a retreat the lame duck would slow down the whole squadron, or else must be left behind.

The conditions of flight and pursuit in this action emphasized the importance of speed and long-range fire.   Owing to their

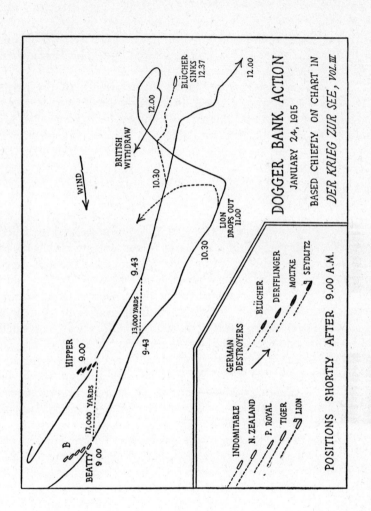

DOGGER BANK ACTION

JANUARY 24, 1915

BASED CHIEFLY ON CHART IN
DER KRIEG ZUR SEE, VOL. III

POSITIONS SHORTLY AFTER 9.00 A.M.

greater angle of elevation, the German 11-inch and 12-inch guns were not outranged by the British 13.5-inch guns, and at 17,000 yards their projectiles had no greater angle of fall.   The chief superiority of the larger ordnance lay in their heavier bursting charges and greater striking energy, 12,800 foot-tons to 8,900 foot-tons.   This was illustrated by the hit that almost proved fatal to the *Seydlitz*.

It is interesting to note that as an aftermath of the battle Admiral Moore, who had been in Beatty's squadron only about two weeks, was soon shifted to another berth; and for his failure to have support available for Hipper, Admiral von Ingenohl was replaced in command of the High Sea Fleet by Admiral von Pohl.

The Dardanelles Campaign

Throughout the war a difference of opinion existed in Allied councils as to whether it was better to concentrate all efforts in the western sphere of operations, or to assail the Central Powers in the Near East as well, where the accession of Turkey (and later of Bulgaria) threatened to put the resources of all south-eastern Europe under Teutonic control, and even opened a gateway into Asia.   Such a division of effort was suggested not only by the necessity of protecting the Suez Canal, Egypt, and Mesopotamia, but by the difficulty of breaking the stalemate on the western front, and by the opportunity that would be offered of utilizing Allied control of sea communications. Furthermore, the Allies had a large margin of predreadnoughts and cruisers ready for action and of no real value elsewhere.

On November 3, 1914, three days after Turkey entered the war, an Allied naval force that had been watching off the Dardanelles engaged the outer forts in a 10-minute bombardment, of no significance save perhaps as a warning to the Turks of trouble later on.   In the same month the First Lord of the British Admiralty, Mr. Winston Churchill, proposed an attack on the Straits as "an ideal method of defending Egypt"; but it was not seriously considered until, on January 2, Russia sent an urgent appeal for a diversion to relieve her forces in the

Caucasus. Lord Kitchener, the British Minister of War, answered favorably, but, feeling that he had no troops to spare, turned the solution over to the Navy.

From the first the decision was influenced by political considerations. Russia needed assurance of Allied solidarity—and it is significant that in February Lord Grey announced that England no longer opposed Russia's ambition to control Constantinople. Nine-tenths of Russia's exports were blocked by the closing of the Straits; their reopening would afford not only access to her vast stores of foodstuffs, but an entry—infinitely more convenient than Vladivostok or Archangel—for munitions and essential supplies. The Balkan States were wavering. In Turkey there was a strong neutral or pro-Ally sentiment. Victory would give an enormous material advantage, help Russia in the impending German drive on her southwestern frontier, and bolster Allied prestige throughout the eastern world.

Faced with the problem, the Admiralty sent an inquiry to Admiral Carden, in command on the scene, as to the practicability of forcing the Dardanelles by the use of ships alone, assuming that old ships would be employed, and "that the importance of the results would justify severe loss." He replied on January 5: "I do not think the Dardanelles can be rushed, but they might be forced by extended operations with a large number of ships." In answer to further inquiries, accompanied by not altogether warranted assurance from the First Lord that "High authorities here concur in your opinion," Admiral Carden outlined four successive operations:

(a) The destruction of defenses at the entrance to the Dardanelles.

(b) Action inside the Straits, so as to clear the defenses up to and including Kephez Point battery No. 8.

(c) Destruction of defenses of the Narrows.

(d) Sweeping of a clear channel through the mine-field and advance through the Narrows, followed by a reduction of the forts further up, and advance into the Sea of Marmora.

This plan was presented at a meeting of the British War Council on January 13. It may be noted at this point that the War Council, though composed of 7 members of the Cabinet,

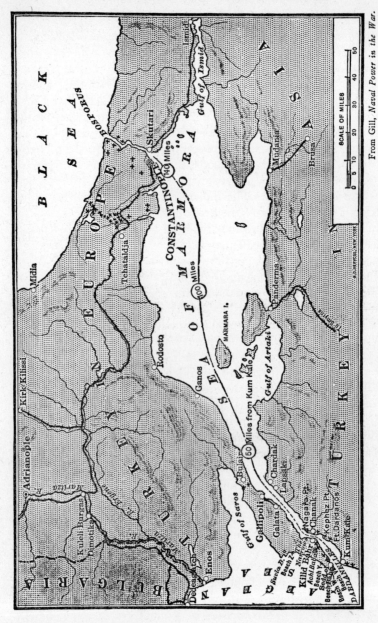

THE APPROACHES TO CONSTANTINOPLE

From Gill, Naval Power in the War.

was at this time dominated by a triumvirate—the Premier (Mr. Asquith), the Minister of War (General Kitchener), and the First Lord of the Admiralty (Mr. Churchill); and in this triumvirate, despite the fact that England's strength was primarily naval, the head of the War Office played a leading rôle. The First Sea Lord (Admiral Fisher) and one or two other military experts attended the Council meetings, but they were not members, and their function, at least as they saw it, was "to open their mouths when told to." Staff organizations existed also at both the War Office and the Admiralty, at the latter consisting of the First Lord, First Sea Lord and three other officers not on the Admiralty Board. The working of this improvised and far from ideal machinery for the supreme task of conducting the war is interestingly revealed in the report[1] of the commission subsequently appointed to investigate the Dardanelles Campaign.

"Mr. Churchill," according to this report, "appears to have advocated the attack by ships alone before the War Council on a certain amount of half-hearted and hesitating expert opinion." Encouraged by his sanguine and aggressive spirit, the Council decided that "the Admiralty should prepare for a naval expedition in February to bombard and take the Gallipoli Peninsula with Constantinople as its objective." In view of the fact that the operation as then conceived was to be purely naval, the word "take" suggests an initial misconception of what the navy could do. The support for the decision, especially from the naval experts, was chiefly on the assumption that if Admiral Carden's first operation were unpromising, the whole plan might be dropped.

Admiral Fisher's misgivings as to the wisdom of the enterprise soon increased, owing primarily to his desire to employ the full naval strength in the home field. He did not believe that "cutting off the enemy's big toe in the East was better than stabbing him to the heart." He had begun the construction of 612 new vessels ranging from "hush-hush" ships of 33 knots and 20-inch guns to 200 motor-boats, and he wished to strike

[1]British ANNUAL REGISTER, 1918, Appendix, pp. 24 ff., from which quotations here are taken.

for access to the Baltic, with a threat of invasion on Germany's Baltic coast. The validity of his objections to the Dardanelles plan appears to depend on the practicability of this alternative, which was not attempted later in the war. The First Lord and the First Sea Lord presented their difference of opinion to the Premier, but it appears that there was no ill feeling; Admiral Fisher later wrote that "Churchill had courage and imagination —he was a war man."

At a Council meeting on January 28, when the decision was made definite, Admiral Fisher was not asked for an opinion and expressed none. (The Investigation Commission declared that the naval experts should have been asked, and should have expressed their views whether asked or not.) But there was a dramatic moment when, after rising as if to leave the Council in protest, he was quickly followed by Lord Kitchener, who pointed out that all the others were in favor of the plan, and induced him once more to take his seat. After the decision, Mr. Churchill testifies, "I never looked back. We had left the region of discussion and consultation, of balancings and misgivings. The matter had now passed into the domain of action."

To turn to the scene of operations, there were now assembled at the Dardanelles 10 British and 4 French predreadnoughts, together with the new battleship *Queen Elizabeth,* the battle cruiser *Inflexible,* and many cruisers and torpedo craft. On February 19, 1915, again on February 25–26, and on March 1–7, this force bombarded the outer forts at Kum Kale and Sedd-el-Bahr and the batteries 10 miles further up at Kephez Point. These were in part silenced and demolished by landing parties. Bad weather, however, interfered with operations, and there was also some shortage of ammunition. The batteries, and especially the mobile artillery of the Turks, still greatly hampered the work of mine sweeping, which at terrible hazards was carried on at night within the Straits.

In the meantime the Government, to quote General Callwell, the Director of Military Operations, had "drifted into a big military attack." But the despatch from England of the 29th Division, which was to join the forces available in Egypt, was delayed, owing to Lord Kitchener's concern about the western situation, from Feb. 22 to March 16—an unfortunate loss of time. By March 17, however, the troops from Egypt and most of the French contingent were assembled at the island of Lemnos, and General Sir Ian Hamilton had arrived to take command. His instructions included the statement that "employment of military forces on any large scale at this juncture is only contemplated in the event of the fleet failing to get through after every effort has been exhausted. Having entered on the project of forcing the Straits, there can be no idea of abandoning the scheme."

On March 11 the First Lord sent to Admiral Carden a despatch asking whether the time had not arrived when "you will have to press hard for a decision," and adding: "Every well-conceived action for forcing a decision, even should regrettable losses be entailed, will receive our support." The Admiral replied concurring, but expressing the opinion that "in order to insure my communication line immediately fleet enters Sea of Marmora, military operations should be opened at once." On March 16 he resigned owing to ill health, and his second in command, Admiral de Robeck, succeeded, with the feeling that he had orders to force the Straits.

The attack on March 18 was the crucial and, as it proved, the final action of the purely naval campaign. At this time the mines had been swept as far up as Kephez Point, and a clear channel opened for some distance beyond. For about an hour during the morning the *Queen Elizabeth* and five other British ships bombarded the Narrows forts at 14,000 yards. Then shortly after 12.00 the French predreadnoughts *Suffren, Gaulois, Charlemagne,* and *Bouvet* approached to about 9,000 yards and by 1.45 had for the time being silenced the batteries at the Narrows. The scene during this bombardment was, as described by participants, one of magnificent though terrible grandeur. Forts, mobile batteries, and the great battleships, as well as a host of destroyers, sweepers and other small craft were all blazing away in this hill-encircled sea arena where Greeks, Romans, and Saracens had fought many centuries before. Turkish reports indicate that at this time conditions in the forts were critical. Communications were destroyed; numerous guns were knocked out, buried in débris, or otherwise put out of action; and ammunition was running low.   On the other hand, though the battleships were hit repeatedly, their actual injuries

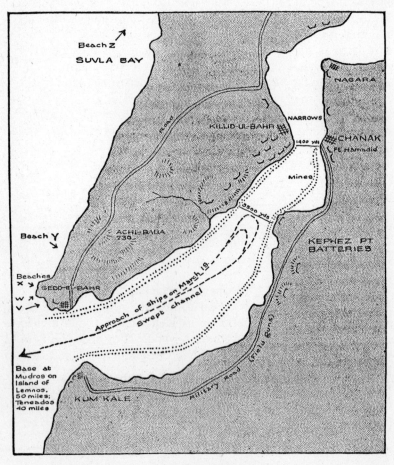

DARDANELLES DEFENSES

from gunfire were not such as to discourage further advance. In the day's action only 6 were killed and 12 wounded by the guns of the forts.

Six British battleships now advanced to relieve the French.

In the maneuvering and withdrawal the *Bouvet* struck a mine
(1.54) and sank in two minutes with the loss of over 600 men.
To cap this startling disaster, the *Gaulois* also was injured by
two shells under water and had to be beached on an island outside the Straits.   The bombardment nevertheless continued, and
at four o'clock, according to Admiral de Robeck's report, "the
forts at the Narrows were practically silenced, the batteries
guarding the mine fields were put to flight, and the situation
appeared most favorable for clearing the mine fields."

But this encouraging aspect of affairs underwent a sudden
change.   At 4.06 the *Inflexible* struck a mine near the Asiatic
shore and was injured so badly she had to be taken to Tenedos.
Ten minutes later the *Irresistible* also struck a mine.   And
finally the *Ocean,* which in the resultant confusion had been
steaming about in the vicinity and standing by her crippled
fellow, struck a third mine about 6 p.m.   Both the *Irresistible*
and the *Ocean* sank that night, after the safe removal of their
personnel.   All these mine injuries were inflicted, as it was
revealed after the war, not by drifting mines as was at first
supposed, but by a single line of about 20 mines moored in Eren
Keui Bay on March 8 and not afterward discovered or removed.

The mine fields unquestionably were the chief menace.
Above the point reached by the battleships on March 18 there
were ten rows of anchored mines staggered across the channel,
amounting in all to about 370.   There was, however, no reserve
supply available in Turkey at that time.   In addition, there were
three fixed torpedo tubes at Nagara Point, but these took twenty
minutes to reload and two of them did not fire half way across
the channel.

Military opinion has very generally pronounced against the
practicability of forcing these obstacles by a purely naval attack.
But there is some good support for the view that it might have
been accomplished—either by a resolute prosecution of the
methods previously followed, or by a "rush through", preferably
at early dawn, in which the fleet in column, protected by dummy
ships, bumpers, or such other devices as naval ingenuity could
suggest, might conceivably have suffered less than in pro-

tracted maneuvering below the forts. Such an attack would have been in the spirit of Farragut's "Damn the torpedoes! Full steam ahead!" at Mobile Bay. Torpedoes, as Farragut called mines, were of course far less of a menace in 1864 than in 1915. But while we are speaking of Farragut, it may be remembered that in dealing with the forts below New Orleans —a situation in many respects analogous to that at the Dardanelles—he was not unduly worried by what the forts could do after he got past them.

On the general feasibility of forcing operations, Admiral Sir Roger Keyes, who was naval chief of staff throughout the Dardanelles campaign, writes as follows in his *Naval Memoirs, The Narrow Seas to the Dardanelles,* p. 186:

"I wish to place on record that I had no doubt then, and have none now—and nothing will ever shake my opinion—that from the 4th April, 1915,[1] onwards, the fleet could have forced the Straits, and with losses trifling in comparison with those the army suffered, could have entered the Marmora with sufficient force to destroy the Turco-German fleet. This operation would have cut the communications—which were sea-borne—of any Turkish armies either in Gallipoli or on the Asiatic side, and would have led immediately to a victory decisive upon the whole course of the war."

General von der Goltz, in command of the Turkish army, is also quoted as having stated that "Although he thought it was almost impossible to force the Dardanelles, still, if the English thought it an important move of the general war, they could by sacrificing ten ships force the entrance, and do it very fast, and be up in Marmora within ten hours from the time they forced it."[2] Admiral Fisher estimated that the loss would be 12 ships.

If such deductions had to be made, there would be no great surplus to deal with the *Göben,* which would fight desperately, or

---

[1] On this date battleship reinforcements arrived.

[2] Repeated by Baron von Wangenheim, German Ambassador to Turkey, to U. S. Ambassador Morgenthau, prior to the attack of March 18, AMBASSADOR MORGENTHAU'S STORY (1919), p. 184.

with the defenses of Constantinople. Indeed such losses would seem absolutely prohibitive if viewed only from the narrow standpoint of the force engaged, without taking account that the old predreadnoughts were (aside from their personnel) of no other value whatever in the naval war, and that immense issues were at stake in the campaign. It is of course easy to see that victory purchased by the loss of 10 predreadnoughts and 10,000 men would be cheap as compared with the loss of 120,000 men killed, wounded, and missing in the later campaign on land.

General Callwell has pointed out that the naval commanders were properly worried about what would happen after they got through the Straits, if the Sublime Porte did not promptly "throw up the sponge." "The communications would have remained closed to colliers and small craft by movable armament, if not also by mines. Forcing the pass would in fact have resembled bursting through a swing door. Soldiers and sailors alike have an instinctive horror of a trap, and they are in the habit of looking behind them as well as before them."[1] But according to Ambassador Morgenthau, who was in a better position than most to form an opinion, "The whole Ottoman State on that 18th day of March, 1915, when the Allied Fleet abandoned the attack, was on the brink of dissolution." The Turkish Government was divided into factions and restive under German domination, and there was an excellent prospect that it would have capitulated under the guns of the Allied fleet. If not, then there might have been nothing left for the latter but to try to get back the way it came.

Feeling in Constantinople during the month before the attack has just been suggested; it was nervous in the extreme. Neither Turks nor Germans felt assured that the Dardanelles could withstand British naval power. Plans were made for a general exit to Asia Minor, and there was a conviction that in a few days Allied ships would be in the Golden Horn. At the forts, postwar evidence indicates that the situation was also serious. The guns, though manned largely by Germans, were not of the latest type, and for a month had been engaged in almost daily

[1] NINETEENTH CENTURY AND AFTER, March, 1919, p. 486.

bombardment. Ammunition was running short. According to a German narrative:

"Most of the Turkish ammunition had been expended. The medium howitzers and mine-field batteries had fired half their supply . . . The long range H. E. shells, which alone were effective against armor, were nearly used up. Ft. Hamadieh had only 17 of them, Kilid Bahr but 10. Also there was no reserve of mines. What, then, was to happen if the battle were renewed on the 19th and following days with undiminished violence?"[1]

To this may be added the statement of Enver Pasha: "If the English had only had the courage to rush more ships through the Dardanelles they could have got to Constantinople, but their delay enabled us to fortify the peninsula, and in 6 weeks' time we had taken down there over 200 Austrian Skoda guns."

If Mr. Churchill was chiefly responsible for undertaking the campaign, he was not responsible for the changed plan after March 18. "It never occurred to me," he states, "that we should not go on." Admiral de Robeck in his first despatches appeared to share this view. On March 26, however, he telegraphed: "I do not hold check on 18th decisive, but having met General Hamilton on 22d and heard his proposals I now consider a combined operation essential to obtain great results and object of campaign." This despatch, Mr. Churchill says, "involved a complete change of plan and was a vital decision. I regretted it very much. I believed then, as I believe now, that we were separated by very little from complete success." He proposed that the admiral should be directed to renew the attack; but the First Sea Lord did not agree, nor did Admiral Sir Arthur Wilson, nor Admiral Sir Henry Jackson. So it was decided to wait for the army, and some satire has been directed at Mr. Churchill and those other "acknowledged experts in the technicalities of amphibious warfare," Mr. Balfour and Mr. Asquith, who were inclined to share his views. The verdict of the Dardanelles Commission was that, "Had the attack been renewed within a day or two there is no reason to suppose that

[1] DER KAMPF UM DIE DARDANELLEN (1915). Quoted in Keyes' *Naval Memoirs*.

the proportion of casualties would have been less; and, if so, even had the second attack succeeded, a very weak force would have been left for subsequent naval operations."

Once decided upon, it was highly essential that the combined operation should begin without further delay. But it was now found that the army transports had been loaded, so to speak, up-side-down, with guns and munitions buried under tents and supplies. Sending them back to Alexandria for reloading involved a six weeks' delay, though Lord Kitchener wired, "I think you had better know at once that I regard such postponement as far too long." The landing on the tip of the Gallipoli Peninsula, which was nearest to the forts in the Straits and said to be the only feasible place, actually began on April 25, and was achieved under the guns of the fleet, and by almost unexampled feats of heroism by boats' crews and the first parties on shore.

Henceforth the campaign belongs to military rather than naval history, though throughout the later operations the navy gave the army vital and unstinted support. "By our navy we went there and were kept there," writes Mr. John Masefield in *Gallipoli*, "and by our navy we came away. During the nine months of our hold on the peninsula over 300,000 men were brought by the navy from places three, four, and even six thousand miles away. During the operations some half of these were removed by our navy, as sick and wounded, to ports from 800 to 3,000 miles away. Every day, for 11 months, ships of our navy moved up and down the Gallipoli coast bombarding the Turk positions. Every day during the operations our navy kept our armies in food, drink, and supplies. Every day, in all that time, if weather permitted, ships of our navy cruised in the Narrows and off Constantinople, and the seaplanes of our navy raided and scouted within the Turkish lines."

On May 12 a Turkish destroyer torpedoed the predreadnought *Goliath;* and on May 25–26 the German submarine *U 23*, which had made the long voyage by way of Gibraltar, sank the *Triumph* and the *Majestic*. It was with prevision of such attacks that Admiral Fisher, according to his own statement, resigned as a protest against the retention of the *Queen Elizabeth* and other capital units in this unpromising field.

On the other hand, the work of British and French submarines, which threaded their way past mines, nets, and torpedo tubes into the Sea of Marmora, forms a heroic if minor chapter in the story of the naval war.   The British *E 11,* Commander Nasmith, made three trips inside and remained in all 96 days, sinking no less than 101 craft of various descriptions, including a battleship, a destroyer, and three gunboats.   Altogether the 13 British and French boats engaged in this work made 27 entries through the Straits.   Eight were lost, but they levied heavy toll on Turkish transports and supply vessels moving between Constantinople and Gallipoli.[1]

So almost unprecedented were the problems involved in a naval attack on the Dardanelles that it appears rash to condemn either the conception or the conduct of an operation that ended in failure when seemingly on the verge of success.   Clearly the campaign was handicapped by lack of unanimous and wholehearted support on the part of the authorities at home, and also by lack of a carefully considered plan.   There was too much of what the historian Cruttwell calls "willing the end without willing the means."   The operation was not thoroughly thought out at the start, and, partly in consequence, suffered thereafter from trying delays and divided councils.   A month after March 18, when the army had already lost 26,000 men, Admiral de Robeck offered in vain to renew the naval attack, and in October, when Admiral Wemyss was in command, his chief of staff Roger Keyes came to London to make another hopeless appeal. The final failure was a tremendous blow to British and Allied prestige throughout the East.   Even so, the operation was not wholly fruitless.   It undoubtedly relieved Russia, kept Bulgaria neutral for at least five months, and immobilized 300,000 Turks for nine months' time.   Upon the withdrawal in December, 1915, many of the Allied troops were transferred to Salonika; and it is noteworthy that there, as at Gallipoli, the army was dependent on the navy for the transport of troops, munitions, and in fact virtually everything needed in the campaign.

Aside from the Dardanelles failure, the naval situation at the

[1]The total was 1 battleship, 1 destroyer, 5 gunboats, 11 transports, 44 steamers, and 148 sailing vessels.

close of 1915 was such as to give assurance to the Western Powers. They had converted potential control of the sea into actual control, save in limited areas on the enemies' sea frontiers. Germany had lost her cruisers and her colonies, and her shipping had been destroyed or driven from the seas. Though the losses from submarines averaged 150,000 tons a month in 1915, they had not yet caused genuine alarm. The German fleet was still a menace, but in spite of attrition warfare, the Grand Fleet was relatively stronger than in 1914.

REFERENCES

British Official HISTORY OF THE GREAT WAR, Naval Operations, Vols. II–III.
DER KRIEG IN DER NORD SEE (German Official Naval History), 2 vols.
MY MEMOIRS, Admiral von Tirpitz, 1919.
GERMANY'S HIGH SEA FLEET IN THE WORLD WAR, Admiral Scheer, 1920.
THE GRAND FLEET, Admiral Jellicoe, 1919.
WITH BEATTY IN THE NORTH SEA, Filson Young, 1921.
NAVAL MEMOIRS: THE NARROW SEAS TO THE DARDANELLES, Admiral Roger Keyes, 1934.
GALLIPOLI DIARY, Sir Ian Hamilton, 1920.
THE WORLD CRISIS, Winston Churchill, 1923–1931.
A HISTORY OF THE GREAT WAR, 1914–1918, C. R. M. F. Cruttwell, 1934.
THE DARDANELLES EXPEDITION, Captain W. D. Puleston, U. S. N., 1926.

CHAPTER XVI

THE WORLD WAR [*Continued*]: THE BATTLE OF JUTLAND

THE commander of the British forces at the battle of Jutland, to quote a familiar phrase of Winston Churchill's, was the only man who could have "lost the war in an afternoon." Perhaps —though this might be disputed—the phrase would be equally true if for "could have lost" were substituted "could have won." As in many another naval engagement we have studied, the stakes at issue in the battle were very great as compared with the human or even the tremendous material forces that were brought to bear. Strategically, Jutland was neither lost nor won, since thereafter the naval situation remained much as it was before. Yet from the standpoint of naval history the battle is of outstanding importance, as the one great fleet action of the World War, and as the most recent in which modern weapons and tactics have come into play. Controversy has raged about almost every move in the battle, and lessons true or false have been drawn which will influence naval construction and methods of fighting until wars end or new wars begin.

Attention has already been drawn to the geographical advantages of England in a naval war with Germany, which enabled her to close Germany's approaches to the Atlantic and cut off her overseas trade; and, on the other hand, to the advantages of Germany arising from her control of the Baltic and her shallow, well-protected North Sea coastline, which, combined with modern weapons such as mines, aircraft, and submarines, made an old-fashioned close blockade impossible. The North Sea itself remained a disputed area throughout the war. From its shelter in the estuaries of the Elbe and Weser the German fleet could undertake raids on the English coast or the Scandinavian trade;

while from its bases far to the northward in the Orkneys and the Scottish firths, supposedly though actually not beyond the reach of German submarines, the Grand Fleet could make periodic sweeps of the North Sea, reënforce the long-range blockade, and, in conjunction with the Dover patrol in the Channel and the cruiser and destroyer forces based at Harwich on the East Coast, afford some protection against German sorties.

Both the main forces in this area were controlled by a cautious naval strategy, very different from that which had marked British conduct of naval war in the past.   By the British this policy was defended on the ground that the fleet stood as a bulwark to guard their shores from invasion, protect their commerce and communications with the Dominions and Continental allies, and, as just stated, support the blockade, on the slow, steady pressure of which they counted to bring the enemy to terms.   The very essence of this "no risks" policy was embodied in Admiral Jellicoe's much-discussed operations memorandum of October 30, 1914.   "Not leaving anything to chance," he wrote, "because our fleet was the one and only factor that was vital to the existence of the empire, as indeed to the Allied cause."   Hence he stated that he would avoid action close to the enemy bases, and would also avoid a direct pursuit of the enemy that would expose his fleet to under-water damage by mine or torpedo.   This, he wrote, "might disable half of our battle fleet before the guns opened fire."   The memorandum was approved by the Admiralty, of which Winston Churchill was then First Lord, though as Commander Frost has remarked, "How so aggressive a leader as Churchill consented to such a defensive attitude in complete variance with the Nelsonian tradition is a mystery that has never been explained."   It had the sanction also of the First Sea Lord, Admiral Fisher, though he had once made the pregnant overstatement that "the most awful thing in war is the careful man."

This matter of policy is of primary importance, for it had its effect on the whole spirit of the Grand Fleet and on every tactical move at Jutland.   Though responsibility for it must rest at least partly with the Admiralty, it is certain that Churchill condemned it severely after the war. In any case, while his function as minister at the head of the Navy Department was to correlate naval and national policies, to assign aims and select leaders, it was not to settle the professional question as to how these aims should be attained. Some responsibility has also been attached to the vigorous writings of Sir Julian Corbett, the naval historian. But his influence has probably been exaggerated, and it is difficult to see how he could have favored ideas so at variance with the traditions illustrated in British naval history over three hundred years. There is some truth, however, in the view that the changes in British naval policy reflected a changed national policy. Britain was no longer a nation aggressively bent on expansion. Her policy, rather, was defensive—"We hold what we have."

As a further basis for the cautious use of the fleet, Admiral Jellicoe himself suggested vaguely that it must be preserved in case it "might later be called upon to confront a situation of much wider scope than that already existing." Was this a reference to possible American intervention on the side of Germany? Aside from the fact that this danger might have been discounted, British statesmanship and strategy were surely not at so low an ebb as to husband a powerful weapon for defeating one enemy, in order to be able later to meet two combined. In any event, these two-fold or divided missions—first to destroy the enemy fleet, and second to preserve one's own fleet against a future contingency—could not be readily combined. As Captain C. C. Gill, U. S. Navy, has remarked:

"In reality there were two 'objectives', one to safeguard British naval supremacy and the other to defeat and annihilate the enemy fleet. Difficulties are increased when two objectives are sought simultaneously. This is particularly true when the two are somewhat in opposition so that the attainment of one interferes with rather than helps the attainment of the other. Singleness of purpose is frustrated, initiative of subordinates is confused and cramped, prompt and concerted action is handicapped."[1]

[1] *The Battle of Jutland, a Strategic and Tactical Study* (Lectures given at the Brazilian Naval War College, 1935).

For Germany a defensive naval policy had more obvious justification. The High Sea Fleet was definitely inferior, in a ratio, roughly, of about 8 to 5. But even as an inactive "fleet in being" it maintained control of the Baltic, cut off Russia's Baltic ports, and gave complete protection to Germany's whole northern sea frontier. In German thought, moreover, the fleet was subordinated to the army, with which the government at first confidently expected to win the war on land. The Kaiser, it is said, wished to keep his splendid navy intact so that, when the land war was won, he could drive a better peace bargain with England. His influence over the naval staff was much greater than it was over the army, and after the Heligoland Bight losses he gave orders that no major operation should be undertaken without his direct approval. But while this caution might be well enough for the main fleet, a basic element in German naval policy had always been the "warfare of attrition", by which British superiority was to be gradually worn down. And yet in the first two years of the war even the lesser fleet elements were not aggressively used to this end. Owing to more rapid construction the British were stronger in the North Sea in 1916 than in 1914. Effective beginnings had been made in German submarine warfare on commerce, but under Admiral von Ingenohl, and in the second year under his successor Von Pohl, the High Sea force had attempted little against the enemy fleet.

A new spirit, however, developed in the High Sea Fleet in the spring of 1916 when the command was taken over by Vice-Admiral Reinhard Scheer. As a squadron commander he had shared the eagerness of the fleet personnel for aggressive action, and his aim now was to employ to this end all the means at his disposal—mines, aircraft, submarines, and also the main fleet. The political and military situations favored such activity. The Verdun offensive was slowing down, blockade strictures were already oppressive, successes at sea would bolster German morale and justify pre-war sacrifices for the building of a navy. Furthermore, in response to President Wilson's vigorous protests after the *Sussex* sinking (March 26, 1916), the German Government had again promised to curb its submarine warfare, and this would release U boats for use with the fleet.

After sorties in March and again in April, 1916, Admiral Scheer conceived the operation which led directly to Jutland. This was to be another raid on the English coast near Sunderland, prior to which all available submarines were to be stationed off the British bases, for a period to extend from May 23 to June 1, in order to strike at the British as they put out to meet the attack.   What was hoped for thereafter was not a fight to a finish, for, as Scheer said, "the ratio of strength prevents us from seeking a battle to a decision with the concentrated enemy fleet;" rather the hope was for a German concentration on some detached enemy force.

On the British side also there was at this time a trend toward more positive action, partly in response to the urgent need for more direct communications with Russia, partly to allay the general dissatisfaction at the passive aspect of the naval war. A plan was conceived for a sweep into the approaches to the Baltic, to begin on June 2, the object of which was very similar to that of Germany's raid toward Sunderland.   In addition to this, owing to the excellent radio information service described in the preceding chapter, the British were well aware of the Germans' contemplated naval activities at the close of May.   On the afternoon of May 30 an Admiralty despatch ordered Admiral Jellicoe with the battleship force at Scapa and Admiral Beatty with the battle cruisers at Rosyth to put to sea.

Thus it happened that at midnight on May 30–31, when the High Sea Fleet was on the point of departure from Jade Roads, the British forces were already steaming eastward, with an appointed rendezvous next day west of the Skagerrak.   At that time there were still about a dozen U boats off the British bases, but there were only two or three contacts.   These resulted in no losses to the British and brought to Scheer only vague radio reports as to the size of the enemy forces or their probable movements.

On the German side, the projected operation had been delayed by repair work and bad weather, and at the last moment, since visibility continued unfavorable for scouting by Zeppelins, the objective was suddenly changed from a raid on the English coast to a shorter movement northward toward the Skagerrak.

The actual sailing of the German divisions, shortly after midnight, and their subsequent movements, were not definitely known either by the British Admiralty or the British commanders at sea, since Scheer, profiting by past experience, had

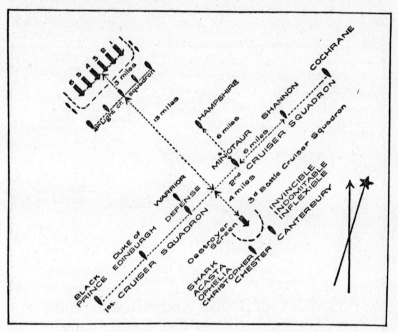

CRUISING FORMATION OF THE BRITISH BATTLE FLEET

(After diagram by Lieut.-Comdr. H. H. Frost, U.S.N., *U. S. Naval Institute Proceedings, Nov., 1919.*)

Forces:
24 Dreadnought Battleships
3 Battle Cruisers
12 Light Cruisers
8 Armored Cruisers
51 Destroyers
Note: One destroyer accompanied each armored cruiser.

arranged to receive and transmit all flagship radio messages indirectly by means of a guardship stationed in the roads.   Hence the meeting of the two fleets on the following afternoon was partly fortuitous; hence also, even throughout the battle, neither side had full data as to the strength of the forces opposed.

At 2 p.m. on the 31st the British main fleet under Admiral Sir John Jellicoe was west of the Skagerrak in the position indicated on the map, page 331, holding a southeasterly course. It consisted of 24 battleships formed in a line of six divisions and screened by cruisers and destroyers. Sixteen miles ahead of the battleships were two armored cruiser divisions of four ships each with the *Hampshire* between to serve as a link for signals to and from the main body. Four miles further ahead

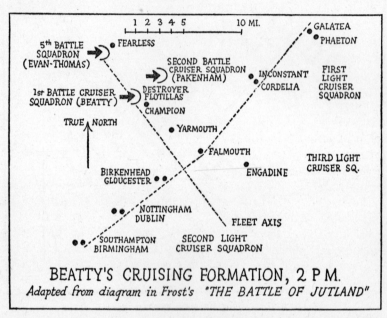

BEATTY'S CRUISING FORMATION, 2 P.M.
Adapted from diagram in Frost's "THE BATTLE OF JUTLAND"

was the 3rd Battle Cruiser Squadron of three ships under Rear Admiral Hood, screened also by destroyers and light cruisers. The diagram on page 353 shows the complete disposition and strength of Admiral Jellicoe's immediate command, and illustrates also the complexity of fleet formation under modern conditions, especially when it is realized that the whole fleet was proceeding on its base course by zigzagging.

Some seventy miles to the southward the scouting forces under Vice-Admiral Sir David Beatty were about to turn from an easterly to a northeasterly course. The 1st Battle Cruiser Squadron of four ships headed by the flagship *Lion* was flanked three miles to the E.N.E. by the 2nd Battle Cruiser Squadron of

two ships, and five miles to the N.N.W. by the 5th Battle
Squadron, consisting of four of the finest battleships in the fleet,
25-knot *Queen Elizabeths,* under Rear Admiral Evan-Thomas.
This squadron had been added to Beatty's command only a week
before, and the two forces had had little or no practice in joint
operations.   The three accompanying light cruiser divisions were
spread out to the southeast at five-mile intervals between ships.

At the same hour, 2 p.m., Vice-Admiral Karl Hipper, with
the German scouting force, was heading northward, some fifteen
or twenty miles southeast of Beatty.   Hipper commanded
Scouting Group I consisting of the battle cruisers *Lützow*
(flag), *Derfflinger, Seydlitz,* and *Von der Tann,* accompanied
by Scouting Group II of 5 light cruisers and by 30 destroyers.
Sixty miles south of Hipper was the main body of the High Sea
Fleet under Vice-Admiral Scheer.   It was in one long column
consisting of two divisions (Divisions I and III) of modern
dreadnoughts, 16 in all, the fleet flagship *Friedrich der Grosse*
being tenth ship in the column, followed by Division II of 6 predreadnoughts.   In battle conditions these last slower and older
ships might prove, like the *Blücher* at the Dogger Bank, more of
a liability than an asset, but sentiment and the pleas of their
gallant commander, Admiral Mauve, induced Scheer at the last
moment to bring them along.   The screen consisted of 6 light
cruisers and 31 destroyers.

Thus the stage was set and the characters disposed for the
great naval drama of that day.   The following table shows the
strength of the opposing forces:

Type	British (Beatty)	German (Hipper)
Dreadnought Battleships	4	0
Battle Cruisers	6	5
Light Cruisers[1]	15	5
Destroyers	27	30

	(Jellicoe)	(Scheer)
Dreadnought Battleships	24	16
Predreadnought Battleships	0	6
Battle Cruisers	3	0
Armored Cruisers	8	0
Light Cruisers	12	6
Destroyers	51	31

[1]Beatty's light cruisers included one seaplane carrier.

The British had a total of 344 heavy guns as compared with the Germans' 244, and owing to their larger size a single discharge of all the British heavy guns would have weighed over 713,000 pounds, as compared with about 213,000 for the Germans. D'Eyncourt in *Naval Construction During the War* estimates that the British weight of broadside was superior by about 3 to 1. The Germans were decidedly better in armor protection and watertight compartmentation. Leaving out of account as of slight fighting value the British armored cruisers and the German predreadnoughts, the British superiority in tonnage was about 7 to 4.

The First Phase

At 2.20 the light cruiser *Galatea,* furthest to the east of Beatty's scouts, reported two enemy vessels engaged in boarding a neutral steamer. Beatty thereupon increased speed on a south-southeasterly course to cut off their retreat. Orders to the division of *Queen Elizabeths* for a similar change of course and speed were communicated by flag signal, but were not received and executed until about ten minutes later, and then only after a "zigzag" to northward, the net result of which was to open the distance between the two divisions to nearly ten miles. In the subsequent maneuvering this gap was only partly closed, so that when the battle cruisers opened fire Beatty's battleship supports were over eight miles astern. To both sides, at this initial stage, quick, accurate information would have been of infinite value. Had Beatty secured this, he might quite possibly have placed his whole force across Hipper's line of retreat, with the *Queen Elizabeths* in close contact with or to south of the *Lions*. On the other hand, had Hipper known that he was dealing not only with 6 battle cruisers but with 4 fast battleships, he might not so readily have advanced into action. Whatever the defects in Beatty's disposition of forces at this time, there has been nothing but praise for his fighting spirit, and for those qualities of dashing leadership which had brought him to flag rank while still under forty.

In actuality, the scouting cruisers on both sides were led far to northward in a kind of mutual pursuit. When Beatty opened fire the 1st and 3rd British light cruiser divisions were 17 miles away, and they had no further part in the battle cruiser action.

At 2.45 Beatty ordered out a seaplane from the carrier *Engadine,* the first instance of air scouting in fleet combat, and its only use that day, since the five Zeppelins later sent out by the Germans saw nothing of the battle. The British plane did not take off till 3.08, and its subsequent information, though accurate, came too late and was not put through to the flagship. Meanwhile the *Galatea* made further reports of "heavy smoke as from a fleet."

At the first message from the *Galatea,* which had been intercepted on Jellicoe's flagship *Iron Duke,* the speed of the main fleet was increased to bring it toward the fighting, and Hood's Third Battle Cruiser Squadron was despatched ahead to cut off a possible retreat of the Germans toward the Skagerrak. Admiral Scheer, also, on receiving reports of contacts with English forces, quickened the speed of his main fleet.

Both Hipper and Beatty during this period of approach had been drawn somewhat to northward by the light cruiser contacts in that quarter. But when they first directly sighted each other at 3.20–3.25 they soon shifted to converging southeasterly courses, both ready to engage. When the German battle cruisers opened fire at 3.48, Beatty had hardly completed the complicated maneuvers of bringing the two battle cruisers of the 2nd Division into position in his rear, shifting his course to E.S.E., and assuming a line of bearing on the enemy. As a result, the Germans had already pushed inside the extreme ranges at which the British guns would be more effective, and opened fire at 16,500 yards. The British began firing less than a minute later. Visibility was at first fairly good on both sides.

The comparative table of Beatty's and Hipper's battle cruisers given below shows at once the superiority of the British in armament and their inferiority in armor. They had 6 battle cruisers to 5, and if the 4 *Queen Elizabeths* could be brought effectively into action their strength might well prove overwhelming. These battleships had 13-inch armor, eight 15-inch guns each, and a speed of 25 knots. The British battle cruisers had a squadron speed of 29 knots and the first four could make 32. Hipper's squadron speed was about 28 knots. This, however, did not prove an important factor, since neither side in the first phase used extreme speeds. It might truly be said that the fate of nations hung on these steel monsters plunging through the low North Sea swell in a light, misty, westerly breeze.

Battle Cruiser Forces

BRITISH				GERMAN			
Name	Armor	Displace-ment	Guns	Name	Armor	Displace-ment	Guns
Queen Mary..	9″	26,350	8 13.5″	Lützow......	13″	26,180	8 12″
Lion.........	9″	26,350	8 13.5″	Derfflinger...	13″	26,180	8 12″
Tiger........	9″	28,500	8 13.5″	Seydlitz.....	11″	24,610	10 11″
Princess Royal	9″	28,350	8 13.5″	Moltke......	11″	22,640	10 11″
Indefatigable..	8″	18,800	8 12″	Von der Tann	10″	19,100	11″
New Zealand..	8″	18,800	8 12″				
		145,150				118,710	

The relative ineffectiveness of the British gunnery in this first stage of the battle seems to have been due partly to over-estimation of the rapidly decreasing range, given by the British as 18,500 instead of 16,500 yards when they opened fire, and partly to faulty distribution of fire such as had occurred before at the Dogger Bank. The two leading British ships at first concentrated on the *Lützow,* and two others on the *Moltke,* leaving the *Derfflinger* for ten minutes not under fire. The German gunnery, on the other hand, showed the results of superior optical instruments and rigorous training for speed and initial accuracy. Once centered on the targets, their 4-gun closely bunched salvos came at 20-second intervals, with the secondary batteries firing in between. Within five minutes the flagship *Lion* was hit twice and the *Tiger* three times. In this period the range had decreased to 13,000 yards, and Beatty turned 5 points away.

The second British hit in the action was made at 3.57 on the *Seydlitz.* This exploded in the midships turret, killing almost its entire crew, but quick flooding prevented a flash to the

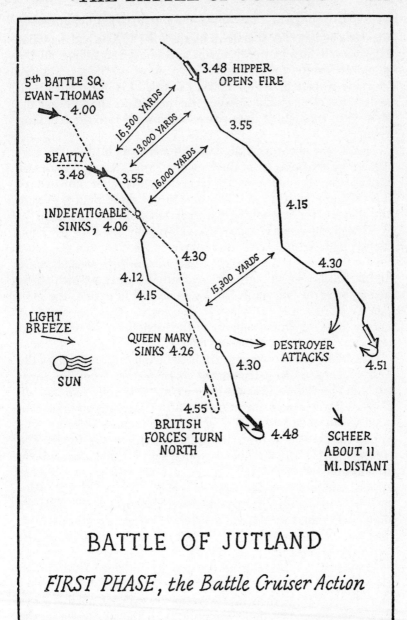

5th BATTLE SQ.
EVAN-THOMAS
4.00

3.48 HIPPER
OPENS FIRE

16,500 YARDS

13,000 YARDS

3.55

BEATTY
3.48

3.55

16,000 YARDS

4.15

INDEFATIGABLE
SINKS, 4.06

4.30

4.12

4.15

15,300 YARDS

4.30

4.30

LIGHT
BREEZE

SUN

QUEEN MARY
SINKS 4.26

DESTROYER
ATTACKS

4.51

4.30

4.55

4.48

BRITISH
FORCES TURN
NORTH

SCHEER
ABOUT 11
MI. DISTANT

BATTLE OF JUTLAND

FIRST PHASE, the Battle Cruiser Action

magazine such as was to destroy three British battle cruisers in the day's action. A fourth hit on the *Lion* at 4.00 had a similar effect, exploding in the Q turret amidships and killing all the gun crew except a major and a sergeant of marines. Though mortally wounded, Major Harvey devoted his last moments to orders for closing and flooding the magazine, thus saving the ship when subsequent fires roared downward into the handling room.

In the rear about 4.05 the *Indefatigable* was hit in quick succession by six shells from the *Von der Tann.* Long tongues of flame from ignited powder bags instantly shot downward. There was a violent explosion and in not more than a minute the ship went down, taking with her 1015 officers and men.

Though the range was now opening rapidly, the *Von der Tann* herself suffered severely, for as the rear German ship she came under the fire of the *Queen Elizabeths,* which at 4.08 were 19,000 yards astern. Hit subsequently by three 15-inch shells and reduced to two main battery guns still in action, the *Von der Tann* still held her place in the line to draw her share of enemy fire. With the support of the battleships, Beatty at 4.13 closed 3 points to a converging course.

The battle cruiser firing again became intense, and at 4.25 the *Queen Mary,* under a temporary concentration from the *Seydlitz* and *Derfflinger,* was hit in quick succession by five 12-inch shells. Two pierced the midships turret, causing an explosion such as had sunk the *Indefatigable* twenty minutes before. The ship went down bow first, her propellers still racing in air. The *Tiger* and the *New Zealand* by quick shifts of helm passed one to port and one to starboard, as a great pall of black smoke rose several hundred feet above the wreckage. At about 4.30 Hipper, now menaced not only by Evan-Thomas but by Beatty's destroyers, was forced to turn definitely away to southeastward, just as both squadrons were getting first intimations of the approach of Scheer.

It is estimated that during the first 12 minutes of this action the Germans made 12 hits to 4 for the British, and that during the first half-hour their hits were in the ratio of about two to one. At the end of that time only 11 of the 16 turrets on the four remaining British cruisers were still in action, while the Germans could operate 17 out of 22. Considered by itself, this battle cruiser action was a decisive victory for the Germans, and Beatty's battleship reënforcements were most opportune.

Shortly after four o'clock both sides ordered destroyer attacks. But these forces had difficulty in getting ahead into favorable positions for attack, and were then kept from their main objective—the major units—by hot combats with each other. The British could put 12 destroyers into action, and these were opposed by 15 smaller enemy craft. There followed, after 4.30, what a British officer describes as "a glorious sort of mêlée, in which the destroyers of both sides were dashing about in all directions." The Germans lost two boats, the *V 27* by gunfire and the *V 29* by torpedo from the *Petard*. Later, at 4.57, when Hipper's force was making its turn to northward in advance of Scheer, five British destroyers finally found themselves in position for attack, and in the face of fire from hostile torpedo craft, from the cruiser *Regensburg,* and from the secondary batteries of the battle cruisers they advanced to ranges of 7,000–5,000 yards in what has been described as "the most gallant destroyer attack of naval history." Of five torpedoes fired, one hit the *Seydlitz,* causing her to take considerable water. Two of the British destroyers, the *Nestor* and the *Nomand,* were disabled, but their heroic crews stood by till they could fire their last torpedoes at Scheer's advancing divisions, which sank them under a rain of shells.

Meantime the 2nd British Light Cruiser Division under Commodore Goodenough, which throughout the day most ably executed its scouting duties, reported from its position ahead of Beatty that it had sighted the German main forces, and pressed in to ranges of about 14,000 yards. By skillful zigzagging and "salvo chasing", i.e., shifting course toward the last enemy splashes to offset corrections for the next salvo, the squadron escaped serious injury, and at this time and later sent valuable information both to Beatty and to Jellicoe. The turn northward of Beatty's battle cruisers was ordered in succession to starboard at 4.42, while Scheer's leading ships were still at extreme range. After the battle cruisers had passed on their northward course the *Queen Elizabeths* turned in their wake, and thus covered them during their northward move.

The Second Phase

At this stage the situation was exactly reversed. Beatty, while escaping from superior forces, was at the same time eagerly luring them toward the Grand Fleet, just as Hipper had previously drawn the British advance forces toward Scheer. Beatty's battered cruisers were again under heavy fire but soon widened the range and for a half hour enjoyed a respite, while during the same time—5.10 to 5.37—Evan-Thomas's battleships were hotly engaged with Hipper and with Scheer's leading ships. As always with a retreating force, their position was highly dangerous, since any injury reducing the speed of a ship would bring it under an overwhelming fire. Scheer was much disappointed that he did not accomplish more at this time. On the other hand, it speaks well for the gunnery of the *Queen Elizabeths* that in this period they inflicted 12 hits to the enemy's 13, scoring most of these with guns of heavier caliber on the weaker armor of the German battle cruisers. Visibility during the northward action was poor for both sides, but favored the British, since the Germans were troubled by the glare of the setting sun. At 5.35 Beatty again shifted course to north-northeast and soon regained contact with Hipper, who also swung off to a more easterly course to avoid being capped. At this point the forces moving northward and the British divisions steaming rapidly southward were already in contact. The main action was about to begin, amid a complexity and uncertainty of dispositions, the account of which, if confusing to the reader, can only faintly suggest the bewildering yet crucial problems that faced the leaders on the scene.

The Third Phase

We have already noted that on first news of contacts with the enemy Admiral Jellicoe had despatched the 3rd Squadron of

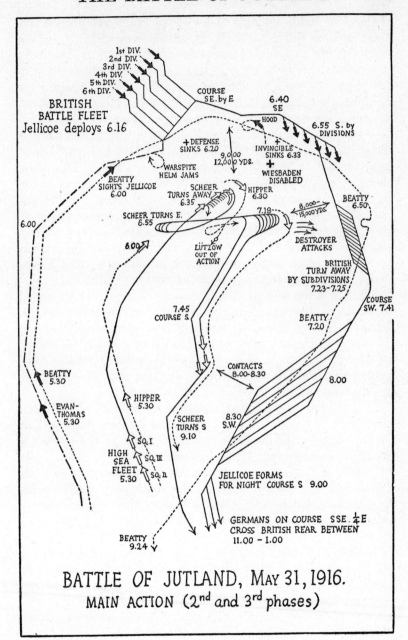

1st DIV.
2nd DIV.
3rd DIV.
4th DIV.
5th DIV.
6th DIV.

COURSE SE. by E

6.40 SE

HOOD

6.55 S. by DIVISIONS

BRITISH BATTLE FLEET
Jellicoe deploys 6.16

+ DEFENSE SINKS 6.20

9,000
12,000 YDS.

+ INVINCIBLE SINKS 6.33

+ WIESBADEN DISABLED

WARSPITE HELM JAMS

BEATTY SIGHTS JELLICOE 6.00

SCHEER TURNS AWAY 6.35

HIPPER 6.30

BEATTY 6.50

7.18

8,000—15,000 YDS.

SCHEER TURNS E. 6.55

6.00

6.00

LÜTZOW OUT OF ACTION

DESTROYER ATTACKS

BRITISH TURN AWAY BY SUBDIVISIONS 7.23-7.25

COURSE SW. 7.41

7.45 COURSE S.

BEATTY 7.20

BEATTY 5.30

EVAN-THOMAS 5.30

HIPPER 5.30

CONTACTS 8.00-8.30

8.00

SCHEER TURNS S 9.10

8.30 S.W.

SQ. I

HIGH SEA FLEET 5.30

SQ. III

SQ. II

JELLICOE FORMS FOR NIGHT COURSE S 9.00

GERMANS ON COURSE SSE. $\frac{1}{4}$E
CROSS BRITISH REAR BETWEEN 11.00 – 1.00

BEATTY 9.24

BATTLE OF JUTLAND, MAY 31, 1916.
MAIN ACTION (2nd and 3rd phases)

three older battle cruisers under Hood to cut off possible retreat into the Baltic. Receiving subsequent orders to support
Beatty, Hood had shifted course toward the gunfire. At about
5.40 one of his light cruisers, the *Chester,* came under heavy
fire from Hipper's advance scouts, and, drawing them after
her, brought them suddenly under the guns of Hood's squadron,
emerging out of the mist only 11,000 yards away. The *Chester* had already been badly crippled, and in the ensuing action
the British destroyer leader *Shark* was disabled and the German
light cruiser *Wiesbaden* was put out of action. This ship,
though wrecked by 12-inch salvos, remained in the center of the
battle area, a target for enemy craft of all types, and did not
sink till early the next day. One highly important effect of
this early contact with Hood's forces was that Scheer, misled by
exaggerated reports of their size, placed the whole British main
body much more to the east than it actually was, and he remained under this impression all through the battle.

Further to the west of Hood, two of Jellicoe's advance guard
of armored cruisers, bent on finishing off the *Wiesbaden,*
plunged directly into close range of both Hipper and Scheer.
The flagship *Defense* blew up at 6.20 with the loss of all hands,
in clear view of most of the ships on both sides, and her com-
panion the *Warrior* was so badly disabled that she withdrew
from action and was abandoned the next day.

Still further to westward, Admiral Beatty's force had been
closing rapidly with the main body, and at about 6.00 was in
visual contact with the *Iron Duke,* the latter to the northeast
about five miles away. Unfortunately, owing to frequent shifts
of course and resultant errors in reckoning, the ships of both
friend and foe coming up from the south were twelve miles
west of the positions where, on the basis of their reports and his
own reckoned position, Admiral Jellicoe had expected them to
appear!

In this and other matters of information, partly no doubt
through defects of his own organization, the commander in
chief was badly served. He knew little even now as to the
enemy's strength, course, or bearing. At 6.01 he signaled
Beatty, "Where is enemy's battle fleet?" to which came the reply

five minutes later, "Enemy battle cruisers bearing SE. (122)"
—but no word as to the enemy battleships.   Not until 6.14,
through bearings received from Beatty, Evan-Thomas, and his
own 6th Battleship Division, was it possible to plot the enemy
position with some accuracy, and about that time Hipper's ships
actually came into view from the *Iron Duke*.   Then, and not
until then, the order went out by flag and radio for deployment
on the port wing.   This meant, in simple language, that his
ships steaming in six divisions were to form one long column or
"line of battle" by turning left in succession at the turning point
of the division leaders (see diagram).

Much criticism has been directed against this deployment to
port, chiefly on the grounds that deployment on the opposite
wing would have put the fast divisions under Beatty and Evan-
Thomas at once in their proper positions in the van, would have
secured quicker and closer contact with the enemy, and would
quite possibly have brought about a concentration on the weaker
predreadnoughts of the enemy rear.   With fuller and earlier
knowledge of the whole situation (such as his critics now have),
Admiral Jellicoe could no doubt have done better.   But his answer seems sufficient—that right-wing deployment would have
meant a sharp turn for all ships under dangerous exposure to
gunfire and torpedo attack, while his own ships would have
masked each other's fire.   His actual deployment was well executed, was in accord with his general policy of safety, and as the
situation developed it put him in excellent position for attack
later on.

At this meeting point of armadas, and especially on the
"Windy Corner" at the southernmost point of the main formation, there was much confusion, requiring, in the words of an
English officer, "such a handling of ships as had never been
dreamed of by seamen before."   Beatty, amid clouds of smoke,
was steaming just south of the line of deployment to gain his
place in the van.   Evan-Thomas, further back, was forced to
take a position in the rear.   As his division veered north to do
so, the *Warspite's* helm jammed and she made two circles to
starboard directly toward the German line.   Though she afforded some cover for the injured *Warrior,* she became a target

for the whole German fleet and was hit 9 times, bringing her total for the day to 13. Badly leaking, she was finally brought under control and steamed toward Rosyth, which she reached safely next day.

The subsequent engagement of the main fleets may be divided into two periods of intensive firing, the first from about 6.30 to 6.40 and the second from 7.05 to 7.30. At the opening of the first period Beatty had already cleared the head of the main column, while at the same time Hipper's force and a few leading ships of Scheer appeared through mist and smoke about 12,000 yards to southward. Successively the *Colossus, Hercules, Iron Duke,* and ten other battleships opened fire. Visibility was wholly favorable to the British and in 42 salvos they scored 12 hits, chiefly on the *Lützow* and *Derfflinger* and on the leading battleship *König.* The *Lützow* at 6.37 dropped out of the line. During the day's fighting she had been hit 20 times and was now badly down by the head and reduced to 15 knots speed. She was sunk by escorting destroyers at 7.00 next morning on the way home. Hipper shifted to a destroyer but did not get aboard the *Derfflinger* till late that night, Captain Hartog of the *Derfflinger* exercising command of the battle cruisers in the intervening time. The *König's* radio was shot away and she took a list of 4.5 degrees.

The *Lützow* and the *Derfflinger,* however, had a little earlier found a target in the old battle cruiser *Invincible,* flagship of Hood's squadron, which had come northward and swung into place ahead of Beatty. Under their combined fire she was hit repeatedly, a final salvo at 6.31 blowing off the roof of her Q turret and exploding the magazine. The ship broke in two and quickly went down. The only survivors, picked up by a British destroyer, were 4 officers and 2 men.

But to the heavy concentration on his battleships Scheer in the poor visibility could make no effective reply. Still placing strong enemy forces to eastward, and fearing envelopment, he made at 6.35 the first of his celebrated battle countermarches (*Gefechtkehrtwendung*) by which, beginning at the rear, the 16 ships of his two leading squadrons reversed course almost simultaneously to westward. As Scheer states in his narrative, it

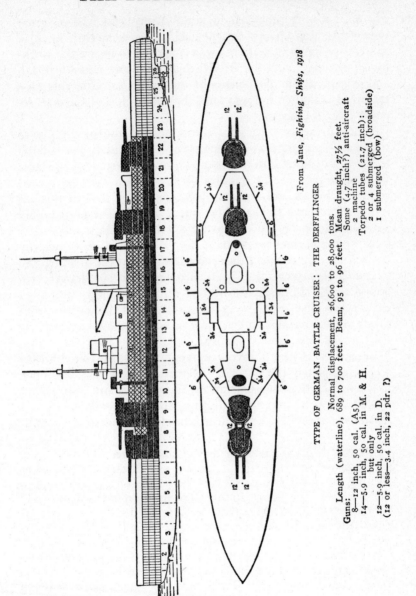

From Jane, *Fighting Ships, 1918*

TYPE OF GERMAN BATTLE CRUISER: THE DERFFLINGER

Length (waterline), 689 to 700 feet. Beam, 95 to 96 feet. Mean draught, 27¼ feet.
Normal displacement, 26,600 to 28,000 tons.

Guns:
8—12 inch, 50 cal. (A5)
14—5.9 inch, 50 cal. in M. & H.
     but only
12—5.9 inch, 50 cal. in D.
(12 or less—3.4 inch, 22 pdr. ?)
Some (4.7 inch?) anti-aircraft
2 machine
Torpedo tubes (21.7 inch):
2 or 4 submerged (broadside)
1 submerged (bow)

was a turn long practiced in peace maneuvers, where "great importance was always attached to its being carried out in a curved line, and every means was employed to insure the working of signals." By the British this turn away was not noted, and in general the movements of the German fleet at this time remained unknown to them until the publication of German reports after the war.

When firing had ceased, Jellicoe shifted course slightly to southeast—a change of but one point and certainly not enough to keep in contact with an enemy steaming west. This course was maintained for 11 minutes till 6.55, when the fleet turned south. Professional students have suggested that in this interim, even more so than later on, it would have been highly expedient to close the enemy by a radical change of course. Fear of submarines might have been discounted, since only by the wildest chance could they have been at a point to which the Germans themselves had been lured at high speed over two hours' time. Mine laying by retreating battleships was a remote possibility, but there is no evidence that the use of either mines or submarines in fleet action was contemplated by the Germans at any stage of the war.

Meantime Scheer's forces moving westward found themselves completely disengaged. Return to their base was open to them. In these circumstances, the motives for Scheer's renewed eastward move at this time are still to some extent a matter for speculation. Scheer himself explains it as follows:

"It was still too early for a nocturnal move. If the enemy followed us, our action in retaining the direction taken after turning the line would partake of the nature of a retreat, and in the event of any damage to our ships in the rear the fleet would be compelled to sacrifice them or else to decide on a line of action enforced by enemy pressure and not adopted voluntarily, which would therefore be detrimental to us from the very outset. Still less was it feasible to strive to detach oneself from the enemy, leaving it to him to decide when he would elect to meet us next morning. There was but one way of averting this—to force the enemy into a second battle by another determined advance, and forcibly compel his destroyers to attack.

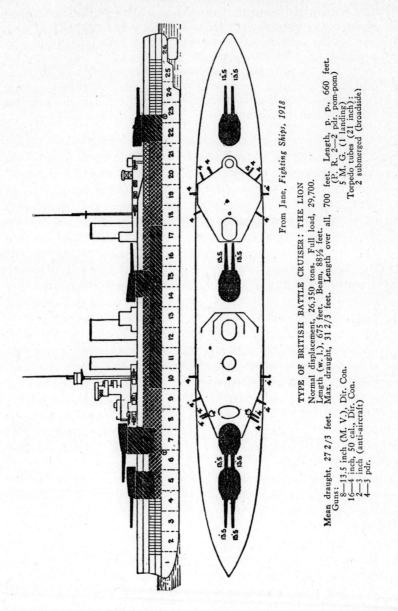

From Jane, *Fighting Ships, 1918*

TYPE OF BRITISH BATTLE CRUISER: THE LION

Normal displacement, 26,350 tons. Full load, 29,700.
Length (w. l.), 675 feet. Beam, 88¼ feet.
Max. draught, 31 2/3 feet. Length over all, 700 feet. Length, p. p., 660 feet.

Mean draught, 27 2/3 feet.

Guns:
8—13.5 inch (M. V.), Dir. Con.
16—4 inch, 50 cal., Dir. Con.
2—3 inch (anti-aircraft)
4—3 pdr.
P. R. 2—2 pdr. pom-pom)
(P. R. 2—2 pdr. pom-pom)
5 M. G. (1 landing).
Torpedo tubes (21 inch):
2 submerged (broadside)

The success of the turning of the line while fighting encouraged me to make the attempt, and decided me to make still further use of the facility of movement. The maneuver would be bound to surprise the enemy, to upset his plans for the rest of the day, and if the blow were powerful enough it would facilitate our extricating ourselves for the night. The plight of the *Wiesbaden* helped also to strengthen my resolve to make an effort to render assistance to her and at least save the crew."

Evidently Scheer was thinking of "extricating" himself, but it was to be by an *offensive defensive*. Admirable as it was in spirit, this second advance eastward at 6.55 was less well conceived tactically, since in ten minutes it would bring the head of his column of 16 ships almost against the center of those 27 dreadnoughts now streaming by divisions to southward. Even the German official history, while praising its "boldness and keen intuition", recognizes that it was "against all the rules of the game."

At about 7.05 the main bodies were again in contact and opened fire at ranges varying from 15,000 yards in the British van to 8,500 yards in the rear. The British, as just stated, were moving southward by divisions, with the van divisions considerably to the eastward, and with some overlapping, but no serious interference with their own fire. Gunnery conditions, in fact, wholly favored the British, for the Germans were subjected to an enfilading fire while silhouetted against the setting sun, but could see nothing to eastward save the flash of guns in a far-extended line. Tables in Frost's *Battle of Jutland* indicate that 20 British ships fired a total of 125 salvos between 7.05 and 7.20 and made about 20 hits, largely on the German battle cruisers, while their only injuries—in fact the only injuries suffered by Jellicoe's six divisions during the entire battle—were two hits on the *Colossus* which injured two men.

Against such a concentration it would seem that only desperate measures could save the Germans from overwhelming disaster. Desperate or not, the measures actually taken were sufficient against an enemy whose answer was "no risks" to each opposing move. To cover their retreat the Germans re-

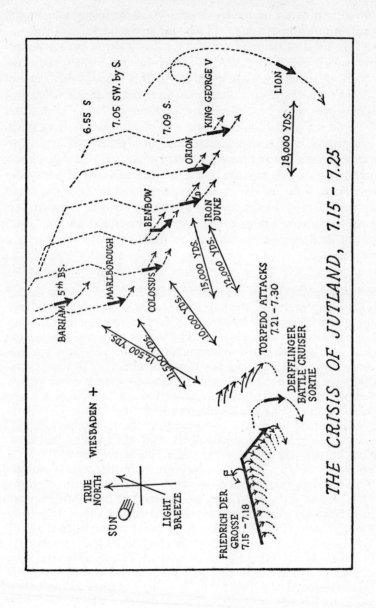

THE CRISIS OF JUTLAND, 7.15 – 7.25

sorted to a sortie of the battle cruisers, a destroyer attack, and another quick turn away.   Each will be considered in turn.

The onset of the depleted and shattered battle cruiser squadron was ordered at 7.13.   Whether or not Scheer knew the condition of the vessels assigned to this "death ride" is not known; the *Derfflinger* had been hit 9 times, the *Seydlitz* had been struck once by torpedo and 14 times by heavy shells, and the *Von der Tann* could use not one of her main battery guns. The direction of their advance was quickly changed at 7.15 to a course more toward the enemy van, and after 7.20 they slowly turned away.   A passage from the narrative of Commander von Hase, gunnery officer of the *Derfflinger,* is here cited, not so much for its factual details as for its vivid account of personal experience under the terrific fire sustained on both sides by the battle cruisers.   It was on them that the brunt of the fighting fell.

"Meanwhile the commander in chief had realized the danger threatening our fleet, the van of which was enclosed by a semicircle of the enemy.   We were, in fact, absolutely 'in the soup' [*in absoluten Wurstkessel*].   There was only one way to get clear of this tactically unfavorable position: to turn the line about and withdraw on the opposite course.   Before everything we must get out of this dangerous enemy envelopment. But the maneuver must be unobserved and executed without interference.   The battle cruisers and destroyers must cover the movements of the fleet.   At about 7.12 the commander in chief made the signal to countermarch, and almost simultaneously gave by wireless the historic order 'Close the enemy!'   [*Ran an den Feind!*]   Without turning a hair the captain ordered 'Full speed ahead, course southeast.'   Followed by the *Seydlitz, Moltke,* and *Von der Tann,* we steamed at first southeast and then from 7.15 on directly toward the enemy van.   The *Derfflinger,* as leading ship, now came under a particularly deadly fire.   Several ships were concentrating upon us.   I selected a target and fired as rapidly as possible.   The range closed from 12,000 to 8,000 yards, and still we steamed at full speed into this inferno of fire, presenting a splendid target to the enemy, while he himself was very difficult to see.   Salvo after salvo

fell around us, shell after shell struck our ship. They were
stirring minutes! I could no longer communicate with Lieut.
von Stosch as the telephones and speaking tubes to the fore-top
had been shot away, so I had to rely on my own observation to
direct the fire. Hitherto all four 12-in. turrets were in action,
but at 7.13 a serious catastrophe occurred. A 15-in. shell
pierced the armor of No. 3 turret and exploded inside. The
gallant turret captain, Lieut. von Boltenstern, had both legs
torn off, and with him perished nearly the whole gun crew. A
charge was ignited in the turret by the explosion. The fire
advanced to the ammunition hoist, where it ignited two more
charges, and thence to the handling room where it ignited two
more. They burned fiercely, flames shooting high above the
turret—but they burned only, they did not explode as our
enemy's had done—and that saved the ship! But the effect was
catastrophic. The flames killed every one within their reach.
Of the 78 men in the turret only five escaped, some badly
wounded, by crawling through the hole for expelling empty
cartridge cases. The remaining 73 died together like heroes,
loyally obeying their turret officer. A few seconds later this
disaster was followed by another. A 15-in. shell pierced the
roof of No. 4 turret and burst inside. The same horrors ensued. With the exception of one man, who was blown out of
the turret hatch by the air pressure, the whole crew of 80 men,
including those in the ammunition room, were instantly killed.
Here, too, the flames ignited the charges not incased in their
protective wrappings. From both after turrets great flames
were now spurting, mingled with clouds of yellow smoke. . . .

"Now hit after hit shook the ship. The enemy had got our
range excellently. We in the armored gun station were pretty
well off, but my heart stood still when I thought of what was
happening inside the ship. My thoughts were rudely interrupted. Suddenly we seemed to hear the crack of doom. A
terrific roar, a tremendous explosion, and then darkness. We
felt a mighty shock, which lifted the conning tower bodily off
its base, to which it sank back vibrating. A heavy shell had
struck the gunnery control station about 20 inches from me.
The shell did not penetrate the thick armor because it had hit at
an angle, but huge pieces of plating were torn away. . . . We
found, however, that the gunnery apparatus was still in order.
Splinters had penetrated the lookout slits of the conning tower,

wounding several people inside. The explosion had forced open the heavy armored door of the station, which jammed so that two men were unable to close it. Then came unexpected assistance. Again we heard a terrific roar and crash, and with the noise of a thunderbolt a 15-in. shell exploded beneath the bridge. The blast of air swept away everything that was not firmly riveted down, and the chart-house disappeared bodily. But the astounding thing was that this same air pressure closed the door of the fore-control! The Englishman was polite; as he had opened the door for us, he again shut it. I looked toward the enemy through my periscope, but though salvos were still falling about us, we could see little of him; all we could see was the huge reddish-gold flames from the guns. Without much hope of hurting the enemy I fired salvo after salvo from the two forward turrets. I could feel how our fire calmed the nerves of the crew. Had we ceased fire the whole ship's company would have been overcome by despair, for every one knew that a few minutes more of this would finish us, but so long as we were firing things could not be so bad. The secondary battery fired also, but of the six 5.9's on the side toward the enemy only two could be used . . ."

—Georg von Hase, Kiel and Jutland

The battle cruisers were recalled just in time—so it would appear—to save them from annihilation. Their ability to stand punishment was, as Commander von Hase remarks, "a splendid testimony to the builders of the German fleet, and particularly to the brilliant Admiral von Tirpitz."

More effective than the battle cruiser sortie, because more feared by the enemy, was the destroyer attack. For this only 14 boats were immediately available. These now advanced and between 7.22 and 7.30 discharged a total of 31 torpedoes, aimed chiefly at the 6th British Division in the rear. Their advance was made under a devastating hostile fire. As seen from a British cruiser, "the destroyers were at times completely hidden by the splashes caused by the secondary armaments of the battle cruisers and battleships." One destroyer, the *S35*, was sunk, and several were severely injured. It was these 31 torpedoes —or a part of them—that caused Jellicoe's 4-point turn away by sub-divisions, two points at 7.22 and two more at 7.25.

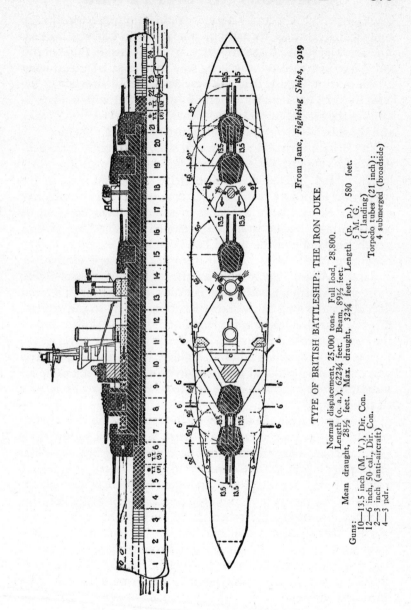

From Jane, Fighting Ships, 1919

TYPE OF BRITISH BATTLESHIP: THE IRON DUKE

Normal displacement, 25,000 tons. Full load, 28,800.
Length (o. a.), 622¾ feet. Beam, 89½ feet.
Mean draught, 28½ feet. Max. draught, 32¾ feet. Length (p. p.), 580 feet.
5 M. G.
(1 landing)
Torpedo tubes (21 inch) :
4 submerged (broadside)

Guns: 10—13.5 inch (M. V.), Dir. Con.
12—6 inch, 50 cal., Dir. Con.
2—3 inch (anti-aircraft)
4—3 pdr.

Though the turns were by no means uniformly executed in the complicated British formation, not a single hit was scored. The *Marlborough's* torpedo injury, which slowed her up but did not force her to leave the line, was the result of an isolated attack a short time before. There were "close shaves" in the 6th Division, but it was a lesson of Jutland that with sea conditions as they were, torpedo tracks could be observed a mile away and the missiles avoided by skillful use of speed and helm.

The British turn away, brief as it was, sacrificed the tremendous advantage of position which had been thrown into their hands. Had Jellicoe closed resolutely, taking the risks of injury from torpedoes, while at the same time using the effective measures of avoidance available in meeting them bows-on, it seems certain that he would have gained the smashing victory which England and the world had been led to expect since the beginning of the war. And therein lies the tragic element of Jutland. Almost unbearable as the weight of responsibility must seem which a naval leader is called upon to bear in a great fleet action, so long as the fate of nations is left to the arbitrament of war that leader must stand or fall by his skillful use of the power entrusted in his hands. After an earlier naval action (see p. 228), a British admiral, Calder, with an inferior force, was court-martialed and reprimanded for "not having done his utmost to renew the said battle and to take or destroy every ship of the enemy."

Quite aside from the opening of the range by the British, this critical contact of the two main fleets was ended by the same German countermarch which had been used twice before. This maneuver, begun at 7.18, was again executed only by Squadrons I and III, for the predreadnoughts in the rear were not involved. To facilitate it, the fleet flagship went to the left, but without distracting the others from their right turn. "Once again," says the German official history, "it was due to the brilliant seamanship of the admirals and commanding officers that the turn of the flagship was not misunderstood and that collisions did not occur." The German fleet was soon lost in the mist and smoke to westward.

In the remaining hour before sunset (at 8.19) we may picture both fleets on southwesterly courses as indicated in the diagram. At 7.47 Beatty made his well-known signal, "Submit that the van of battleships follow battle cruisers. We can then cut off the whole of the enemy fleet." In point of fact, though Jellicoe, upon receipt of the message 12 minutes later, ordered the 1st Division to follow Beatty, the two forces had in general been on similar courses and were about equidistant from the enemy, and Beatty neither at 8.00 nor later made any effective moves to carry out his expressed aim. Owing to the efforts of the Germans to turn southward, there were indeed a number of contacts between 8.15 and 8.30, and firing between the two battle cruiser forces at 10,000 to 15,000 yards. But there was no effort to maintain contact when the weakened German cruisers turned sharply away. Jellicoe also at 8.28 turned 4 points off, to S.W., at a time when from the flagship itself enemy vessels could be seen 18,000 yards distant. Even at this late hour there was time for decisive combat which might center on the weak predreadnoughts of the German rear. But there was to be no second battle of the Nile.

Fourth Phase: The Night Action

As he stated in his report, Admiral Jellicoe "rejected at once the idea of a night action between the heavy ships, as leading to possible disaster, owing, first, to the presence of torpedo craft in such large numbers, and, secondly, to the impossibility of distinguishing between our own and enemy vessels." He also had in mind the element of chance that enters into a night attack, and the German advantage in a night action due to better searchlight system, star shells, and better armor protection against torpedoes. An assertive staff officer might have argued that the enemy fleet was numerically much inferior, that owing to injuries the *Lützow* and other units were limping in the rear, that the German destroyers were fewer in number and had expended most of their torpedoes in the day attacks whereas the British had not, and that every crippled enemy vessel would fall a prey to the pursuing force. Whether or not such considerations were given weight, the decision was to steer for

Horn Reefs, prepared to renew the action at dawn. When dawn came, equally good arguments against renewing the action were at hand.

At 9.00 the British main body was disposed for the night on a course due south in three parallel columns of 8 ships each, with one mile intervals between columns, and half an hour later the battle cruiser force assumed a parallel course ten miles to westward. The destroyer flotillas were placed five miles astern of the main body. Here, in the view of the commander in chief, they would afford a screen for the fleet, would be far enough away to avoid dangerous contacts with it, and would be in good position for attacks on the enemy. It appears, however, that no orders for search or attack were given, and under the influence of the fleet's defensive policy, most of the flotilla commanders felt it their duty to keep in touch with their own fleet rather than seek out the enemy.

Yet their favorable position for contacts is evident from the course of the German fleet during the brief period of darkness, from 9.00 to 2.00. Scheer's situation when night fell was still most difficult. He was in the rear of the British and to westward, where his forces had been pushed by the contacts between 8.00 and 9.00. His one aim now was to thrust through all opposition to the shelter of the German mine fields, as was indicated by his stiff insistence on the course assigned—"SSE. ¼ E. to Horn Reefs Light. Speed 16 knots. *Hold to the course* [*Durchhalten*]."

Aside from a mine-swept passage far away to westward along the Frisian coast, there were two entries available through the mine fields to the German bases—one outside of Heligoland, and the other about 50 miles nearer past Horn Reefs. Subsequent British contacts with the German forces, even as they were meagerly reported to Jellicoe, indicated that this last route was Scheer's choice. In fact Jellicoe's recognition of this as the probable enemy course is evidenced by the direction he assigned to his own fleet for the night, and by the despatch of the mine layer *Abdiel* to place mines south of Horn Reefs Light, a task duly executed before dawn. Scheer's course, as may be seen in the diagram, took his whole fleet diagonally across the rear of the British formation, and across the six columns of destroyers there disposed.

The result of this push through the British rear was a series of fierce, sudden engagements, which swelled the German losses, though the fleet was lucky to come through with so small a toll. With no lights in either force, collisions frequently threatened, and it was difficult to distinguish between friend and foe. In general, the German battleship defense against torpedo attack was highly efficient, consisting of searchlights thrown on approaching destroyers, a quick, accurate fire from the secondary batteries, and then a sharp turn away.

One of the first night encounters came at about 10.30 between Goodenough's 2nd Light Cruiser Squadron and a similar group of German cruisers. Both sides used searchlights and opened fire at the point-blank range of 800 yards! The hotness of the gunnery exchange is indicated by the fact that the *Southampton,* Goodenough's flagship, was hit 18 times and suffered 76 casualties. As an effective counterstroke, a torpedo fired by her struck the old cruiser *Frauenlob,* which went down almost instantly with the loss of all but five of her 324 officers and crew. As she capsized, the men gave three cheers for the Kaiser and the Reich. Goodenough's report of the action, delayed by injury to his radio, reached Jellicoe an hour later.

Between 11.00 and 12.30 there was a confused series of clashes between the main column of Scheer's battleships, now led by the *Westfalen,* and the 4th Destroyer Flotilla of 12 boats on the British right flank. When the *Tipperary* at the head of this flotilla flashed recognition signals at 1,000 yards she was almost shot to pieces by an avalanche of shell and shrapnel from the three leading enemy battleships. The *Spitfire,* next in line, came under heavy fire and shortly afterward narrowly escaped ramming by the dreadnought *Nassau,* which scraped past the destroyer's bow. To quote an officer of the *Spitfire,* "The enemy surged along our port side, clearing everything before her; the boats came crashing down, and even the davits were torn from their sockets, and all this time she was firing her

guns just over our heads." During the same engagement the
Sparrowhawk was fatally injured in a collision with the *Broke,*
whose helm had been jammed by a shell that struck the lower
bridge. One of the torpedoes fired by the 4th Flotilla hit the
light cruiser *Rostock,* which had to be abandoned shortly after
dawn. The Germans also lost the cruiser *Elbing,* which col-
lided with the *Posen* of her own fleet. In this and subsequent
encounters the British lost a total of five destroyers—*Sparrowhawk, Tipperary, Turbulent, Fortune* and *Ardent,* the last four
chiefly as a result of the *Westfalen's* deadly fire at short range.
Despite the rare opportunity for destroyer action as the Germans pierced the British screen, the 4th Flotilla received surprisingly little support from the other flotillas, 44 units in all,
disposed to eastward. The only other attack of consequence
was delivered by the 12th Flotilla, which ran into the rear of the
German line in the mist and drizzle of early dawn. The predreadnought *Pommern* was sunk by one of 12 torpedoes fired
at this time.

It is surprising also that few reports of these contacts were
sent to Admiral Jellicoe, and that of those sent not one reached
him after the *Southampton's* report of the night before. As
early as 2.12 that morning, however, he had reached the decision to turn northward. The chief reason given for this abandonment of pursuit was the dispersion of the British screening
forces. Information as to the enemy's position was also uncertain, though inquiry through the fleet would certainly have
placed the High Sea Fleet fairly definitely to eastward, and a
vigorous advance toward Horn Reefs might still have enabled
the British to cut off its retreat. The Germans passed that
point about 3.00 a.m., and the *Seydlitz* was stranded there for
three hours. It may be assumed that in breaking off the action
Admiral Jellicoe was governed by his fixed policy against operations in proximity to enemy submarines and mines.

By 3 a.m. all the units of the Grand Fleet were on northerly
courses. During the morning they swept over the battle area
of the preceding day and then turned homeward, reaching their
bases at about 7.00 a.m. of June 2nd. It is interesting to note
that the Harwich cruiser and destroyer force, which for rea-

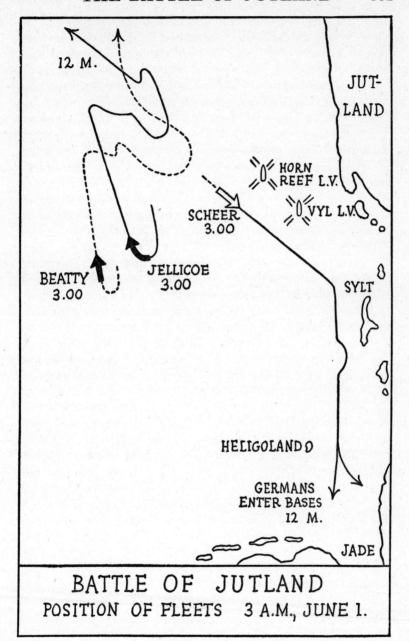

12 M.

JUT-
LAND

HORN
REEF L.V.

VYL L.V.

SCHEER
3.00

BEATTY
3.00

JELLICOE
3.00

SYLT

HELIGOLAND

GERMANS
ENTER BASES
12 M.

JADE

BATTLE OF JUTLAND
POSITION OF FLEETS   3 A.M., JUNE 1.

sons never fully explained was restrained by the Admiralty from going to support Jellicoe on the day of the battle, was sent out at 3.50 a.m. on June 1st.   It came too late to do more than escort the torpedoed *Marlborough* into the Humber.

The exultant German press accounts after the battle, and the "clumsily honest" British *communiqué* which listed three battle cruisers and three armored cruisers lost, with only a vague account of injuries to the enemy, combined to create a profound feeling of disappointment and even alarm not only in the Allied countries but also in America, where sentiment was already swinging toward participation in the war.   But the battle, if it proved anything, proved the hopelessness of any German effort to gain superiority at sea by fleet action, especially against an enemy who would accept action only on his own terms.   This Scheer himself admitted in his subsequent statement that "Even the most favorable issue of a naval combat will not compel England to make peace,"—and he used this as his strongest argument for resort to unrestricted submarine warfare.   However, though the German energies and resources were afterward concentrated on the submarine campaign, it is not true that there were no further fleet activities in the North Sea.   The High Sea Fleet was out again in August and in October of 1916, and in April of 1918 a blow was directed against the Scandinavian convoys which, though broken off because of engine trouble in the *Moltke,* is spoken of by the British historian Newbolt as "the boldest operation undertaken by the German Naval Staff since the war began."

Although the naval situation was unchanged after Jutland, and a retreat cannot be described as a victory, yet from a tactical standpoint the Germans had good reason to be proud of what they had done.   They had met a force superior by a ratio of about 8 to 5 and had escaped after inflicting nearly twice as much damage as they had sustained.   The losses appear on the following page:

Unquestionably the German losses were kept down by the excellent structural features of the newer German ships.   For years prior to the war Admiral von Tirpitz had devoted himself to the problem of under-water protection, to localize the effect of

BRITISH,	Three Battle Cruisers,	QUEEN MARY........26,350 tons
		INDEFATIGABLE.....18,800 "
		INVINCIBLE.........17,250 "

	Three Armored Cruisers,	DEFENSE............14,600 "
		WARRIOR...........13,550 "
		BLACK PRINCE.......13,350 "

	Eight Destroyers,	TIPPERARY.......... 1,430 "
		NESTOR.............. 890 "
		NOMAD.............. 890 "
		TURBULENT......... 1,100 "
		FORTUNE............ 965 "
		ARDENT............. 935 "
		SHARK.............. 935 "
		SPARROWHAWK...... 935 "

Total............111,980 tons

GERMANS,	One Battle Cruiser	LÜTZOW..............26,180 tons
	One Pre-dreadnought,	POMMERN...........13,200 "
	Four Light Cruisers,	WIESBADEN......... 5,400 "
		ELBING............. 4,500 "
		ROSTOCK............ 4,900 "
		FRAUENLOB.......... 2,700 "

	Five Destroyers,	V–4.................... 570 "
		V–48.................. 750 "
		V–27.................. 640 "
		V–29.................. 640 "
		S–33.................. 700 "

Total............60,180 tons

Personnel, killed and wounded: BRITISH, about 6,995: GERMANS, 2,921.

torpedo and mine on the hull of a ship. To quote the words of von Tirpitz:[1]

"We built a section of a ship by itself and carried out experimental explosions on it with torpedo heads, carefully testing the results every time. We tested the possibility of weakening the force of the explosion by letting the explosive gases burst in empty compartments without meeting any resistance. We ascertained the most suitable steel for the different structural parts, and found further that the effect of the explosion was

[1]FIFTY YEARS IN THE ROYAL NAVY, p. 278.

nullified if we compelled it to pulverize coal in any considerable quantity. This resulted in a special arrangement of the coal bunkers. We were then able to meet the force of the explosion . . . by a strong, carefully constructed steel wall which finally secured the safety of the interior of the ship."

The only German ship that succumbed to the blow of a single torpedo was the *Pommern,* an old vessel, built before the fruits of these experiments were embodied in the German fleet. The labor of von Tirpitz was well justified by the results, as may be seen by the instantaneous fashion in which the three British battle cruisers went to the bottom, compared with the ability of the German battle cruisers to stand terrific pounding and yet stay afloat and keep going. The *Lützow* was literally shot to pieces in the battle and even then it took two torpedoes to settle her. Actually she was sunk by opening her seacocks to prevent possible capture. The remarkable ability of the battle cruiser *Göben,* in Turkish waters, to survive shell, mines, and torpedo, bears the same testimony, as does the *Mainz,* which in the action of the Heligoland Bight had to be sunk by one of her own officers, as in the case of the *Lützow.* It is possible that Jellicoe assumed an inferiority of the British armor piercing shell because of this power of the German ships to stay afloat. But photographs published after the armistice showed that British shells penetrated the 11-inch armor of the *Seydlitz* and the 13-inch of the *Derfflinger* with frightful effect. The difference was in the fact that they did not succeed in sinking these ships, which, after all, is the chief object of a shell, and this must be attributed to better under-water construction.

In other matters relating to *matériel,* the British seem to have overestimated the enemy's progress. Mines and submarines had not been developed to a point where Scheer felt it wise to use them in fleet action. In director firing equipment the Germans were actually no better off than the British and the torpedo menace, as shown by the meager results from its use in the battle, did not justify the dominant influence which it exercised over the British tactics. At every crisis it was this threat, real or assumed, that controlled the British moves. It determined the manner of deployment on the wing further from the enemy. At 7.20 14 torpedo boats turned away 27 battleships. At nightfall the peril of under-water attack prevented action, and at dawn the lack of a destroyer screen was the reason given for breaking off the pursuit. One may ask after Jutland whether it is not as dangerous to overestimate as to underestimate what an enemy can do!

For qualities of leadership in the battle, praise is very generally accorded to Admiral Hipper, who displayed a coolness and daring equal to Beatty's and handled more effectively a force which he brought into action highly disciplined and trained. Perhaps more boldness than tactical skill was shown by Admiral Scheer, who twice placed his fleet in "capped" positions in which only quick maneuvering and the enemy's cautious policy saved it from disaster. Acting always in conformity with this cautious policy, the British commander in chief and his subordinate commanders moved their ships throughout the action with a precision in keeping with the high traditions of the British service. This was not equally true of the lighter forces on either side. After the battle, the British took steps to increase the freedom of action of divisional commanders. On this point Admiral Sir Roger Keyes remarks in his discussion of Jutland[1] that "the lesson which struck me most forcibly was the absolute necessity for the senior officers of squadrons, divisions, and subdivisions of the line, and those in command of detached units, to accept responsibility, use more initiative, act promptly, offensively, and, if necessary, independently."

The battle emphasized particularly the cardinal importance of the information service, which calls for a navigational accuracy that will prevent such errors as a twelve-mile discrepancy in plotted positions, and for scouting and communication systems that will supply the high command with prompt, definite, and uninterrupted knowledge of his own and the enemy forces at all times. Air scouting was then in its infancy, but revealed even at this stage how greatly weather conditions may hamper

[1]NAVAL MEMOIRS: SCAPA FLOW TO THE DOVER STRAITS (1935), p. 65.

aerial reconnaissance.   On the general importance of information, Captain Gill writes:[1]

"An outstanding difference between land battles and sea battles is the greater rapidity of movement that characterizes the latter.   Two modern battle fleets can approach each other at the rate of forty miles an hour and hostile light forces can come together at a rate exceeding sixty miles an hour.   In naval operations the factor of time, in minutes and even seconds, may have far-reaching significance.   'Fleet control,' that is to say, efficient leadership of fleets, squadrons, divisions, and flotillas, demands an information service that will operate with maximum speed and clock-like precision.   At Jutland the high command on neither side had such service."

Perhaps the failure to realize the need of the commanders for information arose from the preceding tendency in all navies to emphasize material progress, engineering, and technical proficiency, rather than the art of naval leadership in the field of strategy and tactics.   Such leadership requires in the first place a theoretical knowledge based on history.   As Commander Carylon Bellairs has said, in stressing the neglect of historical studies in British naval training, "Every great leader has been a student of history, and has never ceased to be one."   And, in the second place, the art of naval leadership requires also a practical knowledge based so far as possible on actual experience.   Stressing this need, Captain Gill continues:

"It would seem a fair deduction that one reason for tactical errors committed on the day of Jutland is to be found in the fact that, due to a long period of comparative naval inactivity, the functions of high naval command had become sluggish in disuse, and practice in the art of 'fleet control' on the field of battle had been neglected."

Twenty or more years after Jutland, the heat of the controversies which it excited has subsided.   The four chief leaders have all passed from the scene.   Of their subsequent careers, it

[1] THE BATTLE OF JUTLAND, A STRATEGIC AND TACTICAL STUDY (in MS.).

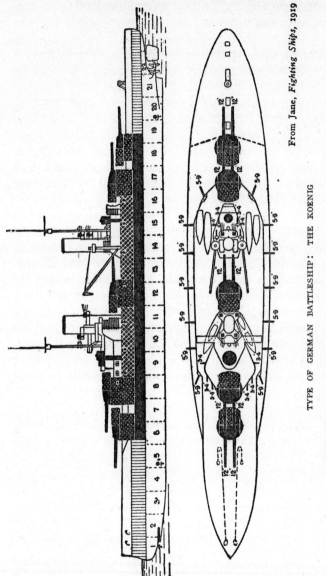

From Jane, *Fighting Ships*, 1919

TYPE OF GERMAN BATTLESHIP: THE KOENIG

Normal displacement, 25,800 tons.
Length (waterline), 573 feet.   Beam, 96¾ feet.   Mean draught, 27¼ feet.
Length (over all), 580 feet.

Guns:—12 inch, 45 cal.
      14—5.9 inch, 50 cal.
      (10 or 4—3.4 inch, 22 pdr.?)
      (2 anti-aircraft?)

2 machine.
Torpedo tubes. (19.7 inch):
      4 (broadside) submerged.
      1 (bow) submerged.

may be noted that Admiral Jellicoe was relieved of the severe
strain of supreme sea command in November, 1916, but was
burdened with even greater responsibilities as First Sea Lord of
the Admiralty in 1916–17 during the height of the submarine
campaign.   He was succeeded as fleet commander in chief by
Admiral Beatty, who remained in this position until the close
of the war and was afterward First Sea Lord from 1919 to
1927.   Jellicoe died in November, 1935, and Beatty four
months later.   Both are buried in St. Paul's Cathedral, London.   Vice-Admiral Scheer was made admiral immediately
after the battle and remained in command of the High Sea
Fleet until August, 1918, when he became Chief of Admiralty
Staff and was succeeded in the fleet by Hipper.   Both went into
retirement at the close of the war.   Scheer's death occurred in
1928 and Hipper's in 1932.

While the preceding account of Jutland has been revised in
the light of later information, the following more general comment on the battle is taken from the first edition, which appeared in 1921.   Written closer to the action, it retains a
warmth which soon passes from the discussion of "far-off
things and battles long ago."   At the same time it relates the
engagement to certain general principles illustrated in the past,
and having an application to future warfare, no matter what
the weapons, and also to undertakings not strictly in the military
field.

Certainly the tactics of Jellicoe do not suggest those of Blake,
Hawke, or Nelson.   They do not fit Farragut's motto—borrowed from Danton[1]—"l'audace, encore l'audace, et toujours
l'audace," or Napoleon's "frappez vite, frappez fort."   War, as
has been observed before, cannot be waged without taking risks.
The British had a heavy margin to gamble on.   As it happened,
23 out of the entire 28 battleships came out of the fight without
so much as a scratch on their paint; and, after deployment, only
one out of the battle line of 27 dreadnoughts received a single
hit.   This was the *Colossus,* which had four men wounded by
a shell.

[1]And borrowed by Danton from Cicero.

The touchstone of naval excellence is Nelson. As Mahan has so ably pointed out, while weapons change principles remain. Dewey, in deciding to take the chances involved in a night entry of Manila Bay did so in answer to his own question, "What would Farragut do?" Hence in considering Jutland one may take a broader view than merely a criticism of tactics. In a word, does the whole conduct of the affair reveal the method and spirit of Nelson?

At Trafalgar there was no need for a deployment after the enemy was sighted because in the words of the famous Memorandum, "the order of sailing is to be the order of battle." The tactics to be followed when the French appeared had been carefully explained by Nelson to his commanders. No signal was needed—except the fine touch of inspiration in "England expects every man to do his duty." In brief, the British fleet had been so thoroughly indoctrinated, and the plan was so simple, that there was no room for hesitation, uncertainty, or dependence on the flagship for orders at the last minute. It is hard to see evidence of any such indoctrination of the Grand Fleet before Jutland.

Again, Nelson was, by example and precept, constantly insisting on the initiative of the subordinate. "The Second in Command will . . . have the entire direction of his line to make the attack upon the enemy, and to follow up the blow until they are captured or destroyed. . . . Captains are to look to their particular line as their rallying point. But in case signals can neither be seen nor perfectly understood, no captain can do very wrong if he places his ship alongside that of an enemy." At Jutland, despite the urgent signals of Beatty at two critical moments, neither Burney of the sixth division nor Jerram of the first felt free to act independently of the orders of the Commander in Chief. The latter tried, as Nelson emphatically did not, to control from the flagship every movement of the entire fleet.

Further, if naval history has taught anything it has established a point so closely related to the responsibility and initiative of the subordinate as to be almost a part of it; namely, a great fleet that fights in a single rigid line ahead never achieves a decisive victory. Blake, Tromp, and de Ruyter fought with squadrons, expecting—indeed demanding—initiative on the part of their flag officers. That was the period when great and decisive victories were won. The close of the 17th century produced the "Fighting Instructions," requiring the unbroken line ahead, and there followed a hundred years of indecisive battles and bungled opportunities. Then Nelson came and revived the untrammeled tactics of the days of Blake with the added glory of his own genius. It appears that at Jutland the battleships were held to a rigid unit of fleet formation as in the days of the Duke of York or Admiral Graves. And concentration with a long line of dreadnoughts is no more possible to-day than it was with a similar line of two-decked sailing ships a century and a half ago.

Finally, in the matter of spirit, the considerations that swayed the movements of the Grand Fleet at all stages were apparently those of what the enemy might do instead of what might be done to the enemy, the very antithesis of the spirit of Nelson. It is no reflection on the personal courage of the Commander in Chief that he should be moved by the consideration of saving his ships. The existence of the Grand Fleet was, of course, essential to the Allied cause, and there was a heavy weight of responsibility hanging on its use. But again it is a matter of naval doctrine. Did the British fleet exist merely to maintain a numerical preponderance over its enemy or to crush that enemy —whatever the cost? If the battle of Jutland receives the stamp of approval as the best that could have been done, then the British or the American officer of the future will know that he is expected primarily to "play safe." But he will never tread the path of Blake, Hawke, or Nelson, the men who made the traditions of the Service and forged the anchors of the British Empire.

*　　*　　*

On the other hand, if the British had destroyed the German fleet the victory would have been priceless. As Jervis remarked at Cape St. Vincent, "A victory is very essential to England at this hour." The spring of 1916 was an ebb point in Allied prospects. The Verdun offensive was not halted, the Somme drive had not yet begun, the Russians were beaten far back in their own territory, the Italians had retreated, and there was rebellion in Ireland. The annihilation of the High Seas Fleet would have reversed the situation with dramatic suddenness and would have at least marked the turning point of the war. Without a German battle fleet, the British could have forced the fighting almost to the very harbors of the German coast—bottling up every exit by a barrage of mines. The blockade, therefore, could have been drawn close to the coast defenses. Moreover, with the High Seas Fleet gone, the British fleet could have entered and taken possession of the Baltic, which throughout the war remained a German lake. By this move England would have threatened the German Baltic coast with invasion and extended her blockade in a highly important locality, cutting off the trade between Sweden and Germany. She would also have come to the relief of Russia, which was suffering terrible losses from the lack of munitions. Indeed it would have saved that ally from the collapse that withdrew her from the war. With no German "fleet in being" great numbers of workers in English industry and vast quantities of supplies might have been transferred to the support of the army. The threat of invasion would have been removed, and the large army that was kept in England right up to the crisis of March, 1918,[1] would have been free to reënforce the army at the front. Finally, without the personnel of the German fleet there could have been no ruthless submarine campaign the year after, such as actually came so near to winning the war. Thus, while the German claim to a triumph that drove the British from the seas is ridiculous, it is equally so to argue, as the First Lord of the Admiralty did, that there was no need of a British victory at Jutland, that all the fruits of victory were gained as it was.

As Winston Churchill, another one-time First Lord of the Admiralty, has written, "It was the policy of Jutland which led directly to the supreme submarine peril of 1917."[2]

[1] A quarter of a million men were sent from England at this time.
[2] THE WORLD CRISIS, Vol. II, p. 154.

REFERENCES

Among the many Jutland sources the following are mentioned as of special interest and value:

THE GRAND FLEET, 1914–1916, Admiral John Rushworth Jellicoe, 1919.

GERMANY'S HIGH SEA FLEET IN THE WORLD WAR, Admiral Reinhard Scheer, N. Y., 1934 (earlier edition, 1920).

THE FIGHTING AT JUTLAND, ed. Fawcett and Hooper, 1920. (Personal narratives.)

A TRUE ACCOUNT OF THE BATTLE OF JUTLAND, Captain T. G. Frothingham, U. S. R. 1920. (The first to draw on German sources.)

WHAT HAPPENED AT JUTLAND, Commander C. C. Gill, U. S. N. 1921.

THE BATTLE OF JUTLAND, Commander H. H. Frost, U. S. N. Published by U. S. Naval Institute, Annapolis, Md., 1936. (An authoritative study, with full bibliography.)

NARRATIVE OF THE BATTLE OF JUTLAND, Admiralty publication, 1924.

REPRODUCTION OF THE RECORD OF THE BATTLE OF JUTLAND, Admiralty publication, 1927.

THE RIDDLE OF JUTLAND, Langhorne Gibson and Admiral J. E. T. Harper, 1934.

ADMIRAL VON HIPPER, H. von Waldeyer-Hartz, 1933.

ZUR SKAGERRAKSCHLACHT, Groos, O., 1921.

CHAPTER XVII

THE WORLD WAR [*Continued*]: COMMERCE WARFARE

INTERDICTION of enemy trade has always been the great weapon of sea power; and hence, though mines, submarines, and the menace of the High Seas Fleet itself made a close blockade of the German coast impossible, Great Britain in the World War steadily extended her efforts to cut off Germany's intercourse with the overseas world. Germany, on the other hand, while unwilling or unable to take the risks of a contest for surface control of the sea, waged cruiser warfare on British and Allied commerce, first by surface vessels, and, when these were destroyed, by submarines. In the policies adopted by each belligerent there is an evident analogy to the British blockade and the French commerce destroying campaigns of the Napoleonic Wars. And just as in the earlier conflict British sea power impelled Napoleon to a ruinous struggle for the domination of Europe, so in the World War, though in a somewhat different fashion, the blockade worked disaster for Germany.

"The consequences of the blockade," writes the German General von Freytag-Loringhoven, "showed themselves at once. Although we succeeded in establishing our war economics by our internal strength, yet the unfavorable state of the world economic situation was felt by us throughout the war. That alone explains why our enemies found ever fresh possibilities of resistance, because the sea stood open to them, and why victories which would otherwise have been absolutely decisive, and the conquest of whole kingdoms, did not bring us nearer peace."

For each group of belligerents, indeed, the enemy's commerce warfare assumed a vital significance. "No German success on land," declares the conservative British Annual Register for 1919, "could have ruined or even very gravely injured the English-speaking powers. The success of the submarine campaign, on the other hand, would have left the United States isolated and have placed the Berlin Government in a position to dominate most of the rest of the world." "The war is won for us," declared General von Hindenburg on July 2, 1917, "if we can withstand the enemy attacks until the submarine has done its work."

Commerce warfare at once involves a third party, the neutral; and it therefore appears desirable, before tracing the progress of this warfare, to outline briefly the principles of international law which, by a slow and tortuous process, have grown up defining the respective rights of neutrals and belligerents in naval war. *Blockade* is among the most fundamental of these rights accorded to the belligerent, upon the conditions that the blockade shall be limited to enemy ports or coasts, confined within specified limits, and made so effective as to create evident danger to traffic. It assumes control of the sea by the blockading navy, and, before the days of mines and submarines, it was enforced by a cordon of ships off the enemy coast. A blockade stops direct trade or intercourse of any kind.

Whether or not a blockade is established, a belligerent has the right to attempt the prevention of *trade in contraband*. A neutral nation is under no obligation whatever to restrain its citizens from engaging in this trade. In preventing it, however, a belligerent warship may stop, visit, and search any merchant vessel on the high seas. If examination of the ship's papers and search show fraud, contraband cargo, offense in respect to blockade, enemy ownership or service, the vessel may be taken as a prize, subject to adjudication in the belligerent's prize courts. The right of merchant vessels to carry defensive armament is well established; but resistance justifies destruction. Under certain circumstances prizes may be destroyed at sea, after removal of the ship's papers and full provision for the safety of passengers and crew.

The Declaration of London,[1] drawn up in 1909, was an attempt to restate and secure general acceptance of these principles, with notable modifications. Lists were drawn up of *absolute* contraband (munitions, etc., adapted obviously if not exclusively for use in war), *conditional* contraband (including foodstuffs, clothing, rolling stock, etc., susceptible of use in war but having non-warlike uses as well), and free goods (including raw cotton and wool, hides, and ores). The most significant provision of the Declaration was that the doctrine of *continuous voyage* should apply only to absolute contraband. This doctrine, established by Great Britain in the French wars and expanded by the United States in the American Civil War, holds that the ultimate enemy destination of a cargo determines its character, regardless of transshipment in a neutral port and subsequent carriage by sea or land. The Declaration of London was never ratified by Great Britain, and was observed for only a brief period in the first months of the war. Had it been ratified and observed, Germany would have been free to import all necessary supplies, other than munitions, through neutral states on her frontiers.

The Blockade of Germany

Unable to establish a close blockade, and not venturing at once to advance the idea of a "long range" blockade, England was nevertheless able to impose severe restrictions upon Germany by extending the lists of contraband, applying the doctrine of continuous voyage to both absolute and conditional contraband, and throwing upon the owners of cargoes the burden of proof as to destination. Cotton still for a time entered Germany, and some exports were permitted. But on March 1, 1915, in retaliation for Germany's declaration of a "war area" around the British Isles, Great Britain asserted her purpose to establish what amounted to a complete embargo

[1] Printed in full in INTERNATIONAL LAW TOPICS of the U. S. Naval War College, 1910, p. 169 ff.

on German trade, holding herself free, in the words of Premier Asquith, "to detain and take into port ships carrying goods of presumed enemy destination, ownership, or origin." In a note of protest on March 30, the United States virtually recognized the legitimacy of a long-range blockade—an innovation of seemingly wide possibilities—and confined its objections to British interference with lawful trade between neutrals, amounting in effect to a blockade of neutral ports.

As a matter of fact, in spite of British efforts, there had been an immense increase of indirect trade with Germany through neutrals. While American exports to Germany in 1915 were $154,000,000 less than in 1913, and in fact practically ceased altogether, American exports to Holland and the Scandinavian states increased by $158,000,000. This trade continued up to the time when the United States entered the war, after which all the restrictions which England had employed were given a sharper application. By a simple process of substitution, European neutrals had been able to import commodities for home use, and export their own products to Germany. Now, in order to secure supplies at all, they were forced to sign agreements which put them on rations and gave the Western Powers complete control of their exports to Germany.

The effect of the Allied blockade upon Germany is suggested by the accompanying chart. In the later stages of the war it created a dearth of important raw materials, crippled war industries, brought the country to the verge of starvation, and caused a marked lowering of national efficiency and morale.

Germany protested vigorously to the United States for allowing her foodstuffs to be shut out of Germany while at the same time shipping to England vast quantities of munitions. Throughout the controversy, however, Great Britain profited by the fact that while her methods caused only financial injury to neutrals, those employed by Germany destroyed or imperiled human lives.

The Submarine Campaign

The German submarine campaign may be dated from February 4, 1915, when Germany, citing as a precedent Great Britain's establishment of a military area in the North Sea, proclaimed a *war zone* "in the waters around Great Britain and Ireland, including the whole English Channel," within

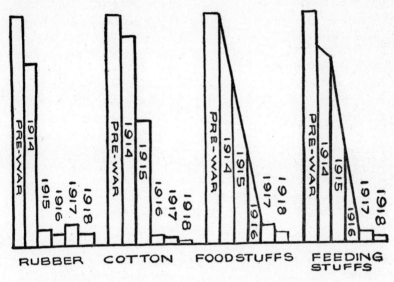

From *The Blockade of Germany*, Alonzo E. Taylor, WORLD'S WORK, Oct. 1919.

EFFECTS OF THE BLOCKADE OF GERMANY

Decreased supply of commodities in successive years of the war.

which enemy merchant vessels would be sunk without assurance of safety to passengers or crew. Furthermore, as a means of keeping neutrals out of British waters, Germany declared she would assume no responsibility for destruction of neutral ships within this zone. What this meant was to all intents and purposes a "paper" submarine blockade of the British Isles. Its illegitimacy arose from the fact that it was conducted surreptitiously over a vast area, and was only in the slightest degree effective, causing a destruction each month of less than one percent of the traffic. Had it been restricted to narrow limits, it would have been still less effective, owing to the facility of countermeasures in a small area.

Determined, however, upon a spectacular demonstration of its possibilities, Germany first published danger notices in American newspapers, and then, on May 7, 1915, sank the unarmed Cunard liner *Lusitania* off the Irish coast, with a loss of 1198 lives, including 102 Americans. In spite of divided American sentiment and a strong desire for peace, this act came little short of bringing the United States into the war. Having already declared its intention to hold Germany to "strict accountability," the United States Government now stated that a second offense would be regarded as "deliberately unfriendly," and after a lengthy interchange of notes secured the pledge that "liners will not be sunk without warning and without safety of the lives of non-combatants, provided that the liners do not try to escape or offer resistance." Violations of this pledge, further controversies, and increased friction with neutrals marked the next year or more, during which, however, sinkings did not greatly exceed the level of about 150,000 tons a month already attained.

During this period Allied countermeasures were chiefly of a defensive character, including patrol of coastal areas, diversion of traffic from customary routes, and arming of merchantmen. This last measure, making surface approach and preliminary warning a highly dangerous procedure for the submarine, led Germany to the announcement that, after March 1, 1916, all armed merchant vessels would be torpedoed without warning. But how were U-boat commanders to distinguish between enemy and neutral vessels? Between vessels with or without guns? The difficulty brings out clearly the fact that while the submarines made good pirates, they were hampered in warfare on legitimate lines.

Germany redoubled U-boat activities to lend strength to her peace proposals at the close of 1916, and when these failed she decided to disregard altogether the cobwebs of legalism that had hitherto hindered her submarine war. On February

GERMAN BARRED ZONES
British mined area and North Sea mine barrage.

1, 1917, she declared unrestricted warfare in an immense
barred zone within limits extending from the Dutch coast
through the middle of the North Sea to the Faroe Islands and
thence west and south to Cape Finisterre, and including also
the entire Mediterranean east of Spain. An American ship
was to be allowed to enter and leave Falmouth once a week,
and there was a crooked lane leading to Greece.

In thus announcing her intention to sink all ships on sight
in European waters, Germany burned her bridges behind her.
She staked everything on this move. Fully anticipating the

hostility of the United States, she hoped to win the war before that country could complete its preparations and give effective support to the Allies. General von Hindenburg's statement has already been quoted. It meant that the army was to assume the defensive, while the navy carried out its attack on Allied communications. Admiral von Capelle, head of the German Admiralty, declared that America's aid would be "absolutely negligible." "My personal view," he added, "is that the U-boat will bring peace within six months."

As it turned out, Germany's disregard of neutral rights in 1917, like the violation of Belgium in 1914, reacted upon her and proved the salvation of the Western Powers. After the defection of Russia, France was in imperative need of men. Great Britain needed ships. Neither of these needs could have been supplied save by America's throwing her utmost energies into active participation in the war. This was precisely the result of the proclamation of Feb. 1, 1917. The United States at once broke off diplomatic relations, armed her merchant vessels in March, and on April 6 declared a state of war.

Having traced the development of submarine warfare to this critical period, we may now turn to the methods and weapons employed by both sides at a time when victory or defeat hinged on the outcome of the war at sea.

Germany's submarine construction and losses appear in the following table from official German sources, the columns showing first the total number built up to the date given, next the total losses to date, and finally the remainder with which Germany started out at the beginning of each year.

After 1916 Germany devoted the facilities of her shipyards entirely to submarine construction, and demoralized the surface fleet to secure personnel. Of the entire number built, not more than a score were over 850 tons. The U C boats were small mine-layers about 160 feet in length, with not more than two weeks' cruising period. The U B's were of various sizes, mostly small, and some of them were built in sections for transportation by rail. The U boats proper, which constituted the largest and most important class, had a speed of

	Boats built	Losses	Remainder (On Jan. 1 of year following)
End of 1914.....	31	5	26
1915.....	93	25	68
1916.....	188	50	138
1917.....	291	122	169
1918.....	372	202	170

about 16 knots on the surface and 9 knots submerged, and could remain at sea for a period of 5 or 6 weeks, the duration of the cruise depending chiefly upon the supply of torpedoes. In addition there were a half dozen large submarine merchantmen of the type of the *Deutschland,* which made two voyages to America in 1916; and a similar number of big cruisers of 2000 tons or more were completed in 1918, mounting two 6-inch guns and capable of remaining at sea for several months. The 372 boats built totaled 209,000 tons and had a personnel of over 11,000 officers and men. There were seldom more than 20 or 30 submarines in active operation at one time. One third of the total number were always in port, and the remainder in training.

It is evident from her limited supply of submarines at the outbreak of war that Germany did not contemplate their use as commerce destroyers. To the Allied navies also, in spite of warnings from a few more far-sighted officers, their use for this purpose came as a complete surprise. New methods had to be devised, new weapons invented, new types of ship built and old ones put to uses for which they were not intended—in short, a whole new system of warfare inaugurated amidst the preoccupations of war. As usual in such circumstances, the navy taking the aggressive with a new weapon gained a temporary ascendancy, until effective counter-measures could be contrived. It is easy to say that all this should have been foreseen and provided for, but it is a question to what

U 71-80 OCEAN-GOING MINE-LAYERS
U B 48-149
U C 80 CLASS OF MINE-LAYERS

OCEAN-GOING TYPES U 30 TO U 39

OCEAN-GOING TYPES FROM ABOUT U 51 TO U 70

OCEAN-GOING TYPES FROM U 19 TO U 28

OCEAN-GOING TYPES FROM ABOUT U 30 UP TO U 39

U 151-157 (OCEAN-GOING)
OCEAN-GOING TYPES OF GERMAN SUBMARINES

extent preparations could profitably have been made before Germany began her campaign. It has already been pointed out in the chapter preceding that, had the German fleet been destroyed at Jutland, subsequent operations on the German coast might have made the submarine campaign impossible, and preparations unnecesary.

Anti-Submarine Tactics

Of the general categories of anti-submarine tactics,—detection, evasion, and destruction—it was naturally those of evasion that were first employed. Among these may be included suspension of sailings upon warning of a submarine in the vicinity, diversion of traffic from customary routes, camouflage, and zigzag courses to prevent the enemy from securing favorable position and aim. The first method was effective only at the expense of a severe reduction of traffic, amounting in the critical months of 1917 to 40 per cent of a total stoppage. The second sometimes actually aided the submarine, for in confined areas such as the Mediterranean it was likely to discover the new route and reap a rich harvest. Camouflage was discarded as of slight value; but shifts of course were employed to advantage by both merchant and naval vessels throughout the war.

Methods of detection depended on both sight and sound. Efficient lookout systems on shipboard, with men assigned to different sectors so as to cover the entire horizon, made it possible frequently to detect a periscope or torpedo wake in time to change course, bring guns to bear, and escape destruction. According to a British Admiralty estimate, in case a submarine were sighted the chances of escape were seven to three, but otherwise only one to four. Aircraft of all kinds proved of great value in detecting the presence of U-boats, as well as in attacking them. Hydrophones and other listening devices, though at first more highly perfected by the enemy, were so developed during the war as to enable patrol vessels to discover the presence and even determine the course and speed of a submerged foe. Along with these devices, a system of information was organized which, drawing information from a wide variety of sources, enabled Allied authorities to trace the cruise of a U-boat, anticipate its arrival in a given locality, and prophesy the duration of its stay.

Among methods of destruction, the mounting of guns on merchantmen was chiefly valuable, as already suggested, because of its effect in forcing submarines to resort to illegal and barbarous methods of warfare. Hitherto, submarines had been accustomed to operate on the surface, board vessels, and sink them by bombs or gunfire. Visit and search, essential in order to avoid injury to neutrals, was now out of the question, for owing to the surface vulnerability of the submarine it might be sent to the bottom by a single well-directed shot. In brief, the guns on the merchant ship kept submarines beneath the surface, forced them to draw upon their limited and costly supply of torpedoes, and hindered them from securing good position and aim for torpedo attack.

Much depended, of course, upon the range of the ship's guns and the size and experience of the gun-crews. When the United States began arming her ships in March, 1917, she was able to put enough trained men aboard to maintain lookouts and man guns both night and day. A dozen or more exciting duels ensued between ships and U-boats before the latter learned that such encounters did not repay the risks involved. On October 19, 1917, the steamer *J. L. Luckenbach* had a four-hour running battle with a submarine in which the ship fired 202 rounds and the pursuer 225. The latter scored nine hits, but was at last driven off by the appearance of a destroyer. To cite another typical engagement, the *Navajo,* in the English Channel, July 4, 1917, was attacked first by torpedo and then by gunfire. The 27th shot from the ship hit the enemy's conning tower and caused two explosions. "Men who were on deck at the guns and had not jumped overboard ran aft. The submarine canted forward at an angle of almost 40 degrees, and the propeller could be plainly seen lashing the air." [1]

[1] For more detailed narratives of this and other episodes of the submarine campaign, see Ralph D. Payne, THE FIGHTING FLEETS, 1918.

In coastal waters where traffic converged, large forces of destroyers and other craft were employed for purposes of escort, mine sweeping, and patrol. Yet, save as a means of keeping the enemy under water and guarding merchant ships, these units had only a limited value owing to the difficulty of making contact with the enemy. During the later stages of the war destroyers depended chiefly upon the depth bomb, an invention of the British navy, which by means of the so-called "Y guns" could be dropped in large numbers around the supposed location of the enemy. It was in this way that the United States Destroyers *Fanning* and *Nicholson,* while engaged as convoy escorts, sank the *U-58* and captured its crew.

The "mystery" or "Q" ships (well-armed vessels disguised as harmless merchantmen) were of slight efficacy after submarines gave up surface attack. In fact, it was the submarine itself which, contrary to all pre-war theories, proved the most effective type of naval craft against its own kind. Whereas fuel economy compelled German submarines to spend as much time as possible on the surface, the Allied under-water boats, operating near their bases, could cruise awash or submerged and were thus able to creep up on the enemy and attack unawares. According to Admiral Sims, Allied destroyers, about 500 in all, were credited with the certain destruction of 34 enemy submarines; yachts, patrol craft, etc., over 3000 altogether, sank 31; whereas about 100 Allied submarines sank probably 20.[1] Since 202 submarines were destroyed, this may be an underestimate of the results accomplished by each type, but it indicates relative efficiency. Submarines kept the enemy beneath the surface, led him to stay farther away from the coast, and also, owing to the disastrous consequences that might ensue from mistaken identity, prevented the U-boats from operating in pairs. The chief danger encountered by Allied submarines was from friendly surface vessels. On one occasion an American submarine, the AL-10, approaching a destroyer of the same service, was forced to dive and was then given a bombardment of depth charges. This bent plates, extinguished lights, and brought the submarine again to the

[1] THE VICTORY AT SEA, *World's Work,* May, 1920, p. 56.

surface, where fortunately she was identified in the nick of time. The two commanders had been roommates at Annapolis.

Work of the United States Navy

Having borne the brunt of the naval war for three years, the British navy welcomed the reënforcements which the United States was able to contribute, and shared to the utmost the experience already gained. On May 3, 1917, the first squadron of 6 American destroyers arrived at Queenstown, and was increased to 50 operating in European waters in November, and 70 at the time of the armistice. A flotilla of yachts, ill adapted as they were for such service, did hazardous duty as escorts in the Bay of Biscay; and a score of submarines crossed the Atlantic during the winter to operate off Ireland and in the Azores. Five dreadnoughts under Admiral Rodman from the U. S. Atlantic fleet became a part of the Grand Fleet at Scapa Flow.

Probably the most notable work of the American navy was in projects where American manufacturing resources and experience in large-scale undertakings could be brought to bear. In four months, from July to November, 1917, the United States Navy constructed an oil pipe line from the west to the east coast of Scotland, thus eliminating the long and dangerous northern circuit. Five 14-inch naval guns, on railway mountings, with a complete train of 16 cars for each gun, were equipped by the navy, manned entirely with naval personnel, and were in action in France from August, 1918, until the armistice, firing a total of 782 rounds on the German lines of communication, at ranges up to 30 miles.

The American proposal of a mine barrage across the entrance to the North Sea from Scotland to Norway at first met with slight approval abroad, so unprecedented was the problem of laying a mine-field 230 miles in length, from 15 to 30 miles in width, and extending at least 240 feet downward in waters the total depth of which was 400 or more feet. Even the mine barrier at the Straits of Dover had proved ineffective owing to heavy tides, currents, and bad bottom conditions, until it was strengthened by Admiral Keyes in 1918. By employing a large type of mine perfected by the United States Naval Bureau of Ordnance, it was found possible, however, to reduce by one-third the number of mines and the amount of wire needed for the North Sea Barrage. The task was therefore undertaken, and completed in the summer of 1918. Out of a total of 70,000 mines, 56,570, or about 80 per cent, were planted by American vessels. The barrage when completed gave an enemy submarine about one chance in ten of getting through. According to reliable records, it accomplished the destruction or serious injury of 17 German sub-

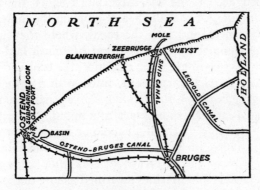

OSTEND-ZEEBRUGGE AREA

marines, and by its deterrent effect, must have practically closed the northern exit to both under-water and surface craft.

The Attack on Zeebrugge and Ostend

At the Channel exit of the North Sea, a vigorous blow at the German submarine nests on the Belgian coast was finally struck on April 22-23, 1918, by the Dover Force under Vice Admiral Roger Keyes, in one of the most brilliant naval operations of the war. Of the two Belgian ports, Ostend and Zeebrugge, the latter was much more useful to the Germans because better protected, less exposed to batteries on the land front, and connected by a deeper canal with the main base 8 miles distant at Bruges. It was planned, however, to attack both ports, with the specific purpose of sinking 5 obsolete cruisers laden with concrete across the entrances to the canals. The operation required extensive reconstruction work on the vessels employed, a thorough course of training for personnel, suitable conditions of atmosphere, wind, and tide, and execu-tion of complicated movements in accordance with a time schedule worked out to the minute.

At Ostend the attack failed owing to a sudden shift of wind which blew the smoke screen laid by motor boats back upon the two block ships, and so confused their approach that they were stranded and blown up west of the entrance.

At Zeebrugge, two of the three block ships, the *Iphigenia* and the *Intrepid,* got past the heavy guns on the mole, through the protective nets, and into the canal, where they were sunk athwart the channel by the explosion of mines laid all along their keels. To facilitate their entrance, the cruiser *Vindictive* (Commander Alfred Carpenter), fitted with a false deck and 18 brows or gangways for landing forces, had been brought up 25 minutes earlier—to be exact, at a minute past midnight—along the outer side of the high mole or breakwater enclosing the harbor. Here, in spite of a heavy swell and tide, she was held in position by the ex-ferryboat *Daffodill,* while some 300 or 400 bluejackets and marines swarmed ashore under a violent fire from batteries and machine guns and did considerable in-jury to the works on the mole. Fifteen minutes later, an old British submarine was run into a viaduct connecting the mole with the shore and there blown up, breaking a big gap in the viaduct. Strange to say, the *Vindictive* and her auxiliaries, after lying more than an hour in this dangerous position, suc-ceeded in taking aboard all survivors from the landing party and getting safely away. Motor launches also rescued the crews of the blockships and the men—all of them wounded—from the submarine. One British destroyer and two motor boats were sunk, and the casualties were 176 killed, 412 wounded, and 49 missing. For a considerable period there-after, all the larger German torpedo craft remained cooped up at Bruges, and the Zeebrugge blockships still obstructed the channel at the end of the war.

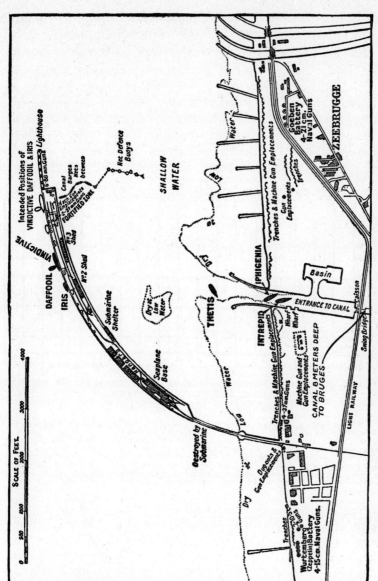

ZEEBRUGGE HARBOR WITH GERMAN DEFENSES AND BRITISH BLOCKSHIPS

The Convoy System

Of all the anti-submarine measures employed, prior to the North Sea Barrage and the Zeebrugge attack, the adoption of the convoy system was undoubtedly the most effective in checking the loss of tonnage at the height of the submarine campaign. Familiar as a means of commerce protection in previous naval wars, the late adoption of the convoy system in the World War occasioned very general surprise. It was felt by naval authorities, however, that great delay would be in-

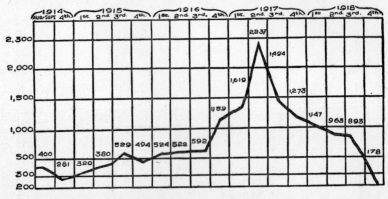

BRITISH, ALLIED AND NEUTRAL MERCHANT SHIPS DESTROYED BY GERMAN
RAIDERS, SUBMARINES AND MINES

(Figures in thousands of gross tons)

The accompanying chart shows the merchant shipping captured or destroyed by Germany in the course of the war. After 1914 the losses were inflicted almost entirely by submarines, either by mine laying or by torpedoes. According to a British Admiralty statement of Dec. 5, 1919, the total loss during the war was 14,820,000 gross tons, of which 8,918,000 was British, and 5,918,000 was Allied or neutral. The United States lost 354,450 tons. During the same period the world's ship construction amounted to 10,850,000 tons, and enemy shipping captured and eventually put into Allied service totalled 2,393,000 tons, so that the net loss at the close of the war was about 1,600,000 tons.

curred in assembling vessels, and in restricting the speed of all ships of a convoy to that of the slowest unit. Merchant captains believed themselves unequal to the task of keeping station at night in close order, with all lights out and frequent changes of course, and they thought that the resultant injuries would be almost as great as from submarines. Furthermore, so long as a large number of neutral vessels were at sea, it appeared a very doubtful expedient to segregate merchant vessels of belligerent nationality and thus distinguish them as legitimate prey.

But in April, 1917, the situation was indeed desperate. The losses had become so heavy that of every 100 ships leaving England it was estimated that 25 never returned.[1] The American commander in European waters, Admiral Sims, reports Admiral Jellicoe as saying at this time, "They will win unless we can stop these losses—and stop them soon."[2] Definitely adopted in May following, the convoy system was in general operation before the end of the summer, with a notable decline of sinkings in both the Mediterranean and the Atlantic. The following table, based on figures from the Naval Annual for 1919, indicates the number of vessels sunk for each submarine destroyed. It shows the decreased effectiveness of submarine operations after September 1, 1917, which is taken as the date

	Vessels sunk per submarine destroyed	Total No. sunk	
Aug. 1, 1914– Feb., 1915	10.4		69 ships sunk, almost entirely by surface cruisers.
Feb. 1, 1915– Feb. 1, 1917	48	544 (two years)	Half by torpedo; 148 without warning; 3,066 lives lost.
Feb. 1, 1917– Sept. 1, 1917	67	736 (7 months)	572 by torpedo; 595 (69%) without warning.
Sept. 1, 1917– April 1, 1918	20.2	548 (7 months)	448 (82%) without warning.
April 1, 1918– Nov. 1, 1918	12	252 (7 months)	239 (91%) without warning.

when the convoy system had come into full use, and brings out the crescendo of losses in 1917.

From July 26, 1917, to October 26, 1918, 90,000 vessels were convoyed, with a total loss from the convoys of 436, or

[1] Brassey's NAVAL ANNUAL, 1919.
[2] World's Work, Sept., 1919.

less than half of one per cent. The convoy system forced submarines to expose themselves to the attacks of destroyer escorts, or else to work close in shore to set upon vessels after the dispersion of the convoy. But when working close to the coast they were exposed to Allied patrols and submarines.

Testifying before a German investigation committee, Captain Bartenbach, of the U-boat section of the German Admiralty, gave the chief perils encountered by his boats as follows: (1) mines, (2) Allied submarines, which "destroyed a whole series of our boats," (3) aircraft of all types, (4) armed merchantmen, (5) hydrophones and listening devices. Admiral Capelle in his testimony referred to the weakening of their efforts due to "indifferent material and second-rate crews."

Transport Work

Dependent in large measure upon the anti-submarine campaign for its safety and success, yet in itself an immense achievement, the transport of over 2,000,000 American troops to France must be regarded as one of the major naval operations of the war. Of these forces 48% were carried in British, and 43% in American transports. About 83% of the convoy work was under the protection of American naval vessels.

The transportation work of the British navy, covering a longer period, was, of course, on a far greater scale. Speaking in Parliament on October 29, 1917, Premier Lloyd George indicated the extent of this service as follows: "Since the beginning of the war the navy has insured the safe transportation to the British and Allied armies of 13,000,000 men, 12,-000,000 horses, 25,000,000 tons of explosives and supplies, and 51,000,000 tons of coal and oil. The loss of men out of the whole 13,000,000 was 3500, of which only 2700 were lost through the action of the enemy. Altogether 130,000,000 tons have been transported by British ships." These figures, covering but three years of the war, are of significance chiefly as indicating the immense transportation problems of the British and Allied navies and the use made of sea communications.

These three main Allied naval operations—the blockade of

Germany, the anti-submarine campaign, and the transportation of American troops to France—were unquestionably decisive factors in the war. Failure in any one of them would have meant victory for Germany. The peace of Europe, it is true, could be achieved only by overcoming Germany's military power on land. A breakdown there, with German domination of the Continent, would have created a situation which it is difficult to envisage, and which very probably would have meant a peace of compromise and humiliation for England and America. It is obvious, however, that, but for the blockade, Germany could have prolonged the war; but for American reënforcements, France would have been overrun; but for the conquest of the submarine, Great Britain would have been forced to surrender.

In the spring of 1918 Germany massed her troops on the western front and began her final effort to break the Allied lines and force a decision. With supreme command for the first time completely centralized under Marshal Foch, and with the support of American armies, the Allies were able to hold up the enemy drives, and on July 18 begin the forward movement which pushed the Germans back upon their frontiers. Yet when the armistice was signed on November 11, the German armies still maintained cohesion, with an unbroken line on foreign soil. Surrender was made inevitable by internal breakdown and revolution, the first open manifestations of which appeared among the sailors of the idle High Seas Fleet at Kiel.

On November 21, 1918, this fleet, designed as the great instrument for conquest of world empire, and in its prime perhaps as efficient a war force as was ever set afloat, steamed silently through two long lines of British and Allied battleships assembled off the Firth of Forth, and the German flags at the mainmasts went down at sunset for the last time.

REFERENCES

BRASSEY'S NAVAL ANNUAL, 1919.
THE VICTORY AT SEA, Vice-Admiral W. S. Sims, U. S. N., 1920.
ANNUAL REPORT of the U. S Secretary of the Navy, 1918

THE DOVER PATROL, 1915-1917, Admiral Sir Reginald Bacon, R. N., 1919.

ZEEBRUGGE AND OSTEND DISPATCHES, ed. by C. Sanford Terry, 1919.

LAYING THE NORTH SEA MINE BARRAGE, Captain R. R. Belknap, U. S. N., U. S. Naval Institute Proceedings, Jan.-Feb., 1920.

AMERICAN SUBMARINE OPERATIONS IN THE WORLD WAR, by Prof. C. S. Alden, U. S. Naval Institute Proceedings. June-July, 1920.

For more popular treatment see also SUBMARINE AND ANTI-SUBMARINE, Sir Henry Newbolt, 1919; THE FIGHTING FLEETS, Ralph D. Payne, 1918; THE U-BOAT HUNTERS, James B. Connolly, 1918; SEA WARFARE, Rudyard Kipling, 1917; etc.

CHAPTER XVIII

NAVAL POWER AFTER 1918

AMONG President Wilson's famous "Fourteen Points" as a basis for ending the World War the second read as follows:

"Absolute freedom of navigation upon the seas, outside territorial waters, alike in peace and in war, except as the seas may be closed in whole or in part by international action for the enforcement of international covenants."

It is evident that this point could have had little significance in time of peace, since aside from national tariff barriers there are no restraints on sea-borne trade. In time of war, however, this "freedom of the seas" would have banned the long-sanctioned weapons of blockade and stoppage of contraband by visit and search, and would thus have placed a tremendous restriction on the exercise of naval power. On the other hand, unless war itself were eliminated by a strong international organization, there could be no assurance that a belligerent, defying the League, would not flout any rules of warfare the League laid down.

For England, as the chief naval power and also the nation chiefly dependent on sea communications, the possible gains from such restrictions seemed not to outweigh the grave risks involved. At her instance, the Allied powers made full reservations on this point, and little was heard of it at Versailles. But its abandonment, together with other disillusionments of the Peace Conference, had much to do with the American decision after the war to complete the big building program of 1916, providing for a fleet comparable to that of the strongest naval power, with seven new super-dreadnoughts and six battle cruisers.

British and Japanese—and Americans also, despite the seemingly immense economic strength of the United States in the post-war period—viewed with much concern the possibilities of a new armament race which would lay a heavy burden on national resources.

To avoid this by joint agreement was a primary motive for the Washington Naval Conference of 1922. Behind it also was the peace and anti-armament sentiment both in this country and abroad, a sentiment especially fervent in the years after the war. And behind it also was the fact that the Anglo-Japanese alliance—still in existence and the most apparent justification for American naval increases—no longer jibed with British imperial interests in the Pacific area. Canada in particular[1] brought pressure to bear to end a commitment that might bring the great English-speaking nations into conflict on issues in which their interests were really akin.

It had been more or less understood that naval parleys would follow the general peace conference, and Anglo-American conversations quickly paved the way for the Conference on Limitation of Naval Armament which, on the invitation of Secretary of State Charles E. Hughes, met at Washington in the winter of 1921-1922. Its triple aims—to end the Anglo-Japanese alliance, secure a settlement of Pacific problems, and limit navies—achieved a large measure of success, in the accomplishment of which the sacrifice of the large American building program proved an effective lever. In capital ships it set up the following ratios and tonnage limits:

Nation	Ratio	Capital Ship	Aircraft Carrier
United States	5	525,000 tons	135,000 tons
Great Britain	5	525,000 "	135,000 "
Japan	3	315,000 "	81,000 "
France	1.75	175,000 "	60,000 "
Italy	1.75	175,000 "	60,000 "

There was also some "qualitative" limitation, notably the restriction of battleships to 35,000 tons and 16-inch guns, of aircraft carriers to 27,000 tons and 8-inch guns, and of cruisers

[1] See "Canada and the Far East," *Foreign Affairs*, April, 1935.

to 10,000 tons and 8-inch guns. The conference failed in its effort to apply the ratio system to cruisers and other auxiliary types, partly because of objections on the part of England, who felt that she needed many cruisers for commerce protection, and partly because of opposition from France and Italy, who could afford no immediate naval increases but found little satisfaction in the inferior ratios dealt out to them by their former allies. There was a separate protocol forbidding the use of gas and limiting submarines to legitimate methods of commerce warfare, but this failed of subsequent ratification, though a submarine agreement was finally reached in 1936.

Chiefly as an inducement to Japan to accept the 5–5–3 ratio, the naval treaty included an important clause providing that the *status quo* be maintained with regard to fortifications and naval bases in certain insular possessions of the Pacific, as follows:

For the United States, the Philippines, Guam, and the Aleutian Islands, but not Hawaii or islands adjacent to Alaska, the Pacific Coast states, or Panama.

For Great Britain, Hongkong, and islands east of 110° East Longitude, but not insular possessions adjacent to Canada, Australia, and New Zealand, and not Singapore.

For Japan, Kurile, Bonin, Amami-Oshima, Loochoo Islands, Formosa, Pescadores, and any others hereafter acquired.

The political agreements at Washington included the so-called Four Power Treaty (United States, Britain, Japan, and France) which ended the alliance between England and Japan and substituted an innocuous pledge that if a controversy arose between any of the signatories they should "invite the other high contracting parties to a joint conference." "A Nine Power Treaty (United States, Belgium, Britain, China, France, Italy, Japan, the Netherlands, and Portugal) attempted to establish the Open Door policy for China; the signatories were to respect the territorial and administrative integrity of China, assist her in establishing a stable government, and "refrain from taking advantage of conditions in China in order to seek special rights or privileges . . ." No term was set for this last treaty, but after the Manchurian crisis of 1931 it was very generally regarded as outmoded by events.

The naval treaty was to run till 1936, and thereafter unless ended by two years' advance notice. Owing to changed political conditions, partly indicated in what follows, later efforts toward naval limitation were much less successful. In 1927 an attempt to extend the ratios to all types failed through disagreement between England and the United States over cruiser requirements, England preferring many small cruisers with 6-inch guns and the United States favoring a larger type that would have a clear superiority over converted merchant vessels and would be more suitable for a nation with few and distant bases. In 1930 this difficulty was settled by compromise, each nation being accorded superiority in its preferred type, and in a treaty signed in London provision was made for extension of the ratios to the smaller categories, with a concession to Japan of a 7 to 10 ratio in cruisers and equality in submarines. France and Italy remained outside the agreement.

The London Treaty expired at the end of 1936. In the meantime the international situation had become much more disturbed both in Europe and in the East. At the conference in London which worked on a new agreement in the winter of 1935–36 Japan insisted on naval equality or at least an abandonment of ratios, and on January 15 withdrew from the negotiations. The subsequent treaty, signed only by the United States, Britain, and France, but with opportunity for future adherence by other nations, preserved a mere remnant of the limitation principle. Most significant among its provisions were those stipulating full exchange of information regarding building programs, a "holiday" in the construction of warcraft between 8,000 and 17,500 tons, and a great number of escape clauses releasing the signatories from restrictions in the event of unforeseen expansion by other powers. In a separate exchange of notes the United States and Great Britain pledged themselves to accept the principle of parity as between their two navies and to avoid competitive building, thus emphasizing the

Anglo-American harmony which was a feature of the 1936 conference.

During the period of the Washington treaties, and after its close, it appeared to many that the strong British and American navies, acting in coöperation, might serve as a potent instrument for the preservation of world peace. Thus a prominent British political figure, the Marquess of Lothian, in discussing "The World Crisis of 1936",[1] offered this suggestion:

". . . if the new world alignment centers about communism, fascism, and democracy, is it not possible that the United States might best preserve its own peace by using its immense power to maintain, in association with the British Commonwealth and the Pan-American Union, command of the oceans of the world as security that democracy and free institutions shall continue to exist over nearly half the globe?"

To most British and Americans this proposal might sound attractive and even idealistic. But it is altogether likely that the rest of the world would regard such a predominance as neither welcome nor beneficent. For example, an Italian writer, commenting on a somewhat similar passage in the first edition of the present work in 1922, remarked, "We want no world hegemony, either by land or by sea." In point of fact, no such solidarity of the major sea powers has been manifested, either in conjunction with the League of Nations or independently. Preoccupied in Europe, Britain has been unwilling to join in concerted action in the Pacific; and the United States has firmly adhered to its traditional policy of non-participation in European affairs. And within the period of the Washington treaties the stabilizing influence anticipated from the strong sea powers was at least thrice successfully challenged.

A brief account of these challenges will serve to indicate the part played by navies in the period covered, during which naval power, though not actually exercised, had a constant influence on the course of events.

[1] In the American quarterly *Foreign Affairs*, October, 1936.

First may be mentioned the rearmament of Germany, in disregard of the Versailles Treaty, which gathered impetus after 1928 and the advent of National Socialist control. Germany's effort, it is true, took the direction chiefly of land and air rearmament; but in the naval field her so-called "pocket battleships", while keeping within the Versailles Treaty limit of 10,000 tons, aroused real concern by their 11-inch guns, heavy armor, and great cruising radius, as compared with the Washington Treaty cruisers of similar size. Then came a general abandonment of Versailles restrictions. In 1936, in a separate naval agreement with Germany, the British Government was apparently very ready to sanction this abandonment upon Germany's promise to limit her fleet to 35 per cent of the strength of the British fleet, with reservations indicating Germany's intention to maintain a naval force capable of coping with either France or Russia in northern waters.

A second and more direct challenge to what may be called the collective peace system, and to the naval powers as its chief guarantors, was Japan's Manchurian adventure of 1931 and her later expansionist program in continental Asia. Whatever her internal economic pressure or external provocation, Japan would hardly have entered upon this course had she not felt an assurance—justified by the sequel—that her disregard of the League Covenant, the Pact of Paris, and the Nine Power Treaty would be met by no effective opposition from the League or the naval powers. The wisdom of undertaking such opposition is open to question, though former Secretary of State Henry L. Stimson[1] has advanced strong arguments, based on the injury to American interests and to the cause of world peace, for the lead which he offered at that time. As a matter of fact, after the Manchurian Commission's verdict against Japan and her withdrawal from the League, no positive action was undertaken. It was negatived by the prevalent anti-war sentiment in the West, by the unsettled conditions in Europe, and above all by the strong Japanese fleet and the increased efficacy of aircraft and submarines which made more than ever difficult a campaign in distant waters.

[1] THE FAR EASTERN CRISIS, 1936.

A third challenge was offered by the Italian conquest of Ethiopia in 1935. Under British leadership, the League opposition now took the form of a munitions embargo against Italy, a withdrawal of all financial assistance, and a virtual stoppage of trade between Italy and the League nations. The United States, acting independently, forbade munitions exports to either belligerent, and made some effort to restrict general exports to peace-time proportions. England heavily reënforced her fleet in the Mediterranean to safeguard her interests in Egypt and the Levant. When the economic sanctions against Italy proved insufficient, it is quite likely that stronger pressure might have been brought to bear had it not been for the increased vulnerability of navies in confined waters, especially to attack from the air.

In fact the limitations placed on the costly surface navies by these new weapons have been regarded by many as marking a revolutionary change in naval warfare. Certainly they have greatly altered strategic problems, particularly for those nations whose geographical situation makes them easily accessible to hostile aircraft. After the Ethiopian settlement, and in view of disturbed conditions in Spain, England took measures for the reorganization of her Mediterranean defenses and the development of Cyprus as a naval and air base, essential to the safety of imperial communications and interests in the middle sea.

The end of the naval ratio system in 1936 and the vigorous rearmament then generally under way were a disappointing sequel to the ambitious plans for international coöperation and arms reduction of the preceding decades. World insecurity had greatly increased.

The aim of these moves to reduce the menace of war must command the strongest sympathy. But less may be said for premature weakening of defenses and open proclamation of unwillingness to defend national interests—measures the effect of which may actually be to give a license to aggression and thus defeat their own aims. Armament restrictions, however desirable, obviously do not strike at the roots of war. And furthermore, proposals of disarmament coming from the satisfied nations, and implying as they inevitably do a stabilization of present conditions, are very naturally viewed askance by nations not satisfied with their position in the world. Nor are these nations ready to accept the argument of the satisfied powers that the conflicts involved in trade and territorial expansion "do not pay."

Of recent years the danger of war has led many Americans not only to oppose all forms of international coöperation but to favor a policy of economic nationalism, the aim of which is to reduce as far as possible our economic dependence on the outside world. Such a policy, while conceivable for this country, would be impossible for most nations, and would seem to run counter to the whole stream of human development, which has brought the peoples of the world into closer material and spiritual interdependence. It is indeed not a policy of peace but one whose best justification is that it makes a nation strong for war.

Closely linked with this trend toward economic isolation, and of special interest in connection with strength at sea, is the new neutrality policy, which would avoid involvement in war by prohibiting munitions exports to belligerents, restricting trade with them, and preventing travel in their ships, even though these steps mean a surrender of certain of the so-called "neutral rights" built up during centuries of strife. Something may doubtless be accomplished by such non-intercourse measures, though they put upon the neutral the difficult task of preventing the movement of trade, and are almost certain to operate strongly in favor of one of the two belligerents. It may be added that no amount of surrender on the part of a weak neutral is likely to satisfy the belligerents' demands.

Discussion of these matters might seem out of place in a study of sea power were it not justified by the close relation between naval and national policies. Naval strength, as is illustrated by the Manchurian and Ethiopian crises, affects national policies; and conversely, national policies and aims determine the size and character of a nation's fleet. These policies cover a wide range. In former times it was assumed that navies existed solely to protect shipping and sea trade. But this is too narrow a view. Even with a limited shipping under its own flag, a nation may need naval power to maintain its communications with foreign markets and vital supply sources, to serve as a first line of defense against aggression from abroad, and to supply backing for national policies and interests that are not strictly limited within its own frontiers. Even such policies as tariff restrictions, immigration barriers, and coöperation with our neighbors to prevent outside interference in the Western Hemisphere may well call for some show of naval power. Quite aside from the Far East, where our diplomacy has at times laid down policies beyond our will or power to support, we have interests and commitments beyond our continental coastline, a clear determination of which will at least help to settle our naval requirements. Finally, as suggested by the quotation on page 419, there is some basis for the belief that naval strength may contribute toward international peace.

Even the briefest review of the naval history here presented will show that, while sea power reaches its most striking manifestations in the clash of battle, and while it has often been the instrument of aggression and conquest, it has also played a part in the maintenance of peace and in the protection and spread of civilization. Naval armament defended the peaceful trader against the pirates and outlaws who infested the ancient seas. Salamis established a barrier against the Persian hordes and gave scope for the glorious if brief expansion of Greek genius in its Golden Age. Naval victories over Carthage paved the way for Roman conquest of the Mediterranean basin, but it was also the strength of the Roman fleet that established the *Pax Romana* for centuries over the seas and rivers of the western world, facilitating the spread of Roman law, engineering, and ideals of practical efficiency, while at the same time it brought back to the center of the empire not only material wealth, but the artistic and spiritual contributions of other lands.

Sufficient has already been said of the service of Byzantine sea power, and of the Christian fleets that fought at Lepanto, in defending Europe against the advance of Saracen and Turk. With the growth of sea trade and colonial interests from the 16th century onward, naval power took on vastly increased importance. Her fleet proved the salvation of England at the time of the Spanish Armada, and for good or ill the British navy in the struggles with the Dutch in the 17th century and with the French in the 18th century was a vital element in the growth of the British Empire.   British naval predominance broke the Napoleonic hegemony of Europe, and was largely responsible for the relative peace of the 19th century, during which British speech and institutions spread throughout the world.   Certainly Allied control of sea communications was also a chief factor in deciding the conflict of 1914–18.   Modern developments in warfare may appear to have lessened the efficacy of surface navies either in guaranteeing national security or assuring sea control.   Yet the building programs of the major powers in the fourth decade of the 20th century would not indicate loss of faith in the value of surface fleets.

So long as wars continue, whether sea control is exerted on the surface or above or beneath, certain fundamental lessons from the past retain their value.   One of these lessons, which has become increasingly important with the more rapid tempo of modern scientific progress, is the necessity of keeping all military branches in close touch with scientific advances.   Now less than ever can any armed force afford to rest on traditions of the past.   Military success has come to depend more and more on the application of new achievements in chemistry, engineering, optics, and other branches of science to the art of war. The corvus won for Rome at Mylæ; better range-finders and gunnery helped decide the battle cruiser action at Jutland.

Another lesson, still more clearly taught by history, is in a way the converse of the first; it is that success in battle cannot be estimated wholly or even chiefly in terms of material strength. One need think only of Salamis, the Armada, Trafalgar, Lissa, and Jutland to realize that it is not always the fleet strongest on paper that has carried off the honors.   Superior weapons are important, but more important still are skilled leadership and the morale and training of personnel.

In the field of leadership and high command there is probably the greatest opportunity for improvement today.   With the modern ease of communications, the management of naval and military operations tends more and more toward centralized control, usually at the seat of government. Here one enters a zone of possible interference and conflict, rather than coöperation, between the civil and the military authorities. Each has its proper functions, but the two are closely interlocked. The experience of the World War indicated that most governments, and especially the more democratic governments, still lacked a well-conceived and efficient organization for the supply of materials, coördination of effort, planning, and general conduct of war. The problem is at least partly met on the more purely military side by the permanent institution of some form of general staff. Much of the planning and preparatory work that falls to such a body may be accomplished in time of peace, enabling it to cope more effectively with the rapid expansion and swift exigencies of war. In this way may perhaps be avoided such uncertainties and delays as marked the conduct of the Dardanelles Campaign, or the Allied adoption of the convoy system in the World War. In the next war a general sent on a day or two's notice to command a distant front, as Sir Ian Hamilton was sent to Gallipoli, will perhaps not find merely a guidebook and travel sketch to help him in the War Office files.

Equal importance is attached to the selection and training of leaders at sea. No task would seem to call for higher qualities of character, theoretical knowledge, and skill based on practical experience than the command of a modern fleet in action. And on the other hand it is unfortunately true that the qualities likely to win promotion in time of peace, such as conformity, industry, and "a clean record," are not always those essential to success in war. Conflict itself can afford the only final test. Yet the aim in time of peace must be to provide in some measure the equivalent of war-time experience, so that leaders not too old for usefulness can be tried out, and have opportunity to develop a sound practical knowledge of the whole difficult art of fleet command.

Solution of all these problems is made easier if a navy steers clear of the evils of cliques, favoritism, inertia, and interference in politics, which beset military as well as civilian organizations, and bears in mind that beyond loyalty to the service there is a higher loyalty to the nation served.

REFERENCES

Reports of the various naval conferences have been published by the Government Printing Office (Washington). A convenient collection of the naval agreements up to that date appears in the Naval Institute *Proceedings* for January, 1932. See also:

THE WASHINGTON CONFERENCE, R. L. Buell, 1922.

THE POLICY OF NAVAL DISARMAMENT, G. Engely, 1932.

A HISTORY OF THE UNITED STATES NAVY, Captain Dudley W. Knox, 1936. (Final chapter deals with naval limitation.)

A HISTORY OF AMERICAN FOREIGN POLICY, J. H. Latané (revised and enlarged edition of 1934).

CHAPTER XIX

THE SECOND WORLD WAR

1939–1941

THE BREAKDOWN of arms limitation and the aggressions of Germany, Italy, and Japan, recounted in the preceding chapter, were sure danger signals pointing to a renewal of European warfare, which would almost inevitably spread throughout the world. The final appeasement efforts at Munich in 1938 proved of slight avail. Firmly supported by the Franco-British alliance, Poland in the next year resisted demands that threatened her national existence. The swift Nazi invasion of Poland was followed by a British ultimatum which expired September 3, 1939. Again British sea power and French land power were pitted against the German nation in arms.

Unquestionably, the engineers of the aggressions in the thirties and of the ensuing conflict itself had seen their opportunity and grounded their hopes, partly, at least, in the decreased effectiveness of sea power. The long *Pax Britannica* of the 19th century had been based on an almost undisputed mastery of the sea and sea communications. With this control England could maintain her far-flung empire, defend her island frontiers, and cut off enemies from trade with the outside world. But this control was weakened in the periods both before and after the First World War. It was weakened in part by the rise of rival naval powers—in Japan, in America, in Continental Europe—which in distant areas, or in coalitions, might effectively dispute the "Mistress of the Seas." It was weakened by the spread of industrialism and by policies of economic self-sufficiency, which made other nations less vulnerable to the paralyzing effects of blockade. It was weakened further by the development of new instruments of war. The submarine had proved in 1914–1918 a dangerous .weapon against an insular nation, dependent on shipping and imports for very existence. Pitted against far superior strength, the sub-surface craft still required most inordinate efforts to put them down. Air power also had grown to be an important factor in sea power. For offense or defense, it could reach out from the coast over great areas of sea.

It would be a great mistake, however, to assume that the increased difficulties of achieving sea control meant that less importance was attached to such control. In fact, its importance increased in warfare on an intercontinental scale. Though the seas separate the continents, they are not the barriers, but the great highways of communications, in peace and war, between the continents and the nations they divide. Wartime control of the sea enables the belligerent possessing it to use these sea communications freely for the movement of its armed forces, supplies, and trade, and forbid such use to its foe. Hence sea control remains vital, whether secured by weapons operating upon, above, or beneath the surface.

To illustrate its continued importance one need merely point to the Mediterranean, the Pacific, and the Atlantic in the Second World War. In the African conflict, troops, supplies, and weapons for both belligerents crossed the Mediterranean, and its importance was not lessened by the fact that neither side could establish exclusive control. In the Pacific, the southward movement of Japan into Malaya, the Philippines, and the Pacific islands was made possible solely by temporary sea mastery, and the hopes of her enemies lay solely in wresting it away. In 1942 the struggle in the Atlantic remained for Britain a conflict to maintain sea communications and for the American nations to maintain an uninterrupted flow of munitions, foodstuffs, and man power overseas.

On the other hand, it may be said truly that modern warfare has broken down the old segregation of land, sea, and air forces. In almost any campaign, weapons of all types are likely to come into play. What is needed is not separation, but closer coöperation and mutual coördination of all weapons under unified command.

I. THE FIRST YEAR

These general considerations, however, have led beyond the conditions which prevailed in the first period of relatively limited war, when Germany's naval efforts were confined to commerce warfare and to such sea operations as were involved in extending her domination over Norway and the Low Countries. Prior to the entry of Italy in June, 1940, the British Navy of some 14 capital ships and corresponding numbers in the lesser categories, though actually far weaker than in 1914, had a relatively greater superiority over the strength opposed. The German fleet consisted only of the 26,000-ton battleships *Gneisenau* and *Scharnhorst,* the "pocket battleships" *Deutschland, Admiral Graf Spee,* and *Admiral Scheer,* a half-dozen cruisers, some 50 destroyers, and 60 to 80 submarines. A threat for the future lay in the big battleships *Bismarck* and *Tirpitz,* nearly completed, and numerous U-boats under construction.

Opening Operations

There was some similarity between the opening naval operations in 1914 and in 1939. The sinking on September 3 of the British liner *Athenia,* almost certainly by German torpedo, as she steamed westward off the Irish coast, gave proof that the sea tragedies of non-combatants would be repeated in this war. Of over 1400 passengers and crew, the death list was 112, including 30 Americans. As another parallel of 1914, the British were driven temporarily from Scapa Flow, but this time by the actual sinking on October 13 of the battleship *Royal Oak,* a veteran of Jutland, by the *U-18.* The feat of Kapitänleutnant Gunther Prien in pushing through the barriers, finding his mark with three or four torpedoes at close range, and getting safely away, was properly described by First Lord of the Admiralty Winston Churchill as "a remarkable exploit of professional skill and daring."[1] Another serious British loss was the torpedoing on September 17 of the old aircraft carrier *Courageous,*

[1]This and other events of the naval war are more fully described in Gilbert Cant's excellent volume THE WAR AT SEA, John Day Co., 1942, the most readable and accurate *ad interim* report on the naval war to the close of 1941.

stationed with aircraft off the western approaches of the Channel to guard traffic before the convoy system was fully under way.   Avoiding her mistake of 1914 in leaving some 500,000 tons of valuable tonnage in American ports, Germany rushed many of her liners homeward in the first days of war. One of these was the big 57,700-ton *Bremen,* which steered far north of Iceland and put in on September 6 at Murmansk, whence after three months she stole safely homeward with aircraft escort along the Norwegian coast.

During these months the U-boat warfare was kept within bounds, and in fact up to June, 1940, the sinking of allied and neutral tonnage by all weapons—U-boats, mines, aircraft, and surface raiders—was held to a monthly average of about 183,000 tons.   This was due partly to immediate employment of the convoy system and to improved detection methods, particularly the "Asdic"[1] device, which, using the reflection of sound waves under water, can detect submarines even when they are not under way.   The Führer's new "secret weapon," first widely used in November, was the magnetic mine, laid on the bottom and brought upward by the magnetic attraction of any large iron body passing within 30 to 50 feet. Its detonation was effected either by contact or by special devices to cause explosion near the surface.   Mines of this type, which would operate only in limited depths and were laid chiefly by aircraft, accounted for heavy losses of both British and neutral[2] shipping until a workable counter-measure was found.   The most effective was a charged electric "de-Gaussing" cable fitted about ships to neutralize the magnetic field set up by the ship's hull.

For surface raiding, the Germans had two pocket battleships at sea in the early days of the war.   The *Deutschland* in October captured only two or three prizes in the North Atlantic, one of which was the U.S. freighter *City of Flint* with a mixed cargo for British ports.   The *Flint* with a prize crew went to Tromsoe, thence to Murmansk, and then back to Norwegian waters, where she was finally released.

[1]Anti-submarine Detection Investigation Committee.

[2]It did not help German-Japanese relations when one of these mines sank the crack Japanese liner *Terukune Maru.*

In company with the cruiser *Emden,* the *Deutschland* on November 23 met in Iceland waters with the auxiliary cruiser *Rawalpindi* of the British Northern Patrol. The big ex-Peninsula and Orient liner had neither the strength to fight nor speed to run, but with her 6-inch guns she stood up valiantly against 11-inch shells. Lights were extinguished and ammunition hoists wrecked at the third salvo, and after thirty-five minutes her last guns were silenced and her whole midships section was a mass of flames. Of her crew of over three hundred, 27 were taken from boats by the Germans and 11 more were saved hours later by a British patrol. Soon after the battle the *Deutschland* and her consort got safely back to home ports.

Battle of the River Plate

It was another story with the *Admiral Graf Spee,* which had slipped into the Atlantic before the outbreak of war. With the big tanker *Altmark,* which had come from Port Arthur with fuel and supplies, the *Spee* operated for three months along the Brazilian and African coasts, capturing in all only eight prizes totaling about 50,000 tons. Her downfall was facilitated by a radio call from the freighter *Doric Prince,* sunk December 2 between Capetown and Sierra Leone, which reached the *Ajax,* flagship of Commodore Henry Harwood of the British South Atlantic patrol. Shrewdly surmising that the Germans would shift westward, Harwood in the briefest possible radio despatch summoned his two other available ships—the 8-inch gun cruiser *Exeter* (8,390 tons) and 6-inch gun cruiser *Achilles* (7,030), sister ship of the *Ajax*—to a rendezvous on December 12 about 150 miles off the River Plate. Fortune and skillful timing favored the British, for here they met and fought the raider on the morning of the next day. In Nelsonian fashion Harwood had worked out tactics with his captains the day before. A guiding principle would be "to act without further instructions so-as to maintain decisive range." The six 11-inch and eight 5.9-inch guns of the *Spee* fired a total broadside of 4,700 pounds, whereas the six 8-inch guns of the *Exeter* and eight 6-inch guns of the *Ajax* and *Achilles* totaled but 3,136. But the British cruisers were handier of maneuver and 6 knots faster, and their smaller guns, though somewhat outranged, could develop a more rapid fire.   By dividing into two groups, they could reduce the effectiveness of director fire control for the enemy's two triple turrets.   Moreover, Harwood, in his own words, had but "one object—destruction," whereas his opponent Captain Hans Langsdorff had orders to concentrate on commerce warfare and to avoid injuries from enemy action that might incapacitate his ship for its primary role.   He seems also to have been hampered by a fuel problem, for according to one report he anchored at Montevideo with oil for only 30 miles.

As shown in the diagram, the *Exeter* advanced directly, while the two smaller cruisers swung on to the northward to bring the enemy under two fires.   The first German 11-inch salvo at 6.18 was split between the two groups, and within four minutes the British were returning the fire at almost 10-mile range. Troubled by the 8-inch broadsides of the *Exeter,* Langsdorff soon concentrated most of his main battery fire on the larger cruiser and in the next 20 minutes gave this ship a hammering which only superb damage control enabled her to survive. At 6.24 a shell from the *Spee's* seventh salvo hit the *Exeter's* forward (B) turret squarely, putting it out of action, and by splinters killing all the men on the bridge but Captain Bell and one other.   To quote a report sent later from the Falklands:

"The *Exeter* closed, receiving 3 or 4 more hits from 11-inch shells. . . .   She returned shot for shot until only one 8-inch gun could be fired, and that by hand. . . .   The steering gear was damaged just after 7 o'clock [the control was shifted at 6.24], and for 45 minutes the Captain conned the ship from the after control, just forward of the mainmast, using a ship's compass.   Through a chain of some 10 sailors, orders were conveyed from man to man to the after steering wheel and the engine-room, until the ship was no longer serviceable and fell out of the action.

"Numerous fires broke out on board but were kept under by gallant men throwing the burning material into the sea, and below decks, where the outbreaks were most numerous, by the staunchness of the fire parties. . . ."

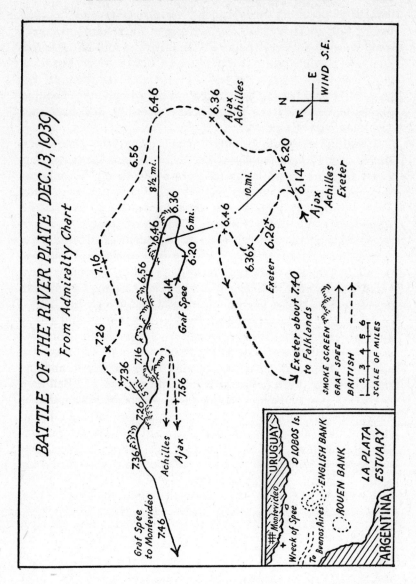

BATTLE OF THE RIVER PLATE DEC. 13, 1939
From Admiralty Chart

WIND S.E.

N E

6.46
6.36 Ajax
       Achilles

6.56
6.20

8½ mi.

10. mi.

6.14

6.46   6.36
6.46   Ajax
       6.56   Achilles
                         Exeter

6.36
6.20   6.46

6.14
Graf Spee

6.36×   Exeter 6.26×

7.16

7.26

Exeter about 7.40
to Falklands

7.36

7.16

7.26 S

7.56

7.36

Achilles   Ajax

SMOKE SCREEN
GRAF SPEE
BRITISH

1 2 3 4 5 6
SCALE OF MILES

Graf Spee
to Montevideo
7.46

URUGUAY
D. LOBOS Is.

Montevideo

ENGLISH BANK

+ Wreck of Spee

To Buenos Aires

ROUEN BANK

LA PLATA
ESTUARY

ARGENTINA

At 6.32 the *Exeter* fired her starboard torpedoes and at 6.38 turned east to fire those of the port side at 9,000 yards. All six went wide, and at this point she suffered her fourth and fifth hits by 11-inch shells. From then on only two of her after guns were in action. She had a 7° list and was down by the head. At 7.30 her last guns were put out of action by flooding below, and at 7.40 she turned away, reaching the Falklands under her own power.

Meantime the 6-inch cruisers had closed the range, the engine-room forces having achieved the feat of increasing the speed from 14 to 28 knots in 20 minutes' time. Their guns were well directed and met only by a less effective fire of the *Spee's* secondary battery. At about 6.36, when the *Exeter's* torpedoes were fired, Captain Langsdorff seems to have reached his decision to fall back on Montevideo. It marked a critical turn in the action. Two 6-inch shells had put the *Spee's* fire-control tower out of commission and greatly hampered effective fire. Langsdorff spoke later of the "inconceivable audacity" of the enemy tactics, and of the high percentage of his men out of action[1]—partly from casualties and partly also, perhaps, from some demoralization among his youthful crew. The turn was covered by the *Spee's* first smoke screen, and the *Ajax* and *Achilles,* working northward to bring all turrets to bear, were temporarily put out of range.

By 6.56 they had again closed, darting through smoke screens to pour in their fire and then turning quickly away. Both had been hit by heavy shells, and the *Ajax* had only three guns still in action, but these and the *Achilles'* entire battery kept up a hot fire. At 7.16 the *Spee* turned southward as if to finish the *Exeter,* but was soon back on a westerly course. She turned again briefly at 7.26 to avoid torpedoes from the *Ajax.* The British temporary swing away about 7.38 was a result of Harwood's decision, in view of the *Exeter's* withdrawal and a very probable ammunition shortage if heavy firing continued, that he would "shadow" at long range for the rest of the day and attempt to close for torpedo attack that night. The rest of the

---

[1]The losses were: *Graf Spee,* 36 k., 60 w.; *Exeter,* 57 k., 25 w.; *Ajax,* 7 k., 2 w.; *Achilles,* 4 k., 3 w.

action was a pursuit at 22 knots with only occasional firing.
The British cruisers separated toward night to close two en-
trances to the La Plata estuary, lest the *Spee* swing around the
English Bank and thus escape.   But the German was bound for
Montevideo and at midnight anchored in the port.

Next night the *Ajax* and *Achilles* on watch outside were
reënforced by the 8-inch cruiser *Cumberland,* which had completed refit and hastened up from the Falklands at the first news
of battle.   Rumors of further reënforcements were rife, but
the *Repulse* and *Ark Royal* were still a thousand miles distant
when the time came for the *Spee* to sail.   On the 15th the
Uruguayan authorities had granted the German ship 72 hours
for temporary repairs.   Before the period ended, Langsdorff
had received direct orders from the Führer to destroy his ship
rather than put to sea.   On the evening of the 17th she
steamed slowly to a point outside the channel, discharged her
crew to tenders, and was blown up at 8.54.   Captain Langsdorff had wished to fight his ship to the end.   Failing this, after
making provision for his crew at Buenos Aires, he shot himself
in his room, wrapped in a flag of the old Imperial Navy, to
which he still gave his true allegiance.

The close-fought naval action and its aftermath of suspense
had attracted world attention and gathered significance from its
test of types and weapons, and especially of the boasted ability
of the pocket battleship to "outshoot anything it could not out-
run."   In England, the rejoicing found expression in the immense crowds which greeted the *Ajax* and *Exeter* men as they
marched through London to a Guildhall banquet; and in Auck-
land a crowd of 100,000 greeted the *Achilles* when this New
Zealand ship returned home.   To quote Winston Churchill,
"In this dark somber winter . . . the brilliant action of the
Plate . . . came like a flash of light and color on the scene."

The "Altmark"

The tale of the *Altmark* still remains.   Upon the news from
Montevideo the tender, with 299 British prisoners aboard, remained several weeks in the South Atlantic, then turned north-

ward in January, eluded patrols, and on February 14 entered Trondheim.   Norwegian officers were suspicious but refrained from search of a naval vessel, though at each of their visits the prisoners broke loose in a pandemonium of shouts and pound-ing in the hold.   But a British aircraft had spotted her as she moved down the coast, and on the night of the 17th the *Cossack,* Captain Vian, and two other destroyers closed in, with cabinet sanction for an invasion of territorial waters.   The *Altmark* had turned up Joesing fjord and rammed her bow in the ice at the upper end.   The *Cossack* pushed in through the dark, narrow channel, brought her bow along the *Altmark's* stern, and at the old cry "Boarders away" the executive officer and 30 men leaped over the rails.   There was little fighting, except that 20 regular German enlisted men had got across the ice and did some shooting from the shore.   With the released prisoners, the *Cossack* steamed away.   In the ensuing diplomacy, the British had a good case in public sympathy and some support in law.   There was no parade of prisoners in Berlin.

The Invasion of Norway

It was within two months of the *Altmark* affair that Germany moved into Norway, by a combination of sea, land, air, and fifth-column action typical of German skill in this kind of campaign.   Little could be expected from Norway's tiny army and navy, but the world had counted on more effective resist-ance by the British fleet—even though it had to work in narrow seas.   The whole campaign illustrated anew the decisive ad-vantage of superiority in the air.   Certainly defeat of the in-vasion was important, for control of Norway meant free Ger-man access to the iron ore of North Sweden, the greater part of which in prewar days had come through the ice-free port of Narvik and down the Norwegian coast.   Possession of Nor-way meant also that German aircraft and submarines would gain bases a third of the way nearer Scapa Flow and North Britain, and that both surface craft and U-boats would find easier access to the outer seas.

Germany's preparations were not unknown—the gathering

of ships and troops in northern ports as early as February for some hidden move. Before the time finally set for the surprise attack, the dawn of April 9, transports were under way, and some of them, with troops and mechanized equipment between-decks, were actually in Norwegian ports. The transport *Rio de Janeiro,* torpedoed April 8 in the Cattegat by the Polish submarine *Orzel,* now operating with the British, astonished Norse fishermen by disgorging on the waters a strange cargo of horses and uniformed Nazi troops. Three German naval squadrons laden with troops and accompanied by destroyers and transports had already left Kiel and Wilhelmshaven, one led by the *Scharnhorst* and *Admiral Hipper* to operate in Narvik and the north, another with the *Gneisenau, Admiral Scheer,* and *Karlsruhe* to attack farther south, and a third with the *Blücher, Lützow* (ex-*Deutschland*), and *Emden* to move up Oslofjord against the capital. It was surprising that, even with the prevailing gales and thick weather, the British fleet should not have made a larger haul.

The Norwegian defense, though completely surprised, was not wholly ineffective. At Oslofjord on the night of the 8th the minelayer *Olav Tryggvasen* sank two enemy mine sweepers and a destroyer and badly damaged the cruiser *Emden.* The *Blücher* and *Lützow,* steaming on up the fjord in confidence that the batteries had been silenced by fifth columnists, were suddenly fired on at 1400 yards by the big guns of the Oscarsborg forts at the narrows, and the *Blücher* was sunk by two torpedoes from fixed tubes on shore. Few of the crew and mass of troops aboard were saved. Oslo itself had already surrendered to air-borne forces when the naval vessels moved in next day.

At Stavanger, Bergen, Trondheim, and other ports there were similar tales of surprise, confusion, and only limited resistance. At Kristiansand, near the southern tip of the peninsula, the *Karlsruhe* was seriously injured by shore batteries, and after landing troops was sunk by the British submarine *Truant* outside. At Bergen the *Königsberg* was also injured by shore defenses and was sunk by British aircraft next day—the first large naval vessel to be sunk in wartime by aerial bombs.

These fine cruisers, and the destroyers sunk later at Narvik, were a serious loss, but the Germans, like the Japanese later, were using ships and crew as expendable weapons, to be sacrificed for adequate gains.

The only contact made by British major units was for ten minutes on the 9th, when in a gale and whirling snow the 32,000-ton battle cruiser *Renown* engaged the *Scharnhorst* and a heavy cruiser. The *Renown* was hit twice but not seriously damaged, and at 14,000 yards landed two 15-inch shells which smashed the *Scharnhorst's* conning tower and silenced an after-turret gun. In the heavy seas and bad visibility, the two German ships escaped under a smoke screen.

Ten German destroyers went into the approaches leading to Narvik, sank two old coast defense ships with heavy loss of life, and on the morning of the 9th landed troops from the 14 German "ore ships" in the port. The Norwegian commander at Narvik, a Quislingite, quickly surrendered.

That night, despite snow squalls and zero weather, five British destroyers led by Captain Warburton-Lee in the *Hardy* made a daring raid up the fjord to Narvik. Taking the Germans completely by surprise, the *Hardy* torpedoed the flotilla leader *Wilhelm Heidkamp* and the *Schmitt* and raised havoc with shipping till the British were in turn attacked by superior forces. H.M.S. *Hunter* was sunk and the *Hardy* was blown up after running ashore. The British again had the upper hand three days later when destroyers supported by the battleship *Warspite* went into the fjord and wiped out every remaining German warcraft. German troops in the Narvik area surrendered to a British expeditionary force late in May. In the subsequent British evacuation in June, the *Gneisenau* and *Scharnhorst* sank the aircraft carrier *Glorious,* the destroyer escorts *Ardent* and *Acasta,* which stuck with the carrier to the end, and the big transport *Orama,* fortunately without troops.

It appears certain that, prior to the German invasion, a Franco-British expeditionary force, originally intended for Finland, was considered for use in a protective occupation of Narvik and the northern ore area. This project was used by the Germans to justify their own move, which in reality had been planned long before. The later Allied expedition of 12,000 men to Norway suffered from overwhelming enemy air and land superiority, and its withdrawal was made inevitable by the bad turn of the war on the Continent. The great difficulty was that of blocking German sea communications. To risk British surface forces in the Skagerrak against superior air power was to court disaster. Though British submarines and mines were said to have sunk 28 transports in three weeks' time, German troops and munitions poured into Norway by sea and air.

The Fall of France

The task of naval forces opposing the Germans in their swift conquest of the Netherlands, May 10–14, 1940, was limited to maintaining sea communications, giving such support as possible on the seaward flank, and safeguarding the evacuation of the government and royal family. Most of the small but well-trained force of Dutch cruisers, destroyers, and submarines escaped to operate later with the British and in the Netherlands Indies.

The evacuation of the allied armies from Dunkirk, May 26–June 4, was a combined operation including not only French and British sea, land, and air forces but all available merchant shipping and small craft on the Channel coasts. The French supplied about 500 such types and the British nearly 900, of which 222 were naval vessels from destroyers down, 91 were tugs and coastwise steamers, and the rest yachts and boats of every description. The French lost 7 destroyers and the British 6. It was only by generally favorable weather, the magnificent work of the R.A.F. in maintaining local air superiority, and the unceasing labors of naval men, merchant seamen, and masses of volunteers, that the miracle was accomplished of saving 335,000, or nine-tenths of the force, when it had been expected that not over 30,000 could be brought away.

Upon the surrender of France in mid-June, there was grave fear that, despite armistice pledges to the contrary, the French fleet might fall into the hands of the Axis. A considerable number of French ships, including the battleship *Lorraine* and three heavy cruisers, were demilitarized by the British at Alexandria; others fled to England during the invasion and in some instances went over to the Free French under General de Gaulle. Of four big battleships building or just completed, the *Richelieu* was on the African west coast, the *Jean Bart* fled from Brest to Casablanca without her after-turret guns, and two were destroyed on the stocks.

Among vessels still unaccounted for, the fast, well-armored battleships *Dunkerque* and *Strasbourg,* the older battleships *Provence* and *Bretagne,* and some light units were at the Mediterranean base of Oran. On the morning of July 3 a British squadron including the battle cruiser *Hood,* two battleships, and the carrier *Ark Royal* appeared off the port. An officer in an accompanying destroyer entered the base and gave the French admiral a choice of courses—his ships could join the British in the war, sail for England with skeleton crews, or be sent for internment in a trans-Atlantic port. Failing a decision in six hours, the British would use force to prevent the ships from falling under Axis control.

When no reply was received and the French were seen to be getting up steam, the British laid a magnetic mine barrier across the entrance and at 6 p.m., hidden by a smoke screen and firing over Mers el-Kebir promontory with aircraft spotting, opened a bombardment at 13,000 yards. The *Bretagne* was heavily hit and capsized after a magazine explosion. The *Dunkerque* and *Provence* were left stranded and in flames. The French fire was limited in volume and effect, but in the smoke of battle the speedy *Strasbourg,* with some cruisers and destroyers, was able to escape to Toulon, suffering a torpedo hit as she got away. The damage inflicted was somewhat less than at first estimated, for in a year or two all these ships except the *Bretagne* were patched up and back at Toulon, where with other French ships they were still a menace, if the Axis could get hold of them and man them with loyal and competent crews. The Oran attack led to a rupture of diplomatic relations and sharper friction between Britain and the Vichy French.

In July, also, the British took similar measures against the

Richelieu at Dakar. This was shortly before the British-Free French expedition to the West African base, which proved a fiasco chiefly because the British were unwilling to start full-scale hostilities when the defenders failed to come over willingly to de Gaulle. In the operations against the battle cruiser, offers like those at Oran were made and rejected. That night eight heroic volunteers in a motor boat succeeded in dropping four depth bombs close under the *Richelieu's* stern. Her propellers and rudder were damaged, and four torpedo hits made later by aircraft left her stranded and probably beyond local repair, though her batteries could be used for defense.

2. THE WAR IN THE MEDITERRANEAN

Upon the defection of France and entry of Italy into the war (June 10), a desperate sea and air conflict ensued to maintain the British life line east and west through the Middle Sea and Axis communications with Libya. While it remained beyond the power of either side to halt the passage of well-guarded enemy convoys, yet the fact that British supply lines through the Mediterranean narrows were not completely blocked stands as evidence of the staying qualities of the British Navy and the shortcomings of Italy's vaunted strength in fast surface vessels, torpedo carriers, and aircraft. The two British advances into Libya at the beginning and the end of 1941, as well as the campaign in Greece, were based upon and made possible by sea power, and in the African campaigns the Navy rendered invaluable service in transport of water, munitions, and prisoners and bombardment of coastal strongholds, supporting the army's right flank. In fact, all these campaigns illustrated the need and value of a close coördination of sea, land, and air weapons.

In contacts during the summer British surface craft more than held their own, and on November 11, 1940, after Admiral Sir Andrew Cunningham's squadron in the Levant had been reënforced by the new aircraft carrier *Illustrious,* the British used their accession of air strength to strike heavily at the Italian main fleet, then concentrated at Taranto. The attack was executed at night with only about 20 aircraft, of which half were torpedoplanes. In two flights they plunged through heavy anti-aircraft fire, dropped flares, and made numerous hits on two new *Littorio*-class battleships and two older ones of the *Cavour* type, as well as on some of the cruisers. The damage, though here again perhaps over-estimated, necessitated a long period for reconstruction, and the *Conte di Cavour* was abandoned.

Of the many convoy attacks and partial fleet actions[1] in the Mediterranean, a few may be taken as typical. One particularly fierce assault on a British convoy south of Sicily was made on January 10, 1941, during which German Stuka bombers joined Italian aircraft in successive waves of 40 or more from noon till dark. The Stukas dived almost vertically as low as 100 feet, sweeping recklessly through a blasting anti-aircraft barrage to reach their targets. At least 12 were shot down. The cruiser *Southampton* of the escort was set on fire and abandoned that night. The carrier *Illustrious* with some of her planes still aboard was almost completely wrecked by repeated hits of 1,000-lb. bombs. She was later laid up in Norfolk, Va., till the next autumn for repairs. During the remainder of the year much of the traffic for Egypt was diverted around Africa, and only the most urgent supplies for Malta and the East went through the central narrows.

The Battle of Cape Matapan

After Taranto, the Italian fleet sought safer bases and remained relatively inactive; but in March, 1941, a squadron appeared east of Sicily—apparently to divert attention from a big transfer of German troops to Libya. This move led to the Cape Matapan action in the Ionian Sea.

Even a meager account of this battle reveals its significance as, in the words of the British Admiralty, "the first skillful coördination of naval operations with attacks launched by aircraft, resulting in the enemy's speed being reduced and our main

[1] One student counts 16 up to January 1, 1942, in 10 of which the British had superior force and in all of which they scored favorable results. W. L. Robinson, "Naval Actions, 1940–1941," *U. S. Naval Institute Proceedings*, 1942.

units being able to force action on a reluctant enemy." On
March 27 aircraft scouts radioed to Alexandria the advance of
an Italian force of 3 battleships, 11 cruisers, and 14 destroyers
east of Sicily, as if bent on raiding British traffic with Greece.
The squadron later separated, with the battleship *Vittorio
Veneto*, 6 cruisers, and 9 destroyers in the more southerly division. The other had little part in the action. The force Admiral Cunningham brought out of Alexandria that afternoon
included the flagship *Warspite*, the *Valiant* and *Barham*, the
carrier *Formidable* (replacing the *Illustrious*), 4 cruisers, and a
considerable body of destroyers.

After cruiser contacts south of Crete on the morning of the
28th (see diagram) and advances and withdrawals suggestive
of the early moves at Jutland, a series of vicious attacks were
launched from 11.30 on by torpedoplanes and bombers from
the *Formidable*. At the first assault the Italians turned back,
but at least three hits at close range slowed the *Vittorio's* speed
to less than 15 knots, and other hits were made on the cruisers.

About 10 that night, as the British battleships came up with
the enemy, a disabled Italian cruiser was reported about three
miles to port. Almost at the same moment a searchlight from
the *Greyhound* destroyer lighted up other cruisers crossing their
bows from the north and hardly 4,000 yards distant. Within
five minutes the 10,000-ton *Fiume*, her sister ship *Zara*, and
probably a smaller cruiser were wrecked by salvos from the
Warspite and her consorts at this close range. The *Pola*, the
cruiser to port, was finished off by a destroyer after the saving
of part of her crew. Subsequently the British main force
seems to have withdrawn to avoid torpedo attack, in which two
Italian destroyers were sunk. The *Vittorio*, badly damaged
under water, had meantime limped away. In the action the
Italians suffered from inadequate air scouting, which gave little
warning of the heavy opposition, and also from weak anti-
aircraft defense, by which only two British planes were shot
down. The loss of the three 8-in. gun cruisers was a heavy
blow. In the morning British destroyers returned to the scene of
the action and picked up about 900 Italians, but the salvage
operations were cut short by an attack of German dive-bombers.

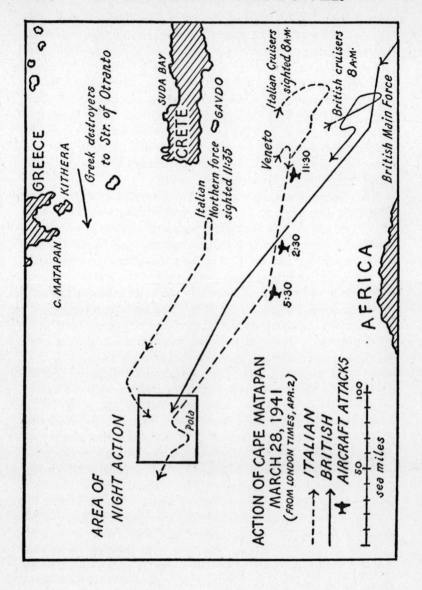

GREECE

C. MATAPAN

KITHERA

Greek destroyers
to Str. of Otranto

SUDA BAY

CRETE

GAVDO

Italian
Northern force
sighted 11:35

Veneto

Italian Cruisers
sighted 8 A.M.

British cruisers
8 A.M.

British Main Force

AFRICA

AREA OF
NIGHT ACTION

Pola

11:30

2:30

5:30

ACTION OF CAPE MATAPAN
MARCH 28, 1941
(FROM LONDON TIMES, APR. 2)

ITALIAN
BRITISH
AIRCRAFT ATTACKS

0   50   100

sea miles

Capture of Crete

In the British evacuation of Greece a month later, and more notably in the operations around Crete in late May, the conditions at Matapan were reversed, and the British fleet suffered from an overwhelming enemy air power.   The evacuation of Greece was creditably accomplished with a loss of but two cruisers and four transports, only one of which was loaded. Crete was too close to Greece for safe tenure, but its capture was a first instance—unless Norway be excepted—of an air-supported overseas invasion in the face of superior sea power. The movement of troops was actually, in the first stages, accomplished by air, since the British fleet effectively smashed up surface transports till its withdrawal was made necessary by swarming torpedoplanes and dive-bombers.   The *Formidable, Warspite,* and other ships had to take the long route to American navy yards for repairs.   Altogether the Germans had over 700 fighters and bombers in the Cretan operations and almost as many transport planes, some of which towed gliders loaded with troops.   During the defense and evacuation the British lost three large cruisers, the *Fiji, York,* and *Gloucester,* the anti-aircraft cruiser *Calcutta,* and six destroyers.

It is little wonder that in the ensuing period the attacks on Axis supply lines across the Sicilian straits was left largely to aircraft and submarines.   Even so, Admiral Cunningham in October claimed damage "up to 50 per cent" of all Axis convoys.   On November 13, 1941, the *Ark Royal,* often claimed previously as a victim, was hit by a single torpedo from a submarine, and sank next morning under tow, about 25 miles east of Gibraltar.   This celebrated carrier had shared in the search for the *Graf Spee,* in the Norway operations, in the chase of the *Bismarck,* and again in the Mediterranean as a valuable weapon, with her planes, for both offense and defense.

Even more than in the broad ocean reaches, the war in the Mediterranean emphasized the new tactics, in which air power is brought into effective combination with other naval weapons. To sea warfare General Wavell's statement regarding land and air power could be applied, "It is the combination of the two

. . . that will bring success in future war." The conflict illustrated also the continued importance of this central waterway, where Phoenicians, Greeks, Romans, Turks, and Christians had fought for 3,000 years.

3. THE WAR IN THE ATLANTIC

Events in the Atlantic area have already been brought down to the summer of 1940. At this time the conquest of Norway and France and the entry of Italy into the war increased British naval preoccupations and made possible a wide extension of the Axis submarine campaign. U-boats could now operate, and aircraft could scout and attack shipping, from a coast line extending from the North Cape to Spain. Tonnage losses in the last seven months of the year mounted to a monthly average, not of less than 200,000, but of more than 400,000 tons.

America and the War

In this situation, and with terrific air raids devastating London during the autumn, America came to a clearer realization that the British Empire was in jeopardy, and that a Germany dominant in Europe, with the possible surrender of the British fleet, meant a very imminent threat to the Western Hemisphere. Democracy was menaced everywhere; and German methods of economic and political penetration, furthermore, could not be met simply by piling up defenses on the home frontiers. Hemispheric protection was the main theme of the Havana Conference of American republics in July, which took steps to prevent transfer of American territory from one to another non-American power. The United States Congress passed legislation for a two-ocean navy and a hitherto unheard-of ten-billion-dollar defense program. The Lend-Lease Act providing "all-out" aid for Britain was still in the offing, to be passed in March of the next year, but the Destroyer-Base deal went through.

This last was an unprecedented forward step in American foreign and naval policy. In exchange for some fifty over-age but thoroughly reconditioned flush-deck destroyers, which England sorely needed, the United States secured 100-year leases of eight bases extending from Newfoundland to British Guiana, including facilities in Bermuda, the Bahamas, Jamaica, Antigua, St. Lucia, and Trinidad. These strengthened control over the Caribbean and pushed American sea defenses into the mid-Atlantic.

In the spring of 1941 German submarine activity was further intensified and brought shipping losses in April to over 589,000 tons. Extending its action accordingly, the United States Government pushed its naval patrol further into the Atlantic, took Greenland under its protection in April, sent troops to Iceland in July, and in early September issued orders that American naval vessels should engage submarines carrying on piratical destruction of shipping "in any waters which America deems vital to its defense." Thus, some time before the declaration of war by the Axis powers on December 11, 1941, the United States was in the war at sea. In this period the U.S. destroyer *Greer* was engaged with a submarine on September 4; the *Kearny* on October 17 was severely damaged by a torpedo hit near the forward engine room but was brought into Reykjavik, Iceland, by excellent work of the engineer force and all hands; and the older destroyer *Reuben James* was sunk on October 31, while engaged in convoy protection, with a loss of over 100 men.

Submarine Warfare

The new submarines which the Germans had put into action in the preceding spring were mostly of small type with surface displacement of from 800 to under 500 tons, which could be built more quickly and cheaply and manned with smaller crews. To meet the regimentation of commerce in convoys, they now employed "wolf-pack" tactics, in which the movements of convoys would be followed by aircraft or submarine scouts and the U-boats would lie in wait and extend their assaults over several nights. Shielded by darkness, they would make concerted attacks with hulls awash and conning towers open, securing thus an advantage in vision, in accuracy of aim, and in speed above that of the slower corvette escorts. In the early days of the war German Focke-Wulfe aircraft also operated freely against commerce from bases on the French coast, but this threat was checked by increasing British air patrols and extending them farther into the Atlantic and by conversion of merchant vessels into catapult carriers for use with convoys. Aircraft thus put to service could be employed effectively against both enemy aircraft and U-boats. These measures, with the addition of many newly constructed corvettes, sloops, and destroyers as escorts, and the increased American aid, brought a sharp reduction of tonnage losses in the latter part of the year. Their efficiency was no doubt one reason, among others, for the extension of submarine activity, early in 1942, to unescorted shipping on the American coast.

In view of the need of secrecy and the reticence of the "silent service" it seems likely that much of the hard fighting, the heroism, and the hardships of both naval and merchant seamen in the submarine war will never be generally known. In a single typical convoy battle, extending from December 17 to 21, 1941, the Admiralty account relates that on the first day a U-boat was brought to the surface by depth bombs and then blown to pieces by gunfire, and that two Focke-Wulfe bombers were driven off by fighter planes from the carrier *Audacity* (converted ex-German merchant ship *Hannover*). The next day another submarine was similarly finished off, and H.M.S. *Stanley* (ex-U.S. destroyer *McCalla*) was sunk by torpedo. On the 19th more Focke-Wulfes came back to the attack and lost two planes. After two more days' fighting in which the *Audacity* was sunk, the action was ended by aircraft reënforcements from the British coast. In the course of the war long-drawn-out actions of this type occurred again and again.

"Gneisenau" and "Scharnhorst"

In addition to a half-dozen ex-merchant vessel raiders active chiefly in the Pacific, Germany threw major units of her navy into the commerce-destroying campaign. The 26,000-ton battleships *Scharnhorst* and *Gneisenau* were out in the first months of 1941 and wrought havoc on almost an entire North Atlantic convoy, but after March 28 they were pinned down at Brest, where they were subjected to repeated R.A.F. bombings.   According to a statement of Prime Minister Churchill (February 17, 1942), these battleships lying on the flank of main British supply routes were subjected to 4,000 tons of bombs.   Though badly damaged, they survived, thanks to sturdy construction and excellent aerial defense measures.   On July 22 the *Scharnhorst* moved to La Pallice, 240 miles to southward, but was soon back again at Brest.   With the *Prince Eugen,* which had joined them, both ships in February, 1942, succeeded in getting back to Germany through the Channel, skirting the French coast and heavily protected by air squadrons, though they were subjected to most violent attacks of British torpedoplanes, bombers, motor torpedo boats, and destroyers.

Chase of the "Bismarck"

On May 21, 1941, British air reconnaissance reported the German battleship *Bismarck,* with the 10,000-ton cruiser *Prince Eugen,* about to sail from Bergen, Norway.   The powerful *Bismarck* was Germany's latest achievement in naval construction, with a full load displacement probably well up toward 45,000 tons, a broad 118-foot beam permitting elaborate compartmentation, eight 15-inch guns, and the best that Nazi skill could provide in fire control, anti-aircraft batteries, and armor protection.

Two nights later, amid snow squalls and thick weather, the Germans were picked up and shadowed by the heavy cruisers *Norfolk* and *Suffolk* in the Denmark Strait between Iceland and Greenland.   The battle cruiser *Hood* and the new 35,000-ton battleship *Prince of Wales* were not far distant and attacked at 6 a.m. next day at about 13 miles' range.   In a heavy swell, with shifting visibility, the *Bismarck* at the second or third salvo scored a hit on the *Hood* amidships, resulting in flames and a magazine explosion which sent great fragments hurtling a half mile through the air.   Within five minutes the big 46,000-ton post-Jutland cruiser went down, the fourth of her type to sink in battle, with the loss of all but 3 of her 1421 men.   Be-

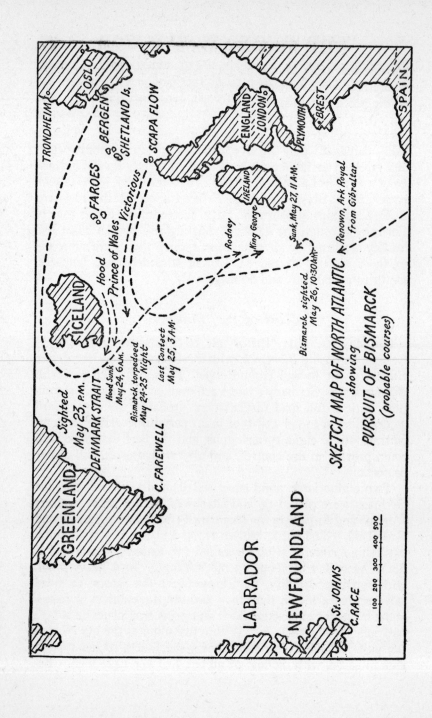

SKETCH MAP OF NORTH ATLANTIC
showing
PURSUIT OF BISMARCK
(probable courses)

fore breaking off the action because of damage to fire control, the *Prince of Wales* made a hit on the *Bismarck's* bow near the water, which seems to have cut down her speed slightly. That afternoon the aircraft carrier *Victorious* was also in striking distance and, guided by the cruisers still hanging to the trail, some of her planes got in a torpedo hit after midnight which further slowed down the *Bismarck*. Then for over thirty hours the German ships were lost in the Atlantic. The *Prince Eugen* had already separated, and finally found refuge in Brest.

At 10.30 a.m., May 26, the *Bismarck* was again spotted some 500 miles west of the Channel by a Catalina aircraft of the Coastal Command, which sent in an alarm and dodged through cloud banks to escape a hail of anti-aircraft fire. Soon the British fleet units, which had put to sea at the first news from Bergen, were closing in, the *King George* from Scapa, the *Rodney* from convoy escort, the *Renown* and *Ark Royal* from Gibraltar. After misdirected efforts in the heavy weather that afternoon, Swordfish planes from the *Ark Royal* pressed home a hard attack that night resulting in at least two hits, one a lucky shot near the stern which damaged propulsion, jammed the steering gear, and cut the enemy's speed to 8 or 10 knots. Destroyers headed by Captain Vian's *Cossack* also swarmed in to the kill and made two hits more. Next morning from 8.47 on the *Bismarck* sustained a terrific hour-and-a-half bombardment from the *King George's* 14-inch and the *Rodney's* 16-inch guns, while the British ships, using their great speed advantage, were uninjured by the enemy's now ineffective fire. About 10.30 the *Bismarck,* a blazing, sinking hulk, was finished off by torpedoes from the cruiser *Sheffield*. As she rolled over slowly and sank by the stern, countless men were washed from her hull or leaped into the sea. A submarine alarm interrupted rescue work, and only 110 out of her complement of 2400 were saved. Among the lost were Admiral Lütjens and 400 naval cadets on their first cruise.

Here, more clearly than at Matapan two months earlier, was illustrated the effective combination of aircraft for scouting and crippling, and heavy surface vessels to strike the final blow. In contrast with the older *Hood,* the *Bismarck* demonstrated the tremendous defensive strength that can be packed into a present-day man-of-war. Six supply ships, sent out to support her in her short-lived mission, presumably of commerce destruction, were later intercepted.

4. THE WAR IN THE PACIFIC

After the Peace of Versailles, Japan continued a consistent policy of economic and political expansion in the Asiatic area, profiting in its accomplishment by the involvements and conflicts of the Western Powers. Steps in this policy, already touched upon in previous chapters, were the immense strategic advantage gained by control, little checked by League supervision, of the former German islands north of the equator; the temporary and slightly regarded restraints of the naval limitation and Pacific treaties, by which Japan still retained predominance in Eastern waters; the unopposed violation of League and treaty pledges in the occupation of Manchuria in 1931; and the final involvement, after July, 1937, in a war to dominate China.

Though the prolongation of this war brought a heavy strain on Japanese resources, it put the aggressive military faction in more complete control of the Japanese government and foreign policy. In the conquest of the Chinese coastal provinces, British and American interests and treaty rights were flagrantly disregarded. Such incidents as the *Panay* attack[1] and the siege of the British concession at Tientsin showed a determination to oust Western influence in China in reckless disregard of the risks involved.

It was the clearly foreseen approach of another European war that had facilitated Japanese aggressions, and in such a conflict Japan's immediate interests lay obviously with the Axis powers. The first link was the Anti-Comintern Agreement of 1936, which was followed finally—after periods of hesitation at Tokio—by open union with Germany and Italy in the Tri-Power Pact of August, 1940. This was primarily a threat to

[1] After the sinking of the U.S. gunboat *Panay* by Japanese aircraft, December 12, 1937, the United States accepted full apologies and reparations, but not the Japanese version of the attack as in any way accidental or unintentional.

keep America out of the war. It pledged all three signatories to join forces if a third power, i.e., the United States, entered against them in either the East or the West. In immediate compensation, Japan received a free hand in French Indo-China, and sanction also, of such value as might be attached to Axis pledges, for the whole grandiose scheme of a "Greater East Asia" dominated by the flag of the rising sun.

Up to this point and thereafter the closely concerted Anglo-American policy was in general one of appeasement, based on a very urgent and natural desire not to take on another enemy, and also on an over-optimistic view of Japan's military strength and of her willingness to stake all in a conflict with the immense economic and productive resources of the major naval powers. All possible aid was given to China, but up to the middle of 1940 the United States supplied Japan with over 54 per cent of her war needs, and from British and Dutch sources also Japan was able to build up great stock piles of scrap iron, oil, and other strategic materials.

It is doubtful if much sincerity can be attached to Japan's final diplomatic moves in November of 1941. Certainly while Japan was prolonging negotiations the Pearl Harbor expedition was already planned and under way, and Envoy Kurusu was delivering a long message to the State Department in Washington at the actual time of the Pearl Harbor attack. The "Japanese High Command" seems to have issued war declarations sometime that day; the British and United States declarations against Japan came on the next day, December 8, and those of Germany and Italy against the United States on December 11.

The Attack on Pearl Harbor[1]

In Japanese major strategy, the attack on Pearl Harbor must be regarded as a secondary move, designed to cripple American naval strength and give additional assurance of the sea and air superiority which Japan already possessed in the

[1]It has seemed desirable to limit the account of the Pearl Harbor action to data given in the report of Secretary of the Navy Knox and the findings of the Roberts Commission, and to end the present narrative of naval events in the Pacific at the close of 1941.

Far Eastern theater and which made possible her rapid moves into Malaya, the Philippines, and the Dutch and British island possessions. The raid was made on December 7 by 150 to 200 fighting, bombing, and torpedoplanes in a series of attacks beginning about 7.55 and ending before 11 a.m. It included the bombing of naval and army air stations in Oahu but was centered primarily on the fleet. Aside from destruction of grounded planes and other damage to shore establishments, the naval losses, according to the Secretary's report, were the battleship *Arizona* of 1916 date, whose boilers and forward magazine were blown up by an accurately placed bomb which went down her stack, the old target ship *Utah,* the destroyers *Cassin, Shaw,* and *Downes,* and the mine-layer *Oglala.* The battleship *Oklahoma* was capsized but could be righted and repaired. Damage to other ships would require repair periods ranging from a week to several months. Naval personnel losses were 91 officers killed and 20 wounded, 2,638 enlisted men killed and 636 wounded.

In addition to the planes, the Japanese used several small, two-man submarines, about 41 feet long, with two 18-inch torpedoes and a cruising radius of some 200 miles. One of these was sunk outside and two were destroyed inside the harbor, to which access was made possible after 5 a.m. by the opening of the gate in the torpedo net across the entrance. The Japanese lost about 40 planes, all of the single-motor type, which bore out the assumption that the entire raid was launched from carriers.

The report of the Roberts Commission indicated that, although definite warnings of the critical situation had come from Washington on November 27 and later, no specific information of Japanese moves was given other than of those down the Asiatic coast. Both Lieutenant General Walter E. Short, in command of army forces in Hawaii, and Admiral Husband E. Kimmel, in command of naval forces, together with their staffs, had regarded an air raid there as improbable. On the Sunday of the attack neither a naval distant reconnaissance nor an army inshore air patrol was operating. A recently installed aircraft detector system was operated from 4 to 7 a.m., but a subsequent report of approaching aircraft made by an inexperienced operator was disregarded. These conditions were fully known by Japanese espionage, which provided the flyers with accurate data regarding airfields and the location of ships.

The Commission in its conclusions held that the preparations were inadequate in view of the warnings given and that it was "a dereliction of duty" on the part of the army and navy commanders in chief "not to consult and confer with the other respecting the meaning and intent of the warnings and the appropriate measures of defense required by the imminence of hostilities." The report spoke in warm praise of the "excellent training and high morale" of both officers and men following the alarm. The Secretary's report also recounted numerous acts of outstanding courage and initiative.

Guam was captured on December 11, but at Wake Island the small Marine garrison beat off repeated air raids and landing attempts extending from December 7 to 22, in the course of which the Japanese lost a cruiser, three or four destroyers, a submarine, a gunboat, and a dozen or more planes. One of the destroyers was sunk by the five aircraft remaining to the island forces after the destruction of seven of their planes on the ground at the first assault. The other surface vessels were sunk by 5-inch and 3-inch guns during Japanese attempts to land. The island was surrendered only after the last plane was disabled and further resistance impossible.

Loss of the "Prince of Wales" and the "Repulse"

In the Japanese advance southward, a main objective was the great British naval base at Singapore. Though the base was finally captured by land attack, the land campaign was dependent on freedom of sea communications, and this in turn was assured by naval and air control. In a risky effort to challenge this superiority, the new British 35,000-ton battleship *Prince of Wales* and the older battle cruiser *Repulse* were both sunk by enemy planes. Operating east of Malaya without air support, the two ships were sighted by Japanese aircraft on December 9 and heavily assailed by torpedoplanes and bombers the next day.

In a series of attacks between 11 and 12 the *Repulse* was reported to have used anti-aircraft fire and high speed to avoid 19 torpedoes. In a final onslaught she was struck a smashing blow amidships and went down after repeated hits. The battleship also was sunk after continued torpedo- and dive-bombing attacks which finally rendered her helpless. Since accompanying destroyers were unmolested in rescue work, they saved about four-fifths of the 3,000 men aboard the two ships.

Ships and Tactics

In transport and landing operations in Malaya and the Philippines, the Japanese even before the end of 1941 had suffered a heavy attrition in combatant ships, transports, and aircraft. These included the older battleship *Haruna,* reported sunk off Aparri in the Philippines by a U.S. Army bombing squadron led by Captain Colin Kelly, severe damage to a battleship of the *Kongo* class by U.S. Navy patrol planes, and a long list of cruisers, destroyers, and submarines sunk or injured by American, Dutch, and British forces. Though the opposition suffered similarly, the Americans at least could count on replacement and expansion by an immense program of new construction, such as was in no wise possible for Japan. Her hopes could lie only in a swift consolidation and exploitation of conquests, coupled with victory for her allies.

The war in the Pacific—involving immense sea distances, limited or non-existent shore communications, contested islands ranging from those of continental size to the tiniest atolls capable of sheltering a ship or plane—could hardly be thought of as other than primarily a naval war. But it was a war requiring the closest integration of sea, land, and air forces. Thus in the Singapore campaign, as already noted, a great naval base was captured by land attack, the success of which hinged largely on air superiority.

Fought chiefly by lighter units, with the battleships held in reserve as all-important elements of defensive and offensive strength, the Pacific campaigns emphasized the increased factor of speed in present-day naval tactics—a speed attained in aircraft scouting and attack, in perfected radio communications, in torpedo carriers of all types and sizes, and in general in the propulsion of surface craft. Since sea warfare, far more than land warfare, is highly mechanized, this heightened tempo of movement put an increased premium, not only on prompt decision and resolute action, but on the most expert handling of ships and weapons.

REFERENCES

THE WAR, FIRST YEAR and THE WAR, SECOND YEAR (2 vols.). By Edgar McInnis, N. Y., 1940, 1941.
THE WAR AT SEA, by Gilbert Kant, N. Y., 1942.
SEA POWER IN CONFLICT, by Paul Schubert, N. Y., 1942.

INDEX

459